W9-BMZ-367

Beginning
MFC COM
Programming

Julian Templeman

Wrox Press Ltd.®

Beginning MFC COM Programming

© 1997 Wrox Press

All rights reserved. No part of this book may be reproduced, stored in a retrieval system or transmitted in any form or by any means - electronic, electrostatic, mechanical, photocopying, recording or otherwise, without the prior written permission of the publisher, except in the case of brief quotations embodied in critical articles or reviews.

The author and publisher have made every effort in the preparation of this book to ensure the accuracy of the information. However, the information contained in this book is sold without warranty, either express or implied. Neither the author, Wrox Press nor its dealers or distributors will be held liable for any damages caused or alleged to be caused either directly or indirectly by this book.

Published by Wrox Press Ltd. 30 Lincoln Road, Olton, Birmingham, B27 6PA , UK.
Printed in Canada
2 3 4 5 TRI 99 98

ISBN 1-874416-87-7

Trademark Acknowledgements

Wrox has endeavored to provide trademark information about all the companies and products mentioned in this book by the appropriate use of capitals. However, Wrox cannot guarantee the accuracy of this information.

Visual C++, Windows 95 and Windows NT are trademarks and ActiveX, ActiveX ControlPack, ActiveX ControlPad, ActiveX SDK, Developer Studio and Internet Explorer are registered trademarks of Microsoft Corporation.

Credits

Author
Julian Templeman

Editors
Jon Hill
Alex Stockton

Managing Editor
John Franklin

Technical Reviewers
Saud Alshibani
Richard Harrison
Jesse Liberty

Technical Reviewers
Richard McCavery
Lynn Mettler
Christophe Nasarre
Marc Simkin
Matt Telles
Gerry Whelan

Cover/Design/Layout
Andrew Guillaume
Graham Butler

Copy Edit/Index
Simon Gilks

About the Author

Julian Templeman lives in London with his wife and three children, two cats, a dog, two PCs, a Mac and a PDP-11. In such spare time as he has, he writes articles and reviews for programming journals, and contributes as an author and technical reviewer to Wrox Press. He's also a keen musician, and can often be found playing guitar, mandolin, Dobro, and bass (although not simultaneously). His skill on the saxophone is not widely appreciated.

Julian first set fingers to keyboard, or more correctly keypunch, while learning Fortran in the course of gaining a B.Sc. in Geology at Imperial College, London, in the late 1970s.

He never became a geologist, recognizing early on that computers were far more fun than rocks, involving a lot more staying indoors, a lot less mud and camping, and a lot more toys to play with. During a stay doing postgraduate work at the Natural History Museum in London, he strayed into programming and has never left. Since then, he's had a number of programming jobs, most of which were in the areas of science or engineering, and all of which involved graphics of one sort or another. For the last two years he's worked for Richford Computer Services in London, doing training and consulting in C++, Windows programming, Java and COM/ActiveX. Oh yes, and occasionally Fortran too, but he tries not to mention it.

Julian can be contacted as **julian@groucho.demon.co.uk**.

Dedications

My thanks are due to the many people who, wittingly or not, have contributed to the development of this book and its author.

Firstly, I owe a debt of gratitude to J. D. Hildebrand, Cecelia Hagen and all the others at Windows Tech Journal both past and present, who encouraged my first attempts at writing, and who still give me a place in their fine magazine.

My thanks are due to all at Richfords, for providing a stimulating and relaxed working environment. I've learnt a lot from my colleagues there, especially Paul Whapham, Roger Woollett and Ken Jackson, and have valued their suggestions and comments (especially the helpful ones!).

The team at Wrox has been unfailingly supportive. Special mention must go to Dave Maclean, for being willing to trust me with this project in the first place; John Franklin, for managing it and being prompt in getting the pay checks out; and Jon Hill, who did all the donkey work, turning my prose into something readable, and not letting me get away with too much. Thanks also to all the technical reviewers, and to those who were willing to be pestered with my questions, including Ken Ramirez, Charlie Kindell and Mike Blaszczak. All of them shed light into previously dark corners, and I learned a lot from them all.

Finally, my thanks must go to my family, who have borne with great good humor the inconvenience and disruption to family life that a project like this inevitably entails. Jane, who has for long periods run the family single-handed, has been wonderfully encouraging in those times when I wondered whether I'd make it to the end. James, Jon and Jessie have also been very understanding about the lack of fatherly attention, and can now have Daddy back.

MFC.COM

Beginning
MFC
COM
Programming

MFC.COM

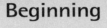

Beginning

MFC COM

Programming

Introduction

Welcome to *Beginning MFC COM Programming*. With this book, you're going to discover how to incorporate COM functionality into your applications without the strain of programming at the API level.

I want to strip away the mystery surrounding terms like OLE, ActiveX, and Automation, and to help you understand how these technologies work. You'll find that behind the terminology, with the help MFC provides, it can be surprisingly straightforward to add powerful features to your applications.

Who this Book is for

This book is primarily for fairly experienced programmers - people who are involved in developing Windows programs. If you need to get to grips with these COM-based technologies and the way the Windows operating system and development tools are evolving, this book is certainly for you. That said, you'll also find quite a lot of *discussion* about COM, OLE and ActiveX in general terms, and these sections can usefully be read by anyone with a programming background who wants to get up to speed on these new technologies.

Every programming book has to define its intended audience by assuming a certain level of expertise (even if that level is 'none at all'), and this one is no exception. In order to get the most out of this book, you should have experience of Windows programming in C++ using Visual C++ and MFC, as that's where we're going to start. You should be familiar with the document/view architecture, and concepts such as message maps and dialog data exchange. Obviously, you don't need to have any experience of COM and its relations, as that's what the book's all about!

What's Covered in this Book

This book is about writing COM-related code using the support given to you by Visual C++ and MFC. Most of the chapters are split into three parts, following a logical sequence. First, there's the discussion of a particular feature - OLE servers, or ActiveX controls, for example - and how it's implemented at the COM level.

These theory sections are written on the basis of containing 'just enough' theory to get you going. COM forms a complex subject area, and while the Visual C++ Wizards and MFC classes shield you from a lot of the underlying technology, it's necessary to appreciate some of the mechanisms (and jargon!) involved in order to use the tools you're given in an effective manner.

Next comes information about how the feature is supported by Visual C++ and MFC, and indeed about how comprehensive that support is. Finally, the subject matter of the chapter is demonstrated in a sample application that illustrates some of the possibilites created by the new things you've learned

Instead of a host of disparate examples, the book focuses on developing a reasonably realistic example program, adding features as you progress. The example I've chosen is a graph-plotting application, capable of producing simple line, bar and pie charts. Although the actual graph plotting aspect isn't developed to any degree of sophistication - this book is about COM programming, not graphics programming, after all - the skeleton is capable of being improved into a genuinely useful tool.

The first three chapters form the foundations of the rest of the book. In Chapter 1, I'll give you a quick tour of the 'state of play' - what COM, OLE and ActiveX are, how to tell the difference between them, and why you'd want to use them. To whet your appetite for the things to come, there's also a simple example program that lets you control Microsoft Word from Visual C++.

Chapter 2 presents the basics of COM. The chapter is quite technical and covers a lot of ground, but that's because COM is a complex subject, with a lot of new concepts and mechanisms that will be unfamiliar to the traditional Windows C++ programmer. It's rounded off with an example of low-level COM coding in C++, which should make you appreciate Chapter 3, because that contains details of the support for COM programming built into Visual C++ and MFC. It discusses the types of COM-enabled applications you can build, the options you can select in AppWizard, and presents an overview of how MFC implements COM features.

The next three chapters come as a set as well. Chapter 4 discusses OLE servers, applications that provide OLE-based services, such as the ability to embed documents or parts of documents in other applications. Chapter 5 introduces containers, which are applications that can contain items from OLE servers. A prime example of a container is Microsoft Word, which can include items such as Paintbrush pictures and Excel spreadsheets in its documents. Chapter 6 explores some of the issues involved in helping servers and containers to work together, such as implementing drag and drop between applications.

Chapter 7 discusses Active Documents (formerly known as DocObjects). If you're intrigued by the prospect of writing an application whose documents can be viewed and edited in programs such as Internet Explorer or the Microsoft Office Binder, then this chapter will be of great interest to you.

This is followed by a chapter on one of the bigger COM-based topics, Automation, which supplies the means by which programs can communicate with and drive one another, and provides a more robust (and easier to code) alternative to the older Dynamic Data Exchange (DDE) mechanism. Automation is also heavily involved in Chapter 9, which discusses ActiveX controls. The successors to Visual Basic's VBXs, ActiveX controls are now widely used both in desktop applications and the Internet. This chapter describes how to create them, and how to use them in various environments.

The final chapter pulls everything together, and we'll develop a simple application which shows how components can be used together to make a complete COM-based system.

What You Need to Use This Book

To get the most out of this book you need Visual C++ 5.0, the latest version of Microsoft's C++ compiler. This version is 32-bit only, so you'll need to install it on Windows 95, Windows NT 3.51 or NT 4, which means a 486 CPU or better, and a minimum 16Mb of memory.

For Visual C++, you'll need quite a lot of hard disk space - a typical installation is 170 Mbytes. You can do a minimal installation that takes up around 40 Mbytes, but this will mean longer compile times, as the CD-ROM will be utilized more often.

In addition, some of the examples we'll build use other Microsoft software - specifically, Visual Basic 5, Word (95 or 97 is fine), the Office Binder (again, 95 or 97), Internet Explorer (version 3+) and the ActiveX Control Pad. I'll tell you how to get hold of the latter when we start talking about ActiveX controls in Chapter 9.

Conventions Used

We use a number of different styles of text and layout in the book to help differentiate between the different kinds of information. Here are examples of the styles we use and an explanation of what they mean:

> *These boxes hold important, not-to-be forgotten, mission critical details which are directly relevant to the surrounding text.*

Background information, asides, references and extra details appear in text like this.

▶ **Important Words** are in a bold type font.

▶ Words that appear on the screen, such as menu options, are in a similar font to the one used on screen, for example, the File menu.

▶ Keys that you press on the keyboard, like *Ctrl* and *Enter*, are in italics.

▶ All filenames are in this style: **Videos.mdb**.

▶ Function names look like this: **sizeof()**.

▶ Code that is new, important or relevant to the current discussion will be presented like this:

```
void main()
{
    cout << "Beginning MFC COM Programming";
}
```

Whereas code you've seen before, or which has little to do with the matter at hand, looks like this:

```
void main()
{
    cout << "Beginning MFC COM Programming";
}
```

Tell Us What You Think

We have tried to make this book as accurate and enjoyable for you as possible, but what really matters is what the book actually does for you. Please let us know your views, whether positive or negative, either by returning the reply card in the back of the book or by contacting us at Wrox Press using either of the following methods:

e-mail:	**feedback@wrox.com**
Internet:	**http://www.wrox.com/**
	http://www.wrox.co.uk/

Source Code and Keeping Up-to-date

We try to keep the prices of our books reasonable, so instead of providing disks, we make the source code for our books available on our web sites:

http://www.wrox.com/
http://www.wrox.co.uk/

We've done everything we can to ensure your download is as fast as possible. The code is also available via FTP:

ftp://ftp.wrox.com
ftp://ftp.wrox.co.uk

If you don't have access to the Internet, then we can provide a disk for a nominal fee to cover postage and packing.

Errata & Updates

We've made every effort to make sure there are no errors in the text or the code. However, to err is human and as such we recognize the need to keep you, the reader, informed of any mistakes as they're spotted and amended.

While you're visiting our web site, please make use of our *Errata* page that's dedicated to fixing any small errors in the book or, offering new ways around a problem and its solution. Errata sheets are available for all our books - please download them, or take part in the continuous improvement of our tutorials and upload a 'fix' or pointer.

For those without access to the net, if you've got a specific problem you can call us on **1-800 USE WROX**. Alternatively, send a letter to:

Wrox Press Inc.,
1512 North Fremont,
Suite 103,
Chicago
IL 60622
USA

Wrox Press Ltd,
30, Lincoln Road,
Olton,
Birmingham,
B27 6PA
UK

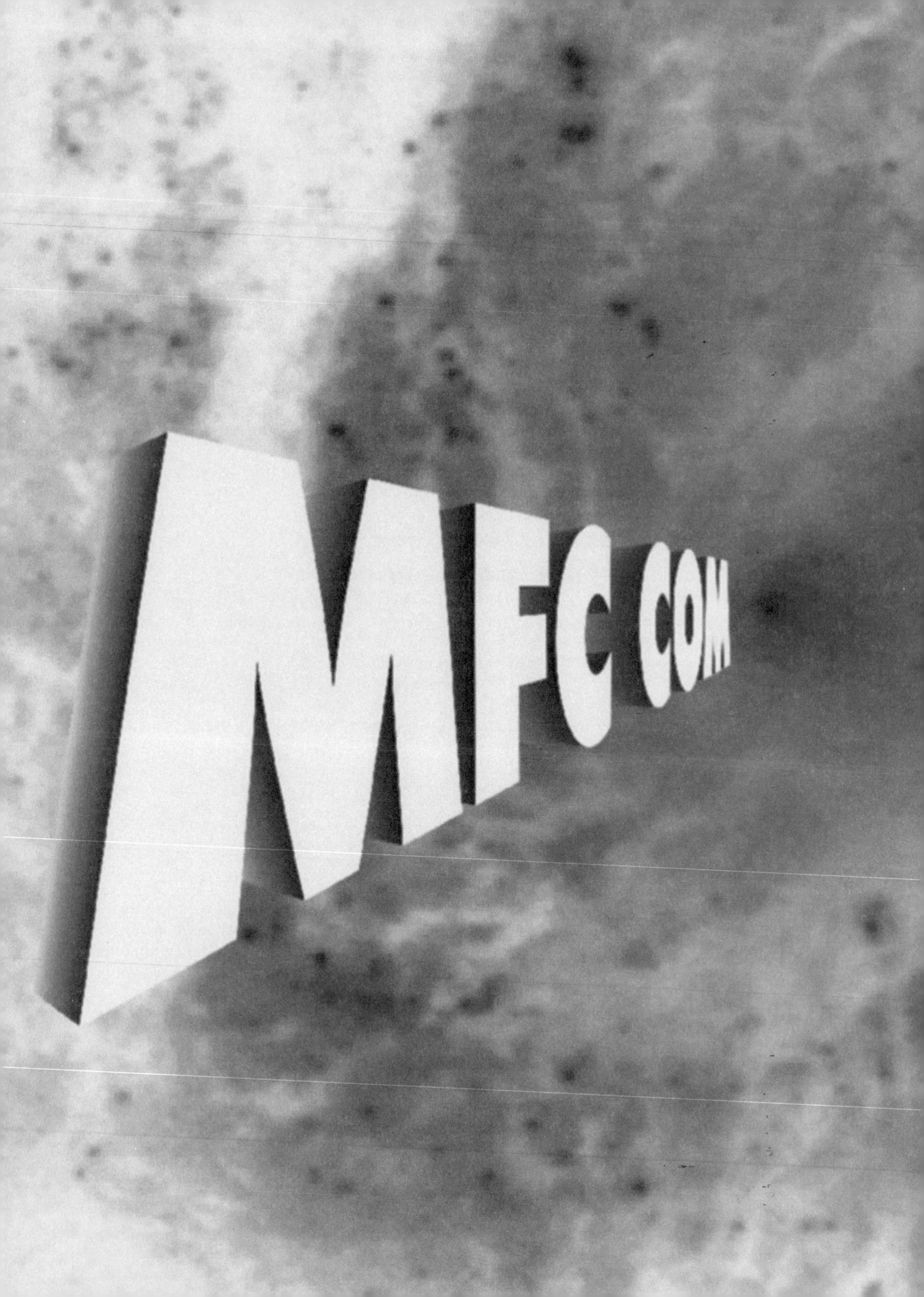
MFC COM

What's in a Name?

You've surely heard about ActiveX and OLE - they're hot topics in the Windows world. Pick up a magazine, read the Usenet newsgroups or browse the Web, and anywhere programming is being discussed you'll find people talking about ActiveX controls, Automation, Active documents... the list goes on. Many programmers are waking up to the fact that these technologies are starting to change the way things work - and that change is as big as the one which faced DOS programmers when Windows first came along.

This book, though, is called *Beginning MFC* **COM** *Programming* - so how does that fit in? As you'll discover, COM is the fundamental technology upon which all the above are built, and as such forms the common thread running through everything else we'll be looking at. Microsoft is using COM-based technologies everywhere, and has built support for them into Visual C++ and MFC. I aim to get you started on understanding and using these technologies, and to show how MFC makes it easy for you to build powerful applications based on them.

COM Evolution

COM, ActiveX and OLE didn't come about by chance. They were created to solve a problem that is, in essence, the complexity of the software environment. Over the past few years, we've seen an amazing increase in the number of software technologies that are available to programmers: GUIs such as Windows and OS/2, networks, client/server computing, databases, the Internet and so on. All these have increased the power and flexibility available to the programmer, but at the same time have brought with them a corresponding increase in the number of APIs, libraries, and techniques which the programmer has to master in order to stay ahead.

The software business being what it is, people expect these technologies to be exploited. It's that expectation which *really* leads to the problems, which fall into a number of areas. Here are the first few I thought of; I'm sure you could add others:

- The sheer quantity of programmer knowledge needed to keep on top of all the new technologies. Once it was possible to be a 'Windows programmer,' and know just about all you needed to write any Windows application you wanted. Now I very much doubt that's true.

- The problems of software bloat. How big is your favorite word processor or compiler? How much of a job do you think it is to maintain and develop monolithic products like these?

▶ Software is becoming more difficult to develop and maintain, both due to software bloat, and other unique problems such as DLL versioning, where two applications want to use the same DLL, but are expecting to find different versions.

▶ Much modern software has a lack of flexibility that fits badly with the advances that have been made in hardware. I can swap my PC-Card 'on the fly'; why can't I do the same with my spell-checker?

▶ Why can't I build my application from this server on this machine, and that database on that Unix box, and that graphics program on that Macintosh, and...

Several ways have been tried to tackle these problems. DLLs, for example, make programs more modular, but they're Windows-specific, and can be language-specific too. C++ classes make software development more manageable, but you can only use C++ objects in C++ programs.

As always in the world of software, there's no one 'silver bullet' that's going to slay the monster of software complexity, but one technique currently stands out above the others in terms of its possibilities: component-based programming.

Let's take the world of electronics as an example. Nowadays, the smallest unit from which electronic apparatus is made is the chip, or in many cases the circuit board. It's years since serious production work was done with individual transistors and resistors soldered together, and today most retail electronic equipment is constructed from components bought in from component manufacturers, or even selected from catalogs.

What advantages does this confer on the vendor and purchaser? Well, consider the PC on which you develop your programs. By using standardized components, we have:

▶ A rapid development cycle for the vendor.

▶ The ability to build from industry-standard components, which leads to flexibility of supply. The vendor can go wherever is best in terms of availability and price.

▶ Flexibility to assemble the product wherever is best.

▶ The benefits of a competitive market for the purchaser.

▶ The ability (or at least the possibility) to upgrade the equipment. You don't like the video card? The hard disk's too small? Fit a new one!

▶ The ability to service the equipment in the field. If your hard disk or power supply fails, you can replace it.

In the PC world, we see larger-scale integration when standard low-level components are used to build higher-level standard assemblies, such as PC-Cards, PCI or VL-bus boards, and so on. Wouldn't it be great if we could do the same thing with software, so that instead of handcrafting huge amounts of software for each application, we could plug together components that were independent of language, and maybe even of operating system? The advantages of using components are manifold:

▶ You get better integration between applications

▶ Developers are forced to define the interfaces between components, so you end up with better modularization

▶ Users are better able to customize applications to suite their needs

▶ Creating parts of an application as components can lead to a healthy market for third-party add-ons, such as has happened for Lotus Notes

We're starting to see this happen, and COM is one of the technologies in the forefront of the search to find ways of writing software objects which can be used in the same versatile way as chips and boards.

COM Revolution

Why is it important that you know about COM? Well, if you're a mainstream Windows programmer - someone who writes applications to run on the desktop rather than, say, device drivers or debuggers - then the answer is, quite simply, your job.

The COM-based technologies are at the very heart of Microsoft's development plans for Windows, and COM is radically affecting how we look at and use just about every aspect of Windows, from operating systems and languages to messaging and databases. Let me give you a few examples:

▶ The controls (called **ActiveX controls**) that you use in Visual Basic and Visual C++, use COM

▶ The controls that you embed in web pages are ActiveX controls, too

▶ If you embed a Paintbrush picture in a Word document, you're using COM

▶ If you write a bit of VBScript to control a Web page, that's using COM

▶ Drag and drop? In a lot of newer programs, it's done with COM

▶ If you want to interact with the Windows 95 shell, you use COM mechanisms

▶ If you write an add-in for Visual Basic 5.0, or run a Visual Basic server program over a network, then guess what... COM again!

There are new COM-based technologies appearing all the time. OLEDB, for example, is the successor to ODBC; where ODBC gives access to relational databases, OLEDB provides a more versatile level of access, so that the same API can be used to retrieve data from all kinds of sources, ranging from flat text files, through spreadsheets, up to ODBC databases.

The next version of Windows will integrate the network and the desktop environment seamlessly, and that's certainly going to be based on COM. It will really pay to get to know something *now* about what COM is, how it works, and how you can use it in your own programs. The Windows programmer who doesn't understand this technology and how to use it is going to be left behind pretty soon.

So just what *is* COM? We'll discover the answer to that at several different levels, from the fairly general to the highly detailed, as we progress through the book; for now, let's take it at an extremely general level, and say that 'COM provides a way for two pieces of code to work together'.

That seems a very simple statement, but consider this: when you double-click on a Paintbrush-generated picture in a Word document to edit it, what's going on? Word provides the space for the picture and Paintbrush does the editing, but it's COM that allows them to communicate.

It certainly doesn't end there. Think about an ActiveX control sitting on a Visual Basic form, or on a Visual C++ dialog. The ActiveX control is a small, self-contained piece of code loaded as a DLL. It sits in a space given to it by the form or dialog, and COM lets the control and its container communicate.

Finally, how about drag and drop? Here, the user selects something in a drag source, drags it across the desktop, and drops it onto a target application. It's COM that provides the mechanism by which the source and target applications communicate during the drag process.

The point hardly needs laboring. At this stage in its evolution, the COM-based technologies cover a lot of ground, precisely *because* COM is a very general mechanism. Some people have trouble grasping exactly what COM is, because there can seem to be so much going on with so little to unify it. What they need to realize is that COM simply defines a standard for the programmer to build on - it's what you do with it that counts.

COM, ActiveX, OLE

It was quite a tough task choosing a name for this book, it really was. Why? Because there are several names which can be used as labels for these related technologies, and it isn't always clear which name should be used for what and when. In fact, Microsoft itself doesn't always seem to know what should be given which name, and sometimes it's seemed as though the names have been changing on a weekly basis, as the marketing people think up new slogans and products.

Let's try to make things a little clearer and get the easy one out of the way. **COM** is the **C**omponent **O**bject **M**odel. The next chapter will explain, in gory detail, what COM actually is and does, but for now let's work on the basis that COM is the standard underpinning OLE, ActiveX, Automation and everything else we're dealing with here: the code which underlies and implements everything else. COM is real nuts-and-bolts stuff, equivalent in some ways to coding at the level of assembler or raw TCP/IP. Relatively few application programmers will tend to get down to the COM level very often, if at all.

Where the confusion really arises is between **OLE** and **ActiveX**. Are they the same? If not, what's different? And what should be called 'OLE' and what 'ActiveX'?

In the blue corner we have OLE. Back in the early 90s, the first OLE technology was introduced. OLE 1.0, as it was then, was limited to using container programs (like Microsoft Word) to hold linked or embedded objects (like Excel spreadsheets), and so the technology was called **O**bject **L**inking and **E**mbedding, which in the circumstances was pretty descriptive and perfectly sensible.

Everything in the garden was rosy until OLE version 2 arrived on the scene. This had rather more functionality than version 1: it supported Automation, controls, and all the other things we're going to discuss in this book - in other words, a whole lot more than plain old linking and embedding. The problem was that by then the name 'OLE' had stuck, like Hoover's name got applied to vacuum cleaners, although it wasn't wholly appropriate any more. If Microsoft had changed the name back then, life would have been a lot simpler for us now.

In the red corner, there's the challenger, ActiveX. Most people know the story of how Netscape, with the Navigator browser, and Sun, with the Java language, revolutionized the use of the Internet through the World Wide Web (WWW). Microsoft suddenly realized that there was a large, technologically advanced and profitable area in which they were very poorly represented. This realization led to a great deal of development getting done very quickly indeed, and a whole slew of new products and technologies emanating from Microsoft; indeed, the flood hasn't stopped, and it sometimes seems as if Microsoft introduces a new technology or product every week.

One thing which Microsoft lacked was an equivalent to Java language applets running on web pages; what it *did* have, however, were OLE controls, and so they set about modifying the specification so that OLE controls could be used in web pages too. In order to make these revamped controls look snazzy and new, a new name was coined, and that name was ActiveX. So, if you want the broadest definition possible, you could say that ActiveX refers to any COM-related technology which is new, or which has anything to do with the Net.

Now the ActiveX label has been stuck on some of the other COM-based technologies too, in order to try to get some sort of consistency in naming, but that's far from the end of the matter. For example, what used to be 'OLE controls' are now 'ActiveX controls', but what used to be called 'OLE Automation' is now just 'Automation'. Microsoft says that the term 'OLE' should only be applied to things which actually deal with linking and embedding, just like we originally had in OLE 1, but at the moment even they aren't consistent in applying the terminology. To give you examples, a lot of the MFC classes still have 'Ole' in their names (even new ones!), and some of the comments which AppWizard generates talk about 'OLE' as well.

The reason, then, that choosing a title was difficult is that to the non-cognoscenti, ActiveX means exciting, up-to-date Internet programming, with web pages and ActiveX controls, while OLE means very difficult, technical, Windows programming. As I hope you'll have gathered from the last few paragraphs, that certainly isn't entirely true. Many of the older technologies are appropriate in the Internet and intranet worlds, while the new ActiveX technologies are vitally important to mainstream Windows programming. The thing that ties them all together, though, is COM; that's what's at the bottom of all these technologies, so that's what this book is *really* about.

Why Visual C++?

Before we move on, let's consider why we should think of using Visual C++ to write COM-based software. There are now several Microsoft tools which enable you to write applications with varying degrees of COM support, including Visual Basic and Visual J++, but (up till now, at any rate) none has the power or the ability to produce industrial strength COM programs that Visual C++ has. Visual Basic 5.0, in particular, is a strong contender with its ability to produce ActiveX controls simply and quickly, but it still lacks the sophistication and power to get down to the nuts and bolts in quite the way that Visual C++ does.

A Simple Automation Application

We'll round off this chapter by writing a very simple application, using the facilities which Visual C++ and MFC provide, to show how to drive Microsoft Word by Automation. That means that we'll be able, from our program, to make Word create a new document and write some text (in our case the ubiquitous "Hello World") to it.

This application will demonstrate how easy it can be to use Visual C++ and Developer Studio to produce COM-based programs; in the next chapter we'll see what programming magic underlies this, and you'll begin to appreciate the help that the Visual C++ Wizards give you.

Before You Start

Using Automation with Visual C++ requires you to have a **type library** for the application you're going to automate, so in order to write this program, you'll need to have the Word type library (plus, of course, a copy of Microsoft Word).

Don't worry about exactly what a type library is for now; I'll explain that later. For the time being, it's reasonable to think of it as performing a similar task to the import libraries that you use with DLLs, in that it provides information to Developer Studio about Word's capabilities, without needing to have Word itself loaded.

Automating Word 95 is simpler than it is for Word 97, so I'll be basing this example around the former. For some reason, Microsoft didn't include the type library file for Word on the product CD, so you need to download the type library file from Microsoft's web site (**http://www.microsoft.com**), or from the Microsoft Software Library.

On the Microsoft site, there's a Knowledge Base article which explains how to get this file (article Q143434, How To Obtain The Word For Windows Type Library); you'll also find the Knowledge Base on the MSDN CDs, and on CompuServe. Once you've got the file containing the type library, unzip it and place the file **wb70en32.tlb** in the same directory as **WinWord.exe**. (It doesn't *actually* matter where you put it, but the Word directory seems a logical place!)

If you're using Word 97, don't despair: there's a way to drive it as if it were Word 95. You'll still require the Word 95 type library, as described above, but you'll also need the one for Word 97. This file *does* come on the product CD, in a file called **Msword8.olb**, which you should be able to find in the **Office** directory.

What Does Automation Do?

Many Windows applications, including Word, have been written so that they can be driven by other applications through Automation. This is a topic you'll come across frequently as you read this book. By making available an **Automation object**, an automated application can expose functions and data that other client applications, written in languages such as Visual Basic, Java or Visual C++, can use.

Automation means that we're able to write applications that can control one another, and it's one of the main ways in which software components can be built together into systems using COM. The number and type of functions and data items which applications expose will differ from application to application. In the case of Word 95, the Automation functionality is due to a single Automation object, and corresponds to a subset of Word's WordBasic macro language. In the case of Word 97, there's a whole hierarchy of Automation objects.

How Does it Work?

This is going to be a *very* simplified explanation of Automation. It gives enough detail that you'll be able to understand what's going on in the programs we're going to write, but I'll skip most of the details and the precise terminology; you'll learn that as we go along.

No matter what language we use to drive an application using Automation, we have to create an object in our code that somehow represents the application we want to drive. Creating this object in our application results in the **server application** being started in the background; the server then creates a COM object that will process our commands - this is the Automation object I referred to above.

Whichever version of Word you're using, Word itself is the server. If you're using Word 95 then the object it creates is a WordBasic object; if you're using Word 97, an Application object is created. If you think of Word as being a 'factory' producing objects for clients to use, you won't be far off the mark.

Once we have a suitable object to talk to, we can tell it to execute our commands. In a Visual C++ program, a true C++ object represents the Automation object, and the commands are member functions of the object's class, for example:

```
myObj.Insert("Some new text");
```

Here I've assumed that the Automation object is called **myObj**, and we've called the **Insert** function to get some text inserted into the document window. In other languages the syntax will vary, but the idea is the same.

Try It Out - Automating Microsoft Word

Since all we want to do is to kick off Word and get it to do something for us, we don't need a complex user interface - a dialog-based application will do nicely. Remember that what I'm giving you here is a simple demonstration of the power of Automation, so don't worry if there are things you don't completely understand - all will be revealed in the chapters to come!

> *I'll mention the differences between coding for the two versions of Word as and when they arise in the discussion. However, the principal change is that where Word 95 only exposes a single, all-encompassing WordBasic object, Word 97 has a whole hierarchy of Automation objects. These are grouped under the Application object, which is always the first to be created.*

1 Start up Developer Studio, and use AppWizard to create a dialog-based application, using all the standard options. Call the application whatever you like - I called mine 'WordTest'.

2 Next, edit the main dialog resource, remove the OK button, and add one labeled Do It instead. We'll use this to do the work for us; you ought to end up with a dialog that looks something like this:

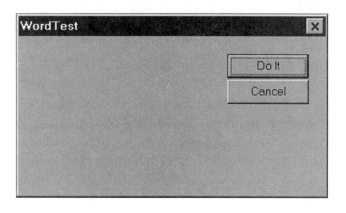

3 Change the properties of the new button so that its ID becomes **IDC_DOIT**, and use ClassWizard to add a handler for the Do It button.

4 In the brief preamble, I said that we communicate with Automation objects through C++ objects. Obviously, these objects must be instances of classes, so our next job is to create the WordBasic class. We do this using the Word 95 type library; when we ask it to, ClassWizard will read the information in the type library which tells it what methods and properties the WordBasic object created by the server supports, and then create a C++ class to represent that object.

This class not only gives us access to the methods and properties of the WordBasic object, but also does a lot of hard work for us - things like telling Word to create the WordBasic object, and translating function arguments into the forms COM needs. To create it, start ClassWizard, press the Add Class... button and choose From a type library... from the drop-down menu:

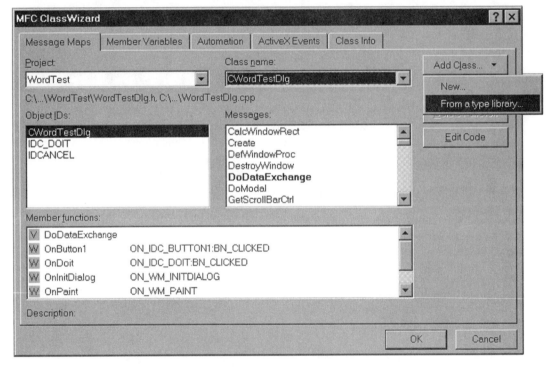

5 ClassWizard will display a file-browsing dialog. Navigate to the directory where you saved the type library file, and select it:

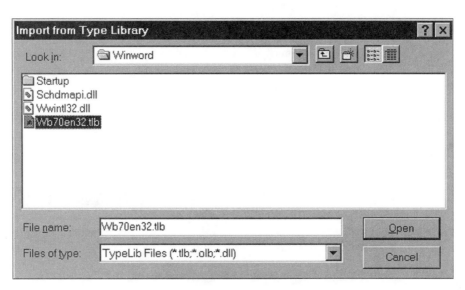

6 When you hit <u>O</u>pen, ClassWizard reads the information in the `.tlb` file, and decides what classes it's going to create for you. In this case, it's going to create a single class called **WordBasic**:

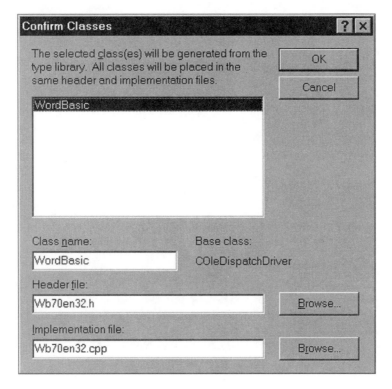

The filenames aren't exactly descriptive, so you can change them if you wish. When you hit OK, ClassWizard creates the C++ code, and adds the class file to your project. If you inspect it, you'll find that the **WordBasic** class contains a huge number of functions; there are hundreds, one for each supported **WordBasic** function.

7 **Word 97 only.** As I mentioned at the beginning of this example, Word 97 Automation begins with an Application object. Once we've created one of those, we can call one of its methods to create a WordBasic object. To communicate with the Application object we need an Application class, and for that we require the Word 97 type library. Follow steps 4 and 5 again, this time choosing the **Msword8.olb** file, and you'll be presented with this dialog:

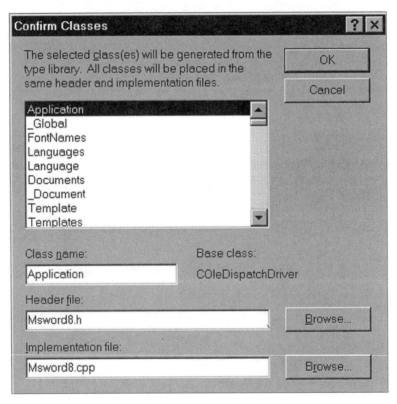

Select Application from the top of the list (I've deleted a leading underline in the Class name box), and generate the **Application** class.

8 Since we didn't opt to include Wizard support for creating the Automation aspect of our project, we need to add some initialization code to the application, placing it right at the top of **InitInstance()** in the application class. The call to **AfxOleInit()** ensures that the OLE DLLs are loaded and ready to go; if it returns **FALSE**, something is fairly drastically wrong, so we need to exit:

```
BOOL CWordTestApp::InitInstance()
{
    AfxEnableControlContainer();
```

```
// Standard initialization
// If you are not using these features and wish to reduce the size
//  of your final executable, you should remove from the following
//  the specific initialization routines you do not need.
```

```
// Initialize OLE libraries
if (!AfxOleInit())
{
   AfxMessageBox("OLE Initialization failed");
   return FALSE;
}
```

9 Now we have the structure in place, let's add the actual code which will automate Word. Open the dialog class implementation file, **WordTestDlg.cpp**, and add the **WordBasic** class header file to the list of includes at the top. If you're using Word 97, you'll need to **#include** the **Application** class header file as well.

10a Word 95. Find the Do It button handler **OnDoit()**, and add the following code:

```
void CWordtestDlg::OnDoit()
{
   // Create a WordBasic object.
   WordBasic wb;

   // Now get its dispatch interface. This will start up the server
   if (!wb.CreateDispatch(_T("word.basic")))
   {
      AfxMessageBox(_T("Call to CreateDispatch on server failed"));
      return;
   }

   // Open a new file
   wb.FileNewDefault();

   // Write some text
   wb.Insert("Hello world!");
}
```

The first thing we do is to create a **WordBasic** object. In the same way that creating a **CDialog** object in MFC doesn't actually create and display the underlying dialog box, creating this object doesn't actually start up Word for us; the actual creation of the underlying object is done later. In the case of a **CDialog**, this would be done by a call to **DoModal()** or **Create()**; here, it's done by the call to **CreateDispatch()**, which starts up Word and creates a **WordBasic** object that we can talk to. If the call returns **TRUE**, then Word was started up and successfully created the object we need.

> Don't worry about exactly what a 'dispatch' is. I'll explain it in the next chapter, and for now it's enough to know that it is, effectively, the interface through which our program can talk to the WordBasic object.

Having got the object, we can now use two member functions of the **WordBasic** class to open a new document and write some text to it. The **FileNewDefault()** function creates a new file, using the default Word document template, **normal.dot**. The **Insert()** function simply inserts a string of text into the document at the current cursor position.

10b   **Word 97.** If you're running Word 97, the code is just a little different. The
OnDoit() handler looks like this:

```
void CWordTestDlg::OnDoit()
{
    // Create an Application object
    Application app;

    // Now get its dispatch interface. This will start up the server
    if (!app.CreateDispatch(_T("word.application")))
    {
        AfxMessageBox(_T("Call to CreateDispatch on server failed"));
        return;
    }

    // Make the application visible
    app.SetVisible(TRUE);

    // Create a WordBasic object
    WordBasic wb(app.GetWordBasic());

    // Open a new file
    wb.FileNewDefault();

    // Write some text
    wb.Insert("Hello world!");
}
```

What difference do these few changes make? For a start, we begin by creating an Application
object, and using that to start up the server, but the syntax should be familiar to you from the
Word 95 example. The call to **SetVisible()**, on the other hand, is new, and makes use of a
feature that's less easy to implement in the older product. By default, applications being driven
by Automation start invisibly in the background, and then silently exit when their task is
finished. This function, as its name implies, makes the application visible.

The final new line creates a WordBasic object for us to interact with, just as we had for Word
95. On this occasion, though, the constructor is called with the result of the **GetWordBasic()**
function, which returns a pointer to the WordBasic object owned by the Word 97 Application
object. After this, the WordBasic object's methods are called as before.

11 The figure below shows the result of running the Word 97 program. In order to actually see
the output from the Word 95 version, you'll have to start Word yourself beforehand, because
of yet another difference in behavior. As I noted in the last step, Automation servers start
up invisibly, and it's not as easy to make Word 95 visible as it is for Word 97. However, if
there's already an instance of Word 95 in existence, the code will use it, and the result will
be the creation of a new document window in the application.

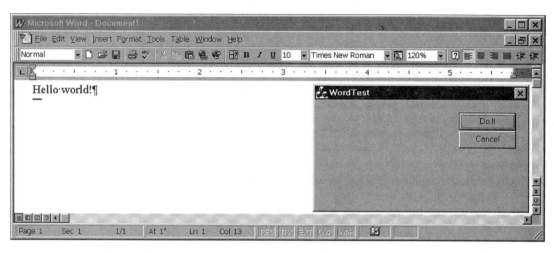

When the Do It button is pressed, Word creates a new document and inserts the text. When we close the dialog application, both Word and the new document persist.

> *I should point out that controlling Word 97 by Automation in this way, by using features of its backward-compatibility with Word 95, is not ideal. However, since this is simply an example of what Automation can do, it seems only sensible to keep the implementations as consistent as possible. If you'd like to see the same task done again using 'real' Word 97 Automation, you can download the code from the Wrox Press web site - but I'd recommend that you read a little further before doing so!*

The thing you should *really* take away from this example, however, is that (apart from the initialization of the OLE DLLs) you only had to write six lines of C++ code in order to take control of Microsoft Word 97 and have it do your bidding. Of course, there was a lot more going on than that, but then that's the point of this book - we're not trying to reinvent the wheel; we're learning how to make best use of the tools already available for implementing COM in our programs. Still, just so you know what you're missing out on, in the next chapter we'll perform this same trick without any help from MFC. Brace yourself!

Summary

In this chapter, you've learned something of COM's history - the reasons for its existence, and its rise to its present position, which is that of lynchpin for many of Microsoft's most important technologies. You should also have clear in your mind the distinctions between these technologies. OLE is all about linking and embedding objects, and the cooperation between applications that allows this to happen, while ActiveX is a general brand name for all of the COM-based technologies, and therefore includes, but is not limited to, OLE.

COM is important, and is going to become more so as time goes by. However, you've just seen how easy it can be to use Automation from a Visual C++ application - it required very little more effort than it would have done using Visual Basic. COM does get more complex than this, but Visual C++, its Wizards and MFC will help to make a lot of the complexity manageable, and give you the ability to create some really great applications.

MFC COM

An Introduction to COM, ActiveX and OLE

Now you've a idea of the things we're going to be looking at, and had a taste of just one of the things COM can do for you, my aim in this chapter is to give you a roller-coaster ride through the world of COM, ActiveX and OLE. I'm going to introduce all the main concepts and jargon, in a fashion that covers 'just enough' material for you to make sense of what follows it, and so that you have a firm (and accurate!) idea of the basics underlying everything we'll be doing with MFC in subsequent chapters.

I'll be going through a range of topics, from the basic fundamentals of the **Component Object Model (COM)**, through traditional **Object Linking and Embedding (OLE)**, and on to the latest COM-based **ActiveX** technologies. That means that this chapter is actually, despite its physical size, a quite brief and fairly superficial treatment of some complex and wide-ranging subjects. Having said that, there's still a lot of material here, and so I've structured it so that you can read it at two levels.

These 'all you need to know' boxes give concise definitions and descriptions, so on a first read through (or if you're reading this book to solve a particular programming problem) you may want to read these sections alone, and then move on to the next chapter. You can then read the whole chapter in depth when you need (or want) to know the details.

This chapter deals with the details and features of COM and its related technologies; the rest of the book focuses on COM programming with MFC. I'll be covering some of the theory in more detail as and when it's needed, but as some of COM's features aren't supported by MFC, I won't be mentioning them again after this chapter. If some of these points are important to you, you'll need to refer to one of the more advanced and specialized texts for details; you'll find a list of resources in Appendix F.

COM Basics

Let's creep up on COM by thinking a little more about two other technologies that are used to create components, albeit at a more fundamental level than COM.

Consider C++ classes, with their use of inheritance and encapsulation. You only have to look at the frameworks used for Windows programming, such as MFC and Borland's OWL, to see how effective classes can be in providing us with software 'black boxes' - top-level wrappers that disguise deeper complexity.

C++ classes are, however, specific to C++ programs, and have an internal structure all of their own. This means that, say, a Smalltalk object and a C++ object won't have much in common, because their internal structures are different, and there is no standard way for them to inter-operate. In fact, many C++ objects often can't even be used with other C++ objects produced by a different compiler, because of the implementation dependencies left open by the C++ language specification. There is no binary standard for compiled C++ objects.

One way to remedy this is to use the second of the two methods I alluded to above: DLLs. These allow run-time linking and have less language dependence. There are problems here too, though, because they only export on a single-routine basis, rather than whole objects at once. And, of course, they're limited to Windows platforms.

Before we move on to look at what COM is, let's go back a step and ask, "What is a C++ object?" A reasonable definition is that it's a software entity that has data, plus methods that make it operate. Some of the functions are private to the object, and are used in its internal operation, while others are visible outside the object, and are used by outside agents to control it.

Think of this in analogy to a real-world object: a car. The steering wheel, brake pedal and so on are 'public' controls, used by the operator to control the car; the actual operation of the steering and brakes, via linkages, cables, pistons and so on, are 'private' to the car. They aren't used directly by the operator, and in many cases the operator may be unaware of their existence.

From the operator's point of view, the important parts of the object are the functions by which it can be manipulated - the object's interface. From the implementor's side, it's important that the interface allows the user to control the object fully, while not allowing them access to parts of the object they shouldn't play with.

> *Why use COM when we've got DLLs? That's a question that is often asked by experienced Windows programmers on first meeting COM. There's no question that DLLs are an essential part of Windows - indeed, Windows wouldn't work without them - but they do suffer from some problems which make true component-based solutions difficult. Here are a few examples; you'll see as we progress how COM provides answers to these (and other) problems.*

> ▶ *DLL names and locations tend to be hard-coded. An application loads a DLL by name, and if the name changes, the DLL becomes 'invisible'. The DLL also has to reside in the application directory, in the Windows system directories, or on the path in order to be found.*

> ▶ *Under Win32, DLLs are hard to share between processes, as they're loaded into the address space of each process that wants to use them, which wastes time and resources. It's possible to load some DLLs, such as the Windows system DLLs, as subsystems so that only one instance services the whole system, but they're expensive and not suited to application software.*

> ▶ *A multiple service DLL requires coordination of ordinal numbers or function names. DLLs have a fixed overhead, so it's often useful to combine functionality (services) into a single DLL, but this may lead to problems if routines from different services have previously been allocated the same ordinal numbers.*

> ▶ *DLLs don't support versioning. Since DLLs are only referenced by name, there's not necessarily any way to tell whether the* **Fred.dll** *present on your system represents version 1.0, 1.1 or even 2.0. It is quite possible (and normal!) to have multiple copies of DLLs of different versions present on one machine, and this can lead to problems which are sometimes very hard to solve. Overwriting older DLL versions is a related problem.*

How COM Works

COM gives us a way to use objects like we do in C++, even when those objects don't live in the same program (perhaps not even on the same machine), and aren't written in the same language. It does this by specifying how software objects should be laid out in binary form (in other words, how they should be laid out in memory), and how they can communicate with one another, in a way that doesn't depend on a particular machine or language, making them **architecture-neutral**.

COM objects consist of a collection of **interfaces**. An interface is the way in which an object exposes its functionality to the outside world. In COM, an interface is a table of pointers to functions implemented by the object. The table represents the interface, and the functions to which it points are the methods of that interface. An object can expose as many interfaces as it chooses.

The defined binary layout of a COM object governs how its tables of publicly-available functions are laid out, and means that the format is independent of the language in which the object was written and the machine architecture on which it runs. The tables, analogous to C++ **virtual function tables**, are known as **vtables**. In Visual C++, COM vtables and C++ virtual function tables have the same structure, which is, I guess, only sensible of Microsoft. This may not be true of other compilers, which means they'd have to do rather more work when representing COM objects in C++.

Standardizing the communication means that one COM object can look for another one at runtime and know how to interact with it. Since the layout of the interfaces is known, it should be possible for any COM object to use a function exposed by another.

Let's nail one other useful piece of jargon before we go any further. You'll see a lot of mention of **servers** and **clients** in the COM literature. A 'server' is a COM object which provides an interface (or interfaces) that someone else might want to use, and a 'client' is a COM object which uses an interface by calling one or more of its functions.

FYI

A COM object is a software object - typically an EXE file or a DLL - exposing one or more interfaces; COM objects communicate with one another by calling functions in each others' interfaces.

A COM interface is a group of pointers to a series of related functions, analogous to the member functions of a C++ class. COM objects can possess one or more interfaces, and the specification for how these are written is language- and architecture-independent.

COM interfaces are implemented as vtables, which are like C++ virtual function tables. An interface thus consists of a table of function pointers that point to functions inside the object.

A server is a COM object that provides one or more interfaces; a client is a COM object that uses a server's interfaces.

Programming with COM

You might well be under the impression that COM programming is difficult - there's lots of new terminology and strange variable types to remember. However, although COM has a reputation for being tricky to understand, it's really quite simple at the core. It's mainly a lack of information and poorly worded documentation that makes it tough to get started.

You'll see in this chapter how it isn't hard to write basic COM-level code, although you should also get a feeling for how tedious it would be to write a whole application in this manner!

Luckily for us C++ programming types, MFC has started to do the same job for COM that it's done for Windows programming, by wrapping up a lot of the tedious, long-winded and error-prone stuff in a set of classes. In addition, Visual C++ provides Wizard support to set up the skeletons of COM-enabled applications. We'll meet these, and see how to use them, as we progress through the book.

Object Packaging

A COM object is an idealized piece of software. In the real world, these objects have to be packaged up somehow, and given somewhere to live. There are three main ways in which objects can be packaged in the Windows environment:

- In a DLL
- In an EXE
- Provided from somewhere else, as a remote service

Objects that never execute on their own, and that are only ever used as components by other applications, can be packaged in DLLs. A typical example of this is the ActiveX control (described later in this chapter), where one or more controls are packaged up into a DLL (usually with the extension **.ocx**), which is loaded by the client when required. Objects in DLLs execute in the client's address space, and are often said to be **in-process** or **in-proc**.

Objects packaged in EXE files execute in their own address space, and are sometimes known as **out-of-process**. This is typically the case where a COM object is provided as part of a larger application, such as the Automation objects exposed by applications such as Microsoft Word and Excel. Note the use of the word 'exposed' here; the inner workings of COM objects are hidden from view, and the only way in which we can know anything about what they're doing is through the interfaces they make available to the outside world. As if to emphasize this rather secretive way of working, COM interfaces and objects are said to be **exposed** by an application.

If we're using a network - a LAN, a WAN, or the Internet - then we may use COM objects packaged up as a **service**, coming to us from another machine, somewhere else. We don't know what is servicing our call at the other end, but something is talking to us over the network!

One very important feature of all this, and one that I'll cover in greater detail later on, is the concept of **location transparency**. Put simply, it doesn't matter to a client where the object it's using is located, or how it is being accessed. As far as the client is concerned, using an object in a DLL is identical to accessing one on another machine across a network, or one on the same machine but out-of-process. We'll take a look at how this is done later on in the chapter.

COM servers come in three basic flavors. An in-process **COM server is packaged as a DLL, so that it shares the address (process) space of the client using it. An** out-of-process **server is packaged as an EXE file, so that it resides in its own address space. A** service **is a COM object provided from Somewhere Else, perhaps elsewhere on a network.**

Location transparency **is the notion that a client doesn't need to know where the object it is using is actually located.**

Interfaces

From what I've said so far, it should be clear that the idea of interfaces is pretty important to COM. It's the only way that COM objects can communicate with one another, and once you understand interfaces and how they work, the rest of COM should fall into place.

An interface is a table of function pointers, which in turn point to functions that are related in some way, such as handling files, or doing a particular calculation. The diagram below shows the idea; the interface consists of a number of function pointers (**pFuncA**, **pFuncB** and so on) that point to the actual functions themselves. If we obtain a pointer to the interface, we can then call the functions.

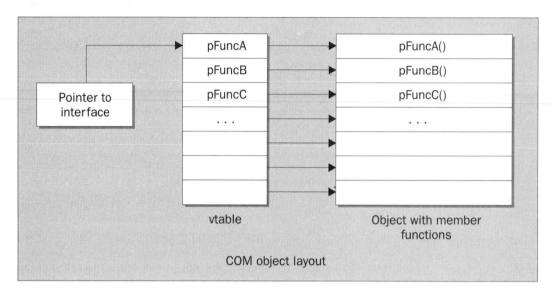

vtable

Object with member functions

COM object layout

It's possible to group any set of functions together into an interface, but like a C++ class, you expect there to be some underlying cohesion between the members. By convention, interfaces are given names starting with **I**, such as **IUnknown** and **IDispatch**. The figure below shows how COM interfaces are commonly drawn, using boxes for the objects and circles for the interfaces exposed by objects.

By convention, names of interfaces always start with **I**, such as **IUnknown** and **IDispatch**.

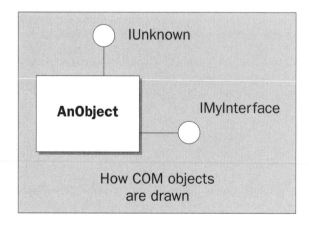

How COM objects are drawn

The idea really is very similar to the virtual function tables used in C++ classes, and it's therefore quite reasonable to implement a COM interface as an 'abstract data type' - a C++ base class consisting solely of pure virtual functions. This makes C++ a natural language for writing COM code, and in fact Microsoft provides C++ classes which wrap all the COM interfaces that they provide.

Since COM has no language dependence, you can write in other languages too, most notably C, but it fits very naturally with C++ classes. It also helps if you have a language with some notion of pointers - I'd hate to think how you'd implement a COM object in FORTRAN-77!

Object Orientation

COM interfaces can be said to act in an object-oriented manner, at least as far as its most famous features - data abstraction, encapsulation and polymorphism - are concerned.

Data abstraction is provided by the interfaces, which provide the client with an abstraction of the underlying object. Encapsulation is supported in that access to the internals of an object is only possible through the functions exposed by an interface. Polymorphism in COM doesn't come via inheritance, as it does in C++, but is supported instead by the fact that any object can support (contain) any other interface, and thus act polymorphically with respect to it. If interface A supports all the functions required by interface B, then A can be treated as if it *is* interface B, since there's nothing you can call in B that isn't also in A.

Objects as Contracts

One of the biggest bugbears of 'traditional' component programmers is the versioning problem. Most of us have had problems created by using the wrong versions of DLLs, and know what headaches it can cause.

When creating a COM component, we can use interfaces in such a way as to minimize the possibility of versioning problems occurring. The way it's done is simple: once an interface has been defined and **published** (in other words, once it's there for clients to use), it is regarded as cast in stone, and nothing should be done which will change the way the interface is used.

The interface is like a contract between the object and a client, specifying that a certain group of services are always going to be available in the same way. This means that you may neither add nor subtract methods, nor change method names, although the *implementations* of methods can change. This 'contract' also states that the interface must support *all* methods documented for that interface, though some method implementations can return an error code saying that they are not supported.

> *This idea of the contract is absolutely central to COM, because without the notion of immutable interfaces, COM isn't a practical solution to component-based development.*

What if you need to change an interface? Under COM, you create a new one, incorporating those elements you need from the existing interface. The important part is that the old interface is still supported by the object, and so can be found by those older clients that require it. The diagram below shows how this works:

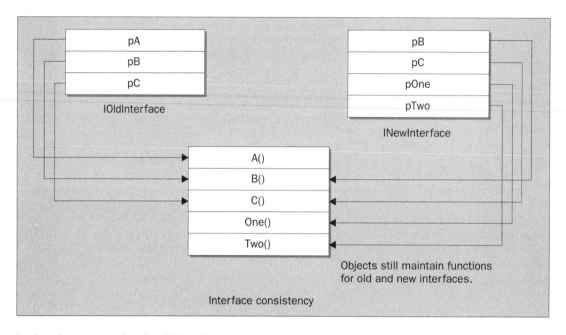

Interface consistency

Objects still maintain functions
for old and new interfaces.

In the above example, the COM object had a simple original interface which supported three functions called **A()**, **B()** and **C()**. Along came some new requirements, and suddenly there was a need to add the functions **One()** and **Two()**, and remove reference to **A()**. So **INewInterface** was born, which incorporates two of **IOldInterface**'s functions and then adds its own. Everyone is happy; older applications can still find **IOldInterface**, while newer ones get **INewInterface**. The overhead is an extra function table - a few dozen bytes in a typical case - plus leaving the old function **A()** in the code. The great advantage is that you've gone a long way toward solving the versioning problems you can get with DLLs.

> **FYI** An interface is regarded as a form of contract between the server and client, in that once a client has used it, the definition of an interface is regarded as fixed, and mustn't be changed. If you need to add, remove or change items in the interface, you must create a new one.

You might wonder why you can't *add* new methods to an interface. The answer is that any client looking for this new method won't find it if the COM server object it's communicating with has an older implementation of the interface. The contract states that the method must be there, or at least return a status code explaining that the function isn't implemented. Neither will be true in this case.

IUnknown

When talking about COM interfaces, we have to start with the most fundamental of them all, **IUnknown**. This interface plays a role in COM not unlike that of **CObject** in MFC; it isn't a whole lot of use on its own, but it provides several services which make everything else work, as we'll see shortly. In C++, **IUnknown** can be defined like this:

```
class IUnknown
{
public:
    virtual HRESULT QueryInterface(REFIID riid, LPVOID FAR* ppv) = 0;
    virtual ULONG AddRef() = 0;
    virtual ULONG Release() = 0;
};
```

Notice that the member functions are implemented as pure virtual functions. Code like this is a *definition* of an interface; one or more applications might decide to implement this interface, in which case they'll have to provide implementations for the member functions themselves. Pure virtual functions provide a way of enforcing this in C++.

> *Don't worry about the precise meanings of the parameter and return types - we'll discover as many as we need to understand as we go along, and there's some further detail in Appendix B. Do note, however, that it's important for the functions making up an interface always to be defined in the same order.*

The unique place of **IUnknown** in the universe of COM interfaces stems from the facts that:

- Every COM object has to implement the **IUnknown** interface. In other words, *all* COM objects implement the three **IUnknown** functions. In fact, the barest minimal COM object is one that only implements **IUnknown**, but that wouldn't be a very useful object!

- Every COM interface starts off with these three **IUnknown** functions, which means that (in a sense) every interface 'inherits' from **IUnknown**.

- **IUnknown** provides the means for COM objects to control their lifetimes, and gives users the ability to navigate between interfaces.

  *Apparently, the name **IUnknown** came about when the developers at Microsoft were designing COM. They had to think of a name for the interface that you used when every-thing else about an object was unknown. To reflect something of its use, they called it **IUnknown**.*

IUnknown is the fundamental COM interface from which all others derive. This interface supports three functions: **QueryInterface()**, which helps navigate to other interfaces supported by the object, and **AddRef()** and **Release()**, which are used to manage the object's lifespan by reference counting.

The important thing to note from the definition given above is that, in C++ terms, the interface is simply a class containing three public, pure virtual functions. If we want to write our own COM object, we know that we need to support the **IUnknown** functions, so we need to inherit from the **IUnknown** class and provide implementations for the virtual functions. In the example below, the derived class name starts with **Co**, a convention denoting that the class implements a COM object:

```
class CoMyObject : public IUnknown
{
public:
```

```
    // Default constructor
    CoMyObject();

    // IUnknown functions
    HRESULT QueryInterface(REFIID riid, LPVOID FAR* ppv);
    ULONG AddRef();
    ULONG Release();
};
```

> *If we want to support more than one interface, there are two main ways to accomplish this. The first is multiple inheritance. Here, we inherit from each of the base interface classes, so that we implement all the necessary functions directly. The second option is to inherit only from* **IUnknown**, *and to use nested classes to handle the other interfaces. This second method is close to how MFC does the job.*

How should **IUnknown**'s three functions be implemented? We'll come to that soon, but before we do there's something else you need to know. If we're going to be calling interface functions, we need a way to refer to objects and interfaces in a way which is portable and, more importantly, unique.

Unique Identifiers

All COM objects and interfaces have distinct and unique identifiers (IDs), which are used to identify them by the system. It would be reasonably easy to make up something unique on a single machine - we could look at all the other COM objects and interfaces installed on that machine, and check that the ID we're proposing for our new item isn't duplicated. However, it's a much bigger problem when we come to work *across* machines - how can you be sure that an ID you pick isn't going to clash with the ID of some object you want to use on another machine? We need something which is guaranteed to be unique across machines, and that's where the idea of a 'universal' ID comes in.

These universal IDs are called either **UUIDs** (Universally Unique IDs) or **GUIDs** (Globally Unique IDs), depending on whose literature you read. How they're constructed is quite interesting in itself, and is covered in the next section.

GUIDs that refer to a COM object are called **class IDs** (or **CLSIDs**), while those that refer to individual interfaces called **interface IDs** (or **IIDs**). In C++ COM programming, you'll sometimes also use *references* to interface IDs, which are called **REFIIDs**.

A couple of new IDs have been recently added to the list. A large application such as Excel or Word can have a lot of different COM objects associated with it, and the **application ID** (or **appID**) is a way of identifying which COM objects belong to a given application. The **category ID** (or **catID**) provides a way to group objects into categories, so that an application can search for all the applications that are spell checkers, or that can import spreadsheet data. You can see some of the standard categories if you look in the registry under **HKEY_CLASSES_ROOT\Component Categories**, and we can expect to see more arriving as the idea catches on.

COM objects and interfaces are identified by (and manipulated using) unique identifiers called GUIDs (Globally Unique Identifiers), also known as UUIDs (Universally Unique Identifiers). A GUID is a 128-bit quantity, generated by an algorithm that makes it very unlikely that duplicates will occur.

A CLSID, or class ID, is a GUID that identifies a COM object.

An IID, or interface ID, is a GUID that identifies an interface.

A REFIID is a C++ type denoting a reference to an IID.

How Identifiers are Generated

An algorithm, specified by the Open Group, is used to generate IDs. The creation process involves computation on data items such as:

- The current date and time
- The machine's network card address (or equivalent information)
- A high frequency counter

The GUID generated is a 128-bit number which is statistically very unlikely to be duplicated; according to the COM specification, unique GUIDs can be generated at a rate of 10 million per second until the year 5770! These IDs are normally handled as strings of hex digits, like this:

```
{000209FE-0000-0000-C000-000000000046}
```

GUIDs in this form aren't very human-friendly (surprisingly, some people find them hard to remember), so COM gives us an easier way to handle them, by letting us associate a name, called a **programmatic ID** or **progID** with the GUID. For example, the name **word.basic** can be used in place of **{000209FE-0000-0000-C000-000000000046}**, the CLSID of the Word 95 Automation object. Note that progIDs aren't required to be unique, so if you're going to use them in code, you need to be aware that there's a chance of name collision, and that it's better to use a CLSID if possible.

A progID, or programmatic ID, provides a humanly-readable alternative to a GUID.

There are several ways to get a GUID, including phoning Microsoft and asking for one (in fact, you get them in batches of 255), but most of the time you don't need to go to that extreme. The basic COM routine for creating GUIDs is **CoCreateGUID()**, which calls the lower-level basic RPC routine **UuidCreate()**. It's this bottom-level routine which contains the algorithm to generate a GUID. You don't usually need to use this yourself, though, and GUIDs tend to be automatically generated by Visual C++ whenever you need them.

When you do need to generate a GUID yourself, there's a Visual C++ utility program called Guidgen that will generate you a GUID and copy it to the clipboard in one of several handy formats. Which one you pick will depend on where in your code you need to paste a GUID.

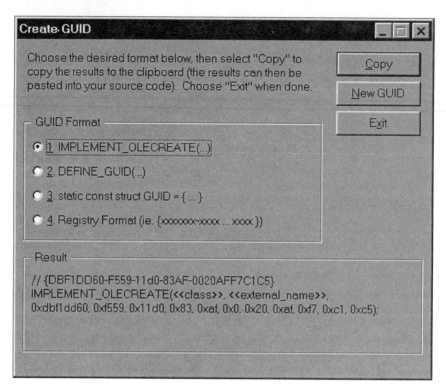

All these IDs need to be stored somewhere, and since the emphasis in COM is on run-time linking of components, it needs to be somewhere central where any object can go to find the information it needs. Enter, the registry!

The Registry

I'm not going to provide a great deal of detail concerning the registry, but if you're working with COM, you need to know something about what the registry is and how it works.

The **system registry** is a repository of information about the machine environment, held in the form of a hierarchical database. The database consists of keys, each of which has an entry of its own and may also contain subkeys. You refer to entries in the registry with a string key made up by concatenating subkeys together with backslashes, rather like a file system path name, e.g. **HKEY_LOCAL_MACHINE\Config\0001**. The example below shows a typical registry entry, and you can see how the key is built up from the various levels in the hierarchy. In this case, the key is **My Computer\KEY_CLASSES_ROOT\PBrush\protocol\StdFileEditing\Verb\0**, and the value associated with the key, shown in the right-hand pane, is **"Edit"**.

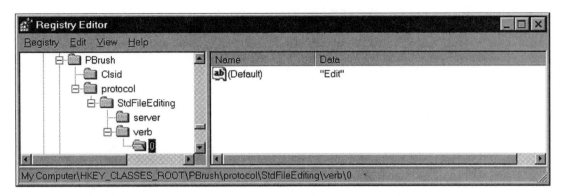

Registry entries can have security control, so that you can control access to particular objects on your machine. The role of the registry in Windows 3.1 was very limited; it has a vastly extended role in Windows NT and 95, holding not only information on COM objects and interfaces, but also much of the information that was previously in **.ini** files.

Location of Information in the Registry

On a Windows 95 or NT 4 machine, the registry information is structured underneath half-a-dozen top-level keys, known as **hives**. The most important of these top-level keys are **HKEY_LOCAL_MACHINE**, which holds all the hardware and software information on the machine, and **HKEY_USERS**, which holds all the user information. Some of the other top-level keys map onto subkeys of these two, as shown in the table below:

Root Key Name	Use
HKEY_LOCAL_MACHINE	Local machine information, including saved configurations
HKEY_USERS	Details of users on this machine
HKEY_CLASSES_ROOT	Holds the COM GUID information. Maps onto **HKEY_LOCAL_MACHINE\Software\Classes**
HKEY_CURRENT_USER	Details of the current user. Maps onto a subkey of **HKEY_USERS**
HKEY_CURRENT_CONFIG	Details of the current machine configuration. Maps onto a subkey of **HKEY_LOCAL_MACHINE\Config**
HKEY_DYN_DATA	Machine performance data

This was slightly different under Windows NT 3.51, in that there was no **HKEY_CURRENT_CONFIG,** *and* **HKEY_DYN_DATA** *was called* **HKEY_PERFORMANCE_DATA.**

From our point of view, the most interesting hive is **HKEY_CLASSES_ROOT**, beneath which all the COM information is stored. The diagram below shows how all the information is stored, and gives you an idea of how an application can find out which server is associated with a particular progID or file type.

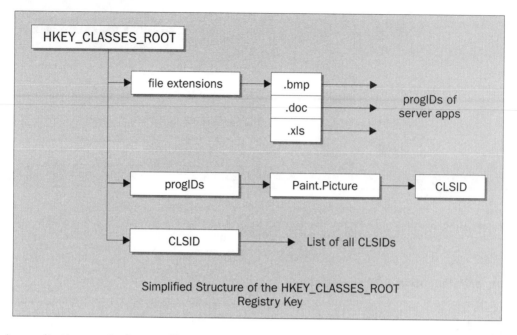

Simplified Structure of the HKEY_CLASSES_ROOT
Registry Key

An application can look up a file extension and find a progID. For instance, in the diagram, **.bmp** has the value **Paint.Picture**. The progID can then be used to find a CLSID, and that CLSID can be looked up in the list that's held under the **HKEY_CLASSES_ROOT\CLSID** subkey. Once there, the **LocalServer32** subkey shows that the server for this file type is (on my machine, anyhow) **C:\Program Files\Accessories\MSPAINT.EXE**.

Manipulating the Registry

You can browse and edit the registry database using the RegEdit utility, although you should make sure you know what you're doing if you do decide to modify it. It's wise always to make a backup first, just in case your activities render your system inoperable. Don't laugh - it can happen, and it could happen to you!

Programs use the Win32 Registry API to edit the database. This is a group of a dozen or so API calls, with names like **RegOpenKey()**, **RegQueryValue()**, and **RegCreateKeyEx()**, which provide the ability to browse the registry, reading and (if security permits) editing and creating entries.

QueryInterface

Now we know how IDs work, we can return to the **IUnknown** interface functions of our tiny COM object, **CoMyObject**. In order to call the functions supported by an interface, we must first get a pointer to the interface itself. Getting these pointers is the job of **QueryInterface()**.

Each interface has a unique identifier, so we can ask an object whether it supports a particular one by calling **QueryInterface()** and passing the ID of the interface we're interested in. Since all interfaces implement **QueryInterface()** (because they all inherit it from **IUnknown**), we can use any interface to find out whether any other interface is supported by the object, and in this way we can navigate around the interfaces that the object supports. Note that you can't easily get a list of the interfaces that an object supports, because the COM team didn't think that was a useful thing to want to do.

When we pass **QueryInterface()** an interface ID, it will return a pointer to the interface if it can (in fact, it's a pointer to the first entry in the vtable comprising the interface), or **NULL** if it can't. You'll notice from the definition of **QueryInterface()** that we pass a pointer variable which is filled in with the address of the first entry in the vtable; since these entries are themselves pointers, we find ourselves dealing a lot with pointers to pointers - ******s.

QueryInterface() is one of the three functions making up the IUnknown interface. Given the ID of an interface, QueryInterface() will return a pointer to an object's implementation of that interface, or NULL if the object doesn't support the interface. The function can be used to navigate from interface to interface around an object.

While we're at it, let's look in closer detail at the syntax of **QueryInterface()**, and especially the data types used:

```
HRESULT QueryInterface(REFIID riid, LPVOID FAR* ppv);
```

The function takes two parameters: a **REFIID** and an **LPVOID FAR***. A **REFIID** is simply a reference to an **IID**, an **IID** being the GUID of an interface. So what we're doing here is passing the GUID of a particular interface by reference. **QueryInterface()** is going to pass us back the address of the interface as a **void*** pointer, so in order to hold that value, we need to pass over the address of a **void*** pointer variable. **LPVOID** is a **typedef** for **void***, so we want an **LPVOID***. The **FAR** keyword is in there because the COM mechanisms will work under 16-bit Windows, where we have to take account of segmentation issues. Under 32-bit Windows the **FAR** is preprocessed away to nothing.

Data Types

COM API calls such as **QueryInterface()** return **HRESULT**s, which are 32-bit quantities used to describe errors or warnings. It's important to realize that the **HRESULT** reflects whether the call worked from COM's, rather than the function's, point of view; if the call to **QueryInterface()** was successful, then the **HRESULT** will reflect this. If COM couldn't make the call work - maybe because the object at the other end had gone away - then the **HRESULT** will reflect this, too. Any result expected from the function will be returned via the argument list. In other words, the **HRESULT** belongs to COM, and the arguments belong to the function called.

COM API calls return HRESULTs, 32-bit quantities holding information on the success (or otherwise) of the call. The SUCCEEDED() and FAILED() macros can be used to test the value of an HRESULT.

HRESULTs aren't just simple numeric error codes, but instead are made up of bit fields, as follows:

Bits	Contents	Description
0-15	The status or error code	
16-27	The facility code	Who set the status code

Table Continued on Following Page

Bits	Contents	Description
28	Reserved bit	
29	Customer code flag	
30-31	Severity flag	00=success, 01=information, 10=warning, 11=error

Clearly, there's quite a lot of information in here, but a lot of the time we're only interested in whether the call succeeded or failed. It wouldn't be particularly convenient to have to test individual bits each time we get back an **HRESULT**, so the Windows API defines several convenient macros for us to use, such as **FAILED(HRESULT)** and **SUCCEEDED(HRESULT)**, which return Boolean values.

You may also see mention of return values called **SCODE**s, especially in older COM code and literature. Originally, an **HRESULT** was just a 'handle to a result' (hence its name), and the actual status data was held in an **SCODE**. When 32-bit operation came along, the two were merged so that the data was stored in the **HRESULT** itself, so that under Windows 95 and NT you can think of **SCODE**s and **HRESULT**s as the same thing.

> *QueryInterface() will return **NULL** if it can't give you a pointer to the interface. This usually means that the object doesn't support the interface you've asked for, but it's possible that the object has, for some reason, decided not to give you a pointer to an interface which it does support - normally because the object doesn't support multiple, simultaneous requests.*

Implementation

Now we know what **QueryInterface()** is supposed to do, we can take a stab at implementing it for our example class:

```
HRESULT QueryInterface(REFIID riid, LPVOID FAR* ppv)
{
    if (riid == IID_IUnknown)
    {
        *ppv = (IUnknown *)this;
    }
    else
    {
        *ppv = NULL;
        return E_NOINTERFACE;
    }
    return S_OK;
}
```

The code is actually pretty straightforward. We check the interface ID which has been asked for against the ones we know about (in this case, only **IUnknown**). The check is done by comparing the ID passed in against the ID for **IUnknown**, **IID_IUnknown**.

> *All the standard interfaces have their corresponding IDs, formed by prefixing the interface name with* **IID_**. *You might expect these to be declared in a header file, but in fact they're defined in some library files -* **uuid.lib, uuid2.lib** *and* **uuid3.lib** *- which can be found along with all the other Visual C++ library files.*

If we find a match, we return a pointer to the interface and a successful result code. The interface pointer is constructed by casting the **this** pointer to an **IUnknown***, which may look rather strange, until you think of what we're trying to do.

Our COM object implements all the **IUnknown** functions, and so it's quite reasonable (and safe) to think of a **CoMyObject** object as an **IUnknown** object. The standard COM header files provide types to represent all the standard interfaces, so there is an **IUnknown** class, and we are quite entitled to cast our **this** pointer and return it, so that the caller can use our object polymorphically as an **IUnknown** object.

If there's no match, we return a **NULL** pointer and an error code **E_NOINTERFACE**, which indicates that the requested interface isn't supported.

This is all very well, but you've probably spotted a problem by now: before we can call **QueryInterface()** for the first time, we need a pointer to an interface! How do we get our first interface in order to start? As you'll discover soon, when we create an object, we get returned a pointer to an interface we specify (usually **IUnknown**), and that gives us a place to begin.

AddRef and Release

C++ objects use constructors and destructors to manage their life spans, and to perform housekeeping such as allocating and deallocating memory. When we want to create a C++ object we can call **new**, and then use **delete** to cause it to be destroyed.

However, these functions are language features, specific to C++. How, then, do we create and destroy COM objects? The answers are:

▶ We call a COM API function, such as **CoCreateInstance()**, to create objects

▶ Objects manage their own destruction

Since objects manage their own destruction, and we already know what **QueryInterface()** does, you've probably guessed that the procedure must have something to do with **AddRef()** and **Release()**, and of course you'd be right.

FYI **AddRef()** and **Release()** are the second and third members of the **IUnknown** interface, and are used to manage object lifetimes through reference counting. Each time a pointer to an interface is handed to a client, **AddRef()** is called; each time a client finishes with an interface pointer, it calls **Release()**.

The management is done by a process of **reference counting**. Each object maintains a reference count, initially set to zero. Every time the object hands a pointer to one of its interfaces to a client, it increments the interface's reference count by calling its **AddRef()** function. When the client finishes with the interface, it calls the interface's **Release()** function, in which the object decrements its reference count.

Usually, when an object implements more than one interface, the **AddRef()** and **Release()** functions for the various interfaces all delegate their functionality to a central point, so that although it may appear to clients that they are dealing with individual interfaces, the reference counting is applying to the object as a whole. When the count reaches zero, no one is using any interfaces any more, so the object can remove itself from memory.

The advantage of this system is that it's simple and robust; the main disadvantage is that it relies on the goodwill of clients, assuming that they'll remember to call **Release()** when they've finished with interfaces. What if a client crashes before releasing an interface? You'll probably get left with a hanging server, in the same way that DLLs can get stuck in memory if their client exits unexpectedly. As you'll see later, MFC makes life somewhat easier by managing interfaces for us in its classes, calling **AddRef()** and **Release()** as appropriate.

Implementation

Now we've seen what **AddRef()** and **Release()** are supposed to do, we can fill in suitable bodies for our simple object's constructor and function implementations, assuming that we have an **int** data member to hold the reference count:

```
CoMyObject::CoMyObject()
{
    // Initialise the reference count to zero, since no-one is
    // using us yet
    m_refCnt = 0;
}

ULONG CoMyObject::AddRef()
{
    // Count one use...
    m_refCnt++;
    return m_refCnt;
}

ULONG CoMyObject::Release()
{
    // Decrement the count, and if it has reached zero, it's goodbye!
    // In this example, assume that the destructor will do what is necessary
    // to shut down the server
    if (--m_refCnt == 0)
        delete this;

    return m_refCnt;
}
```

What I've written above is very simple, and won't be sufficient in some circumstances. If you're concerned about thread-safety, you ought not increment and decrement the reference count directly, but instead use the **InterlockedIncrement()** and **InterlockedDecrement()** Win32 API functions, which prevent more than one thread using the variable at a time.

Now we know what **AddRef()** does, we should also make a change to our definition of **QueryInterface()**. We need to increment the reference count for the interface when we pass a pointer to it back to a client; since that's just what we're doing in **QueryInterface()**, we can save the client a task, and call **AddRef()** ourselves:

```
HRESULT CoMyObject::QueryInterface(IID& riid, void FAR* FAR* ppv)
{
    if (riid == IID_IUnknown)
    {
        *ppv = (IUnknown *)this;
    }
    else
    {
        *ppv = NULL;
        return E_NOINTERFACE;
    }

    // Call AddRef so the client doesn't have to
    ppv->AddRef();

    return S_OK;
}
```

Creating and Using Objects

We know how to find out about an object's interfaces, and how its destruction is managed. Now we finally get around to creating one. In C++, objects are created as static or automatic variables, or on the stack by using the **new** keyword. COM objects, on the other hand, are created using a COM API function, usually **CoCreateInstance()**, as shown in the following example call:

```
IUnknown* pUnk;
HRESULT hr = CoCreateInstance(
            clsid,           // The GUID of the object we want to create
            NULL,            // Reserved - always NULL
            CLSCTX_SERVER,   // The type of thing we're creating,
                             //   in this case a plain server object
            IID_IUnknown,    // When it has been created,
                             //   return us a pointer to this interface
            (void**)&pUnk);  // Store the pointer here
```

CoCreateInstance() does a lot under the surface. It looks up the class ID you give it in the registry, finds the path to the server EXE or DLL which contains the class object, loads the server and gets it to create an object for you, and returns you an interface pointer. We can test the **HRESULT** for success or failure, to tell us whether the object was created or not. Note that **CoCreateInstance()** calls **AddRef()** on the interface whose pointer it returns to us, so we don't have to.

Once we have the initial interface pointer (which is to **IUnknown**), we can use **QueryInterface()** to obtain any other interface that the object supports. We need the ID of the interface we want to find, and a variable of the correct type to hold the interface pointer. Microsoft supplies C++ classes that give us access to all the interfaces it provides. When we have these, we can call **QueryInterface()**, passing the *address* of the pointer. In the following example, we're asking **IUnknown** for a pointer to the object's **IDispatch** interface, which has the ID **IID_IDispatch**:

```
        IDispatch* pDisp;
        hr = pUnk->QueryInterface(IID_IDispatch, (void**)&pDisp);
        if (FAILED(hr))
            AfxMessageBox("QueryInterface on IDispatch failed");
```

Aggregation

COM does support the reuse of existing components, but not through the sort of inheritance we're used to in C++. COM allows us to make up objects out of other objects via a process called **aggregation**. Aggregation is rather a complex topic, and could take several pages of discussion in its own right, so we'll content ourselves with an overview. Again, if you want more details, take a look at Appendix F for a list of some appropriate further reading.

 Aggregation **is a mechanism for building COM objects out of existing COM objects.**

In aggregation, an existing COM object is taken and used in a new object. Some interfaces may be supported by the aggregated object, some by the outer object, and some partly by both; whatever happens, the outside world sees just one object. When you realize that the aggregated object may itself be composed of other aggregations, you can begin to see where some of the complexity starts coming in.

Class Factories

Put simply, a **class factory** is a COM class whose job it is to create other COM objects, and a server will have one class factory for each COM object it can create. When the server is asked to provide an interface, through a call to `CoCreateInstance()` or `QueryInterface()` for example, it's the class factory that will actually create the object.

> *Watch out for the terminology here - it's a bit misleading. Glass factories make glass, but class factories create* instances *of classes. In that sense, 'object factory' might have been a better name.*

The `IClassFactory` interface itself isn't complex, consisting of just two functions:

```
    class IClassFactory : public IUnknown
    {
       virtual HRESULT CreateInstance(LPUNKNOWN pUnk, REFIID riid, void** ppv) = 0;
       virtual HRESULT LockServer(BOOL fLock) = 0;
    }
```

`CreateInstance()` creates an object of the class, and returns a pointer (`ppv`) to an interface whose GUID is specified by `riid`. The first parameter is used in cases where this COM object is being created as part of another, and provides a pointer to the outer, controlling object's `IUnknown` interface. In case you're wondering about the connection between the two, a call to `CoCreateInstance()` in the client ultimately results in a call to the class factory's `CreateInstance()` in the server.

`LockServer()` provides a way for a client to 'lock' a server in memory if, for example, it knows that it needs to create several objects and doesn't want the overhead of the server being loaded and unloaded several times.

A class factory **is a COM class whose job is to create other COM objects of a particular type. It does the same sort of job that new does in C++.**

Why bother with this two-level approach and not just create objects in one go? The main reason is that class factories define how the objects they manage are created. For instance, will a new object get created each time a client requests it, or is there a single object handling multiple clients? Using the class factory as an intermediary gives you the ability to handle these (and other) situations.

There are now two class factory interfaces: **IClassFactory** and **IClassFactory2**. The original interface needed to be extended with functions to handle **licensing**, so a new interface was created. We'll meet licensing later in the book, when we talk about ActiveX controls; for now, all we need to say is that it allows a class factory to check whether a client is allowed to use a class (and so have an object created) or not.

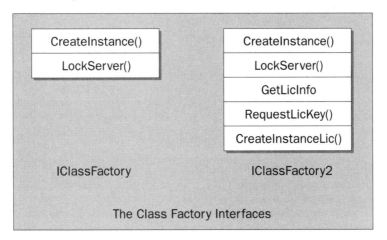

The Class Factory Interfaces

ActiveX and OLE

We've now seen what COM interfaces are and how they work, but what about ActiveX and OLE? As I stated in Chapter 1, COM supplies a standard mechanism for letting objects work together, but it doesn't actually provide anything useful for us to do with them. That's where ActiveX and OLE come in, by providing a bunch of higher-level services, using COM interfaces as their underlying mechanism.

There are services for file handling, drag and drop, persistent objects, linking and embedding, in-place editing, custom controls... the list is quite long. A lot of the complexity that people say comes with these technologies arises from the fact that there are a lot of services covering a lot of ground, and some of them are poorly explained and documented.

It's important to realize that the services currently available reflect those things that Microsoft has found it useful to do with COM; they certainly don't exhaust the possibilities, and I'm sure we'll see new technologies appearing with some regularity. Just as with MFC, you're at liberty to define your own COM objects, your own interfaces, and even your own ActiveX-type services, but you'd have to do quite a lot of work to integrate them with the rest of the COM world.

Common Microsoft Interfaces

In practice, each OLE or ActiveX service is implemented using a number of interfaces. Some of these interfaces are used in the implementation of several different services, while others are particular to just one service.

Drag and drop, for example, uses two interfaces: **IDropSource** and **IDropTarget**. Objects wishing to act as drop sources implement **IDropSource**, while those wishing to be targets implement **IDropTarget**. Applications may implement one, the other, or both of these, depending on the functionality they need. The following diagram shows the interfaces used in some common services:

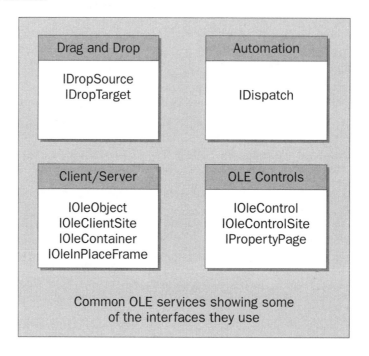

Drag and Drop	Automation
IDropSource IDropTarget	IDispatch

Client/Server	OLE Controls
IOleObject IOleClientSite IOleContainer IOleInPlaceFrame	IOleControl IOleControlSite IPropertyPage

Common OLE services showing some of the interfaces they use

Some services may use well over a dozen interfaces, and some interfaces may have a dozen functions or more. This means that implementing these services at the COM level can be very complex and time consuming. What's going to make things easier for us is that MFC wraps a large amount of the COM-level detail in its classes, so that much of the time you need not be aware that you're using COM functionality at all.

Servers and Containers

Servers and containers are two of the most basic types of COM-enabled application. A **server** is an executable (a DLL or an EXE, depending on server type) which implements one or more COM objects, and provides a class factory for each COM object that it can create. Servers may exist solely for the purpose of providing COM objects, or server functionality can be added to stand-alone applications, such as Word or Excel.

A server **is a piece of code that provides COM objects via class factories.** A container **is an application that can store and display such objects.**

All COM objects are provided by a server, but in this instance we're considering them in their special pairing with **containers**, which are applications that provide space for the storage and display of OLE objects. The container knows nothing about their content or how to manipulate them - that's the responsibility of the objects and their servers.

Linking and Embedding

Linking and embedding represent the two ways in which an object can be held in a container. **Linking** means that the container holds a link (a reference) to an external object. In the current generation of operating systems, this means that the object exists in a separate disk file, so the container effectively stores a path to a file, possibly qualified with some information denoting which portion of the file (such as a range of spreadsheet cells, or paragraphs out of a word-processing document) is being linked.

There are at least two major problems with linking. First, moving the file which holds the object breaks the link; second, the object is in a separate file, so it may be possible for someone else to edit that file and change its layout. If you're linking to a range of cells in a spreadsheet, it isn't inconceivable that someone could modify the formatting of cells within the range (or even add or delete cells), which may well cause problems that are hard to overcome.

 Containers may contain linked and embedded objects. An embedded **object has its data stored by the container, and can only be accessed via the container, so it has no independent existence. A** linked **object stores its data in a separate file, and so can be independently manipulated.**

Embedding means that the container stores the object's data along with its own. Embedded objects don't have an independent existence, so they can't be edited outside the context of their parent document. This removes the problems I just mentioned associated with linking, but the fact that the objects don't have a separate existence means that they can't be shared, and are therefore less useful than linked objects.

Types of Server

You'll recall from our earlier discussion that COM servers can be divided into several different types. In fact, different divisions can be made depending on what criteria you consider. I divided servers up on the basis of where they reside, and ended up with three types:

- In-process servers, packaged as DLLs under Windows
- Local servers, packaged as EXE files
- Remote servers, located somewhere else

For Windows systems, local and remote servers exist as processes in their own right, and so have their own executables. Local servers reside on the same machine as the client, while remote servers are on another system. The diagram below shows the different types of server. Process 1 consists of the client application and an in-process server which shares its address space; Process 2 is a local server, which resides in its own address space, and Process 3 is a remote server, living in its own address space somewhere else on a network.

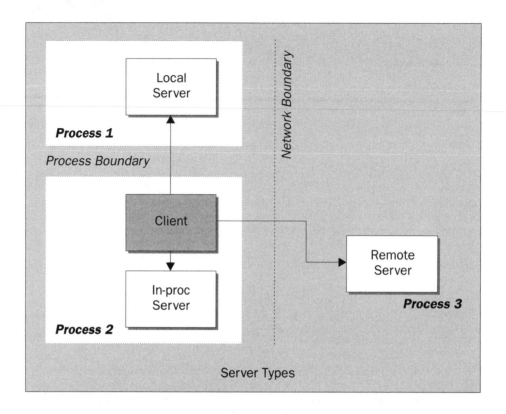

Server Types

There are three types of server. An in-process server is implemented as a DLL, and so lives in the same address space as its client. A local server is an executable, running in its own address space on the same machine as the client. A remote server runs on another machine.

The other way that we can divide up servers is on the basis of what they can do. Visual C++ distinguishes between mini-servers and full servers; both are proper servers, existing as `.exe` files rather than DLLs, but mini-servers cannot execute on their own. Mini-servers check whether they've been called by another application, and if they haven't, refuse to run. The applets that come with Microsoft Word, such as WordArt and the Equation Editor, are mini-servers; they work with Word, but not on their own.

Location Transparency

I've said a few times that a client shouldn't know, or need to know, where the object it's using is located. This principle of **location transparency** means that a client can access in-proc, local, and remote objects in exactly the same way.

Location transparency **means that a client doesn't have to know where a server is located.** It accesses in-process, local and remote servers in the same way, with COM taking care of the connection in each case.

Think for a second about what this implies. We use interfaces via pointers, and one of the requirements of using a pointer is that it has to point to something in your own address space. That means that interfaces in in-proc objects are easy to access, but how does it work for local and remote ones?

If we have to use pointers to something in the local process space, then we'd better provide something to point to. That's where **proxies** and **stubs** come in. Proxies and stubs are small routines that live in the address spaces of clients and servers in order to give them something in-process to call.

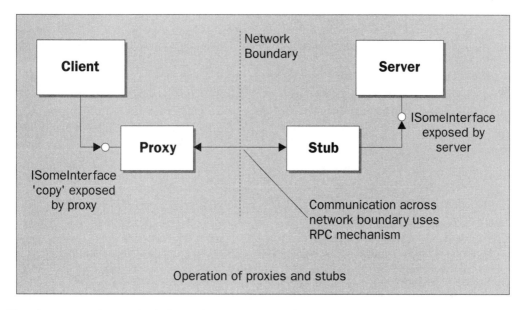

Operation of proxies and stubs

The objects at either end of the RPC (**R**emote **P**rocedure **C**all) don't know that they aren't communicating directly with the other end of the link, because the proxy and stub implement the same interface as the object on whose behalf they're acting. Thus, to the client, the proxy looks exactly like the server, while the stub looks to the server exactly like the client. Behind these 'fronts', the job of sending the data across the network takes place. The use of stubs and proxies ensures that the whole communication process is transparent to the users of the service.

Marshaling

As well as providing a 'local office' at either end of an RPC link, proxies and stubs are responsible for the data transfer across the link. This process, called **marshaling**, involves packaging data from the client into a standard form in the proxy, and then unpacking it in the stub for forwarding to the server. This happens whenever we're communicating across a process boundary, whether that also involves crossing a network or not. It's essential to have some form of neutral data-transfer format, because the server may reside on a machine with another architecture, and the software at both ends may not be written in the same language.

FYI   Marshaling is the process by which data can be packed up, sent to another process, and unpacked into the form needed by that process.

Microsoft provides ready-made stubs and proxies for all its standard COM interfaces, but if you write a custom interface, you will need to create your own. This is done by writing a script in a language called **IDL** (Interface Definition Language) and passing it through the IDL compiler, MIDL, which will generate all the source code needed for your proxy and stub routines.

Structured Storage

When we discussed embedding, we talked about the embedded object's data being stored along with that of the container. The classic example of this is an Excel spreadsheet in a Word document, resulting in a **compound document** - a document that consists of data from several sources. You may have wondered then how documents like this can be saved to disk in such a way that all the information can be reconstructed correctly. **Structured storage** is the solution to this problem, and more besides.

 FYI Structured storage **allows you to impose a file- and directory-like structure on a piece of storage, such as a block of memory or a file. It is commonly used to create structured files called** compound files, **which are heavily used by OLE containers. Structured storage uses analogs of directories and files, called** storages **and** streams.

Structured storage is a mechanism that allows you to impose a hierarchical structure on a piece of storage; in the case of compound files, it allows you to create a file system *within* a file. The normal method of naming data stops at the file level, but using structured storage we can continue down to finer resolutions. The structure of the compound file mimics a file system, using **storages**, which correspond to directories and subdirectories, and **streams**, which correspond to files.

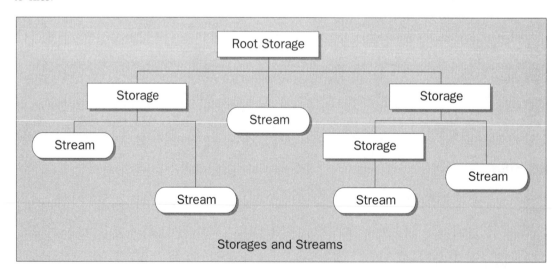

Storages and Streams

A piece of structured storage has a root storage (like a root directory), off which all other structure hangs. The diagram shows how the storages and streams can mimic a traditional filing system, imposing layers of structure upon an otherwise unstructured piece of storage.

If an application knows how to use structured storage, then it can cooperate by storing its data in storages and streams. Our example Word document can therefore create a new stream in which to store each embedded object, and then direct each object to store itself in the appropriate space. When we create an OLE container using MFC, we'll see that the default data storage for serialization switches from a standard binary file to a structured storage file, so that the container can store objects embedded in it. As you'd expect of a COM service, access to structured storage is via interfaces, such as **IStorage** and **IStream**.

> *Although we often think about structured storage in terms of its role in compound files, it's important to realize that it's a general mechanism - all it lays down is how to structure data in a hierarchical manner, not where that data is to be stored. It is quite possible to use a storage mechanism other than disk files.*

Structured storage is important for **object persistence**, a persistent object being one that needs to save its state information; this is accomplished in MFC by the serialization mechanism. Where we're talking about embedded objects in OLE, structured storage is used to make this happen. Generally, a containing object will ask a persistent object to save itself; the container will provide a place in the compound document for the object to save itself, though this is completely hidden from the persistent object.

Automation

Automation was designed to provide a single, uniform method that high-level scripting tools like Word and Excel macros, Visual Basic or VBA could use to control other applications. In the old days, applications had their own, individual, macro languages. This idea could have been extended into the COM world, giving each application its own custom 'macro' interface, but this would have been no better. Why? Because no application would have any way of controlling any other, unless it happened to have prior knowledge of what interface to use.

 Automation**, formerly known as 'OLE automation', provides a way for COM objects to expose functions and data that allows them to be used by other objects. This is done using a standard interface called IDispatch.**

To support Automation, COM defines a single interface, **IDispatch**, which allows objects to expose functions, events and data items that can be manipulated by outside agencies. An object that supports the **IDispatch** interface is called a **programmable object**. The **IDispatch** interface can be queried at runtime in order for a client to establish what Automation functions, events and data items are supported by the object. Instead of having to know what interface and functions you need to use to drive each application, you use one single interface that can tell you what the object supports.

Automation has become a key component of ActiveX controls, as it provides the way in which controls and their containers communicate.

Type Libraries

I stated above that programmable objects can be queried at runtime to find out what functionality they support. However, there's also a way to find out what a programmable object can do *without* having to start up an instance of the object, and that's by using a **type library**.

Type libraries perform a similar function for COM objects to the one import libraries provide for DLLs, in that they contain information about the interfaces supported by the class, and the functions supported by each interface. This information can be read both by tools such as Visual C++, which can build classes to wrap objects at compile-time (called **early-binding**), and dynamically by tools such as Visual Basic, which uses the information to link to objects at runtime (also called **late-binding**).

> A type library **contains information about the interfaces and their constituent functions supported by a COM object. It can be read by tools such as the Visual C++ ClassWizard and Visual Basic's Object Browser, in order to help them construct type-safe code, or display object information to the user. Type libraries are constructed from descriptions written in** IDL (Interface Definition Language).

In Visual C++ 5.0, type libraries are produced by coding up the object and interface definitions in a scripting language called **ODL** (**O**bject **D**escription **L**anguage), which is then compiled by the MIDL utility program. I'll deal with type libraries in a lot more detail later in the book.

Microsoft has now merged ODL into **IDL** (Interface Definition Language), so that one script can be used for both interface and type library creation. The IDL code is then compiled into binary form by the Microsoft IDL compiler, MIDL. This merged scripting language is available in Visual C++ 5.0, and replaces the old ODL for type library description.

IDispatch and How it Works

Automation makes three things available to clients via the **IDispatch** interface:

- Functions, known as **methods**
- Data items, known as **properties**
- Notifications, known as **events**

Automation methods are functions supported by an object that can be called by a client in order to make the object perform some action, such as opening a file, or inserting some text in a buffer.

Automation properties represent the state of the Automation object. They can be made available for clients to read (and write, if required), via 'get' and 'set' functions.

> *You **never** manipulate Automation properties directly, as you can't access data in a COM object. Sometimes, especially when using Visual Basic, it looks as if you're directly modifying data, but you aren't - it's all being done by function calls, with the outward form being provided for the ease of the Visual Basic programmer.*

Automation events allow the object to tell the client when something of interest happens. The object defines a number of events, and the client **subscribes** to those it's interested in. We'll see more about this when we discuss Automation in more detail in Chapter 8.

Automation objects can make properties, methods and events available via the **IDispatch** interface. Properties represent the state of the object, methods represent actions the object can be asked to perform, and events allow the object to signal when something of interest has happened.

IDispatch Functions

IDispatch is a pretty simple interface, with only four new functions. Note the use of the **interface** keyword, which is used as a synonym for **class**:

```
interface IDispatch : public IUnknown
{
public:
    virtual HRESULT GetTypeInfoCount(UINT* pctinfo) = 0;
    virtual HRESULT GetTypeInfo(UINT iTInfo, LCID lcid,
            ITypeInfo** ppTInfo) = 0;
    virtual HRESULT STDMETHODCALLTYPE GetIDsOfNames(REFIID riid,
            LPOLESTR* rgszNames, UINT cNames, LCID lcid,
            DISPID* rgDispId) = 0;
    virtual HRESULT Invoke(DISPID dispIdMember, REFIID riid,
            LCID lcid, WORD wFlags, DISPPARAMS* pDispParams,
            VARIANT* pVarResult, EXCEPINFO* pExcepInfo,
            UINT* puArgErr) = 0;
};
```

The first three functions - **GetTypeInfoCount()**, **GetTypeInfo()** and **GetIDsOfNames()** - allow a client to get type information from the Automation object at runtime using the type library, and we'll see this in action in a short while when we code up an Automation example. The first two of these, respectively, tell you whether the object has any type information, and retrieve it for you.

The third function, **GetIDsOfNames()**, takes a name, which can be that of method or a property. If the object has such a method or property, the function returns you an ID by which it can be used. The first argument is reserved for future use, the second holds an array of names to be looked up, and the third gives the number of names. In fact, only one method can be looked up at a time, so it is common to pass a single name and a count of one. The fourth argument, **lcid**, is the Win32 locale which should be used to interpret the names, while the fifth and final argument will be used by the function to return an array of the IDs which represent the names. We'll see an example of this function in use later in the chapter.

The ID discussed in the previous paragraph is called a **dispID** (or **dispatch ID**), and is similar to the ordinal numbers by which we can refer to functions exported from a DLL. The first property or method will have a dispID of 0, the second will be 1, and so on. All operations on methods and properties are done using these dispIDs rather than names.

It's the last of the four **IDispatch** functions, **Invoke()**, where all the action happens. The idea behind **Invoke()** is pretty simple: you pass it the function you wish to execute, or the property you wish to examine or modify, identifying it using the dispID you got back from **GetIDsOfNames()**. You attach any data which may be required, and **Invoke()** does the work.

The `IDispatch` interface contains four functions: `GetTypeInfoCount()`, `GetTypeInfo()`, `GetIDsOfNames()` and `Invoke()`. The first three allow a client to get type information from the object, to see what Automation functionality it supports. The last one, `Invoke()`, is the way in which properties and methods are used.

More Data Types

As so often, the process isn't *quite* as simple as that, and the complexity arises in passing over the data. Because COM objects are designed to be language- and machine-independent, we can only pass over, and receive back, data types that both ends are guaranteed to understand. This is achieved by the use of the **VARIANT**, a sort of portmanteau data type, which is used to package up the data used in Automation operations. There are a number of API functions to help in constructing and using them, and they can be very useful in areas outside Automation as general data types.

The **VARIANT** is a structure that holds a type identifier and a union which can hold one of a number of standard, portable types (we'll see them in action later, in our example), so when we use `Invoke()`, we pack up arguments into an array of **VARIANT**s (using a structure called **DISPPARAMS**, for 'dispatch parameters') before calling the function.

> *You'll also come across mention of a* **VARIANTARG** *type, and as you might guess,* **VARIANT***s and* **VARIANTARG***s are closely related.* **VARIANTARG***s are used to pass arguments to Automation functions, and can be used to pass data by reference;* **VARIANT***s are general purpose, and can't be used to pass reference data. You will often, however, just hear* **VARIANT** *used to denote both of these.*

A **VARIANT** is a data type used to pass data in Automation, and was originally introduced in Visual Basic. A **VARIANT** is a structure that contains a type flag and a union, and can hold any of numerous data types. The flag denotes the type, and the appropriate member of the union is used to store the data.

Advanced Features

Three advanced features you'll hear mentioned when COM is being discussed are **dual interfaces**, **collections** and **monikers**. MFC gives you no support for implementing or using these features, so I won't describe them in any great detail, but it's certainly worth knowing what they are and what they do.

Dual Interfaces

A dual interface is an extension to `IDispatch` which lets an Automation controller (a client using a programmable object) bind directly to a vtable instead of having to use `IDispatch::Invoke()`.

FYI A dual interface **is an extension to the normal dispatch interface that allows a suitable Automation client to get faster access to Automation methods and properties.**

The difference is mainly one of speed. Using `Invoke()` requires the controller to convert each argument to a **VARIANT**, while with a dual interface, the controller can call the method directly, with no conversion overhead. The table below shows the considerable differences in performance that arise when using three ways of calling functions in a COM interface:

▶ A custom interface, in other words, a specially-written COM interface which directly supports the function we want to call

▶ A dual interface

▶ A traditional dispatch interface, using `GetIDsOfNames()` and `Invoke()`

	Invocations per second		
	Scalars	**Unicode Text**	**ANSI Text**
Custom Interface	3,822,265	73,421	120,337
Dual Interface	3,822,265	60,698	19,503
`GetIDsOfNames()` and `Invoke()`	5,826	4,910	3,891

Essentially, the table shows how quickly functions using different types of data can be called. The traditional dispatch interface comes off worst, while the custom interface is the fastest. The performance of the dual interface is identical to that of the custom interface in the case of scalar data, and only slightly worse for Unicode data. The difference in the case of ANSI data is due to the need to convert to Unicode before sending the data, and back to ANSI at the receiving end.

Win32 programmers, and especially those using COM, now have to deal with two character sets: Unicode and ANSI. The old 8-bit ANSI character set, as used in the **char** *data type, is unsuited for languages that don't use Latin characters. Unicode uses 16-bit characters, and so can hold over 65,000 characters, which is enough for quite a lot of languages!*

Windows NT uses Unicode for its internal character storage; COM also uses it to represent character strings, so if you have an application which uses ANSI characters, you can end up with a lot of conversions.

Visual C++ projects can be compiled either as ANSI or Unicode, and various macros (such as **TCHAR**, **_T()** *and* **LPTSTR**) *are available to enable characters and strings to be declared portably. Various string data types are also defined for use with COM, and we'll meet these as we start writing code.*

A dual interface, as its name implies, serves a dual purpose. It can be used as an ordinary dispatch interface by controllers which need to use this access method, while more sophisticated controllers can call the vtable directly. Visual C++ and Visual Basic (since version 4) are smart enough to use the dual interface if one is present, so implementing Automation via dual interfaces can give considerably better performance in these cases.

> *Now that we've discussed dual interfaces, we've seen the three types of COM interface:*
>
> *The pure COM interface (derived from* `IUnknown`*)*
> *The dispatch interface (an implementation of* `IDispatch`*)*
> *The dual interface (derived from* `IDispatch`*)*

Collections

Many programs that are Automation-enabled will be able to have more than one document open at a time. Some, like Word or PowerPoint, will be true MDI applications, whilst others may simply have a notion of multiple documents. It's recommended that such applications implement a **collection object** to manage this collection of documents. These objects are Automation objects in their own right, with an **IDispatch** interface and their own properties and methods.

Some Automation controllers, such as Visual Basic, are set up to know how to use collection objects. In order for this to work smoothly, there are a set of standard methods which collection objects should implement, such as **Count()** (to return the number of objects in the collection) and **Item()** (to return a given item from the collection). Later versions of Visual Basic (4.0 and above) have direct support for collections in the form of the **for each** construct:

```
for each obj in ObjCollection
    obj.Active = TRUE
next obj
```

These two advanced Automation topics don't strictly fall within the scope of this book, because they aren't supported by MFC and require COM coding. However, they're such useful things to be able to add to an MFC application, that a brief description of how to implement them is provided in Appendix C.

Monikers

If you're not British, you might not know that a **moniker** is another word for a name. COM uses the term to refer to an object that implements the **IMoniker** interface, an interface that provides an intelligent, persistent name for a COM object.

Monikers were designed for use with linked objects in OLE containers, such as a link to a portion of an Excel spreadsheet. Instead of holding the name of the linked file, the container holds one or more monikers, which together define where the object can be found. At runtime, the container can 'bind' to a moniker, which means getting access to its data; note that the container doesn't know how to do this - that's the moniker's job.

If Monikers are important in the context of ActiveX controls, because **URL monikers** can be used to allow controls to access data at a URL on a remote host, and download the data asynchronously. Given the speeds at which some network connections function, it is necessary to have some sort of download mechanism which allows the control to keep functioning while data is downloading, and that is what this asynchronous moniker mechanism provides.

Distributed COM

Finally, we come to **Distributed COM**, or **DCOM**. Quite simply, DCOM is 'COM on a longer wire' - an extension of COM to work over networks, done in such a way that it isn't visible to the majority of applications which want to use it. We used to talk about DCOM being on the horizon, but now it's here, we find that it isn't a separate product at all, but part of COM.

So now, using COM, servers and clients can run on different machines, with communication between them taking place using an RPC mechanism devised by the Open Systems Foundation, called **DCE** (Distributed Computing Environment). The RPC mechanism handles the mechanics of setting up the call to the remote machine and routing data across the connection, performing any data conversion that may be required en route.

 Distributed COM, or DCOM, is an extension of COM that will work across networks. Very little extra work is required on the part of the programmer, unless you start getting involved with security issues. DCOM is built into Windows NT 4.0, and a version is available for Windows 95.

The distributed version of COM was first built into Windows NT 4.0; by the time you read this, there should be a stable version available for Windows 95 as well.

> *For a full discussion of DCOM and what you can do with it, take a look at 'Professional DCOM' by Richard Grimes, ISBN 1-861000-60-X. This and other titles that expand upon information presented in this book are mentioned in the further reading list, in Appendix F.*

A Practical Automation Example

Now that we've covered a lot of the principles behind COM, it's time to put what you've learned into practice. In this section, we're going to write an application that uses the COM API calls to manipulate an object. In fact, it's going to do exactly the same thing we did in Chapter 1, where we wrote that simple MFC program to show how easy it was to do practical Automation coding using MFC, by using Automation to get Microsoft Word to write 'Hello world' in a document window. This example will show you what was going on in those few lines of code.

Here's an overview of the steps making up the application. I'll cross-reference them to the code for the MFC example in the previous chapter, so you can see how they relate. Once again, the differences between Word 95 and Word 97 necessitate slightly different solutions. I'll deal with Word 95 first, and then discuss the changes required to automate Word 97. Here's the sequence of events we'll have to follow:

1 Find the CLSID from the registry

2 Use **CoCreateInstance()** to load the server and create a **word.basic** object. Get back a pointer to a suitable interface, in this case **IUnknown**

3 Use **QueryInterface()** on the **IUnknown** interface to get the dispatch interface, **IDispatch**

4 Use `GetIDsOfNames()` to get the dispID of the `FileNew` method

5 Use `IDispatch::Invoke()` to execute the `FileNew` method, which causes Word to open a new document

6 Use `GetIDsOfNames()` to get the dispID of the `Insert` method

7 Make up an argument block containing the string argument for the `Insert` method

8 Use `IDispatch::Invoke()` to execute the `Insert` method, so that the string appears in Word

9 Tidy up, releasing the interface pointers and other resources we have acquired

The code here is fairly long-winded, by design; it would be possible to make things somewhat more efficient. For example, we could get the `IDispatch` interface directly from `CoCreateInstance()`, rather than first getting `IUnknown` and then using `QueryInterface()`. However, it's presented in this way in order to serve as an example of how all the COM API calls we've seen so far can be used, rather than as a model of good COM programming. Even with that proviso, though, I'm sure you'll agree that basic COM programming is still a rather tedious business!

The table below shows how the steps in the COM code we're about to write correspond to those in the simple MFC example from Chapter 1:

COM Example	MFC Code
	Create WordBasic object
Find CLSID	Call `wb.CreateDispatch()`
Call `CoCreateInstance()`	
Use `QueryInterface()` to get `IDispatch`	
Use `GetIDsOfNames()` to get `FileNew`	
Invoke `FileNew`	Call `wb.FileNewDefault()`
Use `GetIDsOfNames()` to get `Insert`	
Invoke `Insert`	Call `wb.Insert()`
Tidy up	

Try It Out - 'Hello World' the Hard Way for Word 95

We'll need some sort of test-bed application from which to launch our COM code. In this case a vanilla MFC dialog-based application, as created by AppWizard, provides an adequate base - I called mine **WordAuto**. You don't need to specify any support for Automation or ActiveX controls when creating the application; although we're using Automation, we're just calling Win32 API calls.

As we're using COM, we need to add MFC code to include the OLE header files and initialize the OLE libraries. Although we're actually going to use COM and not the higher-level OLE functionality in this program, the MFC code provides an easy way to get what we need. First, add these MFC header files to **stdafx.h** to get the COM support:

```
#define VC_EXTRALEAN        // Exclude rarely-used stuff from Windows headers

#include <afxwin.h>         // MFC core and standard components
#include <afxext.h>         // MFC extensions
#include <afxole.h>         // MFC OLE classes
#include <afxpriv.h>        // MFC OLE classes
#include <afxdisp.h>        // MFC Automation classes
#ifndef _AFX_NO_AFXCMN_SUPPORT
#include <afxcmn.h>         // MFC support for Windows Common Controls
#endif // _AFX_NO_AFXCMN_SUPPORT
```

Next, add a call to **AfxOleInit()** to the application's **InitInstance()** function, which will initialize the OLE DLLs (and hence COM too):

```
BOOL CWordAutoApp::InitInstance()
{
   // Initialize OLE libraries
   if (!AfxOleInit())
   {
      AfxMessageBox("Failed to initialize OLE libraries");
      return FALSE;
   }
```

The dialog will provide a means by which the Automation code can be triggered; we can also use it to display information about the process as it proceeds: the class ID of the object it's working with, and status reports that we'll generate as we go along. If you want to follow this example exactly, give your dialog the title Word Automation Test, and edit the dialog resource so that it looks something like this:

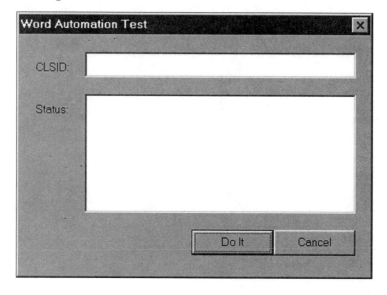

The top box is an edit box; the lower one is a list box. Change their properties so that their IDs are **IDC_CLSID** and **IDC_STATUS** respectively, and make sure that sorting is turned off in the list box. The Do It button replaces the OK button; to agree with the code here, make its ID **IDC_DOIT**. All the code we're going to add will be in the handler for this button, which will be called **OnDoit()** if you have it generated automatically.

Before we start addressing the steps we outlined above, there's a line of code that must go right at the start of the routine:

```
void CWordAutoDlg::OnDoit()
{
    USES_CONVERSION;
```

All the COM API calls use Unicode rather than the MBCS (Multi-Byte Character Set) used by Visual C++, so it's necessary to convert between the two when calling the API. There are a bunch of macros defined, and you need to call the **USES_CONVERSION** macro before you can use them, as it declares a local variable that they use. This macro has to be invoked in every method that makes COM API calls, and it's declared in **afxpriv.h**, which we added to **stdafx.h**.

1 Before we actually get around to finding the CLSID from the registry, the next few lines deal with some more initialization. After switching to the 'wait' cursor, we set up a couple of pointers to the boxes on our dialog, a variable to hold the class ID, and another that we initialize with the progID, **word.basic**.

```
BeginWaitCursor();

CEdit* pCLSID = (CEdit*)GetDlgItem(IDC_CLSID);
CListBox* pList = (CListBox*)GetDlgItem(IDC_STATUS);

CLSID clsid;
LPTSTR tBuff = "word.basic";
```

Next, we use the **CLSIDFromProgID()** function to get the class ID for this progID. The **T2COLE()** macro is used to convert the string in **tBuff** to Unicode in the function call. We then post a diagnostic message to the dialog via the **pList** variable.

```
if (CLSIDFromProgID(T2COLE(tBuff), &clsid) != NOERROR)
{
    AfxMessageBox("CLSIDFromProgID failed");
    return;
}

pList->AddString("Got CLSID");
```

*This method is one of the long-winded ones I alluded to at the start of the example. We could have plugged the progID directly into the API call by casting it to an **OLESTR** on the fly, like this:*

```
if (CLSIDFromProgID(OLESTR("word.basic"), &clsid) != NOERROR)
```

Coding this line would have saved us a variable; using the macro in this case was less efficient than judicious choice of data type.

```
    LPOLESTR lpszOleIID = NULL;
    ::StringFromCLSID(clsid, &lpszOleIID);
    ASSERT(lpszOleIID != NULL);
    pList->AddString("Got string");

    LPTSTR lpszIID = OLE2T(lpszOleIID);
    pCLSID->SetWindowText(lpszIID);


    // Free the memory allocated by the call to StringFromCLSID()
    CoTaskMemFree(lpszOleIID);
```

Finally in this segment, we use the **StringFromCLSID()** API call to retrieve a printable CLSID in the form of a pointer to an OLE string. We retrieve this so that we can back-convert it to an **LPTSTR** using the **OLE2T()** macro, and display it in the dialog's edit control. Note that we pass the *address* of a pointer (i.e. an **LPOLESTR***) to **StringFromCLSID()**, and that this last section of code has nothing to do with the creation of the object - it's just so we can output the CLSID to see what it looks like.

2 Now that we have the CLSID of the object we want to create, we can go ahead and use **CoCreateInstance()** to get COM to create an instance of it for us.

```
    IUnknown *pUnk;

    HRESULT hr = CoCreateInstance(
                    clsid,              // The classID of the object we want
                                        // to create
                    NULL,               // Reserved
                    CLSCTX_SERVER,      // We're creating a local server
                                        // object
                    IID_IUnknown,       // CoCreateInstance will return us a
                                        // pointer to its IUnknown interface
                    (void**)&pUnk);     // in this pointer

    if (FAILED(hr))
    {
        AfxMessageBox("CoCreateInstance failed");
        return;
    }

    // If it worked, update the status listbox
    pList->AddString("Created instance");
    pList->AddString("Got IUnknown");
```

The call to **CoCreateInstance()** takes the CLSID that we've retrieved from the registry. It looks in the registry to find what server ought to be used to create an object, starts up the server, asks it to create the object, and returns us an interface pointer. In this case, we've asked for a pointer to the object's **IUnknown** interface by passing **IID_IUnknown** as the ID of the interface we want retrieved.

In the MFC example of the previous chapter, **CoCreateInstance()** was called as part of the **CreateDispatch()** function, which creates the underlying object and retrieves its **IDispatch** pointer. You'll appreciate from this code that several things could cause **CreateDispatch()** to fail, such as not being able to create the COM object, or not being able to retrieve its **IDispatch** interface.

3 Once we know the object has been created, and have a pointer to its **IUnknown** interface, we can use **QueryInterface()** to ask for the Automation interface, **IDispatch**. Having done that, we can **Release()** the pointer to the **IUnknown** interface, because we won't be needing it again. This code doesn't introduce anything you haven't seen before:

```
IDispatch *pDisp;

hr = pUnk->QueryInterface(IID_IDispatch, (void**)&pDisp);

// Release the IUnknown pointer because we don't need it any more
pUnk->Release();

if (FAILED(hr))
{
   AfxMessageBox("QueryInterface on IDispatch failed");
   return;
}

// If it worked, update status
pList->AddString("Called QueryInterface");
pList->AddString("Got IDispatch");
```

4 We now have a pointer to the Automation interface and the name of the method we want to use (**FileNew** in this case), but before we can invoke it, we have to find its dispID. This is done with a call to the **IDispatch::GetIDsOfNames()** function, which takes the name of an Automation method and returns its dispID, assuming of course that the object's **IDispatch** interface supports the method in question.

```
DISPID disp;
OLECHAR FAR* szFunction = OLESTR("FileNew");

hr = pDisp->GetIDsOfNames(
               IID_NULL,                 // Reserved - must be NULL
               &szFunction,              // Array of function names
               1,                        // Number of names
               LOCALE_SYSTEM_DEFAULT,    // Locale information
               &disp);                   // Address for dispIDs returned

if (FAILED(hr))
{
   AfxMessageBox("GetIDsOfNames failed");
   pDisp->Release();
   return;
}

// If it worked, update status
pList->AddString("Called GetIDsOfNames");
pList->AddString("Got dispID");
```

Note that **GetIDsOfNames()** only takes a single name at a time. Although the second argument is described as holding an 'array of function names', the first entry is used as the name of the function to look up, and any subsequent arguments are taken as names of parameters to the function.

58

> *It's worth noting at this point that this code and the MFC example employ different ways of executing Automation methods. In this example we're doing it all dynamically, querying the object to see whether it supports a given method, and retrieving the dispID. In the MFC example, ClassWizard used information in a type library to find out details of the object's methods and their dispIDs ahead of time, so it didn't need to call* **GetIDsOfNames()**.

A **locale** is a particular language and cultural environment; although we can specify something different, we usually make all calls in the context of the default locale set up for the machine.

5 Once we have the dispID of the **FileNew** method, we're in a position to execute it by calling **IDispatch::Invoke()**. **FileNew** is pretty simple to invoke, because it doesn't take any parameters, so we don't have to concern ourselves with **VARIANT**s and the mechanism of argument passing. All we have to do is to declare an empty parameter block, of type **DISPPARAMS**, and call **Invoke()** with the appropriate dispID.

The arguments to the Automation **Invoke()** function are passed using a **DISPPARAMS** structure, which consists of the array of **VARIANT**s holding the argument data, plus the argument count. **DISPPARAMS** structures can also hold information on named arguments.

```
DISPPARAMS dispNoArgs = { NULL, NULL, 0, 0 };

hr = pDisp->Invoke(disp,                      // Dispatch ID for FileNew
                   IID_NULL,                  // Reserved
                   LOCALE_SYSTEM_DEFAULT,     // Locale info
                   DISPATCH_METHOD,           // We're invoking a method
                                              // (as opposed to getting
                                              // a property or whatever)
                   &dispNoArgs,               // Null parameter block
                   NULL, NULL, NULL);         // Nulls for result (there
                                              // isn't one), exception
                                              // info (not bothered) and
                                              // argument error return

if (FAILED(hr))
{
   AfxMessageBox("Invoke() failed");
   pDisp->Release();
   return;
}

// If it worked, update status
pList->AddString("Called Invoke");
```

The parameters to **Invoke()** are pretty straightforward. First up is the dispID of the method, followed by a (currently unused) second parameter which must be **NULL**. Next comes the locale information, and a flag showing what we're doing in this call, which basically comes down to a choice between invoking a method, setting a property value or getting a property value. This is followed by the address of the parameter block, and then three arguments that take result information. All these last three are **NULL**, because the command doesn't return us a result, and we're not checking error status information.

In the MFC code, the construction of the **DISPPARAMS** block, and the conversion of the arguments to and from **VARIANT**s, is handled for you by the wrapper class, so you can program using normal C++ data types.

6 If you compiled and ran the code we've assembled so far, you'd see a new document window open in Word. To place some text in the window, we need to use the **Insert** Automation method, so we have to retrieve its dispID:

```
DISPID dispIns;
OLECHAR FAR* szFunc1 = OLESTR("Insert");

hr = pDisp->GetIDsOfNames(
                IID_NULL,                 // Reserved - must be NULL
                &szFunc1,                 // Array of function names
                1,                        // Number of names
                LOCALE_SYSTEM_DEFAULT,    // Locale information
                &dispIns );               // Address for dispIDs returned

if (FAILED(hr))
{
   AfxMessageBox("GetIDsOfNames failed");
   pDisp->Release();
   return;
}

// If it worked, update status
pList->AddString("Called GetIDsOfNames");
pList->AddString("Got dispID for 'Insert'");
```

7 **Insert** is a little more complicated than **FileNew**, because it takes a string as a parameter, and that means we have to fill in a parameter block. Here's the code to do it; I'll go through what's happening afterwards:

```
BSTR bstrHello;
bstrHello = SysAllocString(OLESTR("Hello world!"));

// Fill in a parameter block with this one argument...
DISPPARAMS dispArg;
VARIANTARG varg;

V_VT(&varg) = VT_BSTR;
V_BSTR(&varg) = bstrHello;

dispArg.cArgs = 1;
dispArg.cNamedArgs = 0;
dispArg.rgvarg = &varg;
```

In this code, we're storing the parameter in a string variable, packaging that into a **VARIANT** structure, and then putting *that* into a **DISPPARAMS** structure. This already complicated affair is further confused by all the strange macros and variable names it involves. Let's break it down a little.

> A **BSTR** is a length-prefixed string used in Automation functions. There are a number of API functions that help with their creation and manipulation.

The first complication is caused by the way we pass strings to COM routines. COM uses 'binary strings', which have a length at the start, rather than the familiar C++ null-terminated variety. Visual C++ defines a **BSTR** type to hold these binary strings. In fact, they have a null terminator as well, so they're defined as:

```
typedef OLECHAR FAR* BSTR
```

This means they can be used in most places where straight **OLECHAR**s are required. Because of the special formatting of these strings, you have to build and free them using special routines. In the code above, **SysAllocString()** is used to build a **BSTR** out of an **OLESTR**.

The **VARIANTARG** data type is a structure composed of a type field plus a union, so we set the type to **VT_BSTR** to indicate we're passing a **BSTR**, and copy the value into the **bstrVal** field of the union. There are nearly 30 members of this union, covering all the data types that can be stored in a **VARIANT** or a **VARIANTARG**. If you're interested in knowing what they all are, you can look them up in the Visual C++ online help.

The **VT_BSTR** is a member of an enumeration that contains an entry for each type that can be used in a **VARIANT**. Each of them starts with **VT_**, and has a suffix denoting the type, such as **VT_I2** for a two-byte signed integer and **VT_BOOL** for a Boolean.

The **V_VT** and **V_BSTR** macros are provided by Visual C++ to help use **VARIANT**s and **VARIANTARG**s portably. The trouble is that the **VARIANT** structure includes a 'nameless union', a feature not allowed by some C++ implementations, and the code for accessing the members of the **VARIANT** structure will be different on those systems. These macros will be expanded to the correct syntax. If your code is just going to run on a PC under Windows, you're at liberty to either use them or not, as you wish.

Parameters are passed to Automation methods using a **DISPPARAMS** structure, which basically contains an array of **VARIANT**s. We have to set the number of arguments in the **cArgs** member and then fill in each **VARIANT** with its type and content. Automation methods can use named arguments as well as positional ones, but we aren't using them here, so we set the number of named arguments to zero.

8 Once we've set up the data, we can perform the **Invoke()**, and if all has gone correctly, you should see 'Hello world!' appear in your Word document.

```
hr = pDisp->Invoke(dispIns,           // Dispatch ID for Insert
                   IID_NULL,          // Reserved
                   LOCALE_SYSTEM_DEFAULT, // Locale info
                   DISPATCH_METHOD,   // We're invoking a method
                   &dispArg,          // Argument block
                   NULL, NULL, NULL ); // Nulls as before

if (FAILED(hr))
{
   AfxMessageBox("Invoke() failed");
```

```
        pDisp->Release();
        return;
    }


    // If it worked, update status
    pList->AddString("Called Invoke again");
```

9 The last stage is tidying up. We need to free the memory allocated to the **BSTR** object we created, and call **Release()** on the dispatch interface we've acquired so that its reference count is maintained. As you'd expect, the MFC functions of the earlier example release any interface pointers that they use without bothering you with the problem.

```
    // Free up the BSTR object
    SysFreeString(bstrHello);

    // Release the dispatch interface we've acquired
    pDisp->Release();

    EndWaitCursor();
}
```

That's it! All that code just to write 'Hello world!' in a Word document. As in the last chapter, remember to start a copy of Word 95 before you run the application. By default, an Automation server will start up and run invisibly in the background, so unless Word 95 is already running, you won't be able to see what your program is doing!

Try It Out - 'Hello World' the Hard Way for Word 97

To automate Word 97 this way, we have to deal with the same issues that faced us in the Chapter 1 example. That means creating a **word.application** object to start with, then making the application visible, and then getting hold of the application's WordBasic object to work with. Let's deal with them in that order.

1 The first change is the easiest. Just change the **tBuff** variable to hold **word.application** instead of **word.basic**:

```
    CLSID clsid;
    LPTSTR tBuff = "word.application";

    if (CLSIDFromProgID(T2COLE(tBuff), &clsid) != NOERROR)
    {
        AfxMessageBox("CLSIDFromProgID failed");
        return;
    }
```

To provide slightly more helpful feedback, you could also change one of the calls to **AddString()**:

```
    // If it worked, update status
    pList->AddString("Called QueryInterface");
    pList->AddString("Got IDispatch of the Application object");
```

2 To make the application visible, the first thing we have to do is to get hold of the dispID of its **Visible** property. That's going to mean another call to **GetIDsOfNames()**:

```
// If it worked, update status
pList->AddString("Called QueryInterface");
pList->AddString("Got IDispatch of the Application object");

DISPID disp;
OLECHAR FAR* szMethodName = OLESTR("Visible");

hr = pDisp->GetIDsOfNames(IID_NULL, &szMethodName,
                          1, LOCALE_SYSTEM_DEFAULT, &disp);

if (FAILED(hr))
{
   AfxMessageBox("GetIDsOfNames failed");
   pDisp->Release();
   return;
}

// If it worked, update status
pList->AddString("Called GetIDsOfNames");
pList->AddString("Got dispID for Visible");
```

Setting the **Visible** property requires a Boolean **VARIANT**. This is set up in extremely similar fashion to the one we use in the call to the **word.basic** object's **Insert** method:

```
// To set the Visible property, we need to pass it a Boolean variant
VARIANTARG varArg;
V_VT(&varArg) = VT_BOOL;
V_BOOL(&varArg) = TRUE;
```

The **DISPPARAMS** structure, however, is different this time around. Because we're setting a property rather passing a parameter to a method, we have to place a special identifier in the 'named arguments' field. Once that's done, we can call **Invoke()**, and the new instance of Word 97 will be made visible:

```
// Set up the DISPPARAMS structure
DISPPARAMS dispArgs;
DISPID propDispID = DISPID_PROPERTYPUT;
dispArgs.cArgs = 1;
dispArgs.cNamedArgs = 1;
dispArgs.rgdispidNamedArgs = &propDispID;
dispArgs.rgvarg = &varArg;

hr = pDisp->Invoke(disp,                   // Dispatch ID for Visible
                   IID_NULL,               // Reserved
                   LOCALE_SYSTEM_DEFAULT,  // Locale info
                   DISPATCH_PROPERTYPUT,   // We're setting a property
                                           // (as opposed to calling
                                           // a method or whatever)
                   &dispArgs,              // Argument block
                   NULL, NULL, NULL);      // Nulls for result (there
                                           // isn't one), exception
                                           // info (not bothered) and
                                           // argument error return
```

```
if (FAILED(hr))
{
   AfxMessageBox("Invoke() failed");
   pDisp->Release();
   return;
}

// If it worked, update status
pList->AddString("Called Application.Visible = TRUE");
pList->AddString("Application now visible");
```

For more information about getting and setting properties with **Invoke()** *than the cursory explanation given here, take a look at the section called 'Getting and Setting Properties' under* **IDispatch::Invoke()** *in the online help.*

3 Getting hold of the WordBasic object requires us to retrieve the application's **WordBasic** property, and that means going round the **GetIDsOfNames()** loop just one more time to get a dispID:

```
szMethodName = OLESTR("WordBasic");

hr = pDisp->GetIDsOfNames(IID_NULL, &szMethodName,
                                    1, LOCALE_SYSTEM_DEFAULT, &disp);

if (FAILED(hr))
{
   AfxMessageBox("GetIDsOfNames failed");
   pDisp->Release();
   return;
}

// If it worked, update status
pList->AddString("Called GetIDsOfNames");
pList->AddString("Got dispID for WordBasic");
```

This time around, we're not passing any arguments in the **DISPPARAMS** structure (so we can bring forward our **dispNoArgs** declaration), but we *are* receiving a result, for which we'll require a **VARIANT**. The call to **Invoke()** pans out like this:

```
DISPPARAMS dispNoArgs = { NULL, NULL, 0, 0 };

// Variant to take the result of getting the WordBasic property
VARIANTARG varResult;

// Initialize the variant before using it
VariantInit(&varResult);

hr = pDisp->Invoke(
     disp,                      // Dispatch ID for WordBasic
     IID_NULL,                  // Reserved
     LOCALE_SYSTEM_DEFAULT,     // Locale info
     DISPATCH_PROPERTYGET,      // We're getting a property (as opposed
                                // to calling a method or whatever)
     &dispNoArgs,               // Null parameter block
```

```
                      &varResult, NULL, NULL); // Get the result (it's a pointer to the
                                               // WordBasic object), exception info (not
                                               // bothered) and argument error return


    if (FAILED(hr))
    {
      AfxMessageBox("Invoke() failed");
      pDisp->Release();
      return;
    }


    // If it worked, update status
    pList->AddString("Got word.basic object from the WordBasic property");
```

The last thing before returning to the Word 95 code is then to **Release()** the dispatch pointer to the Application object, and set it to the WordBasic object returned from the call to **Invoke()**:

```
    pDisp->Release();
    pDisp = V_DISPATCH(&varResult);
```

```
    OLECHAR FAR* szFunction = OLESTR("FileNew");
```

That was a lot of extra code, but none of it was very different from what we already had for Word 95, and the links with what MFC was doing in Chapter 1 should be clear enough. The presentation here is about as drawn-out as it gets, and you could certainly find ways to abbreviate the code by defining functions - one which called **GetIDsOfNames()** and performed error checking would be a strong candidate, for a start. However, both applications now perform the same task, and if you're a Word 97 user, you should end up with something like this:

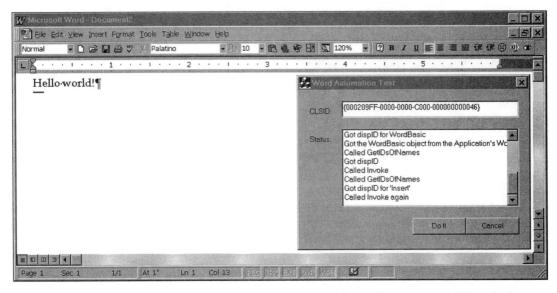

We've already seen how this same task can be accomplished in a few lines of MFC code, but as a final, sobering thought, here's some Visual Basic code that does it again with even fewer lines. This is for Word 95:

```
Dim myObj As Object
Set myObj = CreateObject("word.basic")
myObj.FileNew
myObj.Insert "Hello world!"
```

And this is for Word 97:

```
Dim myApp As Object
Dim myObj As Object

Set myApp = CreateObject("word.application")
myApp.Visible = True
Set myObj = myApp.WordBasic
myObj.FileNew
myObj.Insert "Hello world!"
```

Visual Basic is obviously doing a lot of COM manipulation under the surface, and this is one of its great strengths: the ability to provide a very high-level interface to complex tasks. However, Visual Basic still can't match C++ in terms of performance or flexibility (although some Visual Basic programmers may disagree!).

Summary

We've covered a lot of ground in this chapter, and I'd be quite surprised if you managed to assimilate it fully in one sitting. As you read on, you may want to come back here to re-read topics as you feel the need. In the meantime, I'll summarize the main points of what we've learned:

- ▶ COM objects work by exposing interfaces, which clients can then gain access to and use.

- ▶ COM interfaces are collections of function pointers, implemented in a machine- and language-independent manner. Interfaces are similar in structure to C++ virtual function tables, which makes C++ a natural choice for writing COM code.

- ▶ Everything in COM, including interfaces, is identified by unique 128-bit identifiers called GUIDs, which are stored in the registry.

- ▶ **IUnknown** is the fundamental COM interface, and provides navigation and reference counting functionality through its three functions **QueryInterface()**, **AddRef()** and **Release()**.

- ▶ Location transparency is an important part of COM's operation, and means that a client need not know where the COM object that it's using is located.

- ▶ Microsoft provides a number of standard COM interfaces for doing useful things. These interfaces are used to implement the OLE and ActiveX technologies.

- ▶ The term OLE is now limited to object linking and embedding; just about everything else is ActiveX.

- ▶ Automation is the means COM provides to enable applications to work together, providing a standard way for them to drive one another via the **IDispatch** interface.

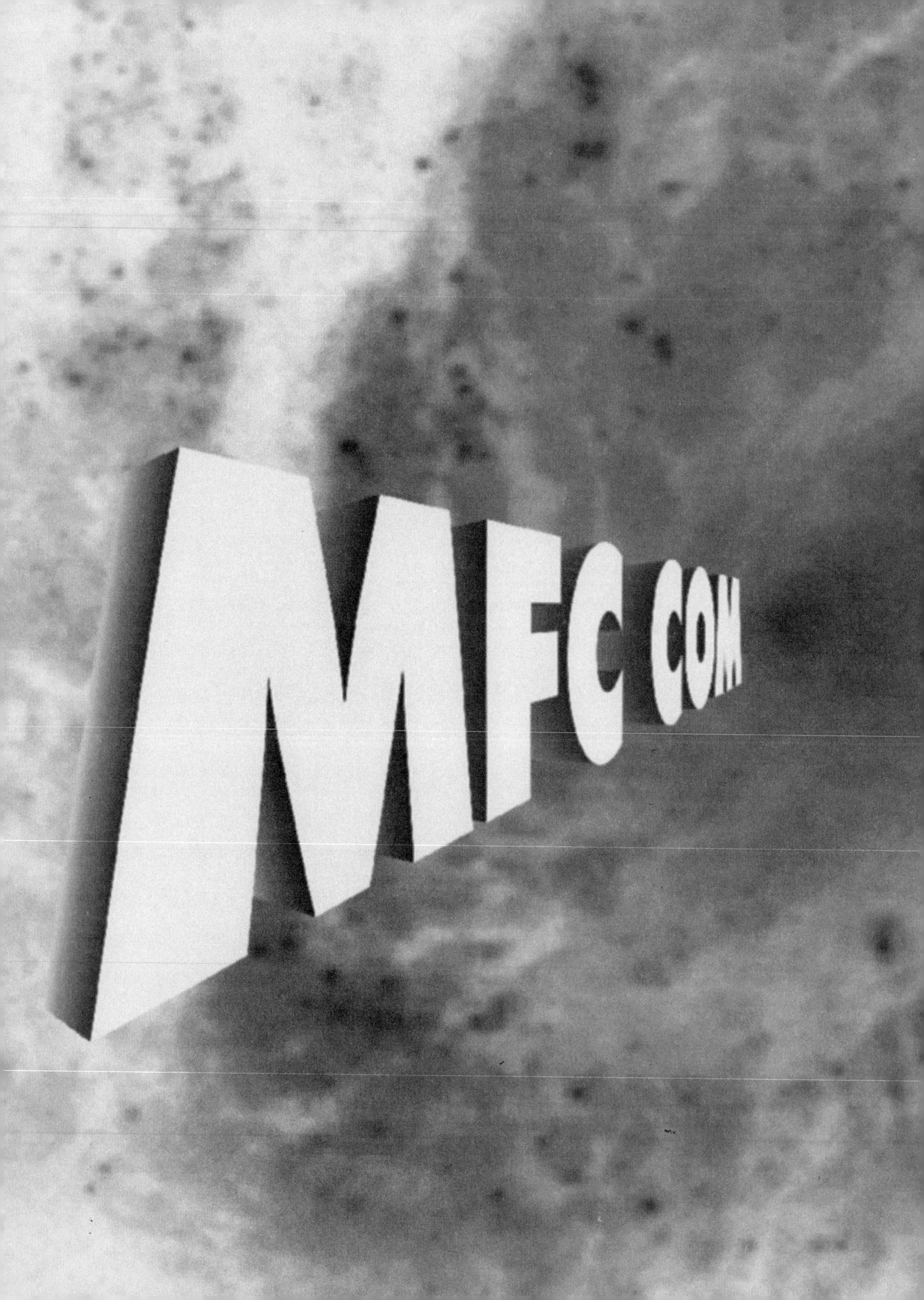
MFC COM

COM Support in Visual C++

This chapter will provide an overview of MFC support for COM, and of the assistance the Visual C++ IDE gives to Windows programmers wanting to include COM support in their applications. I'll start by looking at the ways in which the Developer Studio can add COM support features to applications, and move on to cover the support that MFC provides for program development.

The information I'm presenting here is relevant to Visual C++ releases 4.2 and above, although the specifics of dialog layout pertain to version 5.

COM Support in AppWizard

As you know, the MFC AppWizard is the tool that generates a skeleton application, gathering information via a series of dialog boxes in order to discover what functionality we want included in the skeleton. As the COM-based technologies become increasingly pervasive, the number of related options that we can specify for our applications is on the increase.

All the COM support options are conveniently gathered together on the third of the six MFC AppWizard pages, as shown here:

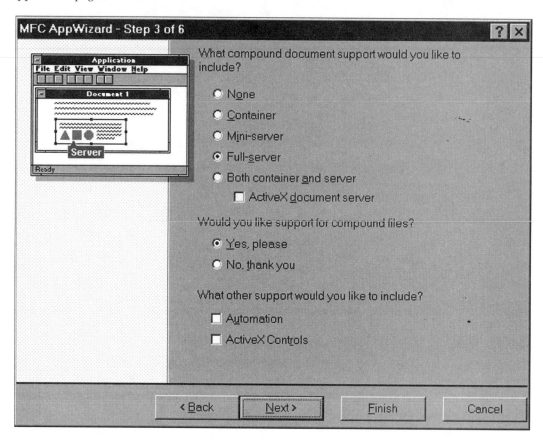

Most of the compound document support involves deriving your application's classes (or at least the view, document and frames) from COM-aware classes, rather than the plain variety. I'll be looking at this further in the second half of the chapter.

Container Support

Selecting this radio button generates the skeleton code for an OLE container application, in other words, one that can contain other OLE objects. The container support offered by AppWizard is fairly rudimentary, mainly because of the wide range of things which you might require a container to do. What you get is the ability for your view and document to support embedded objects. The document will store them, and the view will display them, but they all end up a default size and piled on top of one another, with no metafile image to mark them when they're inactive. There's also no mouse support, so you can't select or move objects either.

The point should be clear: in most cases, you'll have to do quite a lot of work in order to make your container application functional. If you need support for anything particular, you have to add it yourself.

Server Support

AppWizard supports two kinds of server: 'full' and 'mini'. You may remember from the discussion in Chapter 1 that the main difference between these is that mini-servers won't run stand-alone, while full servers will. Both of these are out-of-process servers; you can't easily build in-proc servers, except as ActiveX controls.

What do you get when you build your application as a server? You'll notice quite a few changes to the structure of your project, with at least two new classes being added to support the server functionality. As well as this, code is added to register your application with the registry. Let's not worry about the details now; by the end of this chapter, we'll have generated a skeleton server and taken it apart to see how it works.

One thing you will find is that support for servers is more complete than it is for containers. This is probably because there are fewer options at the server end than there are at the container end, but in any event you'll probably have less work to do to arrive at a functional server than you will to implement a container.

You'll notice that when you check any of the radio buttons that apply to servers, the ActiveX document server check box is enabled. This means that your server items can be used in Active document containers, such as Microsoft Internet Explorer, rather than just in 'ordinary' OLE containers.

> *This is just one of the places where name changes are outpacing Microsoft's dialog designers. The items to which the check box pertains were first called **DocObjects**, and then **ActiveX documents**, and are now correctly referred to as **Active documents**.*

When handling Active documents, the server and container work together just as they do when dealing with embedded or linked objects, but there are several important differences:

▶ The server takes over the entire client area of the container, not just a rectangle

▶ There's no in-place frame with a hatched border or resize handles

▶ Documents can be multi-page, and they're always in-place active.

Compound File Support

If you choose to build a container and/or a server, you can opt to select compound file support. The default is to select this option, and it's best to leave it selected unless you have a good reason for doing otherwise.

If you choose this option, your document's data will be serialized using compound files rather than the standard serialization format - this is the structured storage we talked about in the last chapter. You'll want to choose this when writing a container because OLE objects are used to storing their data in compound files, using the **IStorage** and **IStream** interfaces. This means that you can store OLE objects in your application's serialization files in the same way that Word can store embedded objects in its files.

Automation Support

Choosing Automation support means that your *document class* will be Automation-enabled, making it an Automation server. Note that you don't have to select this option if you're just going to *use* another Automation object, but only if you want your document to be an Automation server. If you want to, you can add Automation-enabled classes afterwards, using ClassWizard.

ActiveX Control Support

If you want to use ActiveX controls in your application, all you need to do is ensure this option is checked, and you're ready to go. A number of controls are supplied with Visual C++, and you can also use any of the dozens of others which are available with packages such as Visual Basic, or as products in their own right.

In fact, all this option does is to insert a call to **AfxEnableControlContainer()** into your application's **InitInstance()** function, so if you don't choose it when you build the application skeleton, it is by no means disastrous.

> *If you don't include ActiveX control support, and then add a control to a dialog in the resource editor, the dialog will not appear at runtime.*

ActiveX Support in ControlWizard

Old versions of Visual C++ came with an add-on extra for developing ActiveX controls (or OLE controls, as they were then), called the Control Developer Kit or CDK. You installed it from the CD, and it integrated itself into the IDE. The old CDK is now fully integrated into Developer Studio (MFC has been extended to include many classes from the CDK), so that ActiveX controls are now one of the standard project types you can build with a Wizard.

Building an ActiveX control with ControlWizard is quite easy, and consists of only two steps. I'll look very briefly here at the options that are available, and discuss them in more detail when we get around to building an ActiveX control in Chapter 9. The first page looks like this:

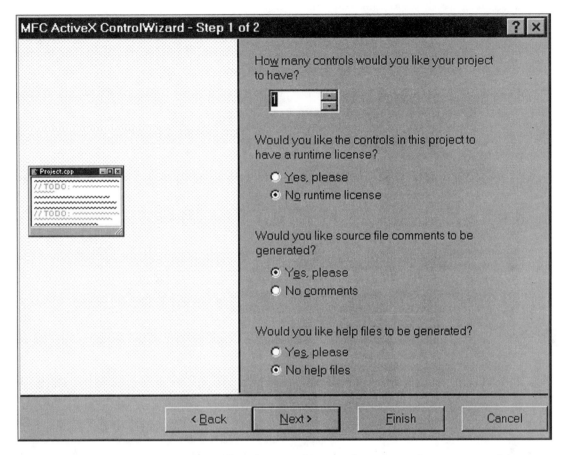

The entries on this page are pretty self-explanatory. You can have more than one control in a project, and can include run-time licensing (which I mentioned in Chapter 2) if you wish. Why might you want to have more than one control per project? You'll end up with multiple **COleControl**-derived classes, but they'll all live in the same DLL; if your project always wants to use the same few controls, you can improve run-time efficiency by including them in a single DLL, rather than in separate ones.

The second page contains some more interesting options:

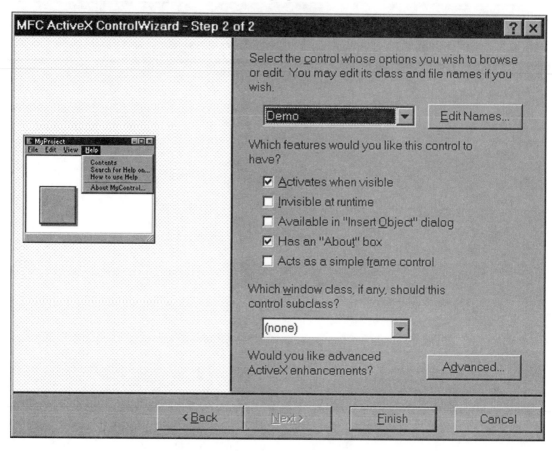

The options on this page are those which determine your control's run-time behavior and appearance. Is it going to be visible or not? If it *is* visible, should it be active as well? We'll discuss these options in detail, along with those illustrated in the next dialog, in Chapter 9.

The next dialog is brought up when you click on the Advanced... button:

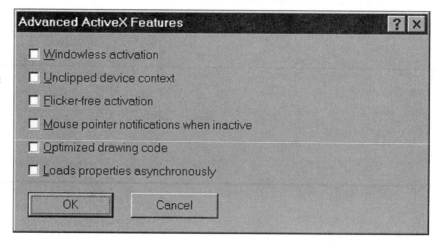

The ActiveX specification allows controls to be quite sophisticated in their behavior, such as allowing them to exist and be active without having to have a window. This dialog allows you to add these features to your control.

> *Windowless controls are an advanced topic, and I won't be mentioning them again in this book. If you're interested in finding out more, have a look at 'ActiveX Controls Inside Out' by Adam Denning, the full reference for which you'll find in the book list in Appendix F.*

COM Support in ClassWizard

ClassWizard is an indispensable tool for maintaining MFC-derived C++ classes, and one of the things it handles particularly well is the implementation of Windows message handlers. What you may not know is that ClassWizard does much the same job in providing support for the COM functionality of your classes.

Adding Automation-enabled Classes

The Add Class... button in ClassWizard drops down a list which enables us to add new classes to our project in two different ways, which I'll talk about here.

Creating a New Class

The first of these methods, accessed via the New... item, creates a totally new class using the parameters we supply in this dialog:

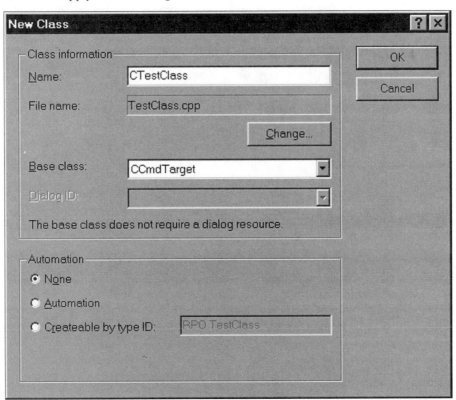

There's a section on this dialog for adding Automation to the class in one of two ways. Selecting the Automation radio button adds the Automation code (which we'll discuss later) to your class, and generates a GUID for the dispatch interface. If you select the third button, this too adds Automation code, but allows you to specify your own progID for the class. This in turn allows an Automation client to create one of these objects directly, rather than having to use a dispatch interface pointer it has been handed from somewhere.

Note that adding Automation to a class in this way assumes that your application is already set up to use COM by initializing the libraries in **InitInstance()**. If it isn't, you'll have to add the code manually, by placing these lines right at the start of **InitInstance()**:

```
// Initialize OLE libraries
if (!AfxOleInit())
{
    AfxMessageBox(IDP_OLE_INIT_FAILED);
    return FALSE;
}
```

Adding Classes from Type Libraries

You'll remember from Chapter 2 that type libraries (**.tlb** files) are used to hold information about the interfaces, methods, properties and events supported by an Automation object. Visual C++ can read these files and create classes that 'wrap' interfaces for us, enabling us to use them easily, and hiding the details of the COM mechanism used in the actual communication. This means that writing Automation clients in Visual C++ is easy, because we just use a C++ object which encapsulates all the Automation methods and properties of the object we're using.

Select the From a type library... entry from the Add Class... drop-down, and ClassWizard will ask you to choose a type library file; these are usually stored with the file extensions **.tlb** or **.olb**. Choose a file, and ClassWizard will offer to create classes for all the interfaces it finds in the file. Here, for example, is the dialog I get when I choose the type library file that comes with the Netscape Navigator browser:

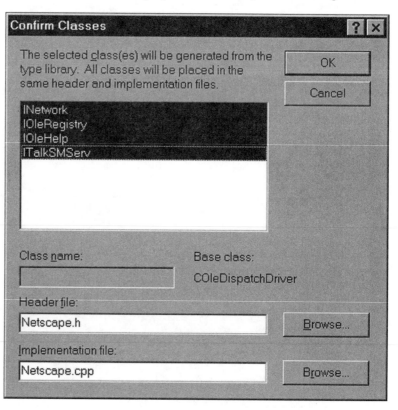

Note that one class is created per interface, that the class name is the same as the interface name, and that all classes are placed in the implementation file shown in the dialog.

Automation and ClassWizard

ClassWizard is also where we develop the Automation support that we've added to our classes. Using the Automation tab, we can add data members and functions to an Automation class that will be used as Automation properties and methods. ClassWizard takes care of all the hard work, generating the underlying COM code and writing the ODL file containing the type information for us, which will get compiled up into a type library.

ActiveX Events and ClassWizard

Using the ActiveX Events tab, you can use ClassWizard to add events to classes that implement ActiveX controls. ClassWizard will generate the code for you to customize, as well as adding appropriate entries to the type information stored in your type library.

I'll be examining in greater detail the features outlined in this and the previous section in Chapter 8, which is all about Automation.

The Components and Controls Gallery

The Components and Controls Gallery is a place where you can store things that you might want to use in several different projects. These 'things' can take the form of C++ classes, ActiveX controls, Wizards that can query you for information and then add functionality to your project's source code, or even whole tools.

The important thing from our current point of view is the ability to store ActiveX controls in the Components and Controls Gallery, because it's from here that we usually choose the controls to use in our C++ development projects. The ability to use ActiveX controls in Visual C++ is a fairly recent development, introduced in version 4.0. Prior to that, you *could* use ActiveX controls, provided you were happy to do the coding to turn your application into a container yourself.

> *It's possible to add controls to your project using ClassWizard, but you have to do more work to use them, as they don't get added to the dialog editor's control palette. In this case, you don't get the help that the dialog editor usually gives you, and you have to create and position the control yourself. You'd do this using the* **Create()** *member function of the control class, and then positioning and sizing it as you would any other window.*

Using ActiveX Controls

Selecting Project | Add To Project | Components and Controls... brings up the Gallery, and as you might expect, all the ActiveX controls which the Gallery finds in the registry are listed in the Registered ActiveX Controls directory:

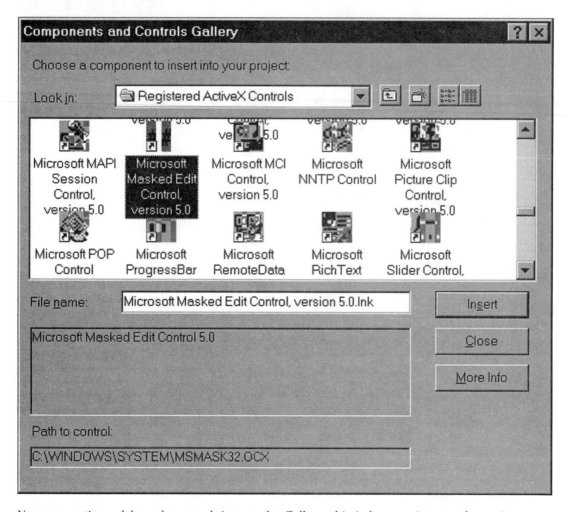

You may notice a delay when you bring up the Gallery; this is because it scans the registry, looking for objects to include in its listings. This means that you can access all the ActiveX controls installed on your machine, regardless of whether they came with Visual C++, Visual Basic or some other package. In fact, since it works on registry entries, you'll see all the controls found in the registry, whether or not they actually exist on the machine! If you try to select an absent control, the Gallery will tell you there's a problem.

Each icon in the list denotes an ActiveX control. You'll find that most of them come with a help file giving details of usage and what properties, methods and events the control supports. This file can be displayed using the **More Info** button. Once you've found the control you wish to use, click on **Insert** to add it to your project. At this point, the Gallery does two things:

▶ It adds the control to the dialog editor's palette

▶ It offers to create classes to wrap the control's Automation interface

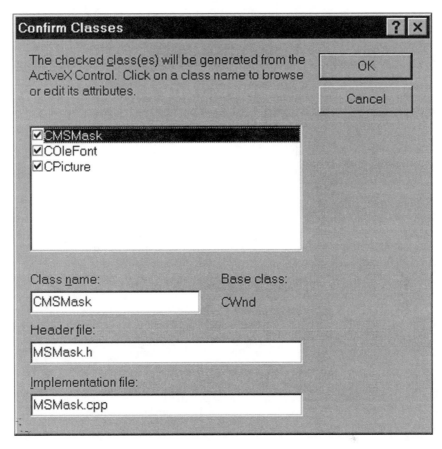

The figure shows the classes that the Components and Controls Gallery will offer to create when you insert the Microsoft Masked Edit control. By default, a class will get created for every suitable interface that the software finds in the type information for the control. You may well not want to use all the classes; in the example above, the only one I'm ever interested in is **CMSMask**, so I can deselect the other two.

What if you find out later that you want to add one of the classes you didn't choose first time around? You can do it like this:

▶ Make a backup of the files (**.cpp** and **.h**) containing the code for the interfaces you selected if you have changed these since they were first generated

▶ Check all the interfaces you want to add, including the original ones

▶ Generate the new files

▶ Verify that the header file and implementation file for the new interface are suitable (because adding **CPicture**, for example, will overwrite any existing **picture.cpp**/**.h** files without warning)

▶ Click OK

Once you've adjusted the classes and file names to your liking and pressed OK, the class code will be generated and added to your application, and the new control will be added to your dialog editor's palette:

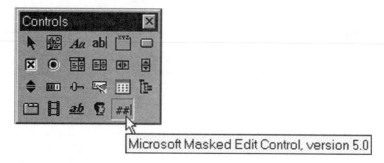

Using these controls is simple. Grab the control off the palette, drop it onto your dialog, and then give it an ID - that much is just the same as for any other control. However, you may well notice that the property sheets for these controls have more tabs than standard Windows controls; these can be used to view and set some of the control's properties at design time, as in Visual Basic.

> *Incidentally, you can also add a new control to a dialog by right-clicking on the dialog and selecting* Insert Active**X** Control... *from the context menu. The ClassWizard will ask you if you want to generate the wrapper class for the control when you create a member variable to represent it.*

When you come to use ClassWizard to associate a variable with the control, ClassWizard will automatically choose the right class to manage it. For example, once I'd installed the Masked Edit control and created one in a dialog, ClassWizard offered to create me a variable for it as follows:

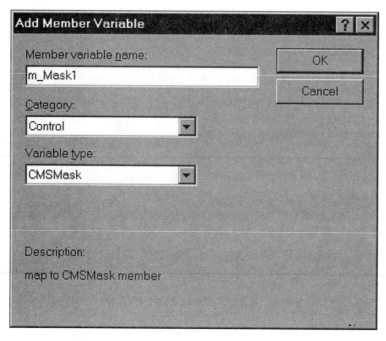

Notice that ClassWizard has automatically picked up the **CMSMask** class from information that's held in the project files. If you look at the contents of the **.dsp** file for your project, you'll see a section at the end that gives the GUIDs of objects used in your project, together with the classes used to handle them.

Once you've passed this stage, you can then control the control (as it were) by calling member functions of the object that represents it, like this:

```
m_Mask1.SetMask("##-???-####");
```

The strange-looking string given as the argument to **SetMask()** represents the mask used to filter the input. The **#** characters represent digits, the **?** characters represent letters, and the dashes are literals. If the control receives invalid input, it will generate a validation error event, which can be caught by the container.

Creating COM-enabled Applications with AppWizard

Shortly, I'm going to move on to start discussing the way in which MFC implements COM functionality, and how that affects the traditional document/view architecture. As a prelude to that discussion, let's generate a couple of skeleton applications: an Automation server and an ActiveX control. I'll look at what makes them different from non-COM applications here, and then dissect them mercilessly in forthcoming chapters.

Try It Out - Creating an Automation Server

1 Create a new project of type MFC AppWizard (exe) and call it **AutoSrv**. For the sake of simplicity, specify it as an SDI application in step one of the Wizard.

2 In step three, choose the Full-server option, and make sure you select the Automation check box. You don't need to check the ActiveX document server box for this example.

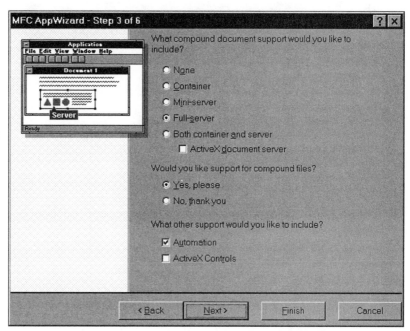

3 In step four, click on the <u>A</u>dvanced... button to bring up the advanced options dialog, and enter a file extension such as **srv**, which will be used to identify the files produced by our server application. Notice also the File type <u>I</u>D field, which sets the progID by which this server's document class will be known in the registry. You are at liberty to change it to something more descriptive if you wish.

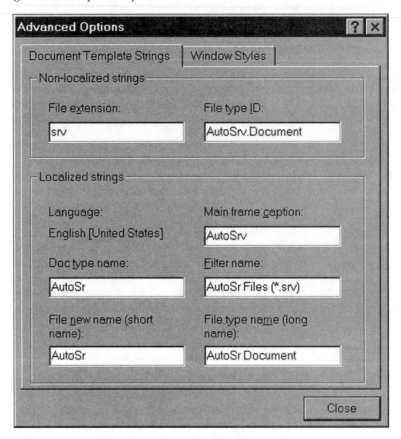

4 Now step through the remaining options to the end (or just press <u>F</u>inish) and generate the source code.

What's Changed?

The skeleton application differs from its non-server counterpart in two areas. Firstly, code has been added to let the application work as an Automation server, and secondly, the MFC structure of the application has been changed in order to add compound document support to the document/view architecture.

The differences in the MFC structure are for the second part of the chapter; in the meantime, let's see what has been added to the code to make it work as an Automation server. The first change you'll notice occurs in **stdafx.h**, where the header files defining the MFC OLE and Automation classes have been added:

```
#define VC_EXTRALEAN            // Exclude rarely-used stuff from Windows headers

#include <afxwin.h>             // MFC core and standard components
#include <afxext.h>             // MFC extensions
#include <afxole.h>             // MFC OLE classes
#include <afxdisp.h>            // MFC OLE automation classes
#ifndef _AFX_NO_AFXCMN_SUPPORT
#include <afxcmn.h>             // MFC support for Windows Common Controls
#endif // _AFX_NO_AFXCMN_SUPPORT
```

All the other significant changes occur in the application class, **CAutoSrvApp**. Because we're now creating an Automation server, our program has to have an entry in the registry, and that means it has to have a CLSID. AppWizard has generated one for us, and it can be found towards the top of **AutoSrv.cpp**:

```
// This identifier was generated to be statistically unique for your app.
// You may change it if you prefer to choose a specific identifier.

// {81F8482C-93AA-11D0-9257-00201834E2A3}
static const CLSID clsid =
{ 0x81f8482c, 0x93aa, 0x11d0, { 0x92, 0x57, 0x0, 0x20, 0x18, 0x34, 0xe2, 0xa3 } };
```

This CLSID will be added to the registry on the first occasion the program is run, along with the matching progID which was given to AppWizard. Don't arbitrarily change the CLSID - if you need to do this, use the Guidgen tool supplied with Visual C++ to generate a new one. Also, if you do change it, you'll need to modify it in the **.reg** file as well.

In case you ever want to find it, the progID is stored in the resource (**.rc**) file, as part of the document template string, in one of the string tables:

```
BEGIN
    IDR_MAINFRAME        "AutoSrv\n\nAutoSr\nAutoSrFiles(*.srv)\n.srv\n
                         AutoSrv.Document\nAutoSr Document"
END
```

Now we've got a CLSID, the server can make sure that the OLE libraries are all initialized, check that it's registered with the system, and then load itself as an Automation server. All this work is done in the application's **InitInstance()** member function.

The code that follows is a typical example from a skeleton server application. The new code is highlighted, and as you can see, there's considerably more going on in this application than there is in the normal, COM-free version. Let's look at each of the additions in turn, so we can build up a picture of what is going on.

Initializing the OLE Libraries

```
BOOL CAutoSrvApp::InitInstance()
{
    // Initialize OLE libraries
    if (!AfxOleInit())
    {
        AfxMessageBox(IDP_OLE_INIT_FAILED);
        return FALSE;
    }
```

The call to **AfxOleInit()** ensures that the OLE DLLs are loaded. If they're already in memory, then this call will have no effect. If the call returns **FALSE**, initialization failed.

Adding OLE Information to the Document Template

```
    // Standard initialization
    // If you are not using these features and wish to reduce the size
    //  of your final executable, you should remove from the following
    //  the specific initialization routines you do not need.

#ifdef _AFXDLL
    Enable3dControls();          // Call this when using MFC in a shared DLL
#else
    Enable3dControlsStatic();    // Call this when linking to MFC statically
#endif

    // Change the registry key under which our settings are stored.
    // You should modify this string to be something appropriate
    // such as the name of your company or organization.
    SetRegistryKey(_T("Local AppWizard-Generated Applications"));

    LoadStdProfileSettings();    // Load standard INI file options (including MRU)

    // Register the application's document templates.  Document templates
    //  serve as the connection between documents, frame windows and views.

    CSingleDocTemplate* pDocTemplate;
    pDocTemplate = new CSingleDocTemplate(
        IDR_MAINFRAME,
        RUNTIME_CLASS(CAutoSrvDoc),
        RUNTIME_CLASS(CMainFrame),         // main SDI frame window
        RUNTIME_CLASS(CAutoSrvView));
    pDocTemplate->SetServerInfo(
        IDR_SRVR_EMBEDDED, IDR_SRVR_INPLACE,
        RUNTIME_CLASS(CInPlaceFrame));
    AddDocTemplate(pDocTemplate);
```

The **SetServerInfo()** function extends the document template so that it can work with compound documents. As you might expect, the document template needs to know rather more for documents that are going to be used with a server. These documents can now be embedded in containers, with their own frame, and can have a menu that's merged with that of the container at runtime.

The template therefore needs to know which menu to use when the application is run stand-alone (resource **IDR_SRVR_EMBEDDED** in the code above), which menu to use when the document is embedded in a container (resource **IDR_SRVR_INPLACE**), and the sort of frame that's used for embedded objects (an object of class **CInPlaceFrame**).

Setting Up the COleTemplateServer Object

An MFC server application, whether it's a 'standard' one or an Automation server, contains a **COleTemplateServer** data member. In Chapter 2, I said that all COM servers have to have a class factory for each class that they support. This means that all MFC programs that implement COM objects have to have class factories for them, and this functionality will be provided by one of two classes:

▶ **COleObjectFactory**, which is used by MFC programs which don't follow the document/view architecture

▶ **COleTemplateServer**, which inherits from **COleObjectFactory**, and which *is* integrated into the document/view architecture

Our application therefore has a **COleTemplateServer** data member, which is used to create server objects at runtime. There needs to be one **COleTemplateServer** object for each document template that the application supports.

```
// Connect the COleTemplateServer to the document template.
//  The COleTemplateServer creates new documents on behalf
//  of requesting OLE containers by using information
//  specified in the document template.
m_server.ConnectTemplate(clsid, pDocTemplate, TRUE);
    // Note: SDI applications register server objects only if /Embedding
    //   or /Automation is present on the command line.


// Enable DDE Execute open
EnableShellOpen();
RegisterShellFileTypes(TRUE);
```

The **COleTemplateServer** member is called **m_server**, and the call to its **ConnectTemplate()** function tells the template server object which CLSID is associated with which document template, so that the correct document, view and frame objects can be created at runtime. The final Boolean parameter determines whether one instance of the application can support multiple instances of the object, or whether a new copy of the application needs to be run for each object.

When the application is requested to create an object with a particular CLSID, the class factory code can use the information supplied in the **ConnectTemplate()** call to request the correct document template object to do its job.

Checking Whether the Application has been Launched as a Server

```
// Parse command line for standard shell commands, DDE, file open
CCommandLineInfo cmdInfo;
ParseCommandLine(cmdInfo);
```

```
// Check to see if launched as OLE server
if (cmdInfo.m_bRunEmbedded || cmdInfo.m_bRunAutomated)
{
    // Register all OLE server (factories) as running.  This enables the
    //  OLE libraries to create objects from other applications.
    COleTemplateServer::RegisterAll();

    // Application was run with /Embedding or /Automation.  Don't show
    //  the main window in this case.
    return TRUE;
}
```

The application can be started as a server in one of two ways: through the activation of an object embedded in a container, or by the use of Automation. In these cases, the application will be started with a command line containing one of the switches **/Embedding** or **/Automation**, and the action of parsing the command line will set the corresponding flags in the

CCmdLineInfo variable. If either of these flags is set, then the **COleTemplateServer** object registers all the application's class factories with the OLE DLLs, so that other applications can create objects.

If the program has been started as a server, **InitInstance()** stops here, returning without creating a main window, so that the program runs invisibly in the background. Just in case you're interested, creating the main window and opening the default new document is done in the bowels of the **ProcessShellCommand()** function.

> *Note that the structure of an MDI application is slightly different, in that the call to* **RegisterAll()** *is placed before the* **if** *statement:*

```
// Register all OLE server factories as running.  This enables the
//  OLE libraries to create objects from other applications.
COleTemplateServer::RegisterAll();
// Note: MDI applications register all server objects without regard
//  to the /Embedding or /Automation on the command line.

// ...

// Check to see if launched as OLE server
if (cmdInfo.m_bRunEmbedded || cmdInfo.m_bRunAutomated)
{
    // Application was run with /Embedding or /Automation.  Don't show the
    //  main window in this case.
    return TRUE;
}
```

> *The clue as to why this happens is given in the comment that follows the statement. An MDI application may be started up stand-alone, and only later be used as a server. This being the case, the application has to register all its class factories when it starts, otherwise it is going to be in trouble when it needs to use them.*

Updating the Registry

```
// When a server application is launched stand-alone, it is a good idea
//  to update the system registry in case it has been damaged.
m_server.UpdateRegistry(OAT_INPLACE_SERVER);
COleObjectFactory::UpdateRegistryAll();
```

Each time the application is run stand-alone, it calls **COleTemplateServer::UpdateRegistry()** to update its entry in the system registry, making sure that it is registered as an in-place server. The first time the application runs, this will register it; on subsequent occasions, it will rewrite the entries, just in case the registry has been damaged in any way.

This behavior is rather typical of the way in which MFC tends to work. It would be possible, although more work, to register the application on the first execution only. It's much simpler to do it every time, and at the expense of a small increase in execution time we get the ability to repair the registry entries.

The second call, to **COleObjectFactory::UpdateRegistryAll()**, makes sure that all the application's object factories are registered.

AppWizard also produces a registry file for your application, which is a text file with a **.reg** extension, holding the registry information for your application. The file contains the same information as that added by the call to **COleObjectFactory::UpdateRegistryAll()**, and is provided so that utilities such as setup programs can register your application or control without having to run it.

Setting Up for Drag and Drop

```
    // Dispatch commands specified on the command line
    if (!ProcessShellCommand(cmdInfo))
        return FALSE;

    // The one and only window has been initialized, so show and update it.
    m_pMainWnd->ShowWindow(SW_SHOW);
    m_pMainWnd->UpdateWindow();

    // Enable drag/drop open
    m_pMainWnd->DragAcceptFiles();

    return TRUE;
}
```

The last thing that the application does in **InitInstance()** is to use a call to **DragAcceptFiles()** to set itself up to accept files dropped on it. This is added as standard to Automation server applications.

That concludes the changes to **InitInstance()**, and if nothing else, this discussion should leave you relieved that AppWizard handles all the complexity for you! Still, the 'traditional' MFC application structure is very much intact, and the changes induced by choosing to create an Automation server are variations on a familiar theme.

Let's go on now to look at a very different kind of AppWizard-generated project: an ActiveX control.

Try It Out - Creating an ActiveX Control

1 Close everything down and bring up the New Project dialog again. This time, choose the MFC ActiveX ControlWizard and give your project the name **ActiveCtl**. When you press OK, you'll be handed over to the two-page Wizard responsible for building controls.

2 For the purposes of this example, make sure you select Yes, please for the runtime licensing option on the first page, and leave the other options at their default settings.

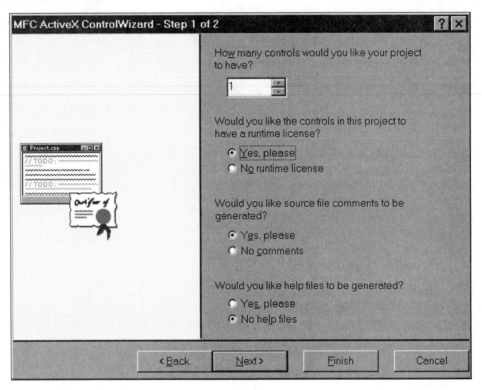

3 Leave the second page with all the default options selected. Click Finish and then OK to generate the source code.

What's Changed?

If you examine the lists of classes and files produced for this application, you'll soon realize that this is nothing like an ordinary AppWizard-generated MFC application. This shouldn't be too surprising, since an ActiveX control isn't really a standard application at all, being instead an in-process server that lives in a DLL. It also needs to support quite a lot of COM functionality, as it communicates with its container by Automation.

ActiveX Support in the Control

Clearly, a large proportion of an ActiveX control project is going to be intimately involved with ActiveX support, but let's single out a few salient points here without getting into too much deep water, and saving detailed discussion for Chapter 9, which is dedicated to controls.

An ActiveX control project involves specifying no fewer than four GUIDs. One of these is for the control's type library, and is declared in the main application class implementation file, **ActiveCtl.cpp**:

```
const GUID CDECL BASED_CODE _tlid =
    { 0x81f8484d, 0x93aa, 0x11d0, { 0x92, 0x57, 0, 0x20, 0x18, 0x34, 0xe2, 0xa3
} };
```

The other three are found in the control class implementation file, **ActiveCtlCtl.cpp**. The first is the GUID for the control itself, as found in the CLSID section in the registry. This is created by the **IMPLEMENT_OLECREATE_EX()** macro, whose task is to create the class factory for the control:

```
IMPLEMENT_OLECREATE_EX(CActiveCtlCtrl, "ACTIVECTL.ActiveCtlCtrl.1",
    0x81f84850, 0x93aa, 0x11d0, 0x92, 0x57, 0, 0x20, 0x18, 0x34, 0xe2, 0xa3)
```

The other two GUIDs define the IIDs of the two custom interfaces implemented by the control - the first for the dispatch interface, and the other for handling outgoing events:

```
const IID BASED_CODE IID_DActiveCtl =
    { 0x81f8484e, 0x93aa, 0x11d0, { 0x92, 0x57, 0, 0x20, 0x18, 0x34, 0xe2, 0xa3
} };
const IID BASED_CODE IID_DActiveCtlEvents =
    { 0x81f8484f, 0x93aa, 0x11d0, { 0x92, 0x57, 0, 0x20, 0x18, 0x34, 0xe2, 0xa3
} };
```

The interfaces supported by the control, including the dispatch interface and its methods and properties, are defined in the project's ODL file. Although you can bring this up in the editor, you should have little need to edit it manually, as ClassWizard maintains it for you.

The Control Skeleton

The **stdafx.h** header file has done away with all of the normal MFC headers, and now only includes the control support file, **afxctl.h**, and the database classes:

```
#define VC_EXTRALEAN      // Exclude rarely-used stuff from Windows headers

#include <afxctl.h>       // MFC support for ActiveX Controls

// Delete the two includes below if you do not wish to use the MFC
//   database classes
#include <afxdb.h>        // MFC database classes
#include <afxdao.h>       // MFC DAO database classes
```

Assuming the project was specified as having only one control, the control application consists of just three classes: **CActiveCtlApp**, **CActiveCtlCtrl** and **CActiveCtlPropPage**. None of these is particularly complicated, due mainly to the fact that a great deal of functionality is implemented for you in various base classes.

CActiveCtlApp

CActiveCtlApp is the control's equivalent of the normal **CWinApp**-derived MFC application class. In the case of an ActiveX control, this class isn't derived directly from **CWinApp**, but from the functionally equivalent **COleControlModule**, which itself inherits from **CWinApp**.

```
class CActiveCtlApp : public COleControlModule
{
public:
   BOOL InitInstance();
   int ExitInstance();
};
```

CActiveCtlApp has only two member functions, **InitInstance()** and **ExitInstance()**, which are called when the control is loaded and unloaded, and to which you can add any special initialization or exit code.

The implementation file contains two more functions which aren't members of the class, called **DllRegisterServer()** and **DllUnregisterServer()**. These functions are exported by in-process servers living in DLLs, and allow external tools such as Regsvr32 to register and unregister the control.

CActiveCtlCtrl

CActiveCtlCtrl is where the functionality of the control is implemented. It inherits from **COleControl** (a **CWnd**-derived class), which is the base class for all MFC-generated ActiveX controls. This base class is huge, containing over 150 member functions, which probably accounts for the deceptive simplicity of the derived control class we see here!

Let's start by looking at the constructor:

```
CActiveCtlCtrl::CActiveCtlCtrl()
{
    InitializeIIDs(&IID_DActiveCtl, &IID_DActiveCtlEvents);

    // TODO: Initialize your control's instance data here.
}
```

The constructor simply calls **InitializeIIDs()**, which passes the IDs of the control's two interfaces - the dispatch and event interfaces, which handle the control's Automation methods, properties and events - to its base class, which takes care of all the work of initializing the COM run-time system and setting up the control.

```
void CActiveCtlCtrl::OnDraw(
        CDC* pdc, const CRect& rcBounds, const CRect& rcInvalid)
{
    // TODO: Replace the following code with your own drawing code.
    pdc->FillRect(rcBounds,
CBrush::FromHandle((HBRUSH)GetStockObject(WHITE_BRUSH)));
    pdc->Ellipse(rcBounds);
}
```

The **OnDraw()** member is the main function of interest, and it's where you put the drawing code for your control. The ControlWizard inserts code to draw a white-filled rectangle containing an ellipse by default, just so you can see where your control is when you place it into a container.

```
void CActiveCtlCtrl::DoPropExchange(CPropExchange* pPX)
{
    ExchangeVersion(pPX, MAKELONG(_wVerMinor, _wVerMajor));
    COleControl::DoPropExchange(pPX);

    // TODO: Call PX_ functions for each persistent custom property.

}

void CActiveCtlCtrl::OnResetState()
{
    COleControl::OnResetState();  // Resets defaults found in DoPropExchange
```

```
        // TODO: Reset any other control state here.
    }
```

OnResetState() is called when the control needs to be reset to the default state found in **DoPropExchange()**, where property persistence is implemented. A control container can ask its controls to save their properties, usually providing some structured storage for that purpose, and this is implemented in a way very similar to dialog data exchange, as we'll see when we discuss controls in detail.

CActiveCtlPropPage

CActiveCtlPropPage is a class that implements your control's single default property page. As with normal AppWizard MFC applications, where you get a single document and a single view class, you get one property page class, and you can add more if you like. For now, just note that from the point of view of an MFC programmer, the property page works very much like a dialog. You edit a dialog resource to create the controls that will appear on the page, and Dynamic Data Exchange connects the controls with the properties of your control. MFC also provides support for some stock property pages, so that you can easily add pages for stock properties such as fonts and colors.

Licensing Support

If (as we've done here) you've chosen licensing support, then extra functionality will be added to the class factory, and a license file (in this case **ActiveCtl.lic**) will be added to the project. The default license file is simply a standard text file, and the default checking function, **VerifyUserLicense()**, simply checks for the presence of a string in the file. You can make the license check as complex as you wish, by altering the contents of the license file and the use that **VerifyUserLicense()** makes of it.

COM and the MFC Model

So far, I've been looking at the scale and diversity of the COM support in Visual C++, and at how the Wizards allow us to build COM-enabled skeletons for applications. Now I want to dive into MFC, and examine how adding COM support to our applications changes the document/view model. During the process, I'll put together a simple MFC server which implements a COM interface, so you can see how it is done, and I'll be using code fragments taken from this server example as often as possible in our discussions.

COM is interwoven into MFC in two ways. There are the visible, on-the-surface classes that you interact with in your programming, and which implement the COM extensions to the MFC programming model; there's also the invisible, behind-the-scenes stuff that actually connects MFC to the COM run-time system. In this chapter, we'll look at the behind-the-scenes stuff, which provides the COM 'engine room' for MFC. In subsequent chapters, we'll look at the visible manifestations of COM, as expressed in the MFC classes we use from day to day.

CCmdTarget and COM

If you're truly going to understand how MFC implements COM, then it's essential to know quite a lot about how **CCmdTarget** works. This class really is the nerve center of MFC, both generally, and especially where COM is concerned. Whenever you're wondering how something dynamic happens in MFC, whether it's messages getting routed, Automation classes getting requests and issuing notifications, or whatever, you can bet that **CCmdTarget** is in there somewhere, acting as a sort of combination of traffic cop, Yellow Pages service and switchboard operator.

We'll see a number of **CCmdTarget**'s capabilities as we explore further. To start with, though, we'll concentrate on two aspects of its operation that are crucial to bringing COM to the rest of MFC. These aspects are

▶ Its mapping support

▶ Its implementation of **IUnknown**

Interface Maps

You probably already know that **CCmdTarget** uses mapping to handle Windows messages, via **message maps**, but you may not know that it also performs several other types of mapping. In this section we'll look at the way the class handles COM interfaces using **interface maps**. Later on, when we come to cover Automation and ActiveX controls, we'll meet **dispatch maps** and **event maps** too.

Fundamentally, all these maps work the same way. A map consists of a series of keyword/value pairs, which map an identifier of some sort onto a pointer. In the case of message maps, the identifiers are Windows message IDs, and the pointers indicate the message-handling routines we create with ClassWizard. When we're using interface maps, the identifiers are interface IDs (IIDs), and the pointers show the start of the vtables for those interfaces.

At this point, great big bells should be ringing in your head, because we've seen interface IDs and pointers together before. In **IUnknown**'s **QueryInterface()** function, we pass a reference to an IID, and get back a pointer to an interface. *That's* what interface maps are used for - they enable MFC to find out whether a given class supports a given interface, and if so, to retrieve a pointer to that interface.

There's one more addition that helps the mechanism to work properly. Each class has a pointer to its base class interface map, so the search for a class which supports an interface can go all the way back up the inheritance chain to **CCmdTarget**, where the chain stops.

Interface Maps at Runtime

Let's begin by taking a look at how **CCmdTarget** actually uses these maps. The process is fairly simple:

1 **QueryInterface()** is called on an object derived from **CCmdTarget**.

2 This results in **CCmdTarget::ExternalQueryInterface()** getting called. The function looks to see whether it is aggregated, and if not, calls **CCmdTarget::InternalQueryInterface()**. I'll cover the difference between the internal and external **QueryInterface()** functions shortly.

3 The internal routine passes the IID on to **CCmdTarget::GetInterface()**.

4 **GetInterface()** gets a pointer to the object's interface map and checks to see whether any entry matches the IID. If so, it returns the interface pointer to **InternalQueryInterface()**, which calls **AddRef()** to increment the interface's reference count.

5   Once the **AddRef()** has been done, the interface pointer is returned as the result of the original **QueryInterface()** call.

6   If the IID isn't found in the map, **GetInterface()** chains back to the base class map, and checks that one. It will continue to process right back up to **CCmdTarget** itself, where the base class map pointer will be **NULL**, and the search will terminate.

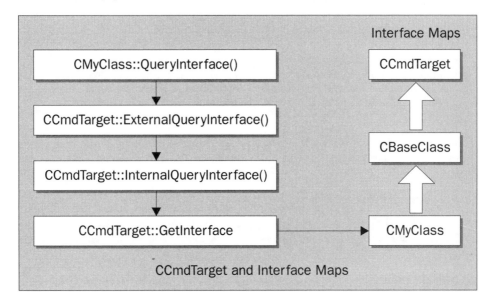

You can see from this process that MFC allows classes effectively to 'inherit' interfaces from their base classes.

Implementing Interface Maps

Let's now dive in and see how this is actually implemented. Here's a piece of the declaration of **CCmdTarget** from **afxwin.h** in Visual C++ 5:

```
class CCmdTarget : public CObject
{
...
#ifndef _AFX_NO_OLE_SUPPORT
    DECLARE_DISPATCH_MAP()
    DECLARE_CONNECTION_MAP()
    DECLARE_INTERFACE_MAP()
...
};
```

As you may have guessed, it's the **DECLARE_INTERFACE_MAP** that interests us at the minute. The other two maps are associated with Automation, and we'll meet them later. The macro is used within a class declaration to set up an interface map for the class. Here's its definition from **afxwin.h**:

```
#define DECLARE_INTERFACE_MAP() \
private: \
    static const AFX_INTERFACEMAP_ENTRY _interfaceEntries[]; \
```

```
protected: \
   static AFX_DATA const AFX_INTERFACEMAP interfaceMap; \
   virtual const AFX_INTERFACEMAP* GetInterfaceMap() const; \
```

> *If you look into the MFC source code, you'll notice that preprocessor symbols such as* _AFXDLL *are used quite frequently. Since MFC's precise use depends on the code in which it is being built, and on the compiler and linker settings, there tends to be a number of 'special cases'.*
>
> *The purpose of* _AFXDLL, *for example, is to handle macros and code that must be declared differently for MFC classes compiled for normal applications than in those for DLLs. In this introductory discussion, I'll tend to skip over these distinctions in the interest of examining the underlying mechanism.*

You can see that the definition sets up two data items and a function. The first item is a static array of interface map entries, each of which holds an IID and the offset into the vtable where this interface can be found:

```
struct AFX_INTERFACEMAP_ENTRY
{
   const void* piid;      // the interface id (IID) (NULL for aggregate)
   size_t nOffset;        // offset of the interface vtable from m_unknown
};
```

The **_interfaceEntries** array frequently only contains a single element, since we often use an MFC class to implement a single COM interface. The second data item is the static interface map:

```
struct AFX_INTERFACEMAP
{
#ifdef _AFXDLL
   const AFX_INTERFACEMAP* (PASCAL* pfnGetBaseMap)(); // NULL is root class
#else
   const AFX_INTERFACEMAP* pBaseMap;
#endif
   const AFX_INTERFACEMAP_ENTRY* pEntry; // map for this class
};
```

In the source of **CCmdTarget**, the **pEntry** pointer is set to point to the first entry in the **_interfaceEntries** array. In derived classes, **pEntry** will point to the **_interfaceEntries** array for the class, while **pBaseMap** will point to the interface map for the parent class. The **GetInterfaceMap()** function returns a pointer to the interface map structure.

CCmdTarget's IUnknown Implementation

You're now used to the fact that interfaces must include the **IUnknown** interface functions, and that's just as true for interfaces buried in MFC code as it is anywhere else. As the main COM-enabling class for MFC, **CCmdTarget** implements **IUnknown**, handles the reference counting, and provides **QueryInterface()** functionality for classes which inherit from it.

Here's **CCmdTarget**'s **IUnknown** code, taken from **afxwin.h**:

```
public:
    // data used when CCmdTarget is made OLE aware
    long m_dwRef;
    LPUNKNOWN m_pOuterUnknown;  // external controlling unknown if != NULL
    DWORD m_xInnerUnknown;  // place-holder for inner controlling unknown

public:
    // advanced operations
    void EnableAggregation();        // call to enable aggregation
    void ExternalDisconnect();       // forcibly disconnect
    LPUNKNOWN GetControllingUnknown();
        // get controlling IUnknown for aggregate creation
    // these versions do not delegate to m_pOuterUnknown
    DWORD InternalQueryInterface(const void*, LPVOID* ppvObj);
    DWORD InternalAddRef();
    DWORD InternalRelease();
    // these versions delegate to m_pOuterUnknown
    DWORD ExternalQueryInterface(const void*, LPVOID* ppvObj);
    DWORD ExternalAddRef();
    DWORD ExternalRelease();
```

Why are there two versions? The 'internal' set is the one that actually handles the **IUnknown** functions; the other, 'external' set is there for use in COM aggregation. I mentioned aggregation briefly in Chapter 2, explaining how an aggregated object is embedded in another, although its interfaces are used as if it was stand-alone. In this case, the object must delegate the reference counting functions to its containing object.

A containing object may implement two interfaces, each of which may be being used by one client. The interfaces will each see a reference count of one, but the actual reference count on the containing object as a whole is two, and it is only the containing object which has the overview necessary in order to manage the reference counting correctly.

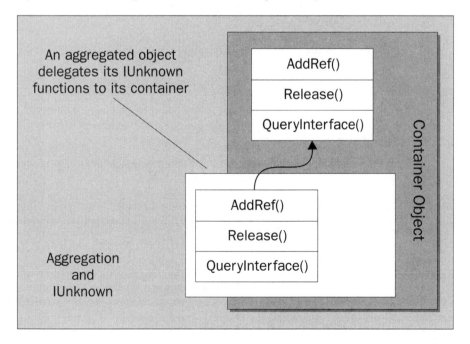

If the object is aggregated, the **m_pOuterUnknown** pointer will point to the **IUnknown** interface of the container object, and so won't be **NULL**. All the 'external' functions do is to check this variable, and if it is set, delegate the action, as you can see from the code for **ExternalAddRef()** in **oleunk.cpp**:

```
DWORD CCmdTarget::ExternalAddRef()
{
    // delegate to controlling unknown if aggregated
    if (m_pOuterUnknown != NULL)
        return m_pOuterUnknown->AddRef();

    return InternalAddRef();
}
```

Adding Interfaces to Classes

We've seen how interface maps fit into a class. The next step is to add an actual interface, or indeed interfaces, to an MFC class. Although we haven't come across an example of it so far, it's perfectly possible for an MFC class to implement more than one COM interface. The process uses aggregation, so all the interfaces have to delegate their **IUnknown** functionality to the containing class.

There are three ways in which we could add one or more interfaces to a class:

▶ Multiple inheritance

▶ Interface implementations

▶ Nested classes

MFC uses the third method, so I'll be explaining that in detail after looking briefly at the others. If you want a more complete explanation of the first two methods, they are covered more fully in Brockschmidt's book, *Inside OLE*.

> *From here on, I'll use the example of a class called **CoDemo**, which implements two interfaces called **IDemo** and **IDemo2**. It will be the basis of theoretical discussion for now, but later on we'll actually code up an example class to demonstrate how it all works in practice.*

Using Multiple Inheritance

Multiple inheritance can be an ideal way to provide multiple interfaces. After all, if we want to implement more than one interface, what could be simpler than writing:

```
class CoDemo: public IUnknown, public IDemo, public IDemo2
{
    // implementation of all three classes
};
```

Although this may indeed work out very well in many cases, there are some disadvantages too. Along with general inefficiencies due to the way some compilers implement multiple inheritance, there are potential problems such as name collisions occurring between functions with the same names in different interfaces.

Using Interface Implementations

The second method, interface implementations, uses a separate class to implement each interface. All the classes - the 'parent' and the classes implementing the interfaces - maintain pointers to one another:

```
class CoDemo : public IUnknown
{
    // Pointers to interface implementation classes
    CDemo* m_pDemo;     // pointer to object implementing IDemo
    CDemo2* m_pDemo2;   // pointer to object implementing IDemo2

    // Make their classes friends, so they can get at protected members
    friend class CDemo;
    friend class CDemo2;

    // Base implementations of IUnknown functions
    virtual HRESULT QueryInterface(REFIID riid, void** ppv);
    virtual ULONG   Release();
    virtual ULONG   AddRef();
};
```

The parent class needs to create objects to handle the interfaces in its constructor, and to delete them in its destructor. The classes that implement the interfaces delegate their **IUnknown** functionality to the parent.

The disadvantage of this method is that the reference counting can get rather complicated, and there's the problem of managing all those forward and backward pointers.

Using Nested Classes

Let's get to the way MFC implements multiple interfaces: nested classes. In some ways, this is similar to the previous method, in that each interface is implemented as a separate class, but this time they're all contained within the parent class, and there's no need for the forward and backward pointers we had in the last example. It also makes the mechanics of reference counting rather simpler. The code fragment below shows how it's done:

```
class CoDemo : public IUnknown
{
    // Base implementations of IUnknown functions
    virtual HRESULT QueryInterface(REFIID riid, void** ppv);
    virtual ULONG   Release();
    virtual ULONG   AddRef();

    class XDemoCls : public IDemo
    {
        // Base implementations of IUnknown functions
        virtual HRESULT QueryInterface(REFIID riid, void** ppv);
        virtual ULONG   Release();
        virtual ULONG   AddRef();

        // Other interface functions...
        virtual void SomeFunc();
    };

    class XDemo2Cls : public IDemo2
```

```
    {
        // Base implementations of IUnknown functions
        virtual HRESULT QueryInterface(REFIID riid, void** ppv);
        virtual ULONG   Release();
        virtual ULONG   AddRef();

        // Other interface functions...
        virtual void SomeOtherFunc();
    };

    friend class XDemoCls;
    friend class XDemo2Cls;

    XDemoCls m_xDemoCls;
    XDemo2Cls m_xDemo2Cls;
};
```

The two interfaces are now implemented as classes nested within the parent, which contains a member of each class type. The nested interface classes, whose names always start with **X**, are declared as **friend**s so that they can access protected and private members in the parent class.

Here's how **QueryInterface()** looks when we're using nested classes. The function simply returns the address of the member corresponding to the required interface:

```
HRESULT CoDemo::QueryInterface(REFIID riid, void** ppv)
{
    *ppv = NULL;

    if (riid == IID_IUnknown)
        *ppv = this;
    else if (riid == IID_IDemo)
        *ppv = &m_xDemoCls;   // return our XDemoCls member
    else if (riid == IID_IDemo2)
        *ppv = &m_xDemo2Cls; // return our XDemo2Cls member
    else
        return E_NOINTERFACE;

    ((LPUNKNOWN)*ppv)->AddRef();
    return S_OK;
}
```

Reference Counting

A few paragraphs ago, I said that the nested class method made it easier to handle reference counting than the interface implementation method, and it's worth taking a quick look at how this is done. What we want to arrange is for calls to the **IUnknown** functions in the nested classes to call the parent class versions *automatically*, without any need for special coding or extra data members holding pointers.

If you looked at the implementation of, say, **QueryInterface()** in one of the nested classes, you'd see something like this:

```
HRESULT CoDemo::XDemoCls::QueryInterface(REFIID riid, void** ppv)
{
    METHOD_PROLOGUE(CoDemo, XDemoCls);
    return pThis->QueryInterface(riid, ppv);
}
```

What's going on? First of all, the `CoDemo::XDemoCls::QueryInterface()` declaration is standard C++ syntax for showing that `QueryInterface()` is a member function of class `XDemoCls`, which is nested inside `CoDemo`.

You'll notice that we're calling another `QueryInterface()` using a variable called `pThis`, which hasn't been declared. In fact, `pThis` is created by the `METHOD_PROLOGUE()` macro, shown below, and is a pointer to the enclosing class.

```
#define METHOD_PROLOGUE(theClass, localClass) \
    theClass* pThis = \
        ((theClass*)((BYTE*)this - offsetof(theClass, m_x##localClass))); \
    AFX_MANAGE_STATE(pThis->m_pModuleState) \
```

The macro itself uses the standard library `offsetof()` macro, which gives the offset of a structure (or class) member from the start of its structure (or class). In this case, we're finding the offset of the nested class from the start of the enclosing class, and then subtracting it from `this` in order to get `pThis`, the address of the enclosing class.

The `AFX_MANAGE_STATE()` macro which follows ensures that the MFC state data being used is correct for the COM object; if you want to know more about MFC state data and how it is managed, look up the macro in Books Online.

> *If you've never come across* `offsetof()` *before, it's worth a look in its own right, as a masterly example of the macro-writers art:*
>
> `#define offsetof(s,m)  (size_t)&(((s*)0)->m)`
>
> *The first time I saw this it took me quite a while to work out quite what was going on! The trick is in the* `(s*)0`*, which casts zero to an* `s*`*, thus (effectively and horribly) giving you an* `s` *with an address of zero. The address of* `m` *then gives you the offset from the start of the structure.*

Enough digression. What we've seen is that nested classes manage to delegate their `IUnknown` functions to their containing class, using a neat coding trick.

The BEGIN_ and END_INTERFACE_PART Macros

Each nested class that represents an interface must, by definition, include the `IUnknown` interfaces. MFC provides a pair of macros, `BEGIN_INTERFACE_PART()` and `END_INTERFACE_PART()`, which do the whole job for us. These macros will create a nested class definition complete with `IUnknown` functions, declare a local variable of the appropriate class type, and declare the nested class to be a friend of the enclosing class:

```
#define BEGIN_INTERFACE_PART(localClass, baseClass) \
    class X##localClass : public baseClass \
    { \
    public: \
        STDMETHOD_(ULONG, AddRef)(); \
        STDMETHOD_(ULONG, Release)(); \
        STDMETHOD(QueryInterface)(REFIID iid, LPVOID* ppvObj); \

#define END_INTERFACE_PART(localClass) \
    } m_x##localClass; \
    friend class X##localClass; \
```

We could therefore code up our example as shown below. We're also using the **STDMETHOD_()** macro to define the virtual functions, rather than spelling them out explicitly, but it amounts to the same thing:

```
class CoDemo : public IUnknown
{
    // Base implementations of IUnknown functions
    virtual HRESULT QueryInterface(REFIID riid, void** ppv);
    virtual ULONG   Release();
    virtual ULONG   AddRef();

    BEGIN_INTERFACE_PART(DemoCls, IDemo)
        STDMETHOD_(void, SomeFunc());
    END_INTERFACE_PART(DemoCls)

    BEGIN_INTERFACE_PART(Demo2Cls, IDemo2)
        STDMETHOD_(void, SomeOtherFunc());
    END_INTERFACE_PART(Demo2Cls)
};
```

Adding the Interface Map to the Class

Once we've created the nested classes to represent the interfaces we wish to support, how do we add a suitable interface map to this class? The first thing we need to do in order to make this an MFC class and use interface maps is to derive the class from **CCmdTarget** rather than **IUnknown**. This works fine because, if you remember, in MFC classes it's **CCmdTarget** that provides the implementation of **IUnknown**.

So, change the base class from **IUnknown** to **CCmdTarget**, and put a **DECLARE_INTERFACE_MAP()** macro in the class definition:

```
class CoDemo : public CCmdTarget
{
    BEGIN_INTERFACE_PART(DemoCls, IDemo)
        STDMETHOD_(void, SomeFunc());
    END_INTERFACE_PART(DemoCls)

    BEGIN_INTERFACE_PART(Demo2Cls, IDemo2)
        STDMETHOD_(void, SomeOtherFunc());
    END_INTERFACE_PART(Demo2Cls)

    DECLARE_INTERFACE_MAP()
};
```

> *Notice that we've lost the **IUnknown** functions; this is because **CCmdTarget** now handles all this for us.*

We've given our class an interface map; what we have to do now is populate it. That's done in the class source file, using the interface map macros.

The INTERFACE_MAP Macros

Three macros are used to actually implement the map and fill in the data structures in the class source code.

▶ `BEGIN_INTERFACE_MAP()` sets up the data structure

▶ `INTERFACE_PART()` declares an entry in the map

▶ `END_INTERFACE_MAP()` completes the map

Here's an example of a map, taken from the application we develop at the end of this chapter:

```
BEGIN_INTERFACE_MAP(CoDemo, CCmdTarget)
    INTERFACE_PART(CoDemo, IID_IDemo, DemoCls)
    INTERFACE_PART(CoDemo, IID_IDemo2, Demo2Cls)
END_INTERFACE_MAP()
```

Let's take this apart and see what it's doing. Here's the code for `BEGIN_INTERFACE_MAP()`:

```
#define BEGIN_INTERFACE_MAP(theClass, theBase) \
    const AFX_INTERFACEMAP* theClass::GetInterfaceMap() const \
        { return &theClass::interfaceMap; } \
    const AFX_DATADEF AFX_INTERFACEMAP theClass::interfaceMap = \
        { &theBase::interfaceMap, &theClass::_interfaceEntries[0], }; \
    const AFX_DATADEF AFX_INTERFACEMAP_ENTRY theClass::_interfaceEntries[] = \
    { \
```

This macro gives us a function to return a pointer to our map, plus a definition of the map itself, and the start of the array of map entries.

The `INTERFACE_PART()` macro defines an entry in the interface map that consists of an interface ID, and the offset of the nested class within the vtable for the class as a whole:

```
#define INTERFACE_PART(theClass, iid, localClass) \
    { &iid, offsetof(theClass, m_x##localClass) }, \
```

Finally, `END_INTERFACE_MAP()` finishes off the map by adding a **NULL** entry:

```
#define END_INTERFACE_MAP() \
    { NULL, (size_t)-1 } \
    }; \
```

That's how interface maps are created, but before we can go on to look at how they get used in practice, we need to look at how **CCmdTarget** handles **IUnknown**.

Using the INTERFACE_MAP Macros

We can now understand a little more about the example we used above:

```
BEGIN_INTERFACE_MAP(CoDemo, CCmdTarget)
    INTERFACE_PART(CoDemo, IID_IDemo, DemoCls)
    INTERFACE_PART(CoDemo, IID_IDemo2, Demo2Cls)
END_INTERFACE_MAP()
```

This tells us the following:

- The **CoDemo** class is derived from **CCmdTarget**
- The class implements two interfaces, which have the GUIDs **IID_IDemo** and **IID_IDemo2**
- The interface **IDemo** is represented by a nested class called **XDemoCls**
- The interface **IDemo2** is represented by a nested class called **XDemo2Cls**

These macros will expand up to look something like this

```
const AFX_INTERFACEMAP* CoDemo::GetInterfaceMap() const
   { return &CoDemo::interfaceMap; }
const AFX_DATADEF AFX_INTERFACEMAP CoDemo::interfaceMap =
   { &CCmdTarget::interfaceMap, &CoDemo::_interfaceEntries[0], };
const AFX_DATADEF AFX_INTERFACEMAP_ENTRY CoDemo::_interfaceEntries[] =
{
   { &IID_IDemo, offsetof(CoDemo, m_xDemoCls) },
   { &IID_IDemo2, offsetof(CoDemo, m_xDemoCls2) },
   { NULL, (size_t)-1 }
};
```

The **offsetof()** macro is used again, this time to find the position of the vtable for the nested class within the parent, and tie it to the interface's IID.

Implementing the Dispatch Interface

CCmdTarget is also the place where Automation is handled for MFC classes, but if you look through the source for **CCmdTarget**, you won't find an implementation of the **IDispatch** interface anywhere in the class definition. What you will find is a **struct** called **XDispatch**:

```
struct XDispatch
{
   DWORD m_vtbl;    // place-holder for IDispatch vtable
   ...
} m_xDispatch;
```

The **IDispatch** interface is actually implemented by a separate class, **COleDispatchImpl**:

```
/////////////////////////////////////////////////////////////////////////////
// COleDispatchImpl - IDispatch implementation

// Note: This class is only designed to be used as a CCmdTarget member
//   (at the offset specified by CCmdTarget::m_xDispatch))
// It WILL NOT work in other classes or at different offsets!

class COleDispatchImpl : public IDispatch
{
public:
   ...

   STDMETHOD_(ULONG, AddRef)();
   STDMETHOD_(ULONG, Release)();
   STDMETHOD(QueryInterface)(REFIID, LPVOID*);
```

```
    STDMETHOD(GetTypeInfoCount)(UINT*);
    STDMETHOD(GetTypeInfo)(UINT, LCID, LPTYPEINFO*);
    STDMETHOD(GetIDsOfNames)(REFIID, LPOLESTR*, UINT, LCID, DISPID*);
    STDMETHOD(Invoke)(DISPID, REFIID, LCID, WORD, DISPPARAMS*, LPVARIANT,
        LPEXCEPINFO, UINT*);

    // special method for disconnect
    virtual void Disconnect();
};
```

You can see that this class implements **IUnknown**, plus the four functions supported by
IDispatch: **GetTypeInfoCount()**, **GetTypeInfo()**, **GetIDsOfNames()** and **Invoke()**.

The connection between **CCmdTarget** and **COleDispatchImpl** is made in the 'magic'
CCmdTarget::EnableAutomation() function, which has to be called in order for Automation
to work. I call it 'magic' because very little detail about this function is provided - just call it,
and Automation will work!

> *We'll look at how* **EnableAutomation()** *actually does work later on, in the chapter on*
> *Automation.*

Another oddity is that the dispatch interface ought to be declared in an interface map, but once
again you won't find one in **CCmdTarget**. This is because **IDispatch** is built into the fabric of
the class, and has been directly entered into the interface map; if you look in the source of
CCmdTarget, in **CmdTarg.cpp**, you'll find the interface map code towards the end of the file:

```
const AFX_INTERFACEMAP_ENTRY CCmdTarget::_interfaceEntries[] =
{
#ifndef _AFX_NO_OLE_SUPPORT
    INTERFACE_PART(CCmdTarget, _IID_IDispatch, Dispatch)
#endif
    { NULL, (size_t)-1 }    // end of entries
};
```

Note the preprocessor usage - the map entry is only included if **_AFX_NO_OLE_SUPPORT** isn't
defined, or in other words, if OLE support *is* defined. The entry links the dispatch interface to
the **CCmdTarget**'s **m_xDispatch** member, which will have been set up by a call to
EnableAutomation(). Remember that the third parameter gives the name of the nested class
(in this case, **XDispatch**), and that **CCmdTarget** will contain a member of this class, called
m_xDispatch, which is set up by the call to **EnableAutomation()**.

The operation of the dispatch interface itself is managed by **dispatch maps**, yet another of MFC's
macro-based mapping mechanisms. We'll discuss dispatch maps more fully when we come to
deal with Automation, but we can afford to take a brief look at how they work here, just for
the curious. A dispatch map is implemented by three macros. In familiar fashion, the first sets
up the declaration of the map in the class definition:

```
DECLARE_DISPATCH_MAP()
```

And the other two are placed in the class implementation, setting up the structure of the map:

```
BEGIN_DISPATCH_MAP(CMyClass, CBaseClass)
    // ...
END_DISPATCH_MAP()
```

As you'd expect by now, this sets up an array that links identifiers to items within the class. In the case of a dispatch map, the link is between the IDs of Automation methods and properties, and their implementations in the class. The map also chains to its base class, so that the hierarchy of maps can be traversed back as far as **CCmdTarget**, just as happens for interface maps.

The entries in the dispatch map are defined by five macros. **DISP_FUNCTION()** defines an Automation function, while the other four (**DISP_PROPERTY()**, **DISP_PROPERTY_EX()**, **DISP_PROPERTY_NOTIFY()** and **DISP_PROPERTY_PARAM()**) provide various different ways of defining properties.

This brief discussion should convince you that dispatch maps are implemented in a similar way to interface maps. The run-time operation of dispatch maps will be discussed in the Chapter 8.

Creating COM Objects

One of the fundamental requirements of a COM object is that it should be creatable at runtime, in response to a request sent to the object's server by a potential client. The way this is done is by requiring servers to implement the **IClassFactory** interface (and perhaps **IClassFactory2**), which in turn is responsible for creating instances of the COM object.

We've already seen how this works. A client calls a COM function to create an object, like this:

```
HRESULT hr = CoCreateInstance(CLSID_CoDemo, NULL, CLSCTX_INPROC_SERVER,
                              IID_ISomeInterface, (VOID FAR **)&pint);
```

The call wants to create an instance of a COM object identified by a CLSID (**CLSID_CoDemo**), which is an in-process server, and to get a pointer to some interface. The COM run-time will interrogate the registry to find the server, and load it if it isn't already loaded. The server will then create a class factory object, whose job is to create the actual object that implements the interface. When the object has been created, a pointer to its vtable gets returned.

As the final part of our tour of the hidden workings of COM within MFC, let's consider how COM objects get constructed. MFC implements the class factory interfaces in the **COleObjectFactory** class which, in addition to the basic object creation needed by **IClassFactory** and **IClassFactory2**, adds some functions to help manage the registration of the COM object. Because each COM object needs its own class factory, and because an MFC application can implement more than one object, it's possible for an application to contain more than one **COleObjectFactory**-derived class.

> *The implementations of* **IClassFactory** *and* **IClassFactory2** *were only merged into* **COleObjectFactory** *in MFC 4.0. Before that, the interfaces were represented by* **COleObjectFactory** *and* **COleObjectFactoryEx** *respectively.*

The **IClassFactory::CreateInstance()** function creates a new instance of the COM object; in **COleObjectFactory** this is handled by **OnCreateObject()**, which creates a new object by using MFC's standard dynamic creation facility - the same one that's used in serialization. One of the parameters **COleObjectFactory**'s constructor requires is the run-time class information for the object, which will have been added to the class by using the **DECLARE_DYNCREATE()** and **IMPLEMENT_DYNCREATE()** macros. Any classes which have been made dynamically creatable in this way will have a **CreateObject()** member function, which **COleObjectFactory** can use to materialize a new instance on the fly.

As you might expect by now, MFC implements its class factory creation using a pair of **DECLARE** and **IMPLEMENT** macros. **DECLARE_OLECREATE()** declares a static instance of **COleObjectFactory** and the GUID associated with the class, so that

```
DECLARE_OLECREATE(CoDemo)
```

expands to

```
protected:
    static COleObjectFactory factory;
    static const GUID _cdecl guid;
```

Note that the class name isn't actually used in the expansion of the macro. **IMPLEMENT_OLECREATE()** constructs the class factory object and the GUID, so that a call of the form

```
IMPLEMENT_OLECREATE(CoDemo,                  // class name
                    "CoDemo",                // external name
                    0x987c0680, 0xd67f,     // GUID in pieces
                    0x11d0, 0x90, 0x4a, 0x44,
                    0x45, 0x53, 0x54, 0x0, 0x0)
```

expands to

```
AFXDATADEF COleObjectFactory CoDemo::Factory(CoDemo::guid,
        RUNTIME_CLASS(CoDemo), FALSE, _T("CoDemo"));
const AFX_DATADEF GUID CoDemo::guid = { 0x987c0680, 0xd67f, 0x11d0,
        {0x90, 0x4a, 0x44, 0x45, 0x53, 0x54, 0x0, 0x0} };
```

COM Objects and the Document/View Architecture

This approach to constructing class factories allows us to link a C++ class with a GUID, so that when a client wants to create an object, the right class will be instantiated. Most MFC applications tend to use the document/view architecture, and that requires a little more structure, because instead of creating a single object, we need to create an MFC document, view and frame.

MFC applications use a document template to link together a set of document, view and frame classes. If our document class is also implementing one or more COM interfaces, as will be the case in Automation, then we need to do two things. First, we need to provide a COM class factory, and second, we need to make sure that a set of document/view/frame objects is created as required.

For document/view programs, these are handled by **COleTemplateServer**, which is derived from **COleObjectFactory**. An application class that is going to implement a COM interface will have a data member of this type:

```
COleTemplateServer m_server;
    // Server object for document creation
```

This member is used in the **InitInstance()** function, like so:

```
CMultiDocTemplate* pDocTemplate;
pDocTemplate = new CMultiDocTemplate(
    IDR_GRAPHSTYPE,
```

```
            RUNTIME_CLASS(CGraphSrvDoc),
            RUNTIME_CLASS(CChildFrame), // custom MDI child frame
            RUNTIME_CLASS(CGraphSrvView));
      pDocTemplate->SetServerInfo(
            IDR_GRAPHSTYPE_SRVR_EMB, IDR_GRAPHSTYPE_SRVR_IP,
            RUNTIME_CLASS(CInPlaceFrame));
      AddDocTemplate(pDocTemplate);
```

```
      // Connect the COleTemplateServer to the document template.
      //  The COleTemplateServer creates new documents on behalf
      //  of requesting OLE containers by using information
      //  specified in the document template.
      m_server.ConnectTemplate(clsid, pDocTemplate, FALSE);

      // Register all OLE server factories as running.  This enables the
      //  OLE libraries to create objects from other applications.
      COleTemplateServer::RegisterAll();
```

AppWizard adds all of the necessary structure into your application when you generate the skeleton. The document template is created in the usual way, and contains (among other things) the **RUNTIME_CLASS()** information for the document class. The template server object's **ConnectTemplate()** function then gets called, which lets the template server pass the document class template information and CLSID down to its underlying **COleObjectFactory** object.

When the **COleObjectFactory** object is asked to create a COM object, it can now use this information to call the document class **CreateObject()** function as required, in order to create new documents.

Anatomy of the MFC Server Application

In the first part of the chapter, I showed how AppWizard can be used to develop the skeleton of an Automation server application, and examined some of the more obvious additions that distinguished the code from a non-server application. Now we'll take a closer look at some more of the functionality of this application. We're going to examine the features we've just been discussing; in other words, the way interfaces are handled in the application. Discussion of what makes it work as a server is left until the next chapter.

All the common interfaces used by COM services will be implemented and handled for us in the API, and so unless we do something out of the ordinary, we won't see any evidence at all of interfaces being used in our application. There is, however, an easy way to cause an interface map to be added to the application without resorting to coding one up ourselves, and that's by adding Automation support, as we did when we built the skeleton application. For an object to support Automation, it needs to implement the **IDispatch** interface, and that will necessitate an interface map being added to the application code. Let's take a look at the sample server application and see how it has been done.

Any C++ class in an MFC program can be driven by Automation; in an AppWizard skeleton, Automation support is added to the default document class, so that's where we need to look for our COM interface support. If you look in the header file for the document class, which in our case was **AutoSrvDoc.h**, you'll notice that the document is now derived from **COleServerDoc** rather than **CDocument**; this new base class, which is derived from **CDocument**, provides the server support. The document class is made dynamically creatable, not only for the purposes of serialization, but also so its class factory can create instances of it.

At the end of the class definition, we come to the section where the maps are declared:

```
class CAutoSrvDoc : public COleServerDoc
{
protected: // create from serialization only
    CAutoSrvDoc();
    DECLARE_DYNCREATE(CAutoSrvDoc)

    // plus the rest of the header file...

// Generated message map functions
protected:
    //{{AFX_MSG(CAutoSrvDoc)
        // NOTE - the ClassWizard will add and remove member functions here.
        //      DO NOT EDIT what you see in these blocks of generated code !
    //}}AFX_MSG
    DECLARE_MESSAGE_MAP()

    // Generated OLE dispatch map functions
    //{{AFX_DISPATCH(CAutoSrvDoc)
        // NOTE - the ClassWizard will add and remove member functions here.
        //      DO NOT EDIT what you see in these blocks of generated code !
    //}}AFX_DISPATCH
    DECLARE_DISPATCH_MAP()
    DECLARE_INTERFACE_MAP()
};
```

We now find that there are three maps: the normal message map for handling Windows messages, and two others: the interface map and the dispatch map.

The interface map itself is implemented at the top of **AutoSrvDoc.cpp**:

```
/////////////////////////////////////////////////////////////////////////
// CAutoSrvDoc

IMPLEMENT_DYNCREATE(CAutoSrvDoc, COleServerDoc)

// Message and dispatch maps omitted for brevity...

// Note: we add support for IID_IAutoSrv to support typesafe binding
//   from VBA.  This IID must match the GUID that is attached to the
//   dispinterface in the .ODL file.

// {81F8482E-93AA-11D0-9257-00201834E2A3}
static const IID IID_IAutoSrv =
{ 0x81f8482e, 0x93aa, 0x11d0, { 0x92, 0x57, 0x0, 0x20, 0x18, 0x34, 0xe2, 0xa3 } };

BEGIN_INTERFACE_MAP(CAutoSrvDoc, COleServerDoc)
    INTERFACE_PART(CAutoSrvDoc, IID_IAutoSrv, Dispatch)
END_INTERFACE_MAP()
```

By now, we know enough to work out what is going on here. We get the GUID referred to in the first comment presented both as a string (in a comment) and in code form. **IID_IAutoSrv** is a static variable defining the IID of a COM interface; in this case, it's a dispatch interface, which supports Automation.

The interface map definition tells us that the class **CAutoSrvDoc** inherits from **COleServerDoc**, and that it supports one interface. As we've already seen from our discussion of the **INTERFACE_PART** macro, this interface has the ID **IID_IAutoSrv**, and its vtable can be found at the offset of **m_xDispatch** within the class **CAutoSrvDoc**. We don't see the **BEGIN_** and **END_INTERFACE_PART()** macros within the class definition, as the declaration of the dispatch interface is handled for us by MFC.

A COM Server Using MFC

To round off this chapter, let's put into practice what we've discussed so far, and use MFC's COM support in an actual application.

The example program defines two custom COM interfaces called **IDemo** and **IDemo2**, each of which has precisely one method. In the case of **IDemo**, the method is called **Square()**, and it returns the square of a number which is passed in as an argument. For **IDemo2**, the method is called **Cube()**, and returns the cube of its argument. Once we've defined the interfaces, we need to implement them, and we'll do it using an in-process server - a DLL in Windows terms. For a simple example like this, it's easier to implement in-process servers, because we don't have to get into the mechanics of marshaling, as we'd have to with local or remote servers.

When the server is complete, we'll use a very simple test program to ensure that the server works as it should.

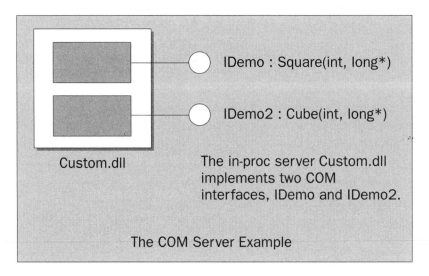

IDemo : Square(int, long*)

IDemo2 : Cube(int, long*)

Custom.dll   The in-proc server Custom.dll implements two COM interfaces, IDemo and IDemo2.

The COM Server Example

Try It Out - An MFC COM Server DLL

1 Use AppWizard to create an MFC DLL project called **Custom**, accepting all the default options on the 1-page dialog.

2 Create a new header file, **IDemo.h**, to hold the declaration of the first interface we're going to implement. The **DECLARE_INTERFACE_()** macro defines an interface, and will expand correctly for both C and C++; the arguments are the name of the interface, and the name of the interface from which it inherits, in this case **IUnknown**. You don't *need* to use this macro, but it does save a little work.

```
// Header for CoDemo COM class demo

// Use the 'include once' pragma to handle multiple inclusions
#if _MSC_VER >= 1000
#pragma once
#endif // _MSC_VER >= 1000

// Declare the interface we're going to implement
#undef INTERFACE
#define INTERFACE IDemo

DECLARE_INTERFACE_(IDemo, IUnknown)
{
    // Interface methods
};
```

Now we can add the method definitions to the macro, using the **STDMETHOD** macros.

```
DECLARE_INTERFACE_(IDemo, IUnknown)
{
    // IUnknown's standard methods
    STDMETHOD(QueryInterface) (THIS_ REFIID riid, LPVOID FAR* ppvObj) PURE;
    STDMETHOD_(ULONG,AddRef) (THIS) PURE;
    STDMETHOD_(ULONG,Release) (THIS) PURE;

    // IDemo's method takes an int and returns its square as a pointer to a long
    STDMETHOD(Square) (THIS_ INT, LPLONG) PURE;
};
```

3 Create a GUID for the interface, using the Guidgen tool:

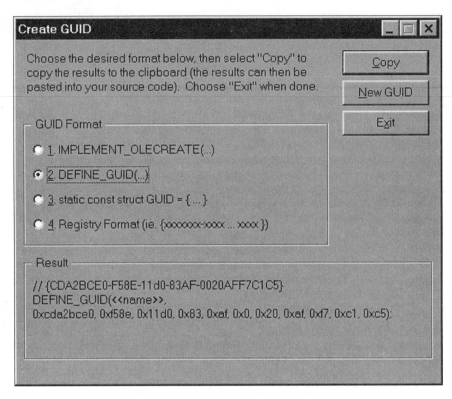

Use the second option to generate the GUID in the right form for including in the header, then copy and paste it, replacing the **<<name>>** marker with **IID_IDemo**:

```
// Define a GUID for the interface
// {CDA2BCE0-F58E-11d0-83AF-0020AFF7C1C5}
DEFINE_GUID(IID_IDemo,
0xcda2bce0, 0xf58e, 0x11d0, 0x83, 0xaf, 0x0, 0x20, 0xaf, 0xf7, 0xc1, 0xc5);
```

Finally, add a useful typedef:

```
typedef IDemo FAR* LPDEMO;
```

4 Follow exactly the same procedure to create the **IDemo2** interface in the **IDemo2.h** header file. You can copy-and-paste the code, provided you remember to:

▶ Change the interface name to **IDemo2**

▶ Change the method name to **Cube()**

▶ Generate a new GUID for the interface

5 The **CoDemo** class is going to implement the **IDemo** interfaces, so create a header file for it called **CoDemo.h**, and add the basic class structure:

```
// Header for CoDemo COM class demo

// Use the 'include once' pragma to handle multiple inclusions
```

```
#if _MSC_VER >= 1000
#pragma once
#endif // _MSC_VER >= 1000

#include "IDemo.h"
#include "IDemo2.h"

// Class must derive from CCmdTarget in order for MFC's interface
// map mechanism to work.
class CoDemo : public CCmdTarget
{
public:
   // Construction and destruction
   CoDemo();
   virtual ~CoDemo();

protected:
   DECLARE_DYNCREATE(CoDemo);
};
```

6 Add two declarations to the class:

```
DECLARE_INTERFACE_MAP();
DECLARE_OLECREATE(CoDemo);
```

The first sets up the interface map that tells MFC which class handles which interface, while the second creates a class factory for the COM class. As you'd expect, these will have matching implementation macros in the implementation code.

7 Declare the interfaces we're going to implement. We need to add two **INTERFACE_PART** blocks, one per interface:

```
// Declare the nested interface class
BEGIN_INTERFACE_PART(DemoCls, IDemo)
   STDMETHOD(Square) (THIS_ INT, LPLONG);
END_INTERFACE_PART(DemoCls)

// Declare the nested interface class
BEGIN_INTERFACE_PART(Demo2Cls, IDemo2)
   STDMETHOD(Cube) (THIS_ INT, LPLONG);
END_INTERFACE_PART(Demo2Cls)
```

This will result in the creation of two nested classes called **XDemoCls** and **XDemo2Cls**, which will implement the **IDemo** and **IDemo2** interfaces respectively.

8 Create a new header file called **CoDemoGUID.h**, and use Guidgen to generate a GUID to represent the CLSID of the **CoDemo** class, in the same way that we did for **IDemo**:

```
// {987C0680-D67F-11d0-904A-444553540000}
DEFINE_GUID(CLSID_CoDemo,
0x987c0680, 0xd67f, 0x11d0, 0x90, 0x4a, 0x44, 0x45, 0x53, 0x54, 0x0, 0x0);
```

9 Create the **CoDemo.cpp** file, and start it off like this:

```
#include <stdafx.h>
#include <initguid.h>     // Necessary for GUIDs to get initialized
                          // properly when using stdafx.h
#include "CoDemo.h"

// Implement dynamic creation
IMPLEMENT_DYNCREATE(CoDemo, CCmdTarget)

// Implement class factory. Cut and paste the GUID from the header file
IMPLEMENT_OLECREATE(CoDemo, "CoDemo",
    0x987c0680, 0xd67f, 0x11d0, 0x90, 0x4a, 0x44, 0x45, 0x53, 0x54, 0x0, 0x0)
```

10 Add the interface map:

```
// Interface map for the class
BEGIN_INTERFACE_MAP(CoDemo, CCmdTarget)
    INTERFACE_PART(CoDemo, IID_IDemo, DemoCls)
    INTERFACE_PART(CoDemo, IID_IDemo2, Demo2Cls)
END_INTERFACE_MAP()
```

The code constructs a map with two entries, which link the **IDemo** and **IDemo2** interfaces with their respective internal classes.

11 Add code for the constructor and destructor to handle the framework's reference counting:

```
CoDemo::CoDemo()
{
    AfxOleLockApp();
}

CoDemo::~CoDemo()
{
    AfxOleUnlockApp();
}
```

These help the framework keep track of the number of active objects in the application.

12 Now add the implementations for the interface methods. First we do the **IUnknown** ones, using the standard technique of delegating their functionality to **CCmdTarget**:

```
STDMETHODIMP_(ULONG) CoDemo::XDemoCls::AddRef()
{
    METHOD_PROLOGUE(CoDemo, DemoCls)
    return pThis->ExternalAddRef();
}

STDMETHODIMP_(ULONG) CoDemo::XDemoCls::Release()
{
    METHOD_PROLOGUE(CoDemo, DemoCls)
    return pThis->ExternalRelease();
}

STDMETHODIMP CoDemo::XDemoCls::QueryInterface(REFIID riid, LPVOID FAR* ppv)
{
    METHOD_PROLOGUE(CoDemo, DemoCls)
    return pThis->ExternalQueryInterface(&riid, ppv);
}
```

The methods for **XDemo2Cls** are exactly the same, apart from the class name in the **METHOD_PROLOGUE()** macro call.

13 Next, add the proper class methods:

```
STDMETHODIMP CoDemo::XDemoCls::Square(INT n, LPLONG lpResult)
{
    METHOD_PROLOGUE(CoDemo, DemoCls)
    *lpResult = n * n;
    return NOERROR;
}

STDMETHODIMP CoDemo::XDemo2Cls::Cube(INT n, LPLONG lpResult)
{
    METHOD_PROLOGUE(CoDemo, Demo2Cls)
    *lpResult = n * n * n;
    return NOERROR;
}
```

14 That's all for the **CoDemo** class, so close that, and add **InitInstance()** and **ExitInstance()** handlers as public members of the application class:

```
BOOL CMyCustomApp::InitInstance()
{
    AfxOleLockApp();
    return COleObjectFactory::RegisterAll();
}

int CMyCustomApp::ExitInstance()
{
    AfxOleUnlockApp();
    return 0;
}
```

15 Add the necessary DLL housekeeping functions to the application class' source file as well:

```
STDAPI DllGetClassObject(REFCLSID rclsid, REFIID riid, LPVOID* ppv)
{
    AFX_MANAGE_STATE(AfxGetStaticModuleState());
    return AfxDllGetClassObject(rclsid, riid, ppv);
}
```

When clients want to create an object of this type, they'll end up calling either **CoGetClassObject()** or **CoCreateInstanceEx()**, and those routines will use **DllGetClassObject()** to get a pointer to the object's class factory interface.

```
STDAPI DllCanUnloadNow()
{
    AFX_MANAGE_STATE(AfxGetStaticModuleState());
    return AfxDllCanUnloadNow();
}
```

DllCanUnloadNow() returns a value to say whether it is safe to unload the DLL. If the DLL still has any clients, it isn't safe to unload it.

```
STDAPI DllRegisterServer()
{
  AFX_MANAGE_STATE(AfxGetStaticModuleState());
  COleObjectFactory::UpdateRegistryAll();
  return S_OK;
}
```

This function creates registry entries for all the COM classes supported by a DLL.

16 Finally, edit the linker definition file to export the DLL management functions:

```
; custom.def : Declares the module parameters for the DLL.

LIBRARY       "custom"
DESCRIPTION   'custom Windows Dynamic Link Library'

EXPORTS
    DllCanUnloadNow    PRIVATE
    DllGetClassObject  PRIVATE
    DllRegisterServer  PRIVATE
```

Once you've completed the coding, you should be able to build the server DLL.

Try It Out - Testing The Server

Before testing the server, the DLL must be entered in the registry. Change to the directory containing the DLL itself, and type:

```
regsvr32 custom.dll
```

Regsvr will display a message box telling you whether it succeeded or failed. Note that if you add or remove interfaces, you'll have to re-register the DLL so that the registry is kept up to date.

Once the DLL is registered, we can write a very simple test program. Create a Win32 application project (not an MFC one!) called **DllTest**, and place the following code into a source file:

```
// Incredibly simple test program to see whether our DLL works

#define INITGUID

#include <windows.h>
#include <stdio.h>
#include "IDemo.h"
#include "IDemo2.h"
#include "CoDemoGUID.h"

int WINAPI WinMain(HINSTANCE hInstance, HINSTANCE hPrevInstance,
                   LPSTR lpszCmdLine, int nCmdShow)
{
    // Interface pointers
    LPUNKNOWN punk;
    IDemo *pDemo;
    IDemo2 *pDemo2;
```

```
// Result of COM calls
HRESULT hr;

// Check COM is initialised
hr = CoInitialize(NULL);

// Create an instance of CoDemo, and get its IUnknown pointer
hr = CoCreateInstance(CLSID_CoDemo,
                      NULL,
                      CLSCTX_INPROC_SERVER,
                      IID_IUnknown,
                      (VOID FAR **)&punk);
if (FAILED(hr))
{
   MessageBox(0, "CoCreateInstance failed for Demo object", "Error", MB_OK);
   return -1;
}


// Get a pointer to its IDemo interface
hr = punk->QueryInterface(IID_IDemo, (LPVOID FAR*)&pDemo);
if (FAILED(hr))
{
   MessageBox(0, "QueryInterface failed for IDemo interface", "Error", MB_OK);
   return -1;
}

// Invoke its Square method
LONG lResult;
char s[80];

hr = pDemo->Square(5, &lResult);

sprintf(s, "The square of 5 is %ld", lResult);
MessageBox(0, s, "IDemo Call", MB_OK);


// Try getting IDemo2
hr = punk->QueryInterface(IID_IDemo2, (LPVOID FAR*)&pDemo2);
if (FAILED(hr))
{
   MessageBox(0, "QueryInterface failed for IDemo2 interface", "Error", MB_OK);
   return -1;
}

hr = pDemo2->Cube(5, &lResult);

sprintf(s, "The cube of 5 is %ld", lResult);
MessageBox(0, s, "IDemo2 Call", MB_OK);

// Release the interfaces we've used
pDemo2->Release();
pDemo->Release();
punk->Release();

// Unload any usused DLLs
CoFreeUnusedLibraries();

// Tell COM we've finished
```

```
    CoUninitialize();

    return 0;
}
```

The program uses the same basic COM calls, and follows the same pattern which we used in our Word example in Chapter 2, so I won't go through the entire code in detail. Note that I take care to check return codes, and to free up all the interfaces and libraries I use. Provided all has gone well, the test program will produce two dialogs like these:

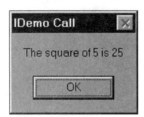
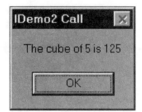

Summary

In this chapter, we've looked at the support that the Visual C++ development environment and the MFC class library give to ActiveX programming.

We've seen how Visual C++ and MFC together provide a structure that allows you to produce several varieties of COM-enabled programs, including

- OLE servers and containers
- Automation servers
- ActiveX controls

We saw how COM objects can be implemented in MFC using nested classes, and the importance of the **CCmdTarget** class as the nerve-centre of MFC's COM capabilities. **CCmdTarget** supplies the interface map mechanism through which COM interfaces are attached to MFC classes.

This chapter marks the end of our general discussions. From this point, we'll be looking in-depth at implementing specific kinds of COM-enabled application for ourselves, starting with OLE servers.

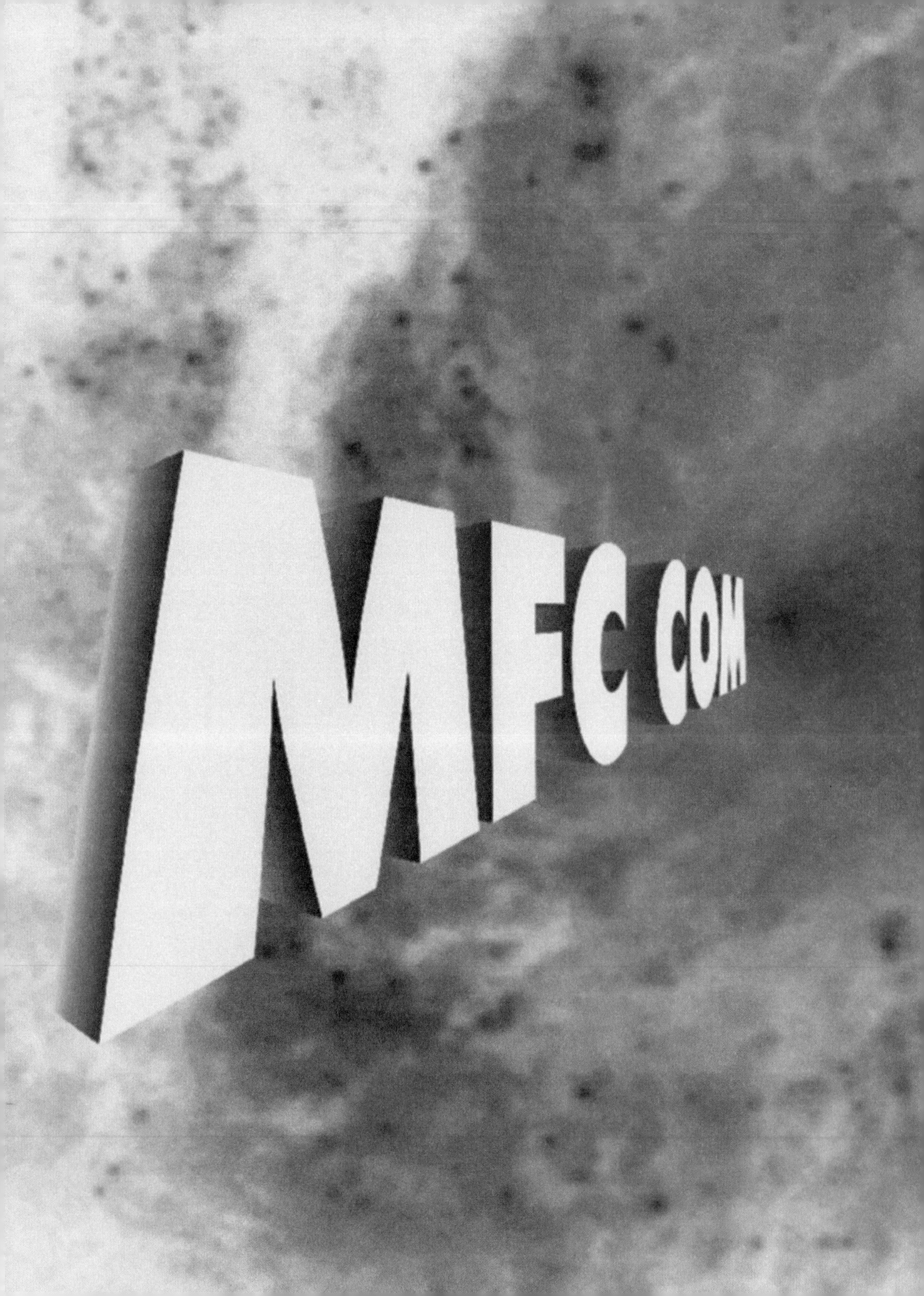
MFC COM

OLE Document Servers

We've already seen how Visual C++ allows us to generate COM-enabled skeletons for applications. In this chapter, we're going to dive into MFC, and examine in much more detail exactly how adding OLE functionality to our applications changes the traditional document/view model.

How OLE Servers are Implemented in MFC

We'll see in this section how the MFC OLE classes enable the application to perform its tasks as a server. There are three main tasks an OLE server application has to perform:

 It needs to be able to store its data in a storage provided by the container

 It needs to notify the container of changes to the item

 It needs to provide menus and toolbars if the object can be edited in-place, and help with the menu and toolbar negotiation

MFC OLE servers are implemented by two classes: **COleServerDoc** and **COleServerItem**. We have two classes because of **linking**; as we'll soon see, some base functionality is needed for the server as a whole, while further functionality needs to be supplied for each linked object. You end up with a **COleServerDoc** for each document, and a **COleServerItem** for each linked item that references the document. If we only supported **embedding**, it would be possible to merge both classes, but because of linking, we need two.

Embedded and linked objects lead a strange existence, split between two applications. They reside in the server but are displayed in a view belonging to the container, and this means that there needs to be communication between the two applications in order for the document to be kept in step with the view, and vice versa. The server item that represents an embedded or linked object has a corresponding client item in the container, and the two items between them manage the content and appearance of the object.

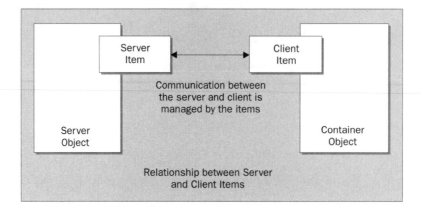

Relationship between Server
and Client Items

Before we can look at the two server classes in more detail, we need to go a couple of steps back up the chain and look at the base classes upon which the whole server-and-container edifice is built: **CDocItem** and **COleDocument**.

The Document Base Classes

CDocItem is used to represent OLE items that are stored in documents in both containers and servers, but it doesn't do much itself. It's mainly used as a base for the server and client object classes, **COleServerItem** and **COleClientItem**. A linked or embedded item has to know the document of which it is a part, so it's always possible for a **CDocItem** to get a pointer back to its document.

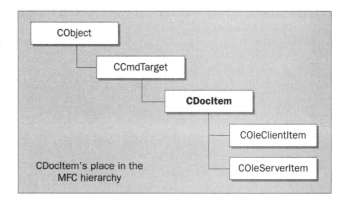

CDocItem's place in the
MFC hierarchy

COleDocument is derived from the **CDocument** class we all know and love, and so it has all the support for the document/view architecture. This class ends up being the base for both server and container documents, and in order to do its job it maintains a list of **CDocItem** objects (actually an MFC **CObList**) called **m_docItemList**.

COleDocument has numerous member functions to help manipulate the list by adding and removing items, iterating over the list and so on. Since the class is used by both servers and containers (and an application can be both), the list can end up holding both **COleServerItem** and **COleClientItem** objects. For those times when you're specifically interested in one type or the other, there are member functions to iterate through either kind exclusively.

The addition of this list to the document class means that we can't use ordinary files to serialize our document data any more. Serialization itself is fine with flat files, but now we need to get the server or client items to save their data too, and ordinary files aren't suited to that task, because we need to maintain divisions between the data belonging to different objects. Instead, servers and containers use structured storage, so that objects can store their data in their own storages and streams.

You'll have noticed that when you create an application in AppWizard, as soon as you choose one of the server or container options, the default setting for the Would you like support for compound files? option becomes Yes, please. This potential problem with serialization is the reason why: if you're writing a container, you should never change this from the default setting, as any attempt to use a standard file for serializing objects will end in tears. The structured storage is enabled by calling a function called **EnableCompoundFile()**, and the root storage for the file is held in a variable called **m_lpRootStorage**.

COleDocument doesn't implement any interfaces itself; that's left to the derived classes that implement the specific server and container functionality. The first of these (and one that we'll look at in more detail in the next chapter) is **COleLinkingDoc**, which adds support for linking to items stored elsewhere. This is the base class from which container documents are derived and, because servers can also be containers, it's used as the base class for server documents as well.

The COleServerDoc Class

And so we reach the server document base class, **COleServerDoc**. This class inherits from **COleLinkingDoc**, so it can both store embedded **COleServerItem** objects, and cope with linked items.

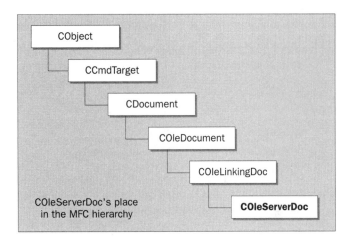

COleServerDoc's place in the MFC hierarchy

COleServerDoc Interfaces

COleServerDoc has to implement several interfaces in order to be able to function as a server:

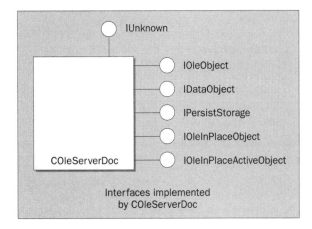

Interfaces implemented by COleServerDoc

The first of these, **IOleObject**, is the main link between a container and a contained object. This interface provides all the functionality needed to enable a container and server to work together, and contains 21 functions (which is probably why Brockschmidt called it the 'interface from hell' in *Inside OLE!*).

The table below briefly describes these functions. We don't need to go into them in any detail, but you can see that they're all to do with communication between an item and its container.

Method	Description
SetClientSite()	Informs the object of its client site in the container
GetClientSite()	Retrieves the object's client site
SetHostNames()	Informs the object of the names of the container application and document
Close()	Moves the object from the running to the loaded state
SetMoniker()	Tells the object its moniker
GetMoniker()	Retrieves the object's moniker
InitFromData()	Initializes embedded object from data
GetClipboardData()	Retrieves a data transfer object from the clipboard
DoVerb()	Requests the object to perform an action - this can be either a custom action, or one of the standards such as 'show properties', 'activate in-place' or 'deactivate'
EnumVerbs()	Returns a list of the actions supported by the object
Update()	Updates an object
IsUpToDate()	Checks if the object is up to date
GetUserClassID()	Returns the CLSID of the object
GetUserType()	Returns the object's user type. For a control, this is the control title
SetExtent()	Called by the container to tell the object its size has changed
GetExtent()	Returns the object's size to the container
Advise()	Sets up an advisory (notification) link between the object and container
Unadvise()	Destroys an advisory link
EnumAdvise()	Lists the advisory links
GetMiscStatus()	Gets the **OLEMISC** status bits which have been set for the object
SetColorScheme()	Informs the object about its color palette

Some of these functions, such as **GetExtent()** and **DoVerb()**, are exposed in the **COleServerDoc** class, while others are handled at lower levels in the MFC hierarchy.

Servers also implement the **IDataObject** interface, which provides **UDT** (Uniform Data Transfer) functions to allow containers and servers to exchange data. **IDataObject** is a general interface which can be used in any situation where it's necessary for two OLE applications to exchange data, whether it be in the context of clipboard operations, drag and drop, or (as here) in a client/server setup. We'll discuss UDT and **IDataObject** more fully in Chapter 6, when we look at the way in which servers and containers interact.

The third interface is **IPersistStorage**, which is implemented by an application to let clients know that it can use structured storage to make its data persistent. The interface includes functions such as **Load()** and **Save()**; when a client needs to serialize its document data, it obtains the object's **IPersistStorage** pointer and uses these functions to serialize the object's data.

COleServerDoc's last two interfaces support in-place activation. **IOleInPlaceObject** gives the container a way to activate and deactivate in-place items, and it also allows it to set the rectangle in which the object is displayed.

IOleInPlaceActiveObject manages communication between parts of the server and container applications. It ties together the in-place object, the document window within the client, and the main frame of the server. It manages the state of the frame and document windows, translates messages, and tells the object when it needs to resize its borders.

COleServerDoc Class Members

COleServerDoc has a number of member functions over and above those supplied by its base class, and they can conveniently be divided into three groups: status, operation and callback functions.

> **Status functions** provide information about the document, such as whether it is embedded in a container or running stand-alone, and whether it is currently in-place active. They also allow access to some data items, such as a pointer to an embedded item.

> **Operation functions** provide ways of notifying the container of various occurrences, such as the document being changed, saved or renamed, and of telling the container to perform actions such as scrolling or activating the document in-place.

> **Callback functions** are called by the framework when certain actions occur. The class members provide default actions, and you can override the functions in your derived document class if you need to provide special processing. There are callbacks for when the document is activated or deactivated, for when it is resized, closed or updated, and so on.

The COleServerItem Class

I've already said that the **COleServerItem** class represents a linked or embedded object at the server end, and the fact that a different server item is needed for every linked object. Let's take a closer look at what it does. Like the server document class, this class implements the **IOleObject** and **IDataObject** interfaces, which support the basic server/container communication and data transfer functions.

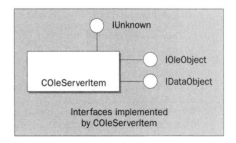

Interfaces implemented by COleServerItem

COleServerItem Class Members

COleServerItem is quite large. In fact, it has over 40 functions, although just as with **COleServerDoc**, these can conveniently be divided into groups, such as:

▶ **Status operations**, like getting the document name, getting/setting the item name, or finding out whether the item is currently attached to a container, and whether it is linked or not.

▶ **Data operations**, including copying data to the clipboard, initiating a drag and drop operation, or serializing the item.

▶ **Object operations**, such including as getting/setting the object extent, requesting the object to perform an OLE action, and so on.

Many of these functions are overridable by derived classes, although simple use of this class in an MFC program only *requires* that you provide code for three functions: **OnDraw()**, **Serialize()** and **OnGetExtent()**. We'll see what these do later on; for now, note that the **On...()** functions are usually called as a result of their counterparts being called on the client side. For instance, **OnDraw()** is called as a result of **COleClientItem::Draw()**, while **OnGetExtent()** is called when **COleClientItem::GetExtent()** is executed.

One function which may be important in more advanced server applications is **OnDoVerb()**, which is executed by a call to **COleClientItem::DoVerb()**. A verb is an action that a server can be asked to perform on an item, such as editing or playing it, and we'll talk about these in more detail in the next chapter.

The MFC Server Implementation

Now we know what classes MFC uses to implement OLE servers, but how do they fit into the structure of an MFC application? We've already explored this a little in preceding chapters, when we looked at the low-level support for COM within MFC, so let's recap what we know. The following table summarizes the main source code files generated by AppWizard for an MDI full-server application that supports Automation but not ActiveX controls. In the second half of the chapter, we're going to develop just such an application called GraphSrv, so let's use that as an example:

File	Description
GraphSrv.cpp	The file containing the **CWinApp**-derived application class, and the **CAboutDlg** class. OLE initialization is performed here.
MainFrm.cpp	The MDI main frame for the application.
GraphSrvDoc.cpp	The document class, derived from **COleServerDoc**.
GraphSrvView.cpp	The view class, derived from **CView**.
SrvrItem.cpp	The server item class, derived from **COleServerItem**.
IpFrame.cpp	The in-place frame class, derived from **COleIPFrameWnd**. This is responsible for handling the frame during in-place activation.

This table doesn't contain all the files created for the project, as some just aren't relevant to this discussion. If you wish, you can create a sample skeleton project and browse the files while you're reading this section, so you can get a feel for what the code looks like on the screen.

By creating a server, we've caused two new files that represent the server item and in-place frame to be generated. In addition, the application class has had the OLE initialization code added to it, and the document class now derives from **COleServerDoc**. The view class is still derived from **CView**, as ever it was, but this shouldn't be too surprising. The OLE server code is designed to support objects being displayed either in a container's view or its own.

Let's now look at these files, see where all the bits fit, and hopefully get a feel for the overall structure of a server application. If some of the descriptions seem a little cursory, that's because they'll get explained in more detail as we develop a server application in the second half of the chapter.

The Application Class

The **CWinApp**-derived application class, **CGraphSrvApp**, has just one addition in its header file, where it declares the **COleTemplateServer** member, **m_server**. Remember that the template server is what links the class factory to the document template.

The application class source file has quite a few changes. The first one you'll notice is that the server's CLSID is defined here:

```
// This identifier was generated to be statistically unique for your app.
// You may change it if you prefer to choose a specific identifier.

// {9A1C8704-96CC-11D0-9257-00201834E2A3}
static const CLSID clsid =
{ 0x9a1c8704, 0x96cc, 0x11d0, { 0x92, 0x57, 0x0, 0x20, 0x18, 0x34, 0xe2, 0xa3 } };
```

The rest of the changes occur in the application's **InitInstance()** member function. I've already covered this function in some detail in Chapter 3, so this is a summary to remind you of what's going on. To start with, the function initializes the OLE DLLs, and exits if initialization fails:

```
BOOL CGraphSrvApp::InitInstance()
{
    // Initialize OLE libraries
    if (!AfxOleInit())
    {
        AfxMessageBox(IDP_OLE_INIT_FAILED);
        return FALSE;
    }
```

After creating the document template, the routine puts the OLE-specific information into the template, and then attaches it to the underlying COM class factory object. This forges a link between being asked to create a COM object, and actually generating the right document, frame and view objects:

```
CMultiDocTemplate* pDocTemplate;
pDocTemplate = new CMultiDocTemplate(
    IDR_GRAPHSTYPE,
    RUNTIME_CLASS(CGraphSrvDoc),
    RUNTIME_CLASS(CChildFrame), // custom MDI child frame
    RUNTIME_CLASS(CGraphSrvView));
pDocTemplate->SetServerInfo(
    IDR_GRAPHSTYPE_SRVR_EMB, IDR_GRAPHSTYPE_SRVR_IP,
    RUNTIME_CLASS(CInPlaceFrame));
AddDocTemplate(pDocTemplate);
```

```
// Connect the COleTemplateServer to the document template.
//  The COleTemplateServer creates new documents on behalf
//  of requesting OLE containers by using information
//  specified in the document template.
m_server.ConnectTemplate(clsid, pDocTemplate, FALSE);
```

The call to **COleTemplateServer::RegisterAll()** registers the server object(s) with the OLE system, so it knows they are running and available:

```
// Register all OLE server factories as running.  This enables the
//  OLE libraries to create objects from other applications.
COleTemplateServer::RegisterAll();
    // Note: MDI applications register all server objects without regard
    //  to the /Embedding or /Automation on the command line.
```

As the comments point out, an MDI application *always* registers its server objects, even if it's being run stand-alone. This is because a client might later ask it to create a document for use in Automation, and the objects need to be registered at that point. SDI applications, on the other hand, are definitely being started up either as an OLE server or stand-alone, so they know from their command line arguments whether to register their servers.

The application next checks to see whether it is being run as a server, because in that case the default action is to run invisibly, without creating a main window. If it *is* running as a server, there will be one of two flags set on the command line (**/Embedding** or **/Automation**) depending on whether the application was started as an ordinary or an Automation server. If either of these flags is found, then **InitInstance()** exits without creating a window:

```
// Check to see if launched as OLE server
if (cmdInfo.m_bRunEmbedded || cmdInfo.m_bRunAutomated)
{
    // Application was run with /Embedding or /Automation.  Don't show
    // the main window in this case.
    return TRUE;
}
```

If the server is launched as a stand-alone application, it updates its registry entries. This happens each time the application is run: the first time, it puts the new entries into the registry; and after that, it rewrites them in case they've been damaged somehow. This sidesteps the need for special code to write the registry entries only when it is run for the first time. Registration is done in two steps:

```
m_server.UpdateRegistry(OAT_INPLACE_SERVER);
COleObjectFactory::UpdateRegistryAll();
```

The call to **COleTemplateServer::UpdateRegistry()** extracts the OLE information from the document template string and loads it into the registry. Then **COleObjectFactory::UpdateRegistryAll()** registers all the application's object factories with the system registry.

The Document Class

The server document class, **CGraphSrvDoc**, shows very little difference from the one you'd see in a non-OLE application, as most of the extra functionality is held in the **COleServerDoc** base class, including the list of **CDocItem** objects and the functions to manipulate this list. All you'll notice 'on the surface' are two extra member functions.

The **OnGetEmbeddedItem()** function creates and returns a new server item which represents the entire document:

```
COleServerItem* CGraphSrvDoc::OnGetEmbeddedItem()
{
    // OnGetEmbeddedItem is called by the framework to get the COleServerItem
    //  that is associated with the document.  It is only called when necessary.

    CGraphSrvSrvrItem* pItem = new CGraphSrvSrvrItem(this);
    ASSERT_VALID(pItem);
    return pItem;
}
```

GetEmbeddedItem() calls **OnGetEmbeddedItem()** in order to return a new server item for the entire document. As an embedded item represents a whole document, you should have little need to change these functions.

The View Class

The view class has one function added to it, **OnCancelEditSrvr()**, which is called if the user presses the *Esc* key when an object is being edited in-place. The function calls the **COleServerDoc::OnDeactivateUI()** function to terminate the editing session, which changes the state of the object server from active to loaded, and removes the object server's menu and toolbar items.

The Server Item Class

This class derives from **COleServerItem**, and is used to provide server items to represent embedded and linked items. As with the document, a lot of the functionality is buried in the base classes, and there are only three significant functions declared in the derived server item class:

```
class CGraphSrvSrvrItem : public COleServerItem
{
    DECLARE_DYNAMIC(CGraphSrvSrvrItem)

// Constructors
public:
    CGraphSrvSrvrItem(CGraphSrvDoc* pContainerDoc);

// Attributes
    CGraphSrvDoc* GetDocument() const
        { return (CGraphSrvDoc*)COleServerItem::GetDocument(); }

// Overrides
    // ClassWizard generated virtual function overrides
    //{{AFX_VIRTUAL(CGraphSrvSrvrItem)
    public:
        virtual BOOL OnDraw(CDC* pDC, CSize& rSize);
        virtual BOOL OnGetExtent(DVASPECT dwDrawAspect, CSize& rSize);
    //}}AFX_VIRTUAL

// Implementation
public:
    ~CGraphSrvSrvrItem();
#ifdef _DEBUG
```

127

```
    virtual void AssertValid() const;
    virtual void Dump(CDumpContext& dc) const;
#endif

protected:
    virtual void Serialize(CArchive& ar);    // overridden for document i/o
};
```

OnDraw() is called in order to generate a metafile for the container to display when the object is inactive. It needs to calculate (and return) the size of the object, and then draw it into the metafile device context provided. The default version of this routine draws nothing, and returns a fixed size of 3000 by 3000 **HIMETRIC** units, so you get a blank square displayed.

OnGetExtent() is called when the container needs to know the size of the item. The default code returns the nominal 3000 by 3000 **HIMETRIC** units used by **OnDraw()**, and needs to be replaced by code to calculate the actual size of the object.

Serialize() is used when the framework needs to get hold of the object's data. An embedded item is, by definition, a whole document, so the operation can simply be delegated to the document's serialization function. Extra code will need to be supplied for linked items, in order to serialize only those parts of the document that are needed for the link.

The In-Place Frame Class

This class is derived from **COleIPFrameWnd**, and represents the in-place editing window. In the same way that we have main frame and child frame classes to represent the frames around 'normal' windows, this class represents the frame around an in-place active object, as shown in the upcoming figure. The functionality in the derived class is mainly concerned with setting up the application's own resources. The class has three data members:

```
protected:
    CToolBar      m_wndToolBar;
    COleDropTarget m_dropTarget;
    COleResizeBar  m_wndResizeBar;
```

The toolbar object represents the bar that will be associated with the in-place editing window. Like the server menus, it's usually a cut-down version of the main toolbar, and can be customized to suit. It's created in the **OnCreateControlBars()** function, which is called when the object is opened for in-place editing. The creation is essentially the same as that of the normal application toolbar.

The third data member (don't worry - I'll come back to the second) is a resize control bar, which is created by the **OnCreate()** member function:

```
int CInPlaceFrame::OnCreate(LPCREATESTRUCT lpCreateStruct)
{
    if (COleIPFrameWnd::OnCreate(lpCreateStruct) == -1)
        return -1;

    // CResizeBar implements in-place resizing.
    if (!m_wndResizeBar.Create(this))
    {
        TRACE0("Failed to create resize bar\n");
        return -1;       // fail to create
    }
```

```
    // By default, it is a good idea to register a drop-target that does
    //  nothing with your frame window.  This prevents drops from
    //  "falling through" to a container that supports drag-drop.
    m_dropTarget.Register(this);

    return 0;
}
```

A resize control bar is a
COleResizeBar object; it appears on
the screen as a tracker rectangle with
a hatched border and resize handles,
and is what the user manipulates in
order to resize the in-place window.
The diagram shows a **COleResizeBar**
object around an in-place frame.

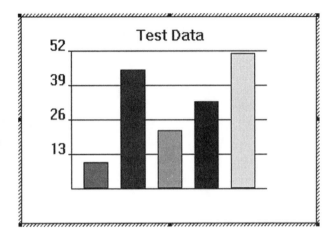

You can see from the code that the second data item, a drag and drop target, is also created in
OnCreate(). You may not want to handle drag and drop in your application, but if you don't
register a target for the frame, any drops that are made will 'fall through' to the container
underneath, which probably isn't what you want (or what your users will expect). The solution
is to register a dummy, do-nothing drop target to catch drops silently.

The Project Resources

Creating your application as a server also adds some extra resources, notably accelerators, menus
and toolbars. The principle behind this is that you may want to show different menus and
toolbars depending on whether the application is being run stand-alone or as a server, servicing
an object in an in-place frame. The added items give you the option of creating custom resources
to fit these circumstances.

The figure shows the extra resources added to server
applications. In each case, those with the **SRVR_IP**
suffix are for use when the object is in-place active,
while those with **SRVR_EMB** will be used when an
embedded object is opened in its own editing
window (rather than in-place).

Note that you need to edit *all* the separate resources,
so that if you make a change to the main menu,
you'll need to propagate it to the **SRVR_IP** and
SRVR_EMB menus manually.

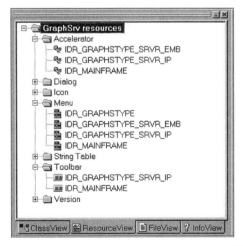

Writing an OLE Server Using MFC

Having looked at how MFC implements OLE servers, we're now going to use Developer Studio to write one, adding such code as we need in order to make the server fully functional. I'll develop the basic application in this chapter, and then show how it can be turned into an ActiveX control and used in component-based systems later on in the book.

Introducing GraphServer

Part of the fun of writing a book like this is thinking up the example code. You have to try to come up with something which is neither too trivial nor too complex, which has some relevance to the real world, and (as a bonus) which might actually be useful to readers as a basis upon which to build.

GraphServer, the application we're going to develop in this chapter, is a simple graph-drawing program, capable of producing output like this:

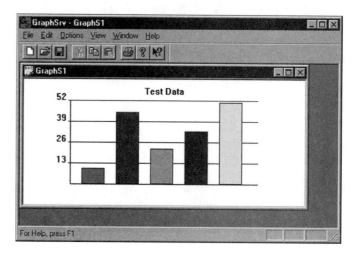

GraphServer is an MDI application that can plot datasets as bar, pie or line charts. In order that the details of the graphics part of the application don't obscure the OLE aspects, I've simplified the functionality of the program as follows:

▶ Only simple, 1-D datasets are supported, consisting of value/label pairs

▶ Datasets can contain only positive, integer values

▶ No editing of datasets via spreadsheets or anything similar is supported

▶ There's no facility for selecting attributes such as color, line type or fill pattern for bars, lines or pie segments

▶ No complicated labeling of axes, bars or pie segments

▶ No feedback from the graph, such as dragging data points to new positions, or deleting them

Any of these features should be fairly easy to add if they're required, but they'd take too much time and space to implement here, and just aren't necessary for a simple OLE server demonstration.

So you know where we're headed, here's the informal specification of the program (and believe me, it's a lot more complete than the specifications provided for many commercial applications!):

> It's an MDI application.

> It will provide line, bar or pie-chart plots of simple datasets.

> There can be a full, half or no frame around the plot.

> Grid lines can be drawn across the graph at suitable *y*-axis values.

> The program will be an OLE server.

> The program will use serialization to store and read data files; it will also be able to import and export text-format files.

> Datasets will have limited support for being edited - values can be changed, but not added or deleted. You can add that if you want!

Try It Out - Creating the Application Skeleton

Most MFC programs start with the creation of the basic application skeleton using AppWizard, and ours is no exception. Select the Projects tab from the New dialog, and select the MFC AppWizard for building executables. Choose a suitable location for your program, and give it the name GraphSrv.

Follow through the steps in the dialogs that follow, making sure that you choose the following options:

> *Step 1:* Leave the type of application at the default setting: Multiple documents.

> *Step 2:* No database support is needed, so you can leave the default setting alone here, too.

> *Step 3:* Choose Full-server as the compound document support option. Don't tick the ActiveX document server or ActiveX Controls check boxes, but do check the Automation box. Make sure that Yes, please is selected as the option for compound file support.

> *Step 4:* Press the Advanced... button, and make sure you enter a file type in the File extension edit control on the Document Template Strings page. I've used **srv** as my file type.

That's all we have to change in the AppWizard dialogs, so press the Finish button to create your application skeleton. You've now got a perfectly valid, working OLE server: you can build the project, and even put GraphServer objects into suitable containers; but there isn't much functionality there, either in the application or OLE departments.

The CGraph Class

At this point, we need to decide how to represent the graph in the program. We could add some data structures and functions to the document class, and let the view use these functions to display the graphs, but this isn't the best (or most flexible) method. It is far preferable, from an OOP point of view, to create a new 'graph' class, which is responsible for storing its own data, and displaying it in a device context on request. The document will then maintain a graph object, using it to store data, and passing its address out to the view, which then uses its device context to allow the graph object to display itself.

The next question is how we're going to structure the graph class itself. We want to be able to plot bar, line and pie charts, and this would tend to suggest a typical class hierarchy:

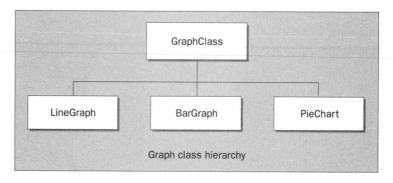

Graph class hierarchy

The problem with this is that we want to allow the user to switch between different graphical views of the same dataset, viewing it as a bar chart one moment and a pie chart the next. We *could* get round this using different sibling classes for the graph types, but that would be rather complex and it's not the point of this exercise, so we'll just have one single graph class, and use member functions to render each type of graph.

Try It Out - Adding the CGraph Class

1 The class will, unsurprisingly, be called **CGraph**, so use ClassWizard to create a new class derived from **CCmdTarget**. This will be useful when we want to use MFC functionality such as serialization later on.

2 Add this highlighted text at the top of the class definition file:

```
//////////////////////////////////////////////////////////////////////////
// CGraph command target
```

```
// Class to hold data items...
class CDatum : public CObject
{
public:
    char name[12];
    int value;
};
```

CDatum is just a helper class, used by **CGraph** to store our label/value data items. Deriving it from **CObject** means that we can use the standard MFC collection classes to store the graph data.

3 The **CGraph** class itself is quite straightforward:

```
class CGraph : public CCmdTarget
{
    DECLARE_DYNCREATE(CGraph)
```

```
    static CGraph* nullObj;

    // Dummy private copy constructor and assignment op to prevent copying
    CGraph(CGraph&) {}
    CGraph& operator=(const CGraph&){ nullObj = new CGraph; return *nullObj; }

    // Enum to describe graph types
    enum TGraphType { BAR, LINE, PIE };
    TGraphType m_type;

    // Enum for framing options on bar and line types
    enum TFrameType { NONE, AXIS, FULL };
    TFrameType m_frame;

    // static array of colors for bars
    enum TColors { NCOL=5 };
    static COLORREF barColor[NCOL];

    // List of data items
    CObList m_data;

    // Current max value in dataset
    int nMaxVal;

    // Offsets and total for pie chart plotting
    int nXoff, nYoff;
    double m_sum;

    // Number of Y-axis lines wanted, and whether to draw them
    int m_YLines;
    BOOL m_bYLines;

    // Current max value for Y axis
    int nYMax;

    // Current bounding rect within which the graph is displayed, plus
    // full client area
    CRect m_rcBnd, m_rcCli;

    // Dataset title
    CString m_sTitle;
```

These data members consist of:

▶ **enum**s for the graph and frame types. The graph can be a bar chart, a pie chart or a line graph, while the frame options are none, half (traditional *x*- and *y*-axes) or full (axes on all four sides).

▶ A single list of **CDatum** objects, plus a title for the dataset.

▶ State data for the appearance, including a color table.

▶ Other 'housekeeping' data members, some of which are there to make calculations quicker, such as the current dataset maximum.

4 After the data members come the member functions:

```
    // Private initialization function
    void Init();

    // Functions to draw the graph types
    void DrawBar(CDC* pDC);
    void DrawLine(CDC* pDC);
    void DrawPie(CDC* pDC);

    void DrawFrame(CDC* pDC);
    void DrawYGrid(CDC* pDC);
    void PieSlice(CDC* pDC, int val, int radius, int nColor);
```

// Attributes
public:
```
    void SetTitle(const char* cs) { m_sTitle = cs; }

    // Set graph and frame types
    void SetBarGraph() { m_type = BAR; }
    void SetLineGraph(){ m_type = LINE; }
    void SetPieChart(){ m_type = PIE; }

    void SetFullFrame() { m_frame = FULL; }
    void SetAxisFrame(){ m_frame = AXIS; }
    void SetNoFrame(){ m_frame = NONE; }

    void SetYLines() { m_bYLines = TRUE; }
    void SetNoYLines(){ m_bYLines = FALSE; }

    // Graph and frame type query functions
    BOOL IsBarGraph() { return m_type == BAR; }
    BOOL IsLineGraph() { return m_type == LINE; }
    BOOL IsPieChart() { return m_type == PIE; }

    BOOL IsFullFrame() { return m_frame == FULL; }
    BOOL IsAxisFrame() { return m_frame == AXIS; }
    BOOL IsNoFrame() { return m_frame == NONE; }

    BOOL HasYLines() { return m_bYLines == TRUE; }

    // Data handling
    void Add(const char* n, int d);
    int Size() { return m_data.GetCount(); }
    void Clear();
    int Total();

    // Cause the graph to be redrawn
    void Display(CRect area, CDC* pDC);
```

// Operations
public:
```
    CGraph(const CString& s);
    CGraph();
    virtual ~CGraph();
```

// Overrides
    // ClassWizard generated virtual function overrides

134

```
    //{{AFX_VIRTUAL(CGraph)
    //}}AFX_VIRTUAL

// Implementation
protected:
    // Generated message map functions
    //{{AFX_MSG(CGraph)
        // NOTE - the ClassWizard will add and remove member functions here.
    //}}AFX_MSG

    DECLARE_MESSAGE_MAP()
};
```

These functions are fairly straightforward: there are functions to get, set and query the graph and frame types, and the public **Display()** routine requests the object to draw itself. This latter function will call the appropriate internal display routine for the current graph type. We have quite a few small, inline member functions, and for simplicity I've coded them in the class definition.

I've changed the default constructor and the destructor to public access, as we'll want to be able to create and delete **CGraph** objects ourselves. I've also provided a private copy constructor and assignment operator, because I've decided that each graph object should be uniquely created, and not copied from another one.

> *I'm using the usual Microsoft convention of starting all class names with a* **C***. Someone once pointed out to me that if you start your class names with a letter other than* **C***, you'll greatly decrease the chances of a class name of yours ever clashing with one of Microsoft's. Whether or not you wish to use this idea, it's worth thinking about!*

5 Let's fill in some of the essential functionality of the graph class in **Graph.cpp**. First, there are a couple of static data members that need to be initialized:

```
CGraph* CGraph::nullObj = NULL;

COLORREF CGraph::barColor[NCOL] =
{
    RGB(127,127,127),  // Dark Grey
    RGB(255,  0,  0),  // Red
    RGB(  0,255,  0),  // Green
    RGB(  0,  0,255),  // Blue
    RGB(255,255,  0),  // Yellow
};
```

The first of these three items, **nullObj**, is described a little later on. The color table is entirely arbitrary for the purposes of this exercise, containing five colors which will be repeated if there are more than five data items. Incidentally, you might have noticed in the header file that the array was dimensioned using an **enum**, a C++ idiom which lets us avoid using preprocessor symbols.

> *The preprocessor is to be avoided when possible, because its symbols are no respecters of scope, and will be substituted wherever they occur. It is far better to use something for which the compiler is responsible if you can.*

6 The next step is to provide constructors (one accepts a title for the graph as a parameter, the other doesn't) and a destructor:

```
CGraph::CGraph()
{
   Init();
}
```

```
CGraph::CGraph(const CString& s)
{
   Init();
   m_sTitle = s;
}
```

```
CGraph::~CGraph()
{
   // Clear the data out of the list
   while (!m_data.IsEmpty())
      delete m_data.RemoveHead();
}
```

```
void CGraph::Init()
{
   m_type = BAR;
   m_frame = AXIS;
   m_YLines = 4;          // Arbitrary choice of four Y-axis lines
   m_bYLines = TRUE;
   m_sTitle = "";

   nMaxVal = -32000;      // Large -ve value for initial comparison
   m_sum = 0.0;
}
```

Not too much explanation required here. The common code for the two constructors has been factored out into a helper routine that sets appropriate default values, and the destructor removes all the data items from the list.

When designing a class, you need to decide whether you want people to be able to copy objects of this class type, either by construction or assignment, using statements like these:

```
CGraph first;
CGraph second(first);   // copy by construction
second = first;         // copy by assignment
```

In this case, although it might make perfect sense to allow people to duplicate graphs by copying, it won't be supported. To this end, the copy constructor and assignment operator are both private, in order to make sure that we avoid possible unpleasant surprises. If we didn't provide them, and someone did try to copy a graph, they'd get the supplied default copy mechanism, which isn't helpful as it copies the pointers from one object to the other.

7 The **Clear()** function is used to 'reset' a graph object. It deletes all the data items in the list, and re-initializes the object:

```
void CGraph::Clear()
{
   // Clear the data out of the list
   while (!m_data.IsEmpty())
      delete m_data.RemoveHead();

   Init();
}
```

8 The other two basic necessities are some way of adding data to the graph, and some way of displaying it. The **Add()** function doesn't contain anything very surprising:

```
// Add a data item to the dataset for this graph.
void CGraph::Add(const char* n, int d)
{
   CDatum* pd = new CDatum;
   ASSERT(pd);

   pd->value = d;
   strcpy(pd->name, n);

   m_data.AddTail(pd);

   // Reset and max value
   if (d > nMaxVal) nMaxVal = d;
}
```

A new **CDatum** object is created, filled with the data passed in, and added to the list. At the same time, we keep track of the current maximum value in the dataset.

Display() is where the work gets done. We get passed an area in which to draw the graph, and from it we can construct a bounding rectangle within which line and bar graphs will get plotted. The rectangle provides the 'data area' of the graph, with axes being plotted on its perimeter. We could just make do with the device context, but this method is a little more flexible, allowing us to position a graph within the device context if we so wish.

Once this has been done, the graph title is drawn, and then the appropriate plotting function is called. Here's the code to do it:

```
// Public function which clients call to display a graph
void CGraph::Display(CRect area, CDC* pDC)
{
   ASSERT(pDC);

   // Save away the graph area
   m_rcCli = area;

   CPoint ptCenter( (m_rcCli.left + (m_rcCli.right-m_rcCli.left) / 2),
                    (m_rcCli.top + (m_rcCli.bottom-m_rcCli.top) / 2) );

   // Set the bounding rectangle for the graph
   m_rcBnd.left = m_rcCli.left + (m_rcCli.right-m_rcCli.left) / 6;
   m_rcBnd.top = m_rcCli.top + (m_rcCli.bottom-m_rcCli.top) / 6;
   m_rcBnd.right = m_rcCli.left + 5*(m_rcCli.right-m_rcCli.left) / 6;
   m_rcBnd.bottom = m_rcCli.top + 5*(m_rcCli.bottom-m_rcCli.top) / 6;
```

```
// Plot the title at the top of the window
pDC->SetTextAlign(TA_CENTER);
pDC->TextOut(ptCenter.x, m_rcCli.top+10, m_sTitle);

switch (m_type)
{
case BAR:
   DrawBar(pDC);
   break;
case PIE:
   DrawPie(pDC);
   break;
case LINE:
   DrawLine(pDC);
   break;
default:
   AfxMessageBox("Bad graph type in CGraph::Display");
   ASSERT(0);
}
}
```

9 This is all very well, but it doesn't really achieve very much. The meat is in the plotting routines themselves. Let's first consider the one that plots the bar chart:

```
void CGraph::DrawBar(CDC* pDC)
{
   ASSERT(pDC);

   DrawFramé(pDC);

   if (m_data.GetCount() == 0)
      return;       // nothing to do

   DrawYGrid(pDC);

   // Calculate the gap between bars. Each bar is 2*gap in width
   int nInt = 3*m_data.GetCount() + 1;
   int gap = (m_rcBnd.right - m_rcBnd.left) / nInt;

   // Calculate the scale factor for the bars
   double scale = double(m_rcBnd.bottom - m_rcBnd.top) / nYMax;

   // Draw bars
   POSITION pos;
   int i = 0;

   for (pos = m_data.GetHeadPosition(); pos != NULL;)
   {
      CDatum* pd = (CDatum*)m_data.GetNext(pos);
      ASSERT(pd);
      int height = (int)(pd->value * scale);

      CBrush cb(barColor[i%NCOL]);
      CBrush* pOldBrush = pDC->SelectObject(&cb);

      pDC->Rectangle( m_rcBnd.left + (i+1)*gap + i*(2*gap),
                      m_rcBnd.bottom - height,
```

```
                        m_rcBnd.left + (i+1)*gap + (i+1)*(2*gap),
                        m_rcBnd.bottom );

        i++;
        pDC->SelectObject(pOldBrush);
    }
}
```

Before we can plot anything at all, we need to find a couple of numerical factors. We know there are n bars and $n+1$ gaps, allowing for a gap at either end. Each bar is twice the width of a gap, so we need to divide the x extent into $(3n+1)$ parts to find the widths of the bars and gaps, as shown in the illustration:

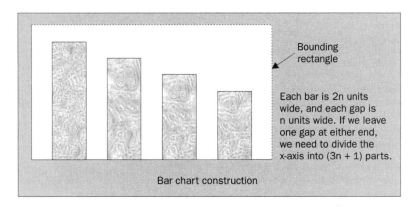

Bounding rectangle

Each bar is 2n units wide, and each gap is n units wide. If we leave one gap at either end, we need to divide the x-axis into (3n + 1) parts.

Bar chart construction

The other factor we need is a scaling factor for the bar heights, based on the dataset maximum, and the size of the rectangle we need to fit it into. Once we've calculated these, plotting is a matter of iterating through the data point list, getting each value and scaling it, then selecting a color and drawing a rectangle of the appropriate size.

10 The helper functions **DrawFrame()** and **DrawYGrid()** are used to draw the frame (if any) around the plot, and to draw the horizontal rules which provide the y-axis scale. This is the former; it just checks the **m_frame** variable and draws lines (or not) accordingly:

```
void CGraph::DrawFrame(CDC* pDC)
{
    ASSERT(pDC);

    if (m_frame == NONE)
        return;

    CPen axisPen(PS_SOLID, 1, RGB(0,0,0));
    CPen* pOldPen = pDC->SelectObject(&axisPen);

    if (m_frame == AXIS)
    {
        // Draw 'axis' lines on the bounding rect
        pDC->MoveTo(m_rcBnd.left, m_rcBnd.top);
        pDC->LineTo(m_rcBnd.left, m_rcBnd.bottom);
        pDC->LineTo(m_rcBnd.right, m_rcBnd.bottom);
    }
```

```
   if (m_frame == FULL)
   {
      pDC->Rectangle(&m_rcBnd);
   }

   pDC->SelectObject(pOldPen);
}
```

DrawYGrid() first makes sure that the maximum *y* value is a multiple of the number of grid lines, incrementing it if necessary. Once we've done this, we can find the numerical increment (**nYinc**) and screen spacing between the grid lines.

```
void CGraph::DrawYGrid(CDC* pDC)
{
   ASSERT(pDC);

   // Check whether we're supposed to be drawing lines
   if (!m_bYLines)
      return;

   // Find the max value for the Y axis, based on the number of Y lines.
   nYMax = nMaxVal;
   while ((nYMax % m_YLines) != 0)
      nYMax++;

   int nYinc = nYMax / m_YLines;
   int nYoffset = (m_rcBnd.bottom - m_rcBnd.top) / m_YLines;

   // Draw the lines
   pDC->SetTextAlign(TA_RIGHT | TA_BASELINE);
   for (int i=0; i<m_YLines; i++)
   {
      char buff[6];
      pDC->MoveTo(m_rcBnd.left-3, m_rcBnd.top+i*nYoffset);
      pDC->LineTo(m_rcBnd.right, m_rcBnd.top+i*nYoffset);

      sprintf(buff, "%d", nYinc*(m_YLines-i));
      pDC->TextOut(m_rcBnd.left-6, m_rcBnd.top+i*nYoffset, buff, strlen(buff));
   }
}
```

11 Plotting the data as a line graph is actually quite similar to the **DrawBar()** function. We calculate the gap between the data points and the *y*-axis scaling factor, as before. Then, when we plot the points, we join each point to the previous one with a line:

```
void CGraph::DrawLine(CDC* pDC)
{
   ASSERT(pDC);

   DrawFrame(pDC);

   if (m_data.GetCount() == 0)
      return;        // nothing to do

   DrawYGrid(pDC);
```

```
// Calculate the gap between points.
int nInt = m_data.GetCount() + 1;
int gap = (m_rcBnd.right - m_rcBnd.left) / nInt;

// Calculate the scale factor for the lines
double scale = double(m_rcBnd.bottom - m_rcBnd.top) / nYMax;

// Draw lines
POSITION pos;
POSITION lastPos = NULL;
int i = 0;
CDatum* pPrev = NULL;

for (pos = m_data.GetHeadPosition(); pos != NULL;)
{
   CDatum* pd = (CDatum*)m_data.GetNext(pos);
   ASSERT(pd);

   int height = (int)(pd->value * scale);

   // If there was a previous point, draw from it to this one
   if (pPrev)
   {
      int prevHeight = (int)(pPrev->value * scale);
      pDC->MoveTo(m_rcBnd.left+i*gap, m_rcBnd.bottom-prevHeight);
      pDC->LineTo(m_rcBnd.left+(i+1)*gap, m_rcBnd.bottom-height);
   }

   i++;
   pPrev = pd;
}
}
```

12 Pie charts are slightly more complicated to draw, mainly because of the way in which the basic GDI 'pie slice' API call works. The call requires you to supply the coordinates of the slice's bounding rectangle, and points defining the start and end points of the arc. It then draws a pie slice whose tip lies at the center of the box. This gives a lot of flexibility for drawing elliptical pie slices, but makes the calculation of coordinates less easy than it might otherwise be.

The easiest way to work would be to set the origin of the coordinate system to the center of the pie, and then use a bounding rectangle equal in size to the diameter of the pie. This way, all the slices would meet up at (0,0), the center of the bounding box. The problem is that when we come to embed a graph into a container such as Word, we'll run into trouble if we're not using a 'normal' coordinate system with (0,0) in the top-left corner.

However, it's still easier to calculate pie coordinates relative to (0,0), so what we'll do is calculate the point where we want the center of the pie (**nXoff**, **nYoff**), and save it away. We'll then calculate the pie coordinates assuming we're at the origin, and apply the offset when we need to do the plotting.

The **DrawPie()** function sets up the radius and center, and then plots the pie slices and the key:

```
void CGraph::DrawPie(CDC* pDC)
{
    ASSERT(pDC);

    // Sanity check - if the data total is zero, we can't plot
    if (Total() == 0)
    {
        AfxMessageBox("Error: data sum is zero - cannot plot");
        return;
    }

    // Calculate the radius
    int radius = min((m_rcCli.bottom-m_rcCli.top)/4,
                (m_rcCli.right-m_rcCli.left/4));

    // Set up the offsets
    nXoff = m_rcCli.left+(m_rcCli.right-m_rcCli.left)/4 + 10;
    nYoff = m_rcCli.top+(m_rcCli.bottom-m_rcCli.top)/2;

    // Display pie slices
    m_sum = 0.0;
    POSITION pos;
    pDC->SetTextAlign(TA_LEFT);
    int i = 0;
    int nColor;

    for (pos = m_data.GetHeadPosition(); pos != NULL;)
    {
        CDatum* pd = (CDatum*)m_data.GetNext(pos);
        ASSERT(pd);

        nColor = i%NCOL;

        // Draw the pie slice
        PieSlice(pDC, pd->value, radius, nColor);

        // And the key entry
        CBrush cb(barColor[nColor]);
        CBrush* pOldBrush = pDC->SelectObject(&cb);

        int xpos = (int)((m_rcCli.right-m_rcCli.left)*0.65);
        int ypos = (m_rcCli.bottom-m_rcCli.top)/4+i*20;
        pDC->Rectangle(xpos, ypos, xpos+15, ypos+15);
        pDC->TextOut(xpos+20, ypos, pd->name, strlen(pd->name));

        i++;
        pDC->SelectObject(pOldBrush);
    }
}
```

You'll need the helper function **Total()**, which returns the total of the values currently held in the dataset:

```
int CGraph::Total()
{
    int nTot = 0;

    // Generate and return dataset total
    POSITION pos;
```

```
    for (pos = m_data.GetHeadPosition(); pos != NULL;)
    {
        CDatum* pd = (CDatum*)m_data.GetNext(pos);
        nTot += pd->value;
    }

    return nTot;
}
```

The **PieSlice()** function is used to plot each segment. The actual data value is converted to a percentage, and **m_sum** is used to hold the running total of percentages; these two values can be used to calculate the start and end points of the slice's arc. In order for the math to work, you'll need to include the **math.h** header file.

```
void CGraph::PieSlice(CDC* pDC, int val, int radius, int nColor)
{
    ASSERT(pDC);

    double dPercent = (double)val * 100 / Total();

    // Do plotting
    int startX, startY, endX, endY;
    double PI = 3.1415927;

    startX = (int)(radius * cos(2*PI*m_sum/100.0));
    startY = (int)(-radius * sin(2*PI*m_sum/100.0));
    endX = (int)(radius * cos(2*PI*(m_sum + dPercent)/100.0));
    endY = (int)(-radius * sin(2*PI*(m_sum + dPercent)/100.0));

    // Add offsets for start and end of arc
    startX += nXoff;
    startY += nYoff;
    endX   += nXoff;
    endY   += nYoff;

    // Calculate bounding box corners
    int X1 = nXoff - radius;
    int Y1 = nYoff - radius;
    int X2 = nXoff + radius;
    int Y2 = nYoff + radius;

    CBrush cb(barColor[nColor]);
    CBrush* pOldBrush = pDC->SelectObject(&cb);

    pDC->Pie(X1, Y1, X2, Y2, startX, startY, endX, endY);

    // Increment the sum
    m_sum += dPercent;

    pDC->SelectObject(pOldBrush);
}
```

That's about it for the basic structure of **CGraph**. There's obviously a lot more that we could add - labeling the pie slices with their percentages, allowing exploded or 3D slices and so on - but what we've done will allow us to build a functional server, and that's what's important here.

13 In order to test the basic operation of the graph class, you can add code to the document. You'll need a **CGraph** object in the document; so, add a variable to **GraphSrvDoc.h**, and a function to get at it:

```
class CGraph;
class CGraphSrvSrvrItem;

class CGraphSrvDoc : public COleServerDoc
{

// Plus all the AppWizard-generated code...

private:
   CGraph* m_pGraph;    // graph object for this document

public:
   CGraph* GetGraph()
      { return m_pGraph; }
};
```

Standard MFC practice would make **m_pGraph** *public, but we'll stick to the recommended OO style, making the data private and using an access function.*

Supply some code to first create a **CGraph** object and assign some data to it in the constructor, and then to delete the object in the destructor:

```
#include "stdafx.h"
#include "GraphSrv.h"
#include "Graph.h"

#include "GraphSrvDoc.h"
#include "SrvrItem.h"

// Plus all the AppWizard-generated code...

CGraphSrvDoc::CGraphSrvDoc()
{
   // Use OLE compound files
   EnableCompoundFile();

   // Create the graph object
   m_pGraph = new CGraph();
   ASSERT(m_pGraph);

   // Test only - give it some data to use, while we're developing
   m_pGraph->SetTitle("Test Data");
   m_pGraph->Add("One", 10);
   m_pGraph->Add("Two", 45);
   m_pGraph->Add("Three", 22);
   m_pGraph->Add("Four", 33);
   m_pGraph->Add("Five", 51);

   EnableAutomation();

   AfxOleLockApp();
}
```

```
CGraphSrvDoc::~CGraphSrvDoc()
{
    delete m_pGraph;
    AfxOleUnlockApp();
}
```

The call to **EnableAutomation()** sets our program up to act as an Automation server, while the calls to **AfxOleLockApp()** and **AfxOleUnlockApp()** are there to make sure that MFC's reference counting for this server is handled correctly.

14 We also need to add code to the view's **OnDraw()** function to get the graph to display itself in the window. It requires a very simple modification:

```
#include "stdafx.h"
#include "GraphSrv.h"
#include "Graph.h"

#include "GraphSrvDoc.h"
#include "GraphSrvView.h"

// AppWizard-generated skeleton...

void CGraphSrvView::OnDraw(CDC* pDC)
{
    CGraphSrvDoc* pDoc = GetDocument();
    ASSERT_VALID(pDoc);

    CRect client;
    GetClientRect(&client);
    pDoc->GetGraph()->Display(client, pDC);
}
```

All we need to do is calculate the area in which we want the graph displayed - in this case, the entire client area - and then tell the object to display itself. When you build and run the application, you should see a display like this:

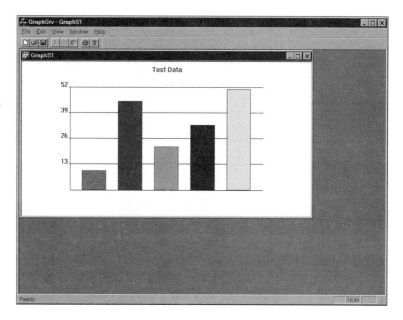

GraphServer Menu Structure

The next step is to add code to the application to interact with the graph class. We need some menu items and associated handlers to interact with the properties of the graph object, such as the graph and frame types.

1 Open up ResourceView and expand the Menu folder; then select the **IDR_GRAPHSTYPE** menu. Insert a new menu, Options, between Edit and View. Under this top-level menu you can add the following sub-menu structure. The diagram shows, using underscores, where to add the accelerator &s:

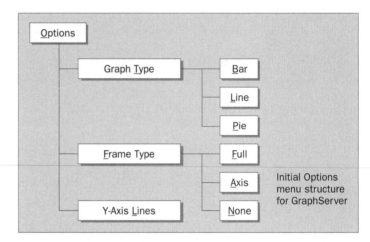

Initial Options menu structure for GraphServer

2 Add handlers for each of the sub-menus to the *document* class. The handlers will all look something like the example for the **ID_OPTIONS_GRAPHTYPE_BAR** menu, shown below:

```
void CGraphSrvDoc::OnOptionsGraphtypeBar()
{
    if (!m_pGraph->IsBarGraph())
    {
        m_pGraph->SetBarGraph();
        SetModifiedFlag(TRUE);
        UpdateAllViews(NULL);
    }
}

void CGraphSrvDoc::OnUpdateOptionsGraphtypeBar(CCmdUI* pCmdUI)
{
    pCmdUI->SetCheck(m_pGraph->IsBarGraph());
}
```

The handler for the Y-Axis Lines option looks like this:

```
void CGraphSrvDoc::OnOptionsYaxislines()
{
    BOOL bLines = m_pGraph->HasYLines();

    if (!bLines)
        m_pGraph->SetYLines();
    else
        m_pGraph->SetNoYLines();
```

```
    SetModifiedFlag(TRUE);
    UpdateAllViews(NULL);
    UpdateAllItems(NULL);
}

void CGraphSrvDoc::OnUpdateOptionsYaxislines(CCmdUI* pCmdUI)
{
    pCmdUI->SetCheck(m_pGraph->HasYLines());
}
```

Once you've added all those functions, you can test the application and make sure that you can alter the properties of the graph object.

File Handling

The last thing we need to do before we get to the server-specific aspects is to add some file handling. We'll give the server two ways in which it can handle files: it will be able to use MFC's serialization to read and write binary files; and it will import and export datasets in a human-readable text format. The ability to read files in a text format is a useful one for any sort of data handling program, and from our point of view it will be handy to be able to create test datasets in a text editor.

Try It Out - Adding Serialization Support

In order to be able to use serialization, a class must inherit from **CObject**, must use the **DECLARE_SERIAL()** and **IMPLEMENT_SERIAL()** macros to instrument the class, and must provide a **Serialize()** function.

1   **CGraph** is already derived from **CCmdTarget** (and hence from **CObject**), so all we need to do is delete the **DECLARE_DYNCREATE()** macro call that ClassWizard inserted, and add the new macro calls and a prototype for **Serialize()** to the class declaration:

```
class CGraph : public CCmdTarget
{
    static CGraph* nullObj;

    // Rest of header file, as before...

// Operations
public:
    DECLARE_SERIAL(CGraph);
    void Serialize(CArchive& ca);

    CGraph(const CString& s);
    CGraph();
    virtual ~CGraph();

    // Rest of header file, as before...

};
```

You'll need to add the same macro and function to the **CDatum** class definition:

```
class CDatum : public CObject
{
public:
    char name[12];
    int value;

    DECLARE_SERIAL(CDatum);
    void Serialize(CArchive& ca);
};
```

2 In the **Graph.cpp** file, remove the old **IMPLEMENT_DYNCREATE()** macro call and replace it with a call to the **IMPLEMENT_SERIAL()** macro for both the **CGraph** and **CDatum** classes. You should also implement the two **Serialize()** functions:

```
// Graph.cpp : implementation file
//

#include "stdafx.h"
#include "GraphSrv.h"
#include "Graph.h"
#include <math.h>

#ifdef _DEBUG
#define new DEBUG_NEW
#undef THIS_FILE
static char THIS_FILE[] = __FILE__;
#endif

/////////////////////////////////////////////////////////////////////////////
// CGraph

IMPLEMENT_SERIAL(CGraph, CCmdTarget, 1)
IMPLEMENT_SERIAL(CDatum, CObject, 1)

...

/////////////////////////////////////////////////////////////////////////////
// Serialization for graph and data objects

void CDatum::Serialize(CArchive& ca)
{
    if (ca.IsStoring())
    {
        ca.Write(name,12);
        ca << (DWORD)value;
    }
    else
    {
        ca.Read(name,12);
        ca >> (DWORD&)value;
    }
}
```

```
void CGraph::Serialize(CArchive& ca)
{
    // Store the miscellaneous data...
    if (ca.IsStoring())
    {
        ca << m_sTitle;
        ca << (DWORD)nMaxVal;
        ca << (short)m_type << (short)m_frame;
    }
    else
    {
        ca >> m_sTitle;
        ca >> (DWORD&)nMaxVal;
        ca >> (short&)m_type >> (short&)m_frame;

        // COblist::Serialize() uses AddTail(); clear the data list
        // first or you'll just be adding to it!
        m_data.RemoveAll();
    }

    // ...and get the data list to serialize itself
    m_data.Serialize(ca);
}
```

3 Finally, in the document class' **Serialize()** function, serialize the graph:

```
void CGraphSrvDoc::Serialize(CArchive& ar)
{
    m_pGraph->Serialize(ar);

    if (ar.IsStoring())
    {
        // TODO: add storing code here
    }
    else
    {
        // TODO: add loading code here
    }
}
```

When you've entered this code, rebuild the project, and check that you can save and restore files.

Try It Out - Adding Import and Export Functionality

1 It's very useful for a utility application like this one to be able to exchange data with other programs using a simple, text-mode file format. Before we start concerning ourselves with the theory, we can add the relevant items to the **Options** menu, giving them the default IDs:

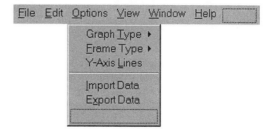

Note that we've added these items to the <u>O</u>ptions menu, when we normally put file-handling commands in the <u>F</u>ile menu. The reason for putting them here is that it will make things much easier when we get to setting up the menus for in-place editing.

2 Let's consider exporting first. It's most sensible for the document class to handle the export menu item; it can get the name of an output file, and then direct its graph object to write itself into the file. Add this code to **GraphSrvDoc.cpp**:

```
void CGraphSrvDoc::OnOptionsExportdata()
{
    // Export the dataset to an ASCII file. First, get a filename
    // to export to...

    CFileDialog cf(FALSE);
    if (cf.DoModal() == IDOK)
    {
        ofstream os(cf.GetPathName());
        if (!os)
        {
            AfxMessageBox("Error opening file for export");
            return;
        }

        // Write the dataset...
        m_pGraph->Export(os);
    }
}
```

3 **CGraph::Export()**, which gets called by the above function, is pretty simple - it just writes the essential data items to the output stream. Personally, I prefer to use the basic C++ file stream classes rather than MFC's **CFile**, as I find them easier to work with. Here's the function header and implementation, for the **Graph.h** and **Graph.cpp** files respectively:

```
void Export(ofstream& os);
```

```
void CGraph::Export(ofstream& os)
{
    os << m_sTitle << endl;
    os << m_data.GetCount() << endl;
    os << nMaxVal << endl;

    POSITION pos;

    for (pos = m_data.GetHeadPosition(); pos != NULL;)
    {
        CDatum* pd = (CDatum*)m_data.GetNext(pos);
        ASSERT(pd);
        os << pd->name << "  " << pd->value << endl;
    }
}
```

4 That will suffice to write us an output file in a human-readable format. What about reading one in? There are several ways in which we could approach this, but we'll take a relatively quick-and-dirty route: we'll give the document class an **Import()** function, so that data can be imported into *any* document. If the document's graph object already has some data, we'll warn the user that it will get overwritten; if they give the go-ahead, then we'll read the file and use it to initialize the graph object.

As before, the document class handles the initial stages: checking whether there is data in the graph object already, and getting the filename.

```
void CGraphSrvDoc::OnOptionsImportdata()
{
    // Import a dataset from an ASCII file. Check if there is any data in
    // this graph object, and alert the user.

    if (m_pGraph->Size() != 0)
        if (IDNO == AfxMessageBox("This operation will overwrite the "
                                   "existing data. Continue?", MB_YESNO))
            return;

    // First, get a filename to read from...
    CFileDialog cf(TRUE);
    if (cf.DoModal() == IDOK)
    {
        ifstream is(cf.GetPathName());
        if (!is)
        {
            AfxMessageBox("Error opening file for import");
            return;
        }

        // Read the dataset and redraw...
        m_pGraph->Import(is);
        SetModifiedFlag(TRUE);
        UpdateAllViews(NULL);
    }
}
```

5 The **Import()** routine isn't too difficult: it just re-initializes the object before reading the data from the file. Here are the function header and implementation:

```
void Import(ifstream& is);
```

```
void CGraph::Import(ifstream& is)
{
    // Clear everything out before we start...
    Clear();

    char buff[80];
    is.getline(buff, sizeof buff);
    m_sTitle = buff;

    int nCount;
    is >> nCount;
    is >> nMaxVal;
```

```
        int i, value;
        for (i=0; i<nCount; i++)
        {
            is >> buff >> value;
            Add(buff, value);
        }
    }
```

6 Because **Graph.h** now makes reference to the **ifstream** and **ofstream** data types, you'll need to add a **#include** for **fstream.h** to the three files that include it, namely **Graph.cpp**, **GraphSrvDoc.cpp** and **GraphSrvView.cpp**. Now you can rebuild the project, and check that exporting and importing data works as expected.

Editing the Data

The final feature we'll add to the basic application is a simple editing dialog, to enable us to edit the values in a graph's dataset. Unfortunately, this isn't as simple a job as it ought to be, because one of the things that is badly lacking from the basic set of Windows controls is some sort of editable list box or grid for data entry and editing. The nearest you can get is the **Grid32.ocx** included with Visual C++, but this has the limitation that it's a read-only grid, and doesn't support cell editing without quite a lot of messing about.

In a full-strength application, you'd use some sort of proper spreadsheet control, or even fire up Excel using Automation. Here, we're constrained to using what comes with Visual C++, and I've chosen to use ordinary combo box controls. What we'll end up with is *not* a serious data editing dialog, but just something that will enable us to test the correct functioning of the graph class when its data changes.

Try It Out - Adding the Editing Dialog

1 Before we get to the dialog, we need to make a couple of changes to the graph class, adding functions to get and set an item in the dataset. Add these definitions to the public section of the **Graph.h** header file:

```
    BOOL GetItem(int index, char* name, int* value);
    BOOL SetItem(int index, char* name, int value);
```

GetItem() takes a zero-based index into the dataset, and if it's valid, returns the name and value of the corresponding items from the dataset:

```
BOOL CGraph::GetItem(int index, char* name, int* value)
{
    ASSERT(name);
    ASSERT(value);

    if (index < 0 || index > m_data.GetCount()-1)
    {
        name[0] = '\0';
        *value = 0;
        return FALSE;
    }
```

```
    POSITION pos = m_data.FindIndex(index);
    if (pos == NULL)
        return FALSE;

    CDatum* pd = (CDatum*)m_data.GetAt(pos);
    ASSERT(pd);
    strcpy(name, pd->name);
    *value = pd->value;
    return TRUE;
}
```

SetItem() is analogous to this, taking an index and using it to replace the values at that position in the dataset. Note that we get the old item from the list and delete it once we've placed the new one, thus avoiding a memory leak. Once a value has been changed, we need to check whether the change has affected the maximum value:

```
BOOL CGraph::SetItem(int index, char* name, int value)
{
    ASSERT(name);
    if (index < 0 || index > m_data.GetCount()-1)
        return FALSE;

    POSITION pos = m_data.FindIndex(index);
    if (pos == NULL)
        return FALSE;

    CDatum* pd = new CDatum;
    ASSERT(pd);

    // Save the old pointer
    CDatum* pOldElement = (CDatum*)m_data.GetAt(pos);
    ASSERT(pOldElement);

    strcpy(pd->name, name);
    pd->value = value;
    m_data.SetAt(pos, pd);

    // Delete the unwanted element
    delete pOldElement;

    return TRUE;
}
```

2 With that done, we can turn our attention to the edit dialog. First, create a new dialog resource, and give it the ID **IDD_DATAEDIT**. Place two combo boxes on the dialog - one to hold the keys for the dataset, and the other to hold the values. Make sure that they're simple combos, and that sorting isn't selected.

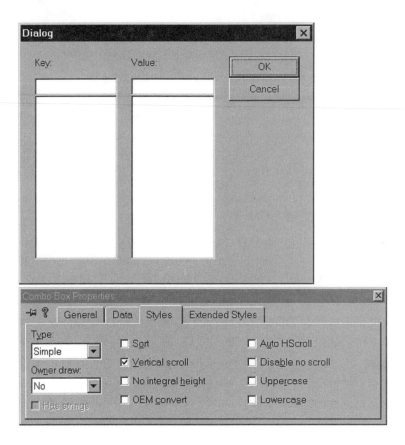

Simple combo boxes are useful here because they really do act like a combination of an edit control and a list box, and don't drop down. We're going to use the list box part to store the items, and the edit control as an editing area. We'll need to provide code to take the data from the edit control and put it back into the list box when the selection changes.

3 Double-click on your new dialog and use ClassWizard to create a new class, **CEditDlg**, based on **CDialog**. Still using ClassWizard, associate **CComboBox** controls with the two combo boxes, with member variables called **m_combo1** and **m_combo2**. In my dialog, **m_combo1** represents the keys, and **m_combo2** represents the values.

4 The dialog is going to display a dataset, so add a **CGraph*** data member to the class to represent this item. Make sure that it's initialized to **NULL** in the constructor, and add a function **SetGraph()** to set it. Lastly, add two integers that will hold the indices of the currently selected items in the combo boxes, and initialize them to -1 in the constructor too.

```
class CEditDlg : public CDialog
{
    CGraph* m_pGraph;
    int m_lastSel1;                    // last selection in combo 1
    int m_lastSel2;                    // last selection in combo 2
```

```
// Construction
public:
    CEditDlg(CWnd* pParent = NULL);    // standard constructor
    void SetGraph(CGraph* pG);

// Dialog Data
    //{{AFX_DATA(CEditDlg)
    enum { IDD = IDD_DATAEDIT };
    CComboBox    m_combo2;
    CComboBox    m_combo1;
    //}}AFX_DATA

// Overrides
    // ClassWizard generated virtual function overrides
    //{{AFX_VIRTUAL(CEditDlg)
    protected:
    virtual void DoDataExchange(CDataExchange* pDX);    // DDX/DDV support
    //}}AFX_VIRTUAL

// Implementation
protected:

    // Generated message map functions
    //{{AFX_MSG(CEditDlg)
        // NOTE: the ClassWizard will add member functions here
    //}}AFX_MSG
    DECLARE_MESSAGE_MAP()
};
```

5 Because of the new member of type **CGraph***, you'll need to include **Graph.h** (and therefore **fstream.h**) at the top of **EditDlg.cpp**. The constructor looks like this:

```
CEditDlg::CEditDlg(CWnd* pParent /*=NULL*/)
    : CDialog(CEditDlg::IDD, pParent)
{
    m_pGraph = NULL;
    m_lastSel1 = -1;
    m_lastSel2 = -1;

    //{{AFX_DATA_INIT(CEditDlg)
        // NOTE: the ClassWizard will add member initialization here
    //}}AFX_DATA_INIT
}
```

And **SetGraph()** is pretty trivial, as you might imagine:

```
void CEditDlg::SetGraph(CGraph* pG)
{
    ASSERT(pG);
    m_pGraph = pG;
}
```

6 Now we need to use ClassWizard again, this time to add a handler for the **WM_INITDIALOG** message, so that we can put the dataset values into the combo boxes when the dialog is initialized:

```
BOOL CEditDlg::OnInitDialog()
{
    CDialog::OnInitDialog();

    // Add the data set to the combo box.
    if (m_pGraph)
    {
        int nItems = m_pGraph->Size();
        for (int i=0; i<nItems; i++)
        {
            char name[20];
            int val;

            BOOL bOK = m_pGraph->GetItem(i, name, &val);
            if (bOK)
            {
                char strVal[20];
                itoa(val, strVal, 10);
                m_combo1.AddString(name);       // add the name
                m_combo2.AddString(strVal);     // and the value
            }
        }
    }

    return TRUE;  // return TRUE unless you set the focus to a control
                  // EXCEPTION: OCX Property Pages should return FALSE
}
```

The function is pretty straightforward: it checks we have a graph, iterates through the items (converting the values to strings as it goes, using the **itoa()** function), and loads the data into the combo boxes.

7   Clicking on an item in the combo box will result in the text being placed in the corresponding edit control automatically. What we have to do is handle the converse situation, so that when the user changes the selection, the edit control content is used to update the combo box. We do this by adding handlers for the **CBN_SELCHANGE** message to both combo boxes. We could link the combos and have them handled by a single routine, but I've left them so they can be edited independently.

We receive the **CBN_SELCHANGE** notification when a *new* selection is made, so we have to remember the old one in order to know where to put back the text; that's the purpose of the selection counters (**m_lastSel1** and **m_lastSel2**) we added to the class. Here's the code for one of the routines (the other is almost identical - just change the **1**s to **2**s):

```
void CEditDlg::OnSelchangeCombo1()
{
    // In the case of a new selection, if there was a previous selection,
    // replace it with the contents of the edit control.

    // Get the edit control associated with the combo box. All CComboBox
    // controls use an ID of 1001 for the edit control, so that's easy!
    CEdit* pEdit1 = (CEdit*)m_combo1.GetDlgItem(1001);
    ASSERT(pEdit1);
```

156

```
    if (m_lastSel1 != -1)
    {
        // Get the text out of the edit control
        CString cs1;
        pEdit1->GetWindowText(cs1);

        // Put it into the last selected position
        m_combo1.DeleteString(m_lastSel1);
        m_combo1.InsertString(m_lastSel1,cs1);
    }

    // Reset the last position
    m_lastSel1 = m_combo1.GetCurSel();
}
```

Combo boxes don't provide a way to replace an item, so we have to resort to the less elegant method of deleting the old item and inserting a new one. Notice a little hack here, used to get the ID of the edit control associated with the combo box. It turns out from the MFC source that **CComboBox**es always use an ID of 1001 for their edit control, so we can easily get at the edit control using that ID.

8 The last function to add to the **CEditDlg** class is a handler for the OK button, using ClassWizard. When the button is pressed, we want to rebuild the dataset from the contents of the edit control:

```
void CEditDlg::OnOK()
{
    // When the user clicks the OK button, we need to rebuild the graph
    // dataset from what's in the combo box. First, though, get the data in
    // the edit controls so we're up to date.
    OnSelchangeCombo1();
    OnSelchangeCombo2();

    for (int i=0; i<m_combo1.GetCount(); i++)
    {
        char s1[20], s2[20];
        m_combo1.GetLBText(i, s1);
        m_combo2.GetLBText(i, s2);

        m_pGraph->SetItem(i, s1, atoi(s2));
    }

    // Call the base class function to dismiss the dialog
    CDialog::OnOK();
}
```

Because the user could edit a value and then click on OK, we need to cause the current contents of the edit controls to be put back into the combo boxes, and this is most easily done by simulating a new selection.

157

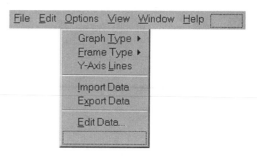

9 That completes the dialog class. Now we need to add code to display it, which we'll do in the view class, so add a new item to the Options menu:

10 Provide a handler for the new item in the view class, and fill in the code to display the dialog. All we need to do is to ensure that the graph gets redrawn if the user returned via the OK button:

```
void CGraphSrvView::OnOptionsEditdata()
{
    CGraphSrvDoc* pDoc = GetDocument();
    ASSERT_VALID(pDoc);

    // Create the dialog, and set its graph member
    CEditDlg dlg;
    dlg.SetGraph(pDoc->GetGraph());

    // If the dialog returned OK, redraw the graph
    if (IDOK == dlg.DoModal())
    {
        CClientDC* pDC = new CClientDC(this);
        ASSERT(pDC);

        CRect client;
        GetClientRect(&client);
        pDoc->GetGraph()->Display(client, pDC);
        pDoc->UpdateAllViews(NULL);
    }
}
```

In order to get our completed example to compile, you should add a **#include** for **EditDlg.h** to the beginning of **GraphSrvView.cpp**.

Testing the Server

Now we've got the basics working, let's see how our application performs as a server. Test it out by starting up a suitable container application (Microsoft Word is good for this) and selecting the Insert | Object... menu item. You'll see this dialog:

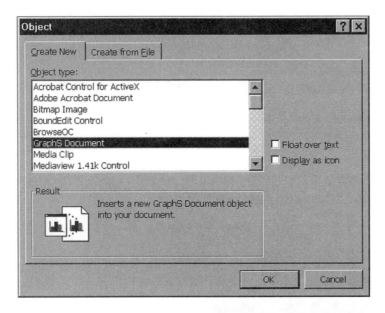

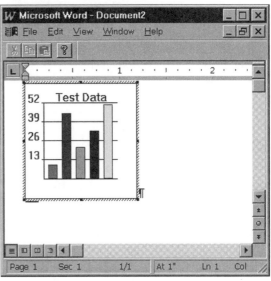

Every time GraphServer is run, it updates its entries in the Registry, one of which says that it is an **insertable object**. The dialog lists all the insertable objects that the Registry knows about. Select the GraphS Document item from the list and click OK; after a pause of a few seconds, during which GraphServer is loaded and an object is created, you should see a display something like this:

Let's examine what we have. The good news is that we have a recognizable object embedded in our Word document; the object is active (as shown by the hatched outline) and the toolbar and menu have changed to GraphServer's. The bad news is that (a) we haven't got the right menu - the one we're showing doesn't contain the graphing functions, and (b) the object size and shape aren't optimal, being square instead of the rectangle we'd like.

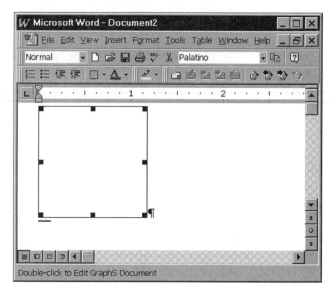

Now click on the Word document anywhere outside the object, and the display will change:

Disaster! Where's the image gone? Well, when the object is active, the server is responsible for providing the screen rendering; when it is inactive, the container displays a **metafile** that shows where the object is and what it looks like. In terms of code, the *active* object displays the output of the **CGraphSrvView::OnDraw()** function, and the *inactive* object ends up displaying the output of server item class' **OnDraw()** function, **CGraphSrvSrvrItem::OnDraw()**. We haven't yet added the code to the server item to generate the metafile for the container, so we get a blank box.

> *The type of border around the object reflects its state. A border with grab handles denotes that the object is selected, while a border with hatching and handles indicates that the object is open for in-place editing. When an object is deselected, it will have no border. Note that the state of the object according to the server is distinct from the state of the server in charge of it, which may well still be loaded even if the object isn't selected at all.*

Improving the Server

We've got three things that we need to sort out:

- The menu being displayed isn't the one we want
- The object size isn't optimal
- The image disappears when the object isn't active

Let's look at these in order. Although we get GraphSrv's menu when the object is active in the container, it obviously isn't the correct menu, as it doesn't have any of the items we've added to support changing the graph type or importing and exporting data. The reason for this is that the server application has *four* menu resources, each of which is used in a particular context:

Menu Resource	Context
IDR_MAINFRAME	Menu shown when the application has no documents open
IDR_GRAPHSTYPE	Menu shown in the application when documents are open
IDR_GRAPHSTYPE_SRVR_EMB	Used by the container when an object is open without using in-place activation
IDR_GRAPHSTYPE_SRVR_IP	Used by the container when an object is open for in-place editing

Try It Out - Adding Server Menus

In order for the correct menu to be displayed when we use objects with containers, we need to duplicate the changes we made to the **IDR_GRAPHSTYPE** menu in the other two **IDR_GRAPHSTYPE_...** menus. This can be done simply by using the copy-and-paste functionality of the menu editor.

When you do this, you'll notice that the **IDR_GRAPHSTYPE_SRVR_EMB** menu is the same as the standard **IDR_GRAPHSTYPE** menu, but that the **..._IP** version is rather different. This is because while the first two are full menus, the in-place menu is a partial one that gets merged with the container's menu when the object is activated.

The **IDR_GRAPHSTYPE_SRVR_IP** menu is divided into three sections by two vertical bars; these sections typically consist of:

▶ Edit and View menus, like the ones displayed when files are open

▶ Object editing menus

▶ The Help menu

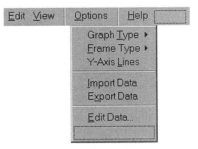

Our Options menu deals with object editing functions, and so should be placed in the middle section, between the two separators:

If you now build and test the server, embedding a GraphS Document object in Word as before, you should find that you can use the Options menu to change the style of the graph and import new datasets.

Another of the problems we noted when we embedded a graph into Word was the size of the object we ended up with, which was much too small. This size is determined by the answer the container gets from the server item representing the object when it calls the item's **OnGetExtent()** member function. As you can see from the code below, the default action is to return a size of 3000 by 3000 **HIMETRIC** units or, in other words, a 3cm square:

```
BOOL CGraphSrvSrvrItem::OnGetExtent(DVASPECT dwDrawAspect, CSize& rSize)
{
    // Most applications, like this one, only handle drawing the content
    //  aspect of the item.  If you wish to support other aspects, such
    //  as DVASPECT_THUMBNAIL (by overriding OnDrawEx), then this
    //  implementation of OnGetExtent should be modified to handle the
    //  additional aspect(s).

    if (dwDrawAspect != DVASPECT_CONTENT)
        return COleServerItem::OnGetExtent(dwDrawAspect, rSize);

    // CGraphSrvSrvrItem::OnGetExtent is called to get the extent in
    //  HIMETRIC units of the entire item.  The default implementation
    //  here simply returns a hard-coded number of units.

    CGraphSrvDoc* pDoc = GetDocument();
    ASSERT_VALID(pDoc);

    // TODO: replace this arbitrary size

    rSize = CSize(3000, 3000);    // 3000 x 3000 HIMETRIC units

    return TRUE;
}
```

Our graph objects consist of a single item - the graph itself - so it's reasonably easy to decide on a size to return. A size of 10000 by 6000 **HIMETRIC** units gives a suitable default size for the object:

```
rSize = CSize(10000, 6000);
```

If your application supports selecting part of the document, such as a range within a spreadsheet, or individual items within a drawing, then calculating the extent may be a considerably more complicated matter.

> *Some strange behavior can occur if you try to resize an embedded object. For instance, you may find that if you resize the object when it is selected but not active for editing, the object will stay the size you chose, and the metafile and active sizes will be the same. If, on the other hand, you try to resize it in the active state, you may well find that the container resets it to its previous size.*
>
> *In fact, it is up to each container how it controls the objects it hosts. Some containers regard it as their job to set the sizes of the objects, and any attempt to resize when the object's server is in control will get overridden when the container regains control.*

You may be wondering about the **DVASPECT** parameter. It's possible for the object to be displayed in any of several ways: in its normal state, as an icon, as a miniature (a 'thumbnail'), or in the form it takes when it prints. Each of these **aspects** will obviously have a different size, and we can check the first parameter to **OnGetExtent()** if we need to handle any of the other aspects. In this case, we don't, so all aspects other than 'normally displayed in a container', denoted by **DVASPECT_CONTENT**, are passed to the base class for default processing.

Try It Out - Providing the Metafile

We need to provide the metafile that the container displays when the inserted object is inactive. A metafile isn't a bunch of pixels, like a bitmap or GIF file, but a list of the GDI instructions that were used to create the image in the first place. These instructions can be 'replayed' to fit into any rectangle, which allows the container to draw the image into the space occupied by the embedded item without having to worry about scaling bitmaps.

The metafile is produced in the server item's **OnDraw()** function. Here's what the default code looks like:

```
BOOL CGraphSrvSrvrItem::OnDraw(CDC* pDC, CSize& rSize)
{
   // Remove this if you use rSize
   UNREFERENCED_PARAMETER(rSize);

   CGraphSrvDoc* pDoc = GetDocument();
   ASSERT_VALID(pDoc);

   // TODO: set mapping mode and extent
   //   (The extent is usually the same as the size returned from OnGetExtent)
   pDC->SetMapMode(MM_ANISOTROPIC);
   pDC->SetWindowOrg(0,0);
   pDC->SetWindowExt(3000, 3000);

   // TODO: add drawing code here.  Optionally, fill in the HIMETRIC extent.
   //   All drawing takes place in the metafile device context (pDC).

   return TRUE;
}
```

The first parameter is a device context – a *metafile* device context. Note the use of the **UNREFERENCED_PARAMETER()** macro, which stops the compiler complaining about unreferenced parameters. Delete this macro, replace the default size with a call to **OnGetExtent()**, and return the value in the **rSize** parameter, which gives the size at which the metafile should be drawn:

```
BOOL CGraphSrvSrvrItem::OnDraw(CDC* pDC, CSize& rSize)
{
   CGraphSrvDoc* pDoc = GetDocument();
   ASSERT_VALID(pDoc);

   // Get the size of the item, convert its coordinates, and use it to set
   // the extent
   CSize size;
   OnGetExtent(DVASPECT_CONTENT, size);
   rSize = size;
```

```
    pDC->SetMapMode(MM_ANISOTROPIC);
    pDC->HIMETRICtoLP(&size);
    pDC->SetWindowOrg(0,0);
    pDC->SetWindowExt(size);

    // TODO: add drawing code here.  Optionally, fill in the HIMETRIC extent.
    //  All drawing takes place in the metafile device context (pDC).

    return TRUE;
}
```

That code makes sure that the metafile will be drawn at the correct size. We now need to add the code to draw the graph using the device context we've been given, so make up a **CRect** object with the same dimensions as the object's extent, and pass it along with the device context to the graph object's **Display()** function:

```
BOOL CGraphSrvSrvrItem::OnDraw(CDC* pDC, CSize& rSize)
{
    CGraphSrvDoc* pDoc = GetDocument();
    ASSERT_VALID(pDoc);

    // Get the size of the item, convert its coordinates, and use it to set
    // the extent
    CSize size;
    OnGetExtent(DVASPECT_CONTENT, size);
    rSize = size;

    pDC->SetMapMode(MM_ANISOTROPIC);
    pDC->HIMETRICtoLP(&size);
    pDC->SetWindowOrg(0,0);
    pDC->SetWindowExt(size);

    // Create a display rectangle, and tell the object to render itself
    CRect area(0, 0, size.cx, size.cy);
    pDoc->GetGraph()->Display(area, pDC);

    return TRUE;
}
```

Once again, because we make reference to the **CGraph** class (by calling **GetGraph()**), you'll need to add **#include**s for **Graph.h** and **fstream.h** to **SrvrItem.cpp**. When you rebuild and test the project, you should find that you now get a metafile image displayed in the container when the object is inactive.

Further Enhancements

We can now embed objects in a container using the Insert | Object... menu item, but there are a couple of other standard ways in which objects can be introduced into a container. We'll deal with the first of those - copy and paste - now.

Try It Out - Adding Support for Copy and Paste

1 Adding support for copy and paste is very simple. Provide a handler for the Edit | Copy operation in the view class, **CGraphSrvView**, and edit the handler code as follows:

```
void CGraphSrvView::OnEditCopy()
{
    // Copy the whole of the document to the clipboard
    CGraphSrvSrvrItem itm(GetDocument());
    itm.CopyToClipboard(FALSE);
}
```

You'll find you also need to include the header file for the server item class, **SrvrItem.h**. The **FALSE** argument to the **CopyToClipboard()** function means that we aren't (yet) supporting linking.

The **CopyToClipboard()** function ends up getting the server item to store itself on the clipboard, using the **CGraphSrvSrvrItem::Serialize()** function. The default action is to check whether it's being called for a linked or embedded item, and to call the document's **Serialize()** function in the case of embedded items, on the assumption that you'll want to handle linked items (which probably represent part of the document) in a different manner. At the moment we don't support linking, so the default code will work just as it is:

```
void CGraphSrvSrvrItem::Serialize(CArchive& ar)
{
    // CGraphSrvSrvrItem::Serialize will be called by the framework if
    //  the item is copied to the clipboard.  This can happen automatically
    //  through the OLE callback OnGetClipboardData.  A good default for
    //  the embedded item is simply to delegate to the document's Serialize
    //  function.  If you support links, then you will want to serialize
    //  just a portion of the document.

    if (!IsLinkedItem())
    {
        CGraphSrvDoc* pDoc = GetDocument();
        ASSERT_VALID(pDoc);
        pDoc->Serialize(ar);
    }
}
```

Rebuild the project, start it up as a stand-alone program, and use Edit | Copy to put the current graph on to the clipboard. You should now be able to use the Edit | Paste Special... menu item in Word (and other containers) to paste an object from the clipboard. Notice that the Paste Link radio button is grayed out, as we haven't implemented linking yet.

2 If you play with the Options menu and try changing the graph type, you'll come across a strange quirk of behavior. While the object is in-place active it shows the changes you've made, but when you deactivate it, Word displays the original metafile. What's going on?

In a non-OLE MFC application, when a change is made to the document, it calls **UpdateAllViews()** in order to make sure that the views are kept up to date. When dealing with linked items, we need to perform an equivalent operation by calling **UpdateAllItems()** to get all linked items to update themselves.

We haven't dealt with linked items yet, but a side effect of this call will ensure that a new metafile gets generated and passed to the container, rather than letting the container use its cached one. All you need to do is add a call to **UpdateAllItems()** after each call to **UpdateAllViews()**. There are eight calls to be added. Here's an example:

```
void CGraphSrvDoc::OnOptionsGraphtypePie()
{
   if (!m_pGraph->IsPieChart())
   {
      m_pGraph->SetPieChart();
      SetModifiedFlag(TRUE);
      UpdateAllViews(NULL);
      UpdateAllItems(NULL);
   }
}
```

That will make sure that the metafile displays properly. Before we move on, however, let's look a little more closely at what's happening in the copy function. This edit operation is a prime example of MFC providing a lot of hidden functionality for you - the code we've added is very simple, but there's more going on under the surface, and it's worth understanding what's really taking place.

In the **OnEditCopy()** handler, we create a server item whose purpose is to represent the object we're about to copy to the clipboard. We then call the item's **CopyToClipboard()** member function which creates an MFC **data object** to represent the data. Data objects are implemented by the **IDataObject** interface, which provides methods for data transfer and notification. MFC provides two classes that implement **IDataObject**, one for each end of a container/server connection. I'll say a lot more about data objects in Chapter 6, when we look at container/server interaction.

Server-side data objects are provided by **COleDataSource**, which can store data in a number of formats, just like normal clipboard operation. Rather like the way Windows messages come in 'standard' and 'custom' flavors, there are a number of standard formats, but you can add your own custom ones, too. If you don't add any others, you'll get data items placed on the clipboard in the three standard formats, each of which is represented by a symbol:

- The **CF_EMBEDSOURCE** format, which represents the native data for your object. The container doesn't have to know anything about this data - all it knows is that it's an embedded object, and so it has to call a server to deal with it.

- The **CF_METAFILEPICT** format, containing the metafile used to display the inactive object.

- The **CF_OBJECTDESCRIPTOR** format, which contains a description of the object, such as its drawing aspect, size and status flags.

If you've enabled linking in the server (as we will very shortly), you'll get a **CF_LINKSOURCE** item as well. The container application can construct an embedded item from the data on the clipboard, as well as storing away the metafile for use when the item is inactive.

Try It Out - Adding Support for Linking

The last thing we'll do in this chapter is to add support for pasting a link to an object, rather than pasting the object itself. In fact, there's very little work to do in order to make the object linkable - you just add a call to **SetItemName()** to the server item's constructor.

1   Each server item must have a unique name if it's going to be a link, because there has to be a way to refer back to the item when the link is activated. In our case, we only have one possible object to link - the whole graph - so we'll pick a simple name: **Graph1**.

```
CGraphSrvSrvrItem::CGraphSrvSrvrItem(CGraphSrvDoc* pContainerDoc)
    : COleServerItem(pContainerDoc, TRUE)
{
    // Set the item name for linking
    SetItemName("Graph1");
}
```

In other applications, the user may be able to select some subset of the document, such as a range from a spreadsheet or some objects from a drawing program. The server items for these have to be given unique names so that they can be identified later when the link needs to be edited. A suitable name for a range of spreadsheet cells might be **A2-B4**, denoting the block of cells whose opposite corners are A2 and B4, and you could modify the constructor for the server item class to pass in the appropriate information.

2   Adding the name to the constructor makes the item linkable, but we also need to modify a couple of other places in the code to support the rest of the linking process. The first is in the view's **OnEditCopy()** function, where we change the call to **CopyToClipboard()** to indicate that we now support linking:

```
void CGraphSrvView::OnEditCopy()
{
    // Copy the whole of the document to the clipboard
    CGraphSrvSrvrItem itm(GetDocument());
    itm.CopyToClipboard(TRUE);
}
```

3   The other bit of code to mend is in the server item's **Serialize()** function. Embedded items always want the whole document serialized, but linked items might need different code in order to retrieve just a portion of the document, hence the **IsLinkedItem()** check. In our case, we're serializing the entire document in both cases, so we can remove the check:

```
void CGraphSrvSrvrItem::Serialize(CArchive& ar)
{
    // CGraphSrvSrvrItem::Serialize will be called by the framework if
    // the item is copied to the clipboard.  This can happen automatically
    // through the OLE callback OnGetClipboardData.  A good default for
    // the embedded item is simply to delegate to the document's Serialize
    // function.  If you support links, then you will want to serialize
    // just a portion of the document.

// if (!IsLinkedItem())
// {
        CGraphSrvDoc* pDoc = GetDocument();
        ASSERT_VALID(pDoc);
        pDoc->Serialize(ar);
// }
}
```

4 Try rebuilding and running the application, saving the document, copying it to the clipboard, and switching to your container. You'll find that the Paste Link radio button in the Paste Special dialog is enabled, because you can now link to the saved file. You'll be able to paste a linked object into the container, but you won't be able to activate it by double-clicking.

> *There are two things that could go wrong at this stage. Firstly, not all containers will allow you to paste the linked object with the server in its present form. This is because they try to activate the object immediately, and so fall foul of the same problem that prevents double-click activation. I'll be dealing with this presently.*
>
> *The second possible cause of failure is that you're only able to paste a link to a document if you've saved it in a file, because a link has to be to something in a file. If you haven't saved the document, you won't be able to link to it.*

The container has a copy of the name that we gave to the item in the server item's constructor. When it's time to edit the object, the container calls the server document's **OnGetLinkedItem()** function with the name of the object, and the document searches its list of items (not a very taxing search, in our case), returning a pointer to a server item which represents the thing we want, which in this case is the whole document.

5 If you now use ClassWizard to provide the **OnGetLinkedItem()** function, the default implementation calls the base class function and returns any **COleServerItem** that it gives you, like this:

```
COleServerItem* CGraphSrvDoc::OnGetLinkedItem(LPCTSTR lpszItemName)
{
    // TODO: Add your specialized code here and/or call the base class

    return COleServerDoc::OnGetLinkedItem(lpszItemName);
}
```

Sadly, that isn't going to work here. The act of constructing a server item adds it to a list maintained by the document, but it turns out there are two flavors of server item: permanent and temporary. A flag on the **COleServerItem** constructor determines whether the item is to be preserved with the document, or whether the framework can delete it when the link operation is over. The constructor of our derived class **CGraphSrvSrvrItem** sets the flag to **TRUE**, so that server items will always be temporary, and the document won't keep a record of them:

```
CGraphSrvSrvrItem::CGraphSrvSrvrItem(CGraphSrvDoc* pContainerDoc)
   : COleServerItem(pContainerDoc, TRUE)
{
   // Set the item name for linking
   SetItemName("Graph1");
}
```

6 We could modify the **COleServerItem** constructor to pass a **FALSE** flag; in that case, all the server items we created would be saved by the document, and we would be responsible for deleting them when the document is destroyed. In this simple example, it gives us no real advantage to save the objects, so we'll keep the default behavior.

This being the case, we need to provide the object ourselves, but it does no harm to keep the base-class call in there, just in case someone does want modify the program in the future to store server items:

```
COleServerItem* CGraphSrvDoc::OnGetLinkedItem(LPCTSTR lpszItemName)
{
   // See if the base class has the item
   COleServerItem* pItem = COleServerDoc::OnGetLinkedItem(lpszItemName);

   if (pItem == NULL)
   {
      pItem = new CGraphSrvSrvrItem(this);
      ASSERT(pItem);
   }

   return pItem;
}
```

The **CGraphSrvSrvrItem** returned by this routine is used by the container to retrieve the server data, via the **Serialize()** function, and the metafile, via **OnDraw()**.

And there you have it. You'll now be able to paste a link into a container, and activate it by double-clicking. The *other* way we might want to get an object into a container - drag and drop - will be covered in Chapter 6, when we look at the interaction between servers and containers.

Summary

MFC uses two classes, **COleServerDoc** and **COleServerItem**, to handle the COM requirements of an OLE server. The document class, **COleServerDoc**, can store a list of server and client items.

An object that's provided by an OLE server and displayed by a container has to be maintained by the two applications acting in concert. This is done by the use of server and client items, which implement each end of the link between the server and container.

To a skeleton application, we've added some of the features required of a real server, such as providing editing functions, linking support, and supplying the metafile to a container. There are still a few things we could add in the area of data transfer, and we'll cover these in a couple of chapters' time.

In this chapter, we've seen how to start developing an OLE server with MFC, and we've got quite a way towards a reasonably functional application. The next step is to provide something into which graph objects can be inserted - in other words, a container.

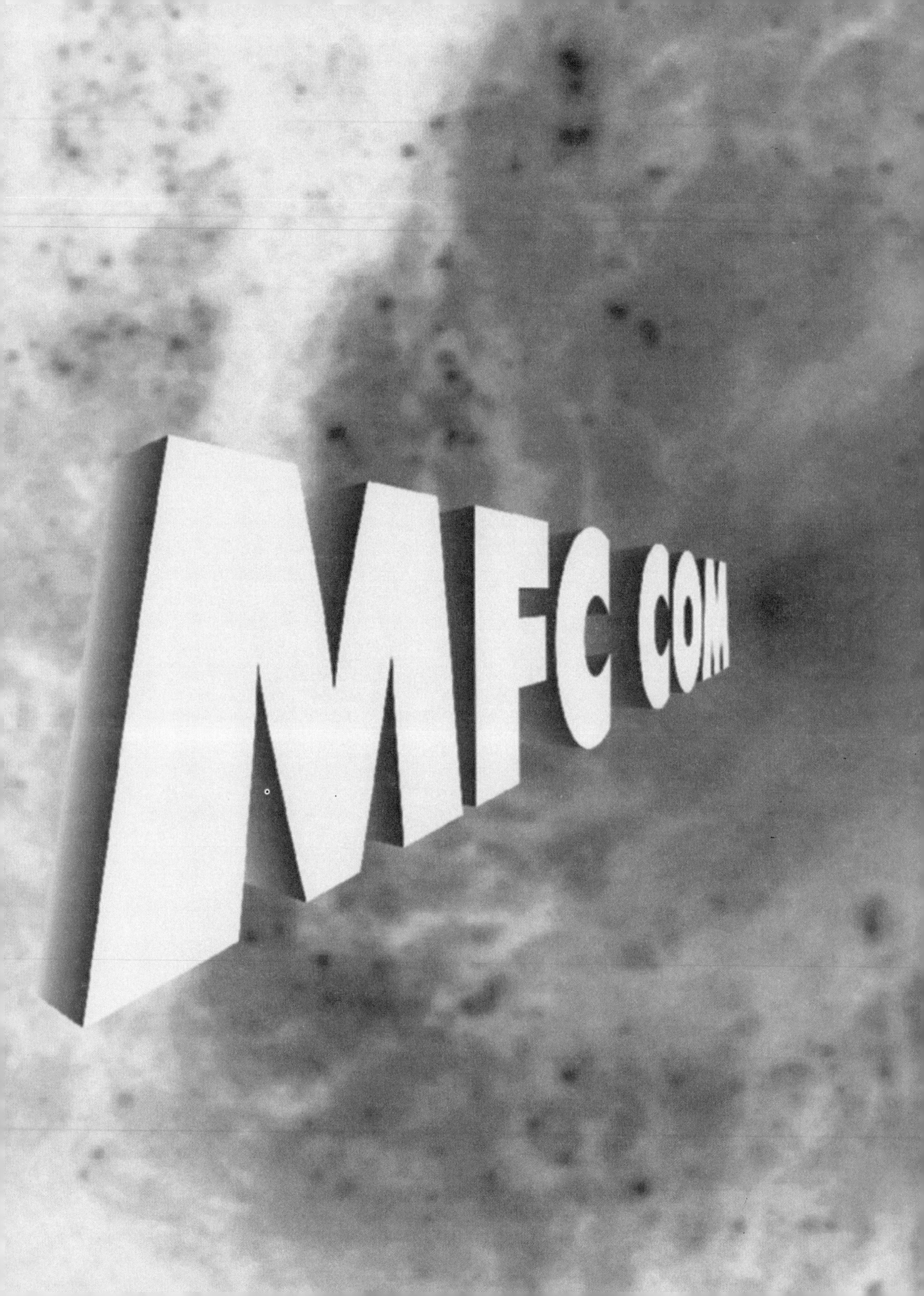
MFC COM

OLE Containers

In the last chapter, we saw how to write a basic OLE server application using MFC. In this chapter, we'll look at how to produce an OLE container application, and in the next chapter we'll look at how servers and containers work together. Hopefully, you can see a logical sequence starting to emerge!

How OLE Containers are Implemented in MFC

OLE containers can be quite complex to program, because of the range of functionality that they have to support. Exactly what they need to do is highly dependent on the nature of the program, but a container may well need to:

- Display embedded and linked objects in its view
- Provide visual feedback on the current state of the object
- Allow the user to move and resize objects
- Allow in-place editing for objects that support it, including menu and toolbar negotiation with the server

MFC gives you a basic structure and a certain amount of help, but because it doesn't know exactly how you want to display and handle the embedded and linked objects, you have to do some of the work yourself. Just as we saw with document servers, the container side of the OLE server/container structure is handled by a set of interfaces that are implemented in custom MFC classes. OLE containers are implemented by two MFC classes.

The first class is **COleDocument**, which is used in place of **CDocument** as the base document class for containers managing embedded and simple linked objects. The second class is **COleClientItem**, which provides the client end of the conversation with the server. If the server has been written with MFC, the object at the other end will be a **COleServerItem**, which we discussed in the previous chapter.

The default view class, as created by AppWizard, holds one **COleClientItem** object to represent the currently selected object.

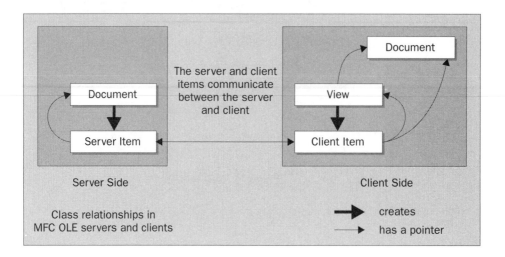

The server and client items communicate between the server and client

Server Side

Client Side

Class relationships in MFC OLE servers and clients

→ creates
→ has a pointer

The COleClientItem Class

The client item class is derived from **COleClientItem**, and one of these is created for each new embedded or linked object in the container document. The item performs two functions: first, it serves as an anchor for the item in the document; and second, it communicates with the server item representing the object at the server end.

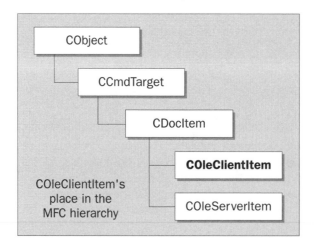

COleClientItem's place in the MFC hierarchy

The MFC base class which implements the client item is called **COleClientItem**, *but the class derived by AppWizard to represent the client item in your container application is called* **CxxxCntrItem** *(rather than* **CxxxClientItem**)*, which sometimes causes confusion.*

COleClientItem's Interfaces

The class implements three COM interfaces: **IOleClientSite**, **IAdviseSink**, and **IOleInPlaceSite**.

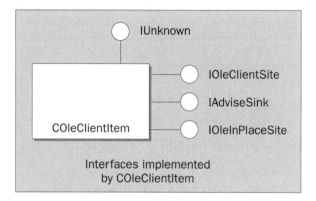

IOleClientSite provides communication between the container and the client item. The server for the item can use this interface to obtain information about the site of the item in the container, and to pass information to the container, such as requests to show the object. The container needs one client site for each item.

IAdviseSink sets up a mechanism so that the container can be notified of changes to the object. The interface contains five functions:

- **OnDataChange()** is called when the content of the object has changed
- **OnViewChange()** is called when the object's view has changed
- **OnRename()** is called when the object has been renamed
- **OnSave()** is called when the object has been saved
- **OnClose()** is sent when the object is closing - when it is going from the active to the loaded state

When a connection is made between the container's **IAdviseSink** and the object's **IDataObject** interface, the object can use these functions to notify the container of changes.

The **IOleInPlaceSite** interface is provided to manage in-place objects, and manages communication between the client site (**IOleClientSite**) and the container. For instance, the **OnInPlaceActivate()** and **OnUIActivate()** functions notify the container that one of its objects is about to be activated; in the latter case, the object is going to become *UI*-active, so the main menu is going to be replaced by a composite menu. The **OnInPlaceDeactivate()** and **OnUIDeactivate()** functions tell the container that one of its objects is about to be deactivated, and in the second case that the container needs to reinstall its user interface.

COleClientItem's Class Members

Now let's take a look at **COleClientItem** itself. It's a *very* large class, bigger even than its server counterpart **COleServerItem**, with over 80 member functions! Here's a brief overview of the main groups the functions fall into.

Clipboard and Data Access Operations

Five functions support clipboard operations relating to the item. **CanPaste()** and **CanPasteLink()** tell whether the clipboard contains an object which is embedded or static (in the case of **CanPaste()**) or linked; static items contain presentation data only, and cannot be edited. We can copy the item data to the clipboard using **CopyToClipboard()**, and customize the data which gets written to the clipboard using **GetClipboardData()**. Finally, **DoDragDrop()** performs a drag and drop operation.

As for data access operations, **AttachDataObject()** gives access to the OLE data in the object, by initializing a **COleDataObject** object. **GetDocument()** returns a pointer to the **COleDocument** object which contains this item.

General Operations

This group contains six functions, including:

▶ **Close()**, which closes the link to the server

▶ **Delete()**, which deletes embedded items or closes linked ones

▶ **Run()**, which runs the application associated with the item

▶ **Draw()**, which draws the item

Activation Operations And Verbs

A number of member functions provide communications with the server object. In particular, the object can be told to **activate** or **deactivate** itself, and that brings us on to the topic of **verbs**.

Consider an object that represents a piece of text. There probably isn't much you'd want to do with such an object apart from edit it. How about a sound clip? Most of the time you'll want to play it to hear the sound, but the server might also be able to *edit* sounds, so you'd want to give the user the option of either playing *or* editing the sound clip.

These actions are called **verbs** in OLE-speak, and the dominant one - 'play' in the case of the sound clip, or 'edit' for the text object - is called the **primary verb**. This is the action that's performed when the user double-clicks on an object in a container. Other, secondary verbs can be accessed via menu items, either on the frame's menu, or on a local menu presented when the user right-clicks on the object.

The **DoVerb()** function takes a numeric value which specifies a verb and calls the **OnDoVerb()** member of the corresponding **COleServerItem** to perform the action. The verb can be one of the built-in actions - the primary verb, the secondary verb, activate the object in-place, edit in a separate window, or hide the object - and it's also possible for an object to define its own verbs, which can be retrieved by a client.

DoVerb() also handles any exceptions which may occur by displaying a standard dialog box. If you want to handle exceptions yourself, use **Activate()** instead, which is what **DoVerb()** calls. It follows that **DoVerb()** and **Activate()** both call the server item's **OnDoVerb()** member in the end; as you can see from the listing below, there isn't much mystery to it:

```
void COleServerItem::OnDoVerb(LONG iVerb)
{
   switch (iVerb)
   {
   // open - maps to OnOpen
   case OLEIVERB_OPEN:
   case -OLEIVERB_OPEN-1:   // allows positive OLEIVERB_OPEN-1 in registry
      OnOpen();
      break;

   // primary, show, and unknown map to OnShow
   case OLEIVERB_PRIMARY:   // OLEIVERB_PRIMARY is 0 and "Edit" in registry
   case OLEIVERB_SHOW:
      OnShow();
      break;

   // hide maps to OnHide
   case OLEIVERB_HIDE:
   case -OLEIVERB_HIDE-1:   // allows positive OLEIVERB_HIDE-1 in registry
      OnHide();
      break;

   default:
      // negative verbs not understood should return E_NOTIMPL
      if (iVerb < 0)
         AfxThrowOleException(E_NOTIMPL);

      // positive verb not processed --
      //   according to OLE spec, primary verb should be executed
      //   instead.
      OnDoVerb(OLEIVERB_PRIMARY);

      // also, OLEOBJ_S_INVALIDVERB should be returned.
      AfxThrowOleException(OLEOBJ_S_INVALIDVERB);
   }
}
```

The standard verbs, which have IDs of zero or less, cause the corresponding **On...()** function to be called. Any negative verb which isn't understood causes an **E_NOTIMPL** exception to be thrown, while positive numbered verbs which haven't been recognized cause the primary verb to be executed instead, via a recursive call to the handler.

You'd override this routine if you wanted to add other verbs, and also if your primary verb wasn't going to call **OnShow()** to edit the object in-place.

Linked and Embedded Item Functions

Some functions are provided to assist in working with linked and embedded items, such as setting the text which will be used as the window title when an embedded item is in-place edited, and setting its bounding rectangle.

For linked items, it's possible to update the metafile that's used to display the item, and to check whether the display data is up-to-date with the actual source of the link.

Status Functions

There are a number of functions (sixteen in MFC 4.2) which return status information about the item. For example, **IsActive()** tells you whether the object is in-place active (being edited), and **IsModified()** tells you whether the item has been modified since it was last saved. **GetType()** tells you whether the object is linked, embedded or static. As you might expect, a static object is one that is for display only, and cannot be edited.

The purpose of most of these functions is pretty self-explanatory, but note that there are two functions to return the object's extent (in other words, its bounding rectangle) - **GetExtent()** and **GetCachedExtent()**. The difference between them is that **GetExtent()** retrieves the object's 'native size' (how big the server thinks the object ought to be) while **GetCachedExtent()** uses the saved extent information from the last time the object was drawn. The MFC documentation says that **GetExtent()** shouldn't be called if you need to find the object's size in another OLE handler routine, such as **OnChange()**, when you might be in the middle of changing the object; in that case, you should use **GetCachedExtent()** instead.

Callback Functions

COleClientItem has a number of functions that are called by the framework in order to tell the object that something has happened. The most important of these from the point of view of the MFC programmer are:

- **OnChange()**, which is called by the framework when the object is modified or saved, or when the connection is closed.

- **OnChangeItemPosition()**, called when the object has moved or changed its size.

- **OnGetItemPosition()** must be implemented to provide the position of the object within the container view.

- **OnActivate()**, called to warn the item that it has just been activated. AppWizard generates code to close any other currently active item.

- **OnDeactivateUI()** is called when an in-place edit is terminated. The base class implementation restores the application's user interface. AppWizard generates code that will cause inside-out objects to hide their user interface.

> *Microsoft talks of servers as being either 'outside-in' or 'inside-out'. When you insert something like an Excel spreadsheet into a container, Excel is only loaded when the user wants to edit the object; this is called* **outside-in activation.** *Many lightweight objects, such as ActiveX controls, want to have their servers loaded the whole time that the object is visible, regardless of whether it is being used or not; this is called* **inside-out activation.** *The latter may not be supported by some older containers.*

There are a number of other callback functions (14 in all) which can be overridden if the need arises.

More Complex Containers - COleLinkingDoc

The combination of classes derived from **COleDocument** and **COleClientItem** does well for many containers, but sometimes an application may want to create more complex links. For example, an application may want to grab a link to a picture embedded in my container, without wanting to know where the original object lives. It's to cope with these situations that **COleLinkingDoc** has been provided.

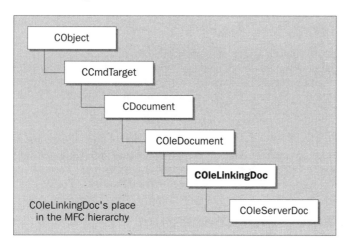

COleLinkingDoc's place in the MFC hierarchy

COleLinkingDoc's Interfaces

COleLinkingDoc implements **IPersistFile**, **IOleContainer**, **IOleItemContainer** and **IParseDisplayName**. Let's take a quick tour of these interfaces to find out what they're for.

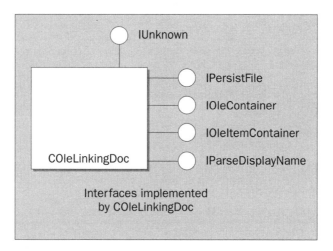

Interfaces implemented by COleLinkingDoc

I mentioned object persistence in the previous chapter, showing how **COleServerDoc** implements the **IPersistStorage** interface. **IPersistFile** is similar, indicating that this document can serialize itself to a disk file rather than a storage. The document object is responsible for handling the actual opening of the file.

IOleContainer supports features such as the enumeration of objects in a compound document, and the ability to lock the container so that silent updates of link sources can be carried out safely, by ensuring that the container keeps running.

The other two interfaces are mainly concerned with monikers, the objects that provide a link between the name of a linked item and where it actually lives. **IOleItemContainer** (not to be confused with **IOleContainer**!) is actually used to get the item named by a moniker, while **IParseDisplayName** takes a human-readable name and converts it into a moniker.

COleLinkingDoc's Class Members

Unlike **COleServerDoc**, this class has few members. Two functions handle registering and de-registering the document with the OLE run-time system, while another two are callback functions. **OnFindEmbeddedItem()** is called to pass back a pointer to a given **COleClientItem** object, given a name string, and **OnFindLinkedItem()** does the same for linked items, this time passing back a pointer to the corresponding **COleServerItem** object.

I won't go into this class in any great detail, because you won't find **COleLinkingDoc** used in an application generated by AppWizard. All AppWizard-generated applications use **COleDocument**, and you'll need to use this class manually if you want to implement advanced linking.

The MFC Container Implementation

Now we've seen something of how OLE implements containers, let's move on to look at how MFC works this out in its document/view architecture. AppWizard will generate you a skeleton container, but you'll be left with quite a lot of work to do in order to make even a basic container application functional. Why is this?

Well, the basis of the container application is that it provides you with a view in which OLE objects can be embedded, but it has no idea what you are trying to accomplish in your application. Because of this, there's very little help that it can give you in providing code for mouse operations - positioning, drawing and things like that - which depend completely upon the nature of your application.

If you generate a skeleton container application using AppWizard, you'll get numerous source files generated. You may care to generate a skeleton application, so that you can browse through it as you're reading. If you call the application **Cont**, you'll have a head start on the practical section later on, as that is what we'll call our sample container application.

You'll need to make the following selections in the AppWizard dialog steps:

- *Step 1:* Select <u>S</u>ingle document as the application type.

- *Step 2:* We don't need any database support, so you can leave the default option.

- *Step 3:* Choose <u>C</u>ontainer as the compound document support type, and ensure that compound file support is selected. There's no need to choose support for either A<u>u</u>tomation or ActiveX Cont<u>r</u>ols in this application.

- *Step 4:* Click on the <u>A</u>dvanced... button, and give the application a file extension. I chose **cnn**, mainly because it doesn't clash with anything else on my system!

Steps 5 & 6 need no changes, so you can click on Finish and let AppWizard get on with generating the skeleton files. Here's a list of the source files that are of interest from our point of view:

File	Description
Cont.cpp	The file containing the **CWinApp**-derived application class and the **CAboutDlg** class. OLE initialization is performed here.
MainFrm.cpp	The SDI main frame for the application.
ContDoc.cpp	The document class, derived from **COleDocument**.
ContView.cpp	The view class, derived from **CView**.
CntrItem.cpp	The container item class, derived from **COleClientItem**.

Let's look at each of the classes contained in these files in turn.

The Application Class

The changes made to the application class are similar in kind to those made for a server application, but the task is quite a lot simpler as none of the registry manipulation associated with the server needs to be done. Unlike a server, a container application needn't be a COM object in its own right (unless, of course, it's a server as well as a container). In that case, the application doesn't need to have a CLSID, and as it has no COM functionality, it doesn't need to register itself.

The first thing that's done in the **InitInstance()** member function is to initialize the OLE DLLs, and exit if initialization fails:

```
BOOL CContApp::InitInstance()
{
    // Initialize OLE libraries
    if (!AfxOleInit())
    {
        AfxMessageBox(IDP_OLE_INIT_FAILED);
        return FALSE;
    }
```

After creating the document template, the routine puts the OLE container information into the template:

```
    CSingleDocTemplate* pDocTemplate;
    pDocTemplate = new CSingleDocTemplate(
        IDR_MAINFRAME,
        RUNTIME_CLASS(CContDoc),
        RUNTIME_CLASS(CMainFrame),          // main SDI frame window
        RUNTIME_CLASS(CContView));
    pDocTemplate->SetContainerInfo(IDR_CNTR_INPLACE);
    AddDocTemplate(pDocTemplate);
```

The call to **SetContainerInfo()** informs the template of the resources which will be used when an object is in-place activated. The default resource ID is provided by AppWizard, and specifies a menu that will be merged with the in-place menu provided by the server when the object is activated. You can edit this menu as you wish, to provide the functionality that you want to be available when a server is active.

The Document Class

There is very little visible difference between the document class for a container application and an ordinary one, apart from the fact that it's derived from **COleDocument** rather than **CDocument**. We've already seen how the OLE document classes store a list of **CDocItem** objects, and this is reflected in the document's **Serialize()** function:

```
void CContDoc::Serialize(CArchive& ar)
{
    if (ar.IsStoring())
    {
        // TODO: add storing code here
    }
    else
    {
        // TODO: add loading code here
    }

    // Calling the base class COleDocument enables serialization
    //  of the container document's COleClientItem objects.
    COleDocument::Serialize(ar);
}
```

The base class **Serialize()** function is called in order to serialize the document items, and this call will also handle all the communication which is needed with the server and the items it holds.

The Client Item Class

As noted above, the client item class is derived from **COleClientItem**, and the document holds one of these objects for each embedded or linked object. The client item class contains nineteen **On...()** functions, which are called when the framework needs to interact with the item. The following paragraphs discuss the most important of them.

OnChange() is called by the framework when the state of an item being edited changes, and causes the document to redraw all views of the item. We'll look at the details of this function when we write a container application later in the chapter.

OnChangeItemPosition() is called when the size or position of the item changes, while **OnGetItemPosition()** is called to return the position and size of the item.

OnActivate() is called when the item has been activated for in-place editing, but before its user interface elements (menu and toolbar) have been put in place; **OnActivateUI()** is called when that happens. The function checks whether there is already an in-place active item, and closes it if there is, as it only wants to allow one such item per view. After that, it calls the base class **OnActivate()**, which in turn calls back to **OnChange()** to signal that the item's state has changed.

OnDeactivateUI() is called when the user deactivates the object, typically by pressing the *Esc* key. The function calls the base class implementation and then hides any menus and toolbars created by the object, returning the container's UI to its normal state.

The **Serialize()** function works very nearly as normal, except that it first calls the base class serialization function. It's important to do this first, because the base class function sets up the pointer to the item's document, which is available through the **GetDocument()** function. This behavior is in contrast to the container's document class **Serialize()** function, where the base class function gets called last.

The View Class

The container's purpose is to hold and display linked or embedded items, so it's not surprising that there are quite a few changes made to the view class. The following listing highlights the OLE-related additions and changes to the class:

```
class CContView : public CView
{
protected: // create from serialization only
    CContView();
    DECLARE_DYNCREATE(CContView)

// Attributes
public:
    CContDoc* GetDocument();
    // m_pSelection holds the selection to the current CContCntrItem.
    // For many applications, such a member variable isn't adequate to
    //  represent a selection, such as a multiple selection or a selection
    //  of objects that are not CContCntrItem objects.  This selection
    //  mechanism is provided just to help you get started.

    // TODO: replace this selection mechanism with one appropriate to your app.
    CContCntrItem* m_pSelection;

// Operations
public:

// Overrides
    // ClassWizard generated virtual function overrides
    //{{AFX_VIRTUAL(CContView)
    public:
    virtual void OnDraw(CDC* pDC);  // overridden to draw this view
    virtual BOOL PreCreateWindow(CREATESTRUCT& cs);
    protected:
    virtual void OnInitialUpdate(); // called first time after construct
    virtual BOOL OnPreparePrinting(CPrintInfo* pInfo);
    virtual void OnBeginPrinting(CDC* pDC, CPrintInfo* pInfo);
    virtual void OnEndPrinting(CDC* pDC, CPrintInfo* pInfo);
    virtual BOOL IsSelected(const CObject* pDocItem) const;// Container support
    //}}AFX_VIRTUAL

// Implementation
public:
    virtual ~CContView();
#ifdef _DEBUG
    virtual void AssertValid() const;
    virtual void Dump(CDumpContext& dc) const;
#endif

protected:

// Generated message map functions
protected:
```

```
//{{AFX_MSG(CContView)
    // NOTE - the ClassWizard will add and remove member functions here.
    //    DO NOT EDIT what you see in these blocks of generated code !
    afx_msg void OnDestroy();
    afx_msg void OnSetFocus(CWnd* pOldWnd);
    afx_msg void OnSize(UINT nType, int cx, int cy);
    afx_msg void OnInsertObject();
    afx_msg void OnCancelEditCntr();
//}}AFX_MSG
    DECLARE_MESSAGE_MAP()
};
```

The data member **m_pSelection** points to a client item. The default mechanism is initially to set it to **NULL**, and whenever an object is inserted into the container, to set it to point to the client item which is managing the object. In a more fully featured container program that implemented mouse handling, you'd change the code to use this data item to point to the currently selected item. Note the comments above the declaration of **m_pSelection**; this is the default way of representing a selection, and may well be replaced in more sophisticated applications.

The **OnDraw()** provided by AppWizard only draws the item pointed to by **m_pSelection**; if the variable is currently **NULL**, the function searches the item list to find the first item, and draws it.

```
void CContView::OnDraw(CDC* pDC)
{
   CContDoc* pDoc = GetDocument();
   ASSERT_VALID(pDoc);

   // TODO: add draw code for native data here
   // TODO: also draw all OLE items in the document

   // Draw the selection at an arbitrary position.  This code should be
   //   removed once your real drawing code is implemented.  This position
   //   corresponds exactly to the rectangle returned by CContCntrItem,
   //   to give the effect of in-place editing.

   // TODO: remove this code when final draw code is complete.

   if (m_pSelection == NULL)
   {
      POSITION pos = pDoc->GetStartPosition();
      m_pSelection = (CContCntrItem*)pDoc->GetNextClientItem(pos);
   }
   if (m_pSelection != NULL)
      m_pSelection->Draw(pDC, CRect(10, 10, 210, 210));
}
```

In the skeleton application, the first item in the list will be the last item added to the container; in a real-world container, this routine would draw *all* the visible items, as well as the container's own native data.

The **COleClientItem** object pointed to by **m_pSelection** is given an arbitrary rectangle in which to draw itself, which is why all new objects end up positioned on top of one another, at least to begin with. The **Draw()** operation provides an image by replaying the metafile which was created for the item by the server program, as described in the last chapter.

The **WM_SETFOCUS** message needs special handling in the **OnSetFocus()** function, since if an item is being in-place edited, its window (rather than the container itself) should be passed the focus. The function first gets a pointer to the current in-place active item, and then gets a pointer to its window. If both these steps work, the focus is set to the item's window; otherwise, it's passed to the view.

The other message that needs special handling is **WM_SIZE**. **OnSize()** resizes the window, and then passes the information to the in-place active item so that it can resize itself accordingly.

OnCancelEditCntr() provides a handler for the *Esc* key, which calls **COleClientItem::Close()** to deactivate any item undergoing in-place editing.

OnInsertObject() is a handler for the I̲nsert | O̲bject... menu item. This is one of the more complicated functions in the container application, handling as it does the whole process of obtaining and inserting an object into the container. Here's a walk-through of the function:

```
void CContView::OnInsertObject()
{
   // Invoke the standard Insert Object dialog box to obtain information
   //  for new CContCntrItem object.
   COleInsertDialog dlg;
   if (dlg.DoModal() != IDOK)
      return;
```

The function first puts up a standard Insert Object dialog. This is one of the OLE common dialogs, used to perform tasks normally associated with OLE-enabled applications. The dialog scans the registry for objects that can be inserted, displays a list of names, and the user picks the name of the type of object they wish to insert.

The next step is to create a new client item to represent this object. The act of creating the object adds it to the list maintained by the container's document:

```
   BeginWaitCursor();

   CContCntrItem* pItem = NULL;
   TRY
   {
      // Create new item connected to this document.
      CContDoc* pDoc = GetDocument();
      ASSERT_VALID(pDoc);
      pItem = new CContCntrItem(pDoc);
      ASSERT_VALID(pItem);
```

The function then tries to initialize the object using the data retrieved from the dialog. If this doesn't work, it throws an exception:

```
      // Initialize the item from the dialog data.
      if (!dlg.CreateItem(pItem))
         AfxThrowMemoryException();  // any exception will do
      ASSERT_VALID(pItem);
```

Any **CException**-derived exception can be thrown, and will be caught by the **CATCH** block later in the function. If the object was to be a new object, rather than one inserted from a file, then the function needs to start up the server so the user can edit the new object:

```
// If item created from class list (not from file) then launch
//  the server to edit the item.
if (dlg.GetSelectionType() == COleInsertDialog::createNewItem)
   pItem->DoVerb(OLEIVERB_SHOW, this);

ASSERT_VALID(pItem);
```

The final action is to set the selection to the last item inserted. This can be changed by the user to implement the desired selection mechanism.

```
// As an arbitrary user interface design, this sets the selection
//  to the last item inserted.

// TODO: reimplement selection as appropriate for your application

m_pSelection = pItem;   // set selection to last inserted item
pDoc->UpdateAllViews(NULL);
}
```

The Resources

An MFC container application has some resources added: an extra accelerator table and an extra menu for use when an object is in-place active. You can see them in the following figure:

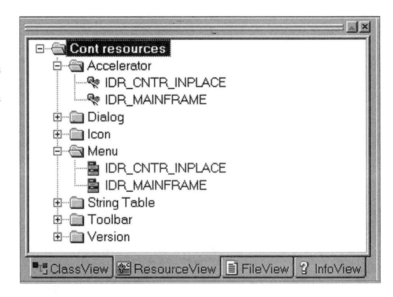

The most interesting thing from our point of view, however, lives on the main menu under Edit, where the AppWizard has generated a menu with several new additions.

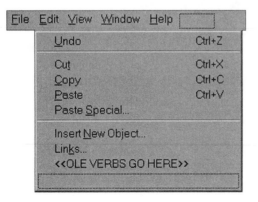

We've got the usual copy and paste commands, plus a section at the bottom that deals with OLE objects. The first of these, Insert <u>N</u>ew Object..., brings up the OLE object insertion dialog, so that the user can select the type of object to insert.

If the document contains one or more linked objects, the second item, Lin<u>k</u>s..., will be enabled. Selecting it will bring up a **COleLinksDialog** dialog box. This is achieved by the framework calling **COleDocument::OnUpdateEditLinksMenu()**, which looks at each item in the document's item list and sees whether it represents a link. If it does, the menu item is enabled. The Edit Link dialog is used to control the link, by allowing such things as causing the presentation data to be updated, or breaking the link.

The last item, <<OLE VERBS GO HERE>>, is a placeholder, where the framework inserts the OLE verbs applicable to the selected item at runtime. You can see in the figure below how the placeholder has been replaced with a sub-menu showing the OLE verbs supported by our GraphServer object, which are <u>E</u>dit (for in-place editing) and <u>O</u>pen (for opening a separate editing window).

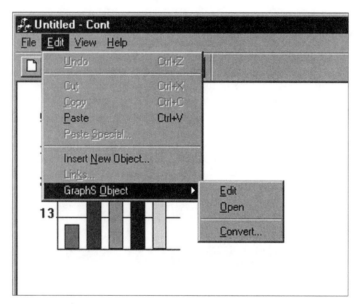

The last item, <u>C</u>onvert..., brings up a **COleConvertDialog** dialog box, with which the user can (if it makes any sense!) convert the object to another type - in other words, they can open it with another server application.

Writing an OLE Container Using MFC

You should now have an idea of how OLE containers work, and how the MFC classes implement them. For the rest of the chapter, we're going to put together a basic container application, into which you should be able to insert GraphServer graphs, Excel spreadsheets - in fact, *any* insertable object.

How you place the objects in the container's view depends entirely on what the application is designed to do, and there's no such thing as a general way to position items. Here's a brief, informal specification for the container application we're going to produce. It's shorter than the server specification, because the application is going to support only the functionality for a simple container:

- It will be an OLE container application
- It will accept objects chosen from an Insert Object dialog
- It will paste objects or links from the clipboard
- It will position inserted items at the last place the mouse was clicked
- It will let the user move and resize items
- It will provide an appropriate appearance for the in-place frame, to show when the object is selected or active for editing
- It will handle menu and toolbar merging with the server

Producing the Skeleton Application

If you've been following along with the chapter to this point by generating the code on your machine, you'll already have the skeleton application in place. If not, the description of what options to select in AppWizard in order to produce our basic container is given in the section called *The MFC Container Implementation*. Follow the instructions there, and then rejoin this discussion.

If you build and run the application, you'll find that the Edit | Insert New Object... menu item will bring up a standard Insert Object dialog, used to choose an object to insert into the container. This menu item is handled by the view class' **OnInsertObject()** function, whose default action is to display a **COleInsertDialog** dialog box:

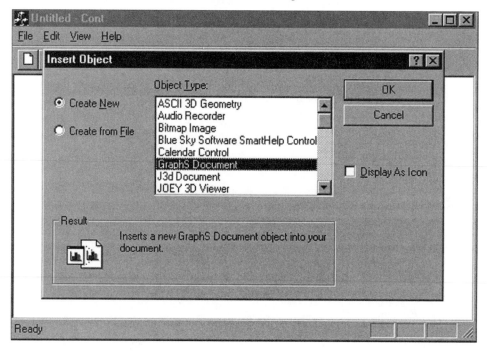

If you insert an object, you'll see that the server's menu and toolbar have been correctly merged with those of the container, but the object isn't correctly sized, using a default size given to it by the container instead. You'll also find that you can't deactivate the object using the mouse, because we have no mouse event handling yet.

At present, the only way to deactivate the object is to use the *Esc* key, which calls the view's **OnCancelEditCntr()** function to cancel the in-place edit of the object. The object can be reactivated using the Edit menu, by choosing the GraphS Object | Edit option to activate the item for in-place editing.

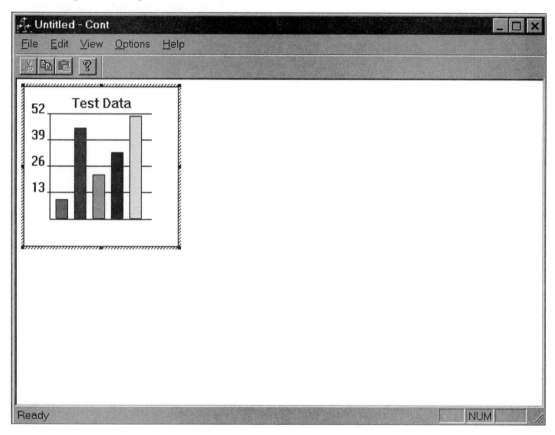

There's another problem too. You'll find that you can insert more than one object, but they all occupy the same space and are incorrectly sized - and since we have no mouse control yet, we can't do much about moving or resizing them within the container. You may be able to move and resize them when they are in-place active and the server is in control, but when they aren't active, they're firmly fixed in one place It's obvious that we have quite a lot of work to do before we can display objects properly.

Providing Basic Container Functionality

A good starting point for adding functionality is to sort out object sizing and placement. In order to do this, we need to modify the client item class, **CContCntrItem**, quite a lot, providing several small utility functions, and editing some of the skeleton code that has been provided for us.

189

Try It Out - Dealing with Object Size and Position

1 Start off by adding a **CPoint** and a **CSize** object as private data members of the **CContCntrItem** class, which will represent the position and size of the object in the container:

```
class CContCntrItem : public COleClientItem
{
    // ...
private:
    CSize  m_Size;
    CPoint m_Position;
    // ...
};
```

Make sure they have a sensible initialization in the class constructor:

```
CContCntrItem::CContCntrItem(CContDoc* pContainer)
    : COleClientItem(pContainer), m_Position(10,10), m_Size(200,200)
{
    // TODO: add one-time construction code here

}
```

Also, modify the item's **Serialize()** function so that these two items are correctly handled:

```
void CContCntrItem::Serialize(CArchive& ar)
{
    ASSERT_VALID(this);

    // Call base class first to read in COleClientItem data.
    // Since this sets up the m_pDocument pointer returned from
    //   CContCntrItem::GetDocument, it is a good idea to call
    //   the base class Serialize first.
    COleClientItem::Serialize(ar);

    // now store/retrieve data specific to CContCntrItem
    if (ar.IsStoring())
    {
        ar << m_Size << m_Position;
    }
    else
    {
        ar >> m_Size >> m_Position;
    }
}
```

2 Next is a pair of small member functions: one to set the item's position, and the other to return a **CRect** describing the item's size and position:

```
class CContCntrItem : public COleClientItem
{
    // ...
public:
    void SetPosition(CPoint pt)
        { m_Position = pt; }
```

```
CRect GetRect() const
   { return CRect(m_Position, m_Size); }
// ...
};
```

3 The next of these utility functions is **UpdateSize()**, which will get the size of the object from the server. In addition, it will return **TRUE** or **FALSE**, depending on whether the size of the object is different from the stored size:

```
BOOL CContCntrItem::UpdateSize()
{
   CSize Size;

   GetCachedExtent(&Size,DVASPECT_CONTENT);
   CClientDC DC(NULL);
   DC.HIMETRICtoDP(&Size);

   if (Size == m_Size)
      return FALSE;    // Return FALSE if the size hasn't changed...

   m_Size = Size;
   return TRUE;        // ...and TRUE if it has.
}
```

Notice the use of the base class **GetCachedExtent()** function, which returns the size of the object in **HIMETRIC** units, and which we promptly convert to device coordinates. Remember that both **GetExtent()** and **GetCachedExtent()** can be used to return the size of a client item; the difference between them is that **GetCachedExtent()** can be called while processing other OLE handlers, such as **OnChange()**, while **GetExtent()** can't.

4 The client item class has a member function, **OnChangeItemPosition()**, which is called when the object position and/or size has changed. It is passed a **CRect** that holds the object's new extent, so we need to update our position and size variables to reflect this:

```
BOOL CContCntrItem::OnChangeItemPosition(const CRect& rectPos)
{
   ASSERT_VALID(this);

   // During in-place activation CContCntrItem::OnChangeItemPosition
   //  is called by the server to change the position of the in-place
   //  window.  Usually, this is a result of the data in the server
   //  document changing such that the extent has changed or as a result
   //  of in-place resizing.
   //
   // The default here is to call the base class, which will call
   //  COleClientItem::SetItemRects to move the item
   //  to the new position.

   if (!COleClientItem::OnChangeItemPosition(rectPos))
      return FALSE;

   // TODO: update any cache you may have of the item's rectangle/extent
   m_Size = rectPos.Size();
   m_Position = rectPos.TopLeft();

   return TRUE;
}
```

5 The next function to modify is **OnGetItemPosition()**. This is called to set the location of the item during in-place activation and by default is set to a hard-coded value, which explains why all the inserted objects end up in the same place with the same size. Replace the hard-coded value with a call to the **GetRect()** function, so that the object's extent is returned:

```
void CContCntrItem::OnGetItemPosition(CRect& rPosition)
{
    ASSERT_VALID(this);

    // During in-place activation, CContCntrItem::OnGetItemPosition
    //  will be called to determine the location of this item.  The default
    //  implementation created from AppWizard simply returns a hard-coded
    //  rectangle.  Usually, this rectangle would reflect the current
    //  position of the item relative to the view used for activation.
    //  You can obtain the view by calling CContCntrItem::GetActiveView.

    // TODO: return correct rectangle (in pixels) in rPosition

    rPosition = GetRect();
}
```

Handling Changes of Object State

At this point we've got all the code in place to handle the sizing and placing of the object. The next step (still with me?) is to consider the **OnChange()** function. This is called when the user has modified, saved, or closed the item, giving you a chance to act on the changes. It has the following prototype:

```
virtual void CContCntrItem::OnChange(OLE_NOTIFICATION nCode, DWORD dwParam);
```

The first argument to **OnChange()** is a code describing the reason the item has been changed:

Code	Meaning
OLE_CHANGED	The aspect of the item has changed, e.g. from **DVASPECT_CONTENT** to an icon, **DVASPECT_ICON**
OLE_SAVED	The item has been saved
OLE_CLOSED	The item has been closed
OLE_CHANGED_STATE	The item has changed state

The meaning of the second parameter is dependent on the first, as shown in the table below:

Code	Second Argument
OLE_CHANGED	Specifies the aspect of the item which has changed: **DVASPECT_CONTENT, DVASPECT_ICON, DVASPECT_THUMBNAIL**, or **DVASPECT_DOCPRINT**
OLE_SAVED	Not used, so pass **NULL**
OLE_CLOSED	Not used, so pass **NULL**
OLE_CHANGED_STATE	Details the state being entered, and can be one of the constants **emptyState, loadedState, openState, activeState**, or **activeUIState**

All we want to do on this occasion is to invalidate the item and force it to redraw itself by calling **UpdateAllViews()**, which is exactly the functionality AppWizard supplies by default:

```
void CContCntrItem::OnChange(OLE_NOTIFICATION nCode, DWORD dwParam)
{
   ASSERT_VALID(this);

   COleClientItem::OnChange(nCode, dwParam);

   // When an item is being edited (either in-place or fully open)
   //  it sends OnChange notifications for changes in the state of the
   //  item or visual appearance of its content.

   // TODO: invalidate the item by calling UpdateAllViews
   //  (with hints appropriate to your application)

   GetDocument()->UpdateAllViews(NULL);
      // for now just update ALL views/no hints
}
```

The call in the code passes just one argument to **UpdateAllViews()**. Remember, though, that it's possible to pass two more arguments: a **long**, and a pointer to an object of a **CObject**-derived class. The purpose of these optional arguments is to act as 'hints', passing some information to the view so that it can optimize its redrawing. If you don't want to pass hints, don't specify the arguments.

Try It Out - Drawing the Object

A function we certainly do need to modify is **OnDraw()**, the routine which draws the object. The default version draws the single, most recent object using the default placement and size as used in **OnGetItemPosition()**. This was fine for the default implementation, because all the objects occupied the same space. We were only ever able to see the top one, so that's all that needed to be drawn.

Now, however, we're going to be able to place objects in the container in different positions, so we must ensure that *all* of them get drawn. This is the view's job, and we implement it by iterating over the list of client items held in the document, getting each one to draw itself:

```
void CContView::OnDraw(CDC* pDC)
{
   CContDoc* pDoc = GetDocument();
   ASSERT_VALID(pDoc);

   POSITION pos = pDoc->GetStartPosition();

   // Iterate through all client items in the document, getting
   // each one to draw itself
   while(pos)
   {
      CContCntrItem* pItem = (CContCntrItem*)pDoc->GetNextClientItem(pos);
      if (pItem)
         pItem->Draw(pDC, pItem->GetRect());
   }
}
```

Instead of using a hard-coded rectangle, we now use the extent of the client item itself.

Try It Out - Choosing the Object's Position

Now we've sorted out the sizing of the object, we need to decide where to position it. How you do this will depend on the precise nature of your application; maybe you want to lay objects out in a grid, or position them at a text caret, or (as we'll do here) place them at the last-clicked mouse position.

1 Add a **CPoint** data member to the view class, and use it to store the position each time the left mouse button is pressed by adding a handler for **WM_LBUTTONDOWN**:

```
class CContView : public CView
{
   // ...
private:
   CPoint m_LastClick;
   // ...
};
```

```
CContView::CContView() : m_LastClick(0,0)
{
   m_pSelection = NULL;
   // TODO: add construction code here
}
```

```
void CContView::OnLButtonDown(UINT nFlags, CPoint point)
{
   // Keep track of where the mouse was last clicked
   m_LastClick = point;

   CView::OnLButtonDown(nFlags, point);
}
```

2 After all that, we can add the code to position an item. Positioning is handled in the view's **OnInsertObject()** function; this is one of the more complex of the skeleton functions provided for you, and we looked at it in detail earlier in the chapter.

We'll leave most of the code alone, as the default operation works fine for our purposes. What we *will* do is add a couple of lines of code to set the position of the item to our last-saved mouse position, and then save its size:

```
   // Initialize the item from the dialog data.
   if (!dlg.CreateItem(pItem))
      AfxThrowMemoryException();  // any exception will do
   ASSERT_VALID(pItem);

   // Give the item position and set its size
   pItem->SetPosition(m_LastClick);
   pItem->UpdateSize();

   // If item created from class list (not from file) then launch
   //   the server to edit the item.
   if (dlg.GetSelectionType() == COleInsertDialog::createNewItem)
      pItem->DoVerb(OLEIVERB_SHOW, this);

   ASSERT_VALID(pItem);
```

3 That's about it for this stage, so rebuild and run the application, and look at what you get. Click the mouse somewhere in the view, and then insert a GraphServer object; you should find that the object is inserted where you clicked, and that it's now the size specified by the server.

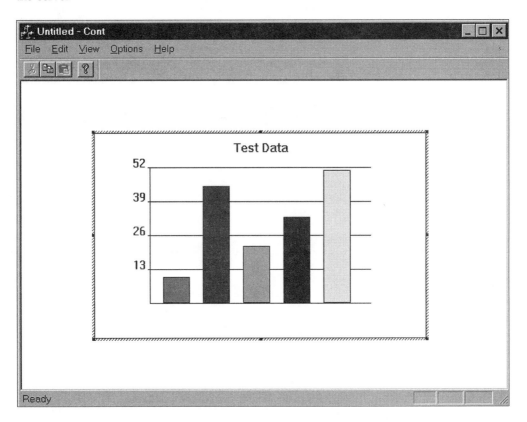

Selecting Objects

We still have no way to interact with the embedded object via the mouse - we can't activate it, deactivate it or resize it. It seems a good idea to add this capability as the next step. Before we get into the coding, though, I want to introduce you to the **CRectTracker** class.

This isn't specifically an OLE class (it's actually a graphics class), but it *is* often used in OLE container applications like this one. A **tracker** is simply a rectangle that can be displayed in a variety of styles - it can have solid, dotted, or hatched borders, for example. It can also be filled with a hatched pattern, and have resize handles on the inside or outside. Trackers are useful in any application where you need to show the state of a graphical object.

What we'll do is associate a tracker with each client item in the container, setting its size to that of the item, and setting its appearance according to the item's state, as shown in the following table. Although there's nothing to enforce using these combinations of states and appearances, they are standard, so you'll risk confusing people if you depart from them:

Tracker Appearance	Item State
Dotted border	Item is linked
Solid border	Item is embedded in your document
Resize handles	Item is currently selected
Hatched border	Item is currently in-place active
Hatched pattern overlays item	Item's server is open

Try It Out - Setting Up a Tracker

1 The initialization of the tracker can be done conveniently by providing a **SetupTracker()** function in the client item class, which will set the tracker object to reflect the state of the item. Given the fact that this is such a common operation, it is perhaps odd that MFC doesn't provide you with a standard way to handle it; this routine will, however, handle all the usual options, and is generally very useful:

```
// Set up a tracker according to the item's current state.
void CContCntrItem::SetupTracker(CRectTracker& Tracker, BOOL Selected) const
{
   Tracker.m_rect = GetRect();

   // set minimum size for our OLE items
   Tracker.m_sizeMin.cx = 8;
   Tracker.m_sizeMin.cy = 8;

   Tracker.m_nStyle = 0;

   // setup resize handles if item is selected
   if (Selected)
      Tracker.m_nStyle |= CRectTracker::resizeInside;

   // put correct border depending on item type
   if (GetType() == OT_LINK)
      Tracker.m_nStyle |= CRectTracker::dottedLine;
   else
      Tracker.m_nStyle |= CRectTracker::solidLine;

   // put hatching over the item if it is currently open
   UINT State = GetItemState();
   if (State == COleClientItem::openState
                        || State == COleClientItem::activeUIState)
      Tracker.m_nStyle |= CRectTracker::hatchInside;
}
```

We check whether the object is selected, and if it is, then we set the tracker style to show resize handles. We then determine the object type using **GetType()**, which may return one of three values:

▶ **OT_LINK** means it's a linked object

▶ **OT_EMBEDDED** denotes an embedded object

▶ **OT_STATIC** denotes a static (that is, uneditable) object

If the object is a link, we use a dotted border; otherwise, the border is solid. The final step is to determine the object's state using **GetItemState()**, which returns one of the following values:

Return Value	Meaning
COleClientItem::emptyState	The **COleClientItem** exists as an MFC object, but isn't yet associated with any OLE data.
COleClientItem::loadedState	The OLE data has been associated with the **COleClientItem**.
COleClientItem::openState	The item is open for editing in the server's window, rather than in-place in the container. In this state, the representation of the item in the container window is usually crosshatched.
COleClientItem::activeState	The item briefly passes through this state on the way to the next one.
COleClientItem::activeUIState	The item is in-place active, with UI elements such as menus and toolbars in place.

If the item is in the **open** or **activeUI** states, we set the style to place hatching over the tracker rectangle.

2 Now, in the view's **OnDraw()** function, we create a **CRectTracker** object as each item is drawn, and pass it to **SetupTracker()** to be initialized. The **m_pSelection** variable will point to the currently selected item, so we can easily set the flag to tell **SetupTracker()** whether to draw this item as selected or not:

```
void CContView::OnDraw(CDC* pDC)
{
   CContDoc* pDoc = GetDocument();
   ASSERT_VALID(pDoc);

   POSITION pos = pDoc->GetStartPosition();

   // Iterate through all client items in the document, getting
   // each one to draw itself
   while(pos)
   {
      CContCntrItem* pItem = (CContCntrItem*)pDoc->GetNextClientItem(pos);
      if (pItem)
      {
         pItem->Draw(pDC, pItem->GetRect());

         CRectTracker trk;
         pItem->SetupTracker(trk, pItem == m_pSelection);
         trk.Draw(pDC);
      }
   }
}
```

Once we've initialized the tracker, we draw it. This means all items have at least a rectangle to show where they are, and the selected item will have sizing handles, although they can't be used yet.

Try It Out - Enabling Selection

We can place more than one item in the container, and we want to be able to click on items to select them, and double-click on items to activate them. The first thing we need, therefore, is some way of telling whether a mouse click has hit an object or not. The obvious place to put this is the document, since it's that which maintains the list of container items.

1 We'll provide a document member function called **HitTest()** which will take a point and see whether it lies inside an object. If so, it will return a pointer to the client item that contains the point, otherwise it will return **NULL**:

```
CContCntrItem* CContDoc::HitTest(CPoint pt) const
{
   CContCntrItem* pObj = NULL;

   // Get the head of the document object list in the document
   POSITION pos = GetStartPosition();

   while (pos)
   {
      CContCntrItem* pItem = (CContCntrItem*)GetNextClientItem(pos);
      ASSERT(pItem);
      if ((pItem->GetRect()).PtInRect(pt))
      {
         pObj = pItem;
         break;
      }
   }

   return pObj;
}
```

Because we're now making mention of the **CContCntrItem** class in the document header file, you'll need to add a forward declaration to the top of the file when you add this function:

```
class CContCntrItem;
```

2 We can use the **HitTest()** function in the **WM_LBUTTONDOWN** handler to see whether the mouse has been clicked over an object:

```
void CContView::OnLButtonDown(UINT nFlags, CPoint point)
{
   // keep track of where the mouse was last clicked
   m_LastClick = point;

   // Have we hit an object?
   CContCntrItem* pItem = GetDocument()->HitTest(point);

   CView::OnLButtonDown(nFlags, point);
}
```

3 If we *have* hit an object, we want to save it in the view's **m_pSelection** variable. The purpose of this variable has changed: instead of denoting the last item added, it will now hold a pointer to the last item the user clicked on, which is a lot more sensible. We can do this by adding a new member function to the view called **SetSelected()**:

```
void CContView::SetSelected(CContCntrItem* pItem)
{
    // Don't bother doing anything if the user has reclicked on
    // the same item
    if (pItem != m_pSelection)
    {
        // If there isn't a current selection, don't try to close it
        if (m_pSelection != NULL)
        {
            // Close the current selection if it is active
            UINT state = m_pSelection->GetItemState();

            if (state == COleClientItem::openState ||
                state == COleClientItem::activeState ||
                state == COleClientItem::activeUIState)
            m_pSelection->Close();
        }

        // Set the selection and force a redraw
        m_pSelection = pItem;
        Invalidate();
    }
}
```

If there's a current selection, the function checks to see whether it's open. It could be open in one of three states: in-place active, UI-active, or open in its own window. If the object is in any of these three states, then its **Close()** function is called, since there can only be one item selected at a time.

4 Lastly, add a call to this function to the left button down handler, so that **SetSelected()** is called on the pointer returned from the hit-test:

```
void CContView::OnLButtonDown(UINT nFlags, CPoint point)
{
    // keep track of where the mouse was last clicked
    m_LastClick = point;

    // Have we hit an object?
    CContCntrItem* pItem = GetDocument()->HitTest(point);
    SetSelected(pItem);

    CView::OnLButtonDown(nFlags, point);
}
```

Try It Out - Enabling Activation

We can now select objects using the mouse, so the logical next step is to be able to *activate* them using the mouse as well. In OLE containers, a double-click on an embedded or linked object is normally expected to open it for in-place editing, unless the *Ctrl* key is pressed, in which case the object is opened in its own window.

> *Remember that this rule isn't a strict one. The double-click is actually used to perform the object's primary OLE verb, and although most of the time this verb will be 'edit' or an equivalent, it could be 'play' for something like a sound or AVI clip.*

199

All we need to do is to add a handler to the view for the double-click event, which we'll use to call the **DoVerb()** function for the client item:

```
void CContView::OnLButtonDblClk(UINT nFlags, CPoint point)
{
    if (m_pSelection != NULL)
    {
        if (nFlags & MK_CONTROL)
            m_pSelection->DoVerb(OLEIVERB_OPEN, this);
        else
            m_pSelection->DoVerb(OLEIVERB_PRIMARY, this);
    }

    CView::OnLButtonDblClk(nFlags, point);
}
```

If the *Ctrl* key is pressed when the button is double-clicked, **DoVerb()** is passed **OLEIVERB_OPEN** and will launch the server to do an out-of-place edit. Otherwise, **OLEIVERB_PRIMARY** is used to perform an in-place edit (provided the server supports it).

If you build and test the application now, you should be able to produce behavior like this:

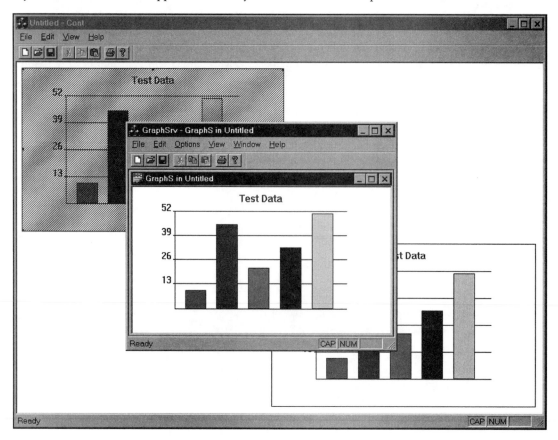

Here you can see a container containing two GraphSrv objects. The bottom one is inactive, as indicated by the solid border, while the top one is being edited out-of-place, caused by double-clicking on it with the *Ctrl* key held down. The hatched background to the object shows that it is open for out-of-place editing.

Moving and Resizing Objects

We can now insert objects and activate them for editing. It would be useful if we could also move and resize objects we've already inserted into the container, and it turns out that this isn't too hard to achieve.

The secret lies in using a tracker in the view's **OnLButtonDown()** handler. Hit testing will tell us whether we've hit an item or not; if we have, we can set up a tracker to fit around the item, and the tracker will then handle all the mouse interaction required for moving and resizing the item. All we have to do is to pass the information on the new size and/or position to the item, and get it to redraw itself.

Try It Out - Tracker Manipulation

1 Start by adding the tracker code to the button handler:

```
void CContView::OnLButtonDown(UINT nFlags, CPoint point)
{
   // Save the last mouse position
   m_lastClick = point;

   // Have we hit an object?
   CContCntrItem* pItem = GetDocument()->HitTest(point);
   SetSelected(pItem);

   // Nothing else to do if no object selected
   if (pItem != NULL)
   {
      // Set up a tracker
      CRectTracker trk;
      pItem->SetupTracker(trk, pItem == m_pSelection);

      // Update window before using tracker
      UpdateWindow();

      if (trk.Track(this, point))
      {
         pItem->Move(trk.m_rect);
         GetDocument()->SetModifiedFlag();
      }
   }

   CView::OnLButtonDown(nFlags, point);
}
```

The new code checks whether we've hit anything before continuing. If we have, we create a tracker and set it up as before, and then ensure that the window is up to date before using it. The call to **CRectTracker::Track()** causes the tracker to capture the mouse, keeping the capture until the user releases the left mouse button, presses the *Esc* key, or clicks the right button. If the tracking operation is aborted, the call will return **FALSE**. When the call to **Track()** returns, the tracker's **m_rect** member will hold the size of the tracker rectangle. We can pass this on to the item, and then tell the document that it has been modified.

2 The client item's **Move()** routine resets the size and position members from the rectangle passed in:

```
void CContCntrItem::Move(CRect& rc)
{
   GetDocument()->UpdateAllViews(NULL);
   m_Position.x = rc.left;
   m_Position.y = rc.top;

   m_Size.cx = rc.right - rc.left;
   m_Size.cy = rc.bottom - rc.top;

   GetDocument()->UpdateAllViews(NULL);

   // Call SetItemRects() when the position or size of the item changes
   if (IsInPlaceActive())
      SetItemRects();
}
```

We get the document to update the view before and after resetting the size, and if the item is in-place active, we call **SetItemRects()** to reset the bounding rectangle of the item. It's recommended in the online help that this function be called whenever the size or position of the item changes; if the item isn't in-place active, we don't need to call the function, as the server will discover the object's new size when it is next made active.

If you now rebuild and run the application, you should be able to move items by clicking the mouse pointer in the tracker rectangle, and resize them by dragging the tracker handles.

Implementing Paste

If there's an OLE item on the clipboard, most programs will respond to Edit | Paste by embedding the object in the current document. There will be an item on the clipboard if the user selected an item in a server document and then copied it. The Paste menu item is enabled by the framework if the **CanPaste()** member function returns a non-zero value.

This behavior is implemented by one of the three member functions that **COleClientItem** possesses for creating objects from the clipboard:

- **CreateFromClipboard()** creates an embedded item
- **CreateLinkFromClipboard()** creates a link
- **CreateStaticFromClipboard()** creates a static item that can't be edited

Try It Out - Adding a Handler For Edit | Paste

The actual code is similar to that provided for inserting a new object, except that in this case the object already exists. Use ClassWizard to create a handler for Edit | Paste in the view class:

```
void CContView::OnEditPaste()
{
    // Create a new embedded object from data on the clipboard.

    CContCntrItem* pNewItem = NULL;

    try
    {
        // First create a client item, and add it to the document
        CContDoc* pDoc = GetDocument();
        ASSERT_VALID(pDoc);
        pNewItem = new CContCntrItem(pDoc);
        ASSERT_VALID(pNewItem);

        // Set it as the selected item
        SetSelected(pNewItem);

        // Fill it with the data from the clipboard. If this call
        // fails, throw an exception (anything will do!)
        if (!pNewItem->CreateFromClipboard())
            AfxThrowMemoryException();
        ASSERT_VALID(pNewItem);

        // Set its position and size
        pNewItem->SetPosition(m_LastClick);
        pNewItem->UpdateSize();

        // Activate the object for in-place editing
        pNewItem->DoVerb(OLEIVERB_SHOW, this);
    }

    catch(CException*)
    {
        if (pNewItem != NULL)
        {
            ASSERT_VALID(pNewItem);
            delete pNewItem;
        }

        AfxMessageBox("Failed to paste OLE item");
    }
}
```

We create a new client item, set it as selected, and then try to initialize it with the data from the clipboard. If this call fails, we throw an exception. It doesn't have to be any particular exception, so an **AfxMemoryException()** is as good as any other. The **catch()** block deletes the item and displays a message box informing the user of the error. If the object *was* initialized correctly, we place it and then cause it to be activated for in-place editing.

You can test the program by firing up GraphServer and choosing Edit | Copy to copy the document onto the clipboard. Now try pasting the item into the container.

Implementing Paste Special

A container application's main menu has an Edit | Paste Special... item, which can be used to control completely how objects are pasted into the application.

The **COlePasteSpecialDialog** class will do much of the work for us. This is one of the standard OLE dialogs - it shows the user a list of the formats in which the object on the clipboard can be rendered, and when the user chooses one, it creates a client item from the data present on the clipboard. Here's a typical Paste Special dialog:

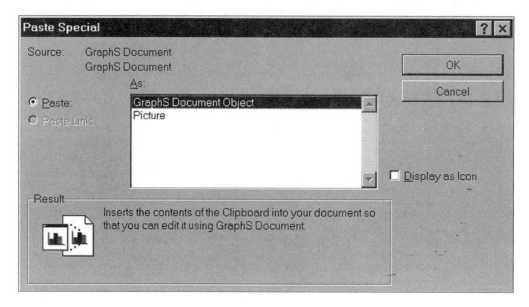

The clipboard may contain data in a number of formats, depending on what was supported by the server. The dialog class function **AddStandardFormats()** causes the dialog to look for **CF_BITMAP**, **CF_TEXT** and **CF_METAFILEPICT** in addition to linked and embedded object data. More specific control may be obtained by calling **AddFormat()**, which you can use to add new formats to the list shown in the dialog; these can either be standard formats, or custom ones which you've invented and registered with the system.

Try It Out - Adding a Handler for Edit | Paste Special

1 Use ClassWizard to add a handler for **ID_EDIT_PASTE_SPECIAL**, and create a **COlePasteSpecialDialog** object:

```
void CContView::OnEditPasteSpecial()
{
    COlePasteSpecialDialog dlg;
```

2 Before using this object, call the dialog's **AddStandardFormats()** function. This adds the standard data formats to the list the dialog will handle, which are:

▶ **CF_BITMAP** (device-dependent bitmap data)

▶ **CF_DIB** (device-independent bitmap data)

▶ **CF_METAFILEPICT** (metafile data)

▶ Embedded object

▶ Link source (optional)

You can prevent the inclusion of the link source type by passing a **FALSE** argument to the function. Add the formats, show the dialog, and if the user cancels, the function can exit:

```
dlg.AddStandardFormats();
if (IDOK != dlg.DoModal())
   return;
```

3   Assuming the user didn't close the dialog without making a selection, we need to handle the selection they made. We can find out what that was by calling the dialog's **GetSelectionType()** function, which will return one of four values:

▶ **COlePasteSpecialDialog::pasteLink** if the user wants to paste a link to the object

▶ **COlePasteSpecialDialog::pasteNormal** if they want to embed the object

▶ **COlePasteSpecialDialog::pasteOther** if the format chosen is not a standard OLE format

▶ **COlePasteSpecialDialog::pasteStatic** if they chose to create a static item and paste a metafile

In this example, we don't use non-standard formats or static items, so we'll only handle embedded and linked objects:

```
UINT type = dlg.GetSelectionType();
switch (type)
{
   case COlePasteSpecialDialog::pasteLink:
   case COlePasteSpecialDialog::pasteNormal:
   {
      // Create an item
      CContCntrItem* pNewItem = NULL;
      CContDoc* pDoc = GetDocument();
      ASSERT_VALID(pDoc);
      pNewItem = new CContCntrItem(pDoc);
      ASSERT_VALID(pNewItem);

      if (!dlg.CreateItem(pNewItem))
      {
         delete pNewItem;
         MessageBox("Failed to create item",
                    AfxGetAppName(), MB_ICONEXCLAMATION | MB_OK);
         return;
      }

      // Set the position and size
      pNewItem->SetPosition(m_LastClick);
      pNewItem->UpdateSize();
```

```
                // Convention asys that this becomes the selected object
                SetSelected(pNewItem);
                Invalidate();

                // Tell the document it has been modified
                pDoc->SetModifiedFlag();
                break;
        }

        case COlePasteSpecialDialog::pasteOther:
        case COlePasteSpecialDialog::pasteStatic:
            MessageBox("Unsupported clipboard format",
                        AfxGetAppName(), MB_ICONEXCLAMATION | MB_OK);
            break;

        default:
            MessageBox("Unknown clipboard format",
                        AfxGetAppName(), MB_ICONEXCLAMATION | MB_OK);
            return;
    }
}
```

If you look at the code that creates the linked and embedded items, you'll see that it has distinct similarities to the object insertion and pasting code we've already provided. The main difference here is that the dialog class does all the work for us with its **CreateItem()** function, which creates a new client item and returns a pointer to it. A final thing to note is that, by convention, the pasted object becomes the selected object.

Try It Out - Controlling the Paste Special Menu Item

One last thing we can usefully do is to make sure the Paste Special... menu item is only enabled when there's something valid on the clipboard - something which can be made into an embedded or a linked object. To do this, use ClassWizard to create an **UPDATE_COMMAND_UI** handler for the Paste Special... menu item:

```
void CContView::OnUpdateEditPasteSpecial(CCmdUI* pCmdUI)
{
    // See whether there's an object on the clipboard at all
    COleDataObject clipObj;
    BOOL bEnable = clipObj.AttachClipboard();

    // If there is an object, see whether it is usable for
    // creating linked or embedded objects
    if (bEnable)
    {
        bEnable = COleClientItem::CanCreateFromData(&clipObj);
        bEnable |= COleClientItem::CanCreateLinkFromData(&clipObj);
    }

    pCmdUI->Enable(bEnable);
}
```

Objects of class **COleDataObject** are used to pass OLE data around between processes. I'll talk about them more in the next chapter; for now, just note that we create one and then try to attach it to the data on the clipboard. If this works, then there was an OLE object there. Next we use two client item functions which take a **COleDataObject** and determine whether it can be used to create an embedded or a linked item respectively. Either of these will do for us, so we OR the results together, and use the final Boolean value to determine whether the menu item should be enabled or not.

Time to build and test the application again. Check that the Paste Special... item works, and also that the menu item is disabled if you copy some non-OLE data, such as a line of text, to the clipboard.

Summary

We've seen in this chapter how OLE containers work. MFC supports containers using the **COleDocument** and **COleLinkingDocument** classes to manage container documents, and the **COleClientItem** class to provide client item support. The client item class works with the **COleServerItem** class on the server side to implement the container/server communication needed to manage embedded and linked objects.

Containers don't get as much support in the MFC skeleton application as servers do, because AppWizard doesn't know what you're going to want to do with the objects that are going to be placed into the container.

We've created a basic MFC OLE container application to match the server we wrote in the previous chapter. The application is pretty basic, but it does illustrate most of the principles involved in writing real containers. What we need to look at now is how servers and containers interact, and that's our subject in the next chapter.

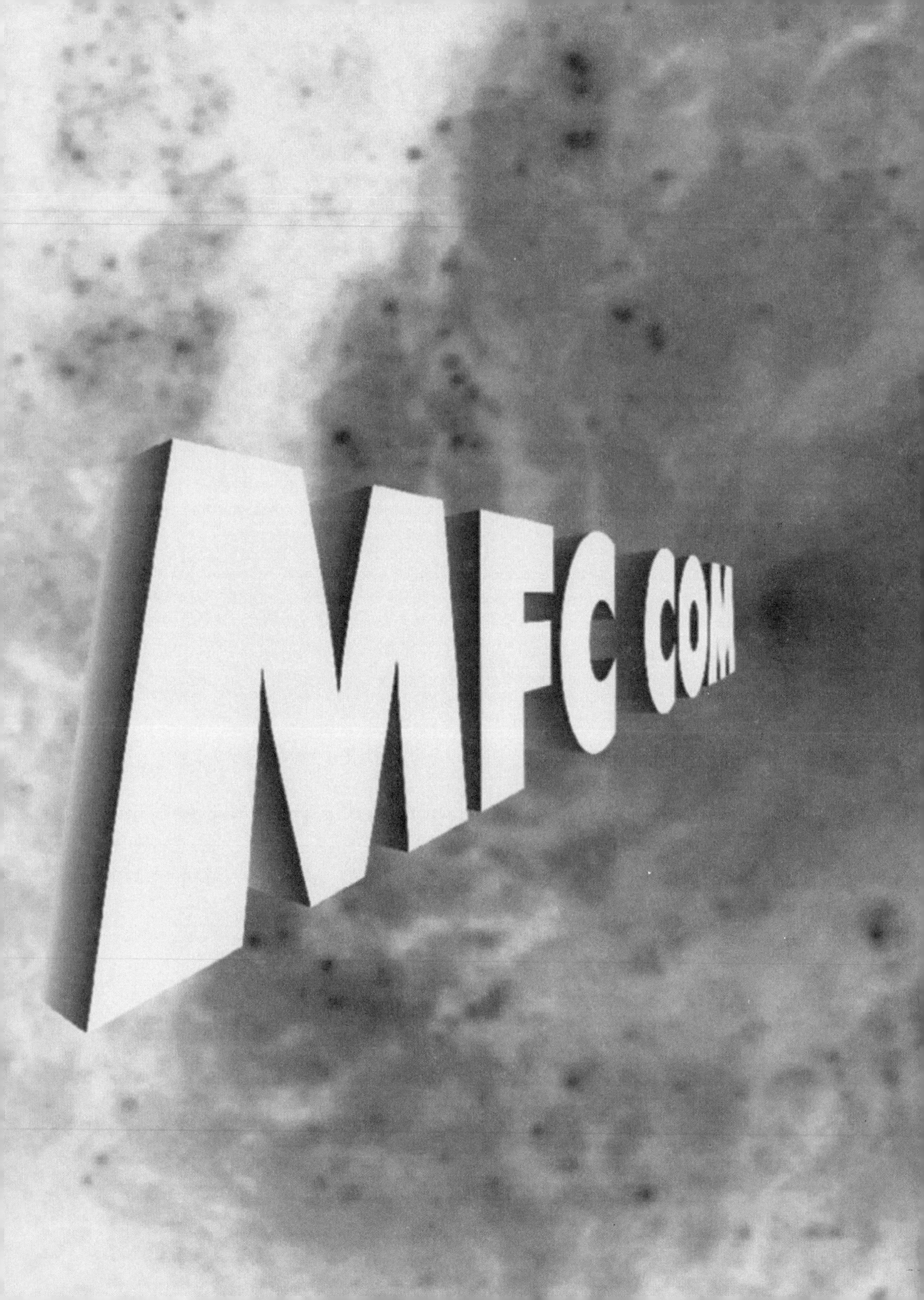
MFC COM

Servers and Containers in Action

We've now seen how to write basic OLE server and container applications, and we've allowed them to work together in a rather limited way by implementing copy and paste via the clipboard. In this chapter, we'll move on to look at how data exchange between OLE applications works, and we'll use this to enhance the data exchange between our client and server applications.

Server/Container Cooperation

I'll start, though, by taking a look at exactly what takes place when servers and containers work together with embedded and linked objects. In other words, "Just what happens when you double-click on that Excel spreadsheet?"

The Activation Process

Activation usually occurs when the left mouse button is double-clicked. If the server isn't loaded at this point, it's the job of the **in-process handler** to load the server and tell it to make sure the object is ready for use.

> *The in-process handler is the 'caretaker' that's responsible for handling the affairs of an object when the server isn't loaded. If you look in the registry under the CLSID for a typical server object, you'll see entries called* LocalServer32, *which gives the path to the server, and* InprocHandler32, *which identifies the in-process handler. The default handler is part of* `Ole32.dll`, *and will usually be all that's needed.*

As we saw in the last chapter, activation is achieved by calling the `COleClientItem::DoVerb()` function, which activates the object either in-place or in a window of its own. This function call actually kicks off a whole train of events, summarized in the diagram on the next page:

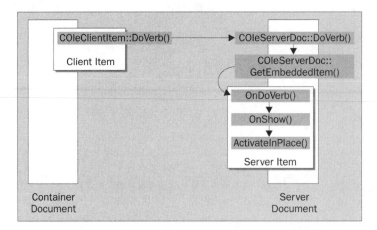

The call to **COleClientItem::DoVerb()** results in a call to **COleServerDoc::DoVerb()**, which gets the embedded object by calling **GetEmbeddedItem()**, and then gets the item to do the work using its **OnDoVerb()** function. We saw **COleServerItem::OnDoVerb()** in the previous chapter; the default action for the primary verb is to call **OnShow()**:

```
// primary, show, and unknown map to OnShow
case OLEIVERB_PRIMARY:
case OLEIVERB_SHOW:
    OnShow();
    break;
```

OnShow() tries to get the document to activate itself in-place. If, for any reason, it can't then it opens the document out-of-place in its own window instead:

```
void COleServerItem::OnShow()
{
    ASSERT_VALID(this);

    // attempt in place activation (if not supported, fall back on "Open")
    COleServerDoc* pDoc = GetDocument();
    if (!pDoc->ActivateInPlace())
    {
        // by default OnShow() maps to OnOpen() if in-place activation
        //  not supported
        OnOpen();
    }
}
```

ActivateInPlace() is where the actual work of activation takes place. It comprises over 200 lines of heavy-duty code, and it performs five main tasks:

- ▶ Creating the in-place frame window
- ▶ Positioning this window
- ▶ Linking the server and container windows together so that commands are handled correctly
- ▶ Handling the menu negotiation
- ▶ Scrolling the item into view and giving it the focus

You'll be relieved to hear that I won't go into great detail about this function, because you don't need to know how the routine operates in order to implement in-place activation. In case you're intrigued, though, the diagram below shows a summary of the activation procedure in flowchart form. I think you'll agree that it's a fairly involved process!

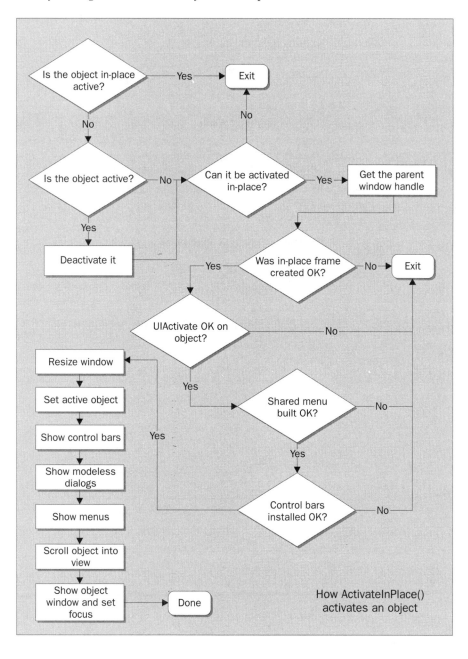

How ActivateInPlace() activates an object

The Deactivation Process

In the same vein, let's consider briefly what happens when the user deactivates an object, by clicking somewhere outside its boundaries, or by pressing the *Esc* key. Once again, you don't need to understand the fine detail of this procedure to be able to use servers and containers, but it may be helpful to appreciate something of what is involved.

The process is not as complex as activation, although there's still quite a lot happening, with the usual to-and-fro going on between the server and container. This diagram summarizes the main events:

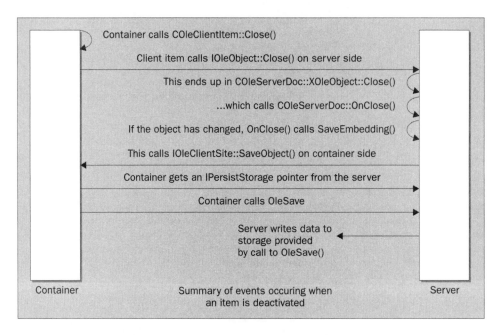

Container   Summary of events occuring when   Server
                                 an item is deactivated

When the container detects that the object is to be deactivated, it calls the active object's **Close()** function, passing it one of three flags:

Flag	Meaning
OLECLOSE_SAVEIFDIRTY	Save the item if it has been changed
OLECLOSE_NOSAVE	Don't save the item
OLECLOSE_PROMPTSAVE	Ask the user whether to save

If the item doesn't need saving, the server closes it and that's that. If the close flag was **OLECLOSE_SAVEIFDIRTY**, a series of calls is made which culminates in using the **OleSave()** API call to write the data out to a storage. The pointer to a storage which is passed in the call to **OleSave()** is used to construct a **CArchive**, so that the normal document serialization can be used.

Uniform Data Transfer

Uniform Data Transfer, known as **UDT**, provides a standard way of transferring data between applications, using the COM interface **IDataObject** as the medium. UDT was originally designed for use with compound documents, but also provides a very useful way of implementing clipboard operations and drag and drop. As usual, MFC encapsulates the OLE mechanisms for the clipboard and drag and drop in classes, but you still need to appreciate something of what's involved if you're intending to use these operations in your own applications.

UDT, DDE and the Clipboard

You may be wondering how UDT differs from older data transfer methods like DDE and clipboard exchange. Those methods suffer from several limitations, of which three in particular stand out:

▶ The problems of global memory use. Both of the older methods use global memory for data transfer, which may result in a lot of swapping memory to disk and back if large amounts of data are being transferred.

▶ The traditional Windows clipboard mechanism allows you to specify the clipboard data format, but you only have a single integer to play with, so you can't specify how the data should be rendered.

▶ The DDE mechanism works by sending some special Windows messages between the applications which are trying to communicate. This is a fairly simple way to implement inter-process communication, but you have to manage all the protocols yourself, and it's quite easy to get lockups and unreliable behavior.

Another serious drawback of the older methods becomes apparent when we start considering distributed objects, since neither DDE nor global memory will work across a network. Microsoft did introduce **NetDDE**, but this was never entirely satisfactory, in that it would never work across a heterogeneous network, as COM is supposed to.

The UDT Data Structures

Data can be passed between processes in many different forms, and it's necessary to provide some **metadata** that describes the transferred data to the receiving process. The Uniform Data Transfer process uses two important structures to accomplish this:

▶ The **FORMATETC** structure (pronounced 'format et cetera') describes the data itself, providing a fuller description than the standard Windows clipboard format.

▶ The **STGMEDIUM** structure describes the 'storage medium' that's being used to transfer the data. DDE only allowed global memory, but with UDT you can choose from several storage methods.

FORMATETC describes the actual data format, but only does half the job - it says what format data is in, but nothing about where it is. The second structure, **STGMEDIUM**, describes the way the data is stored, including details of where it is.

Why do we need two structures? The **FORMATETC** structure can be used by servers *and* clients to specify either the format(s) in which data is available, or the format in which data is required. So, a client could send a server a **FORMATETC** structure to tell it that it wanted some data in a particular format, and if the data were available, the server would reply with a **STGMEDIUM** structure giving details of exactly where the data is to be found.

Here's what the **FORMATETC** structure looks like:

```
typedef struct tagFORMATETC
{
    CLIPFORMAT      cfFormat;   // Clipboard format
    DVTARGETDEVICE *ptd;        // Device for which the data was rendered
    DWORD           dwAspect;   // Data aspect - full content, icon etc
    LONG            lindex;     // Index used if data is split across page
                                // boundaries. -1 means that the data isn't
                                // split
    DWORD           tymed;      // Type of storage medium
}FORMATETC, *LPFORMATETC;
```

We can pass over most of the detail, but we'll look at the **tymed** member, which holds the storage medium for the data. The value is taken from the **TYMED** enumerated type, and can take one of the following values:

TYMED Enumeration Value	Medium
TYMED_HGLOBAL	A global memory handle
TYMED_FILE	A traditional disk file
TYMED_ISTREAM	A COM **IStream** object
TYMED_ISTORAGE	A COM **IStorage** object
TYMED_GDI	A Windows GDI object
TYMED_MFPICT	A metafile picture
TYMED_ENHMF	An enhanced metafile picture
TYMED_NULL	No medium (i.e. no data)

This shows the range of possible data media that we can use for transferring data; it's certainly much more flexible than the old clipboard!

When we have a **FORMATETC** defining the format of some data, a **STGMEDIUM** structure can then be used to say exactly where it is. The **STGMEDIUM** structure definition shows how the details of the medium are passed over. It contains a union that has one member for each of the types in the **TYMED** enumeration:

```
typedef struct tagSTGMEDIUM
{
    DWORD tymed;
    union
    {
        HBITMAP hBitmap;                // Bitmap
        HMETAFILEPICT hMetaFilePict;    // Metafile
        HENHMETAFILE hEnhMetaFile;      // Enhanced metafile
```

```
    HGLOBAL hGlobal;                 // Memory handle
    LPOLESTR lpszFileName;           // Filename
    IStream __RPC_FAR *pstm;         // IStream pointer
    IStorage __RPC_FAR *pstg;        // IStorage pointer
  };
  IUnknown __RPC_FAR *pUnkForRelease;
} STGMEDIUM;
```

The IDataObject Interface

As you'd expect, UDT is implemented using interfaces, and in this case the interface of interest is **IDataObject**. Any object which wants to be a source of data implements the **IDataObject** interface, and clients can use a pointer to the interface to access the data, regardless of where that pointer has come from - the clipboard, a drag and drop operation, or whatever.

The interface provides a client with the ability to do things like:

▶ Send and receive data

▶ Find whether the object supports a particular format, and enumerate the formats it does support

▶ Set up and break **advisory connections**, a callback mechanism through which the client can be notified when the data changes

The OLE Clipboard Mechanism

OLE extends the standard Windows clipboard mechanism to work with COM objects and use UDT, and in fact the entire clipboard mechanism is now COM-based. If you don't need to use such things, you can stick to using it in the original way, but all COM-based operations (such as ActiveX controls and compound documents) need this support.

Four API functions support the OLE clipboard:

▶ **OleSetClipboard()** puts an **IDataObject** on the clipboard and calls **AddRef()** on it.

▶ **OleGetClipboard()** retrieves an **IDataObject** from the clipboard, calling **AddRef()** on it. The user of the object must release it.

▶ **OleFlushClipboard()** clears the clipboard, releasing the data object.

▶ **OleIsCurrentClipboard()** says whether a given data object is the one currently on the clipboard.

The figures below show how the OLE clipboard works. An object that wants to make data available to clients on the clipboard implements the **IDataObject** interface. When it wants to copy data, it uses **OleSetClipboard()** to pass a copy of its interface pointer to the OLE run-time code, which stores it.

215

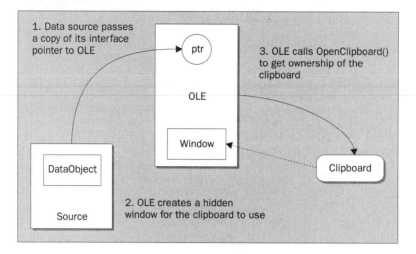

1. Data source passes a copy of its interface pointer to OLE

ptr

OLE

3. OLE calls OpenClipboard() to get ownership of the clipboard

Window

Clipboard

DataObject

Source

2. OLE creates a hidden window for the clipboard to use

OLE uses the clipboard in normal Windows fashion, calling **OpenClipboard()** to claim temporary ownership of the clipboard. The problem here is that Windows requires a window handle to be passed to this function, so before it can call the function, OLE creates its own hidden window to work with clipboard operations.

> *This window is one of the things set up by the call to* **OleInitialize()** *in an MFC application. The equivalent COM routine,* **CoInitialize()**, *doesn't create a window, so any subsequent clipboard operations would fail.*

OLE uses **delayed rendering** for its clipboard operations. In other words, it only puts a *pointer* to the data onto the clipboard, in this case the pointer to the **IDataObject** interface. The actual data won't get passed over until someone asks for it. The figure below shows what happens when an OLE-aware client wants to retrieve data.

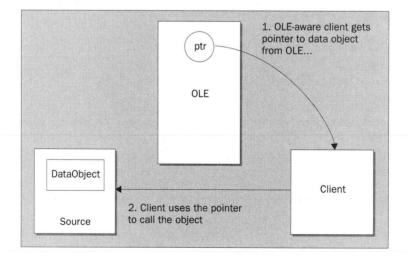

ptr

OLE

1. OLE-aware client gets pointer to data object from OLE...

Client

DataObject

Source

2. Client uses the pointer to call the object

When such an OLE-aware client wants to get the data from the clipboard, it uses **OleGetClipboard()** to get the **IDataObject** pointer from the clipboard. Once it has this, it can use **IDataObject::GetData()** to request the data directly from the object.

On the other hand, if a client (OLE-aware or not) uses the **GetClipboardData()** API call to retrieve data, then a **WM_RENDERFORMAT** message gets sent by Windows to the hidden window, and OLE then arranges to retrieve the data from the data object in the source. This is less efficient than calling ·**OleGetClipboard()**, and will usually be used by non OLE-aware clients.

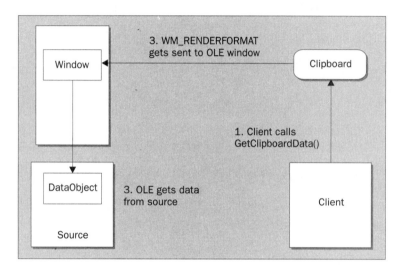

OLE Drag and Drop

Like the clipboard, drag and drop is a way of transferring an **IDataObject** from a source to a client, and, as with the OLE clipboard, the capability of the original Windows drag and drop mechanism is extended through the flexibility provided by **IDataObject**.

There are several different ways in which you can use drag and drop: to move data, to copy data, or to establish a link between a server and a container. OLE drag and drop uses two interfaces: **IDropSource** and **IDropTarget**.

The data source needs to understand how to use **IDataObject**, and in addition provides a **drop source** object, which implements the **IDropSource** interface. The client implements a **drop target**, which (as you might expect) uses the **IDropTarget** interface.

IDropSource possesses two functions:

▶ **QueryContinueDrag()**, which can be called periodically in order to decide whether to continue or cancel a drag and drop operation.

▶ **GiveFeedback()**, which allows the source to change the mouse cursor depending on the type and state of the operation. It may be a copy or move operation; it may be a link; or a drop may not be allowed here. A flag signaling the state is passed to the routine.

IDropTarget is implemented by the client end of a drag and drop operation. The client has to call the **RegisterDragDrop()** API function in order to associate a window handle with the COM object implementing the drop target. After this, Windows will notify the target whenever drag and drop movement occurs over the target's window. The **IDropTarget** interface has four functions:

- **DragEnter()**, called when a drag operation is occurring and the mouse pointer enters the window
- **DragOver()** is like a **WM_MOUSEMOVE** message, in that calls to it are generated repeatedly as the pointer moves around the window
- **DragLeave()** is called when the pointer leaves the target window
- **Drop()** is called if the user releases the mouse button while over the target window

The actual operation is kicked off by calling the **DoDragDrop()** API function, which monitors the state of the mouse and keyboard, and doesn't return until the user either drops the data on the target, or presses the *Esc* key to cancel the operation.

How MFC Implements UDT

MFC has several classes that work together to implement UDT functions. We'll look at them in the twin contexts of clipboard operations and drag and drop.

The Clipboard Classes

Clipboard operation is supported by two classes: **COleDataSource** and **COleDataObject**. Both are similar in operation, but **COleDataSource** is a full COM object, whereas **COleDataObject** is a wrapper class to help manipulate an **IDataObject** pointer.

COleDataSource, as its name implies, is used to originate data for transfer. When the user wants to copy data to the clipboard, or wants to start a drag and drop operation, the data to be transferred is stored in a **COleDataSource** object. Conversely, **COleDataObject** is used on the receiving end, and is used to provide access to the data stored by a **COleDataSource**.

The COleDataSource Class

You can create a **COleDataSource** object yourself if necessary, but the MFC server and client item classes will create one for you when you call their **CopyToClipboard()** or **DoDragDrop()** member functions.

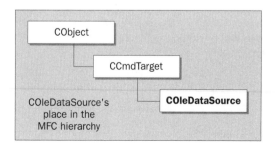

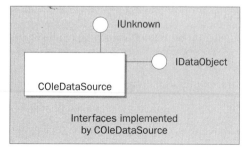

We saw how simple it was to use this mechanism from MFC when we implemented clipboard copy in the GraphSrv application in Chapter 4:

```
void CGraphSrvView::OnEditCopy()
{
    // Copy the whole of the document to the clipboard
    CGraphSrvSrvrItem itm(GetDocument());
    itm.CopyToClipboard(TRUE);
}
```

Adding those two lines to the Edit | Copy handler were all that was needed to get the server item to cache its data in a **COleDataSource** object and copy it to the clipboard.

For a **COleDataSource** object you create yourself, the process is slightly more complex. You can use **FORMATETC** and **STGMEDIUM** structures and call **CacheData()** to cache their data into the data source; alternatively, you can use the Windows **GlobalAlloc()** API function to grab some memory, put the data into it, and then use **CacheGlobalData()** to put this into the data source. Once you've associated the data with the source, a call to **SetClipboard()** will put the data source onto the clipboard, ready to be retrieved.

Here's a code fragment showing the sort of thing you'd do using **CacheData()**:

```
// Set up a data source
COleDataSource *pDS = new COleDataSource;

// Declare a STGMEDIUM to hold the data
STGMEDIUM stg;

// Store the data, which is in a block of memory with handle hG
stg.tymed = TYMED_HGLOBAL;
stg.hGlobal = hG;

// Cache the data in the source, and put it onto the clipboard
pDS->CacheData(CF_SOMEFORMAT, &stg);
```

And for completeness, here's the way you'd do it using **GlobalAlloc()**:

```
COleDataSource *pDS = new COleDataSource;

// Grab the appropriate amount of memory
HGLOBAL hG = GlobalAlloc(GHND | GMEM_SHARE, nBytes);
GlobalLock(hG);

// Copy the data...

// Cache the data in the source, and put it onto the clipboard
GlobalUnlock(hG);
pDS->CacheGlobalData(CF_SOMEFORMAT, hG);
pDS->SetClipboard();
```

We create a data source and allocate some memory. After doing whatever we need to do to copy the data into the memory, we call **CacheGlobalData()** to put it into the data source, specifying the appropriate clipboard format. Finally, we put the data source itself on the clipboard.

Immediate and Delayed Rendering

Much of the time, the data is cached into the **COleDataSource** at the time it is created and kept in memory, so that it's immediately available when required. This is called **immediate rendering** of data, and it may not be the best solution where you need to transfer a large amount of data. There's always a chance that something placed on the clipboard will never be retrieved, in which case the effort of putting it there will have been wasted.

Instead, it's possible to use **delayed rendering**. This is one of the more advanced UDT techniques, so we'll just mention it in passing here. The basic idea is that the data source puts the *format* of the data onto the clipboard, using a **FORMATETC** structure, but not the data itself. Clients can verify that the sort of data they want is on the clipboard, and then tell the source to supply it. In this way, the data is only transferred when it's going to be used, and the overhead in maintaining the **COleDataSource** is much lower.

Delayed rendering is supported in **COleDataSource** through five functions:

▶ **DelayRenderData()** puts the **FORMATETC** data onto the clipboard.

▶ **DelayRenderFileData()** does the same, but uses **CFile** as the storage medium for the data.

▶ **OnRenderData()** is called to retrieve the actual data. It is passed format details using a **FORMATETC** structure, and will end up calling either **OnRenderFileData()** to get the data back from a **CFile**, or **OnRenderGlobalData()** to retrieve it via a global memory handle.

You may have noticed that some applications, like Microsoft Word, warn you if you have a large amount of data on the clipboard when you exit, asking whether you want to make it available after the program has finished. If the data has been placed on the clipboard by delayed rendering, the actual data needs to be supplied in place of the format, since the source won't be around to provide the delayed data after the application has exited.

The COleDataObject Class

COleDataObject is used to retrieve the data from a **COleDataSource**. You *can* do it yourself, but as with data sources, the MFC client item class will handle it for you. Again, we saw this in the previous chapter, when we implemented Edit | Paste for the container application, and used the

> COleDataObject
>
> COleDataObject doesn't have a base class...

CreateFromClipboard() member function to create a client item from the data on the clipboard.

In order to do it yourself, you must first create a **COleDataObject**, and call its **AttachClipboard()** function to get the data from the clipboard.

Now you need to find out whether the data has the format you want. If you only want to check for one or two formats, you can call **IsDataAvailable()** to check a specific format; alternatively, you can enumerate through all the formats available on the clipboard by using **BeginEnumFormats()** and **GetNextFormat()**, until you've either found the one you want, or run out of formats.

Once you've found the format you require, you can retrieve the actual data using one of three functions:

▶ **GetData()** uses **FORMATETC** and **STGMEDIUM** to retrieve the data

▶ **GetFileData()** returns a pointer to a **CFile** which is storing the data

▶ **GetGlobalData()** returns a global memory handle

As an example, the following fragment shows how we might retrieve the data we placed on the clipboard when we were discussing **COleDataSource**:

```
COleDataObject cd;

cd.AttachClipboard();

if (cd.IsDataAvailable(CF_SOMEFORMAT)
{
    HANDLE h = cd.GetGlobalData(CF_SOMEFORMAT);

    // Use the data somehow...

    GlobalUnlock(h);
    GlobalFree(h);
}
```

It's also possible to use this class with a **COleDataSource** which isn't on the clipboard, in which case you can use the **Attach()**, **Release()** and **Detach()** functions to manage the use of the data source.

The Drag and Drop Classes

MFC implements drag and drop using two specialized classes - **COleDropSource** and **COleDropTarget** - in addition to the **COleDataSource** and **COleDataObject** classes we've just been discussing.

The COleDropSource Class

COleDropSource implements the **IDropSource** interface, and works along with **COleDataSource** to provide the source for drag and drop operations. MFC drag and drop will work quite happily with the default **COleDropSource**, but you may wish to override it if you're unhappy about some of the defaults which this class uses for cursors, escape keys and suchlike.

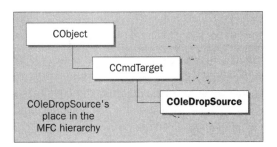

COleDropSource's place in the MFC hierarchy

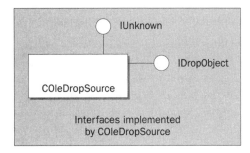

Interfaces implemented by COleDropSource

COleDropSource has three functions, the first two of which implement the corresponding **IDropSource** functions:

▶ **QueryContinueDrag()** is called repeatedly when the object is being dragged over the target window. It gets passed the state of the mouse and modifier keys, and returns an **SCODE** value saying whether the drag should continue (**S_OK**), whether a drop should occur (**DRAGDROP_S_DROP**), or whether the operation should be canceled (**DRAGDROP_S_CANCEL**).

▶ **GiveFeedback()** returns a **DROPEFFECT** value (see below for a discussion of **DROPEFFECT**) indicating what would happen if a drop occurred at this point, and is used by the framework to set the appropriate cursor.

▶ **OnBeginDrag()** is called by the framework to capture the mouse at the start of the drag process.

The COleDropTarget Class

COleDropTarget implements **IDropTarget**, and works with **COleDataObject** to implement the drag and drop target. The **COleDropTarget** member functions closely follow those of the interface it implements:

▶ **OnDragEnter()** implements **IDropTarget::DragEnter()**

▶ **OnDragOver()** implements **IDropTarget::DragOver()**

▶ **OnDragLeave()** implements **IDropTarget::DragLeave()**

▶ **OnDrop()** implements **IDropTarget::Drop()**

I've already mentioned the purposes of these interface functions, so I won't dwell on them here. Note, though, that the default implementations of these functions do nothing; we need to override them because only we know how our drop target is going to handle dropped objects.

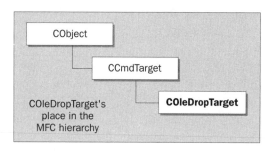

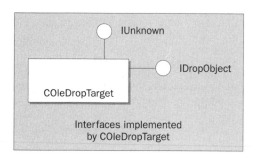

COleDropTarget also implements a few other functions:

▶ **OnDragScroll()** is called by the framework before **OnDragEnter()** and **OnDragOver()** in order to determine whether the mouse pointer is in the window's scrolling region.

▶ **OnDropEx()** is called first when a drop occurs. You can override this function to handle special drop activity, like drag and drop using the right mouse button. If this function hasn't handled the drop, the framework then calls **OnDrop()**.

▶ **Register()** registers the drop target with Windows.

▶ **Revoke()** de-registers the target.

The Drag and Drop Operation

What actually happens in a drag and drop operation? First of all, the client creates a **COleDropTarget** variable as a member of each view class that it wants to be a drop target. In the view's **OnCreate()** functions, the target object must register itself, using **COleDropTarget::Register()**. The target will automatically be de-registered when the view's destructor is called.

How the drop source handles its data depends on what sort of application and data we're dealing with. If the application is a container and the data to be transferred is a client item, then you can call **COleClientItem::DoDragDrop()**. If it isn't a client item, then you need to construct a **COleDataSource** object, initialize it with the data, and then call the object's **DoDragDrop()** member function. Finally, if the application is a server, use **COleServerItem::DoDragDrop()**. We'll see this being done in earnest later in the chapter, when we add drag and drop support to our server application.

The client and server item **DoDragDrop()** functions both take the same parameters:

```
DROPEFFECT DoDragDrop(LPCRECT lpItemRect,
                      CPoint  ptOffset,
                      BOOL    bIncludeLink = FALSE,
                      DWORD   dwEffects = DROPEFFECT_COPY | DROPEFFECT_MOVE,
                      LPCRECT lpRectStartDrag = NULL);
```

The first parameter is the item's bounding rectangle in pixels, while the **CPoint** describes the point within this rectangle where the mouse position was located at the time the drag started. The third parameter says whether the application supports links; if it's set to **TRUE**, link data can be copied.

The drop effects determine which types of drag and drop operation are supported by this drag source, with the defaults being moving and copying data. If we supported linking by setting **bIncludeLink** to **TRUE**, we'd want to include **DROPEFFECT_LINK** in the list of effects.

The last parameter defines a rectangle within which dragging won't occur. By using this, you can arrange things so that dragging doesn't occur until the user has moved a certain distance away from the actual object. If the parameter is **NULL**, a one-pixel rectangle is used.

> *There's also a time delay built into dragging, so that the operation will be aborted if the mouse hasn't moved within 200ms of* **DoDragDrop()** *being called.*

COleDataSource::DoDragDrop() is slightly different:

```
DROPEFFECT DoDragDrop(
    DWORD             dwEffects = DROPEFFECT_COPY|DROPEFFECT_MOVE|DROPEFFECT_LINK,
    LPCRECT           lpRectStartDrag = NULL,
    COleDropSource*   pDropSource = NULL);
```

223

The operations supported by default are slightly different, but we still have the notion of the starting rectangle. We also have a pointer to a **COleDropSource** object which will handle the user interface aspects of the drag, such as altering the cursor to reflect what would happen if an object were dropped at a particular point. If you've created your own custom **COleDropSource**-derived class, you can use it here. Otherwise, you can leave the pointer as **NULL**, and the standard MFC implementation will get used.

When the mouse pointer enters the window associated with the drop target, the window starts getting drag and drop notification messages. These notifications are handled by the **On...()** members of the **COleDropTarget** class, such as **OnDragEnter()**. In actual fact, the notifications get sent to the drop target object, which then delegates them to the view. **CView** has default handlers for these messages that you can override in order to obtain specific behavior.

The **OnDragEnter()** and **OnDragOver()** functions are pretty similar in the way they work. They each get passed

- A pointer to a **COleDataObject**
- A **DWORD** containing the state of the control keys, which is useful because the *Ctrl* key differentiates a move from a copy operation
- The position of the mouse

The functions can use this data to determine what kind of operation is being attempted, and return a **DROPEFFECT** value which tells the framework which cursor to display. There are five possible return values:

DROPEFFECT Value	Meaning
DROPEFFECT_NONE	No drop is allowed
DROPEFFECT_COPY	A copy operation is in progress
DROPEFFECT_MOVE	A move operation is in progress
DROPEFFECT_LINK	A link operation is in progress
DROPEFFECT_SCROLL	A drag/scroll operation is in progress

If no drop is allowed, the cursor will change to a circle with a line through it. For a copy, the cursor is the regular arrow with a small plus sign to the upper right; for a move, it's an arrow with a square to the lower right.

OnDragLeave() is called when the mouse pointer leaves the target window, and is called so that you can do any tidying up you might need to do.

OnDrop() is called when the user releases the mouse button while over the window. It takes the same parameters as the **OnDragEnter()** and **OnDragOver()** functions, and returns a **DROPEFFECT** showing what actually occurred. The code for getting the data into the client is very similar to that for pasting from the clipboard, and many developers use a single routine for performing both operations.

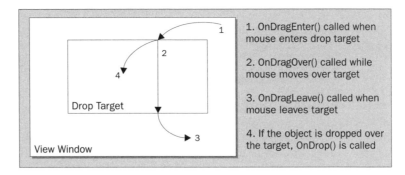

1. OnDragEnter() called when mouse enters drop target

2. OnDragOver() called while mouse moves over target

3. OnDragLeave() called when mouse leaves target

4. If the object is dropped over the target, OnDrop() is called

Adding UDT Features to the Server and Container

Let's see, now, how to add some of these UDT features to the applications we've already created. We'll add drag and drop to both the container and server, and also look at how we can support other clipboard formats (such as a text representation of the data) in the server.

Initiating Drag and Drop in the Server

It's really very easy to add drag and drop support to GraphServer. All we need to do is provide a drag and drop handler for when the left mouse button is pressed. As I explained above, if the user takes no action, then the operation will silently abort itself without any further intervention being needed on our part, so it really is a 'fire-and-forget' operation as far as we're concerned.

Try It Out - Adding Drag and Drop Support to the Server

1 Start by adding a **WM_LBUTTONDOWN** handler to the view class, and creating a new server item to represent the data. If this were an application like a drawing program, where we could select individual items in the document, then we'd need to create a server item to represent the selected item. Here, we're going to use the server item to represent the entire document, so we create a **CGraphSrvSrvrItem** item, passing it a pointer to the document object:

```
void CGraphSrvView::OnLButtonDown(UINT nFlags, CPoint point)
{
    // Construct a server item for the document
    CGraphSrvSrvrItem itm(GetDocument());

    CView::OnLButtonDown(nFlags, point);
}
```

2 All we need to do now is to call the server item's **DoDragDrop()** function. This needs to know the rectangle giving the size and position of the object, which is easy in this case because we can just use the view's client rectangle. It also needs to know where the mouse was inside this rectangle, which is similarly easy to calculate.

225

Here's the code:

```
void CGraphSrvView::OnLButtonDown(UINT nFlags, CPoint point)
{
    // Construct a server item for the document
    CGraphSrvSrvrItem itm(GetDocument());

    // Get the bounding rectangle and the mouse point
    CRect rect;
    GetClientRect(&rect);

    CPoint pt(point - rect.TopLeft());

    // Initiate the drag-and-drop operation
    itm.DoDragDrop(&rect,
                   pt,
                   TRUE,
                   DROPEFFECT_COPY | DROPEFFECT_LINK);

    CView::OnLButtonDown(nFlags, point);
}
```

The other arguments determine whether to include link information (**TRUE** in our case, since we added support for linking to the server) and what drag and drop operations are supported. We're supporting copying and linking, but not moving, since it doesn't really make much sense to move a whole document.

3 If you now rebuild the project, you should find that you can click on a GraphServer graph, drag it over, and drop it onto a suitable container, such as Word. Notice the cursors that are displayed as you perform the drag and drop operation. I think you'll agree that was a very small amount of effort required to implement quite a powerful feature.

Accepting Dropped Objects in the Container

We now need to add functionality so that the container can accept dropped objects. This is a little more complicated and involves rather more effort than the drag side of the operation, so we'll take it in stages.

Try It Out - Registering as a Drop Target

1 Remember that any view that wants to be a drop target has to have a **COleDropTarget** member object, so the first step is to add one of these to the view class:

```
class CContView : public CView
{
    COleDropTarget m_dropTarget;

protected: // create from serialization only
    CContView();
    DECLARE_DYNCREATE(CContView)

    // Rest of class omitted...
};
```

2 The target needs to be registered before it can be used, and it makes sense to do this when the view is created. Use ClassWizard to provide a handler for **WM_CREATE** and use the handler to register the drop target object, passing the view itself as the drop window:

```
int CContView::OnCreate(LPCREATESTRUCT lpCreateStruct)
{
    if (CView::OnCreate(lpCreateStruct) == -1)
        return -1;

    // Register the drop target
    m_dropTarget.Register(this);

    return 0;
}
```

Now, in order to make the drag and drop work, we have to provide implementations of **OnDragOver()**, **OnDrop()**, **OnDragEnter()**, and **OnDragLeave()**. Before we continue, prepare by using ClassWizard to provide skeleton overrides for these functions in the view class.

Try It Out - Implementing OnDragOver()

OnDragOver() needs to determine what effect dropping the object at this point would have. The function is passed a **COleDataObject** pointer, a **DWORD** describing the states of the modifier keys (*Alt*, *Ctrl* and *Shift*) and mouse buttons, plus the current mouse position relative to the client area.

The online documentation for **IDropTarget::DragEnter()** suggests that the modifier keys affect the drop operation in the following manner:

▶ The *Ctrl* and *Shift* keys together cause a link operation

▶ *Ctrl* alone causes a copy

▶ *Shift* alone, or no modifier keys at all, causes a move

We can implement this in the code like this:

```
DROPEFFECT CContView::OnDragOver(COleDataObject* pDataObject,
                                 DWORD dwKeyState, CPoint point)
{
    // Decide what action to report
    DROPEFFECT dr;

    DWORD state = dwKeyState & (MK_CONTROL | MK_ALT | MK_SHIFT);

    if (state == (MK_CONTROL | MK_SHIFT))
        dr = DROPEFFECT_LINK;
    else if (state == MK_CONTROL)
        dr = DROPEFFECT_COPY;
    else if (state == 0 || state == MK_SHIFT)
        dr = DROPEFFECT_MOVE;
    else
        dr = DROPEFFECT_NONE;

    return dr;
}
```

We declare a **DROPEFFECT** object, and then mask the state argument to leave only the modifier key settings. Once we've done this, we can simply test for equality against the combinations we require.

Try It Out - Implementing OnDrop()

The code for the **OnDrop()** function is quite similar to the client item creation code we saw when we were inserting objects and pasting from the clipboard. Just as before, we create a new client item and attach it to the document, and then tell the item to get its data from the dropped object:

```
BOOL CContView::OnDrop(COleDataObject* pDataObject,
                       DROPEFFECT dropEffect, CPoint point)
{
    CContCntrItem* pItem = NULL;

    try
    {
        // Try creating a new item
        CContDoc* pDoc = GetDocument();
        ASSERT_VALID(pDoc);
        pItem = new CContCntrItem(pDoc);
        ASSERT_VALID(pItem);

        // Let the object get its data, depending on the type
        // of drop operation
        if (dropEffect == DROPEFFECT_LINK)
        {
            if (!pItem->CreateLinkFromData(pDataObject))
                AfxThrowMemoryException();
        }
        else
        {
            if (!pItem->CreateFromData(pDataObject))
                AfxThrowMemoryException();
        }

        // Set the item's position and size in the container
        pItem->SetPosition(point);
        pItem->UpdateSize();

        // Make this the selected item
        SetSelected(pItem);
        Invalidate();

        // Tell the document it's been modified
        pDoc->SetModifiedFlag();
    }

    catch(CException* pCE)
    {
        // Tidy up if there was an error.
        if (pItem != NULL)
        {
            ASSERT_VALID(pItem);
```

```
        pItem->Delete();
    }

    AfxMessageBox(IDP_FAILED_TO_CREATE);
    pCE->Delete();

    // The drop wasn't successful, so return FALSE
    return FALSE;
    }

    // Return TRUE to show the drop worked
    return TRUE;
}
```

We check the **DROPEFFECT** that has been passed to us, and if it's a **DROPEFFECT_LINK**, we tell the item to initialize itself accordingly. Once the item has got its data, we position it as before. Notice the error handling mechanism here: if an error occurs, we delete the item by calling **COleClientItem::Delete()**, rather than by using the C++ **delete** keyword. **Delete()** handles clearing up after the item, making sure that the document containing the item is updated.

If you rebuild the application, you'll find that it will now accept dropped objects, but there are two problems. Firstly, there's no feedback on the size and position of the object as you're dragging; it would be nice to see the outline of the object as we drag it, in order to help with positioning. Secondly, the container doesn't put the new object in quite the right place; I may have clicked in the center of the object when I began the drag, but when I drop it, the object gets placed with its *origin* at the mouse position.

Try It Out - Implementing OnDragEnter() and OnDragLeave()

Let's solve these two problems. We'll give feedback when dragging by showing a **focus rectangle** that is the correct size for the item being dragged. In case you haven't met one before, a focus rectangle is a rectangle that a **CDC** object can draw, usually used to indicate that something has the focus. It's drawn using an XOR technique, so you just need to draw it a second time in order to erase it.

1 In order to draw the focus rectangle correctly, we must find the size of the item and the offset of the mouse pointer within the rectangle; the obvious place to do this is in **OnDragEnter()**, so that we get the information as soon as the mouse pointer enters the target window. Start by adding two new data members to the view class, both **CSize** objects:

```
class CContView : public CView
{
    COleDropTarget m_dropTarget;

    CSize m_dragItemSize;
    CSize m_dragOffset;

    // Rest of class definition omitted...
};
```

The first of these is going to be used to store the size of the dragged object (we don't need a **CRect** because we're only interested in relative size, not coordinates); the second holds the position where the mouse pointer was clicked relative to the server item, in device coordinates.

2 How are we going to get this information? When the server constructed the data source at the start of the drag and drop operation, a data structure was added which provides useful information about the object being transferred. The **OBJECTDESCRIPTOR** structure looks like this:

```
typedef struct tagOBJECTDESCRIPTOR
{
    ULONG   cbSize;
    CLSID   clsid;
    DWORD   dwDrawAspect;
    SIZEL   sizel;
    POINTL  pointl;
    DWORD   dwStatus;
    DWORD   dwFullUserTypeName;
    DWORD   dwSrcOfCopy;
    /* variable sized string data may appear here */
} OBJECTDESCRIPTOR;
```

This structure contains information such as the CLSID of the object and its drawing aspect, along with the two items which interest us, which are the object size (**sizel**) and the mouse offset (**pointl**).

The data is available via global memory, and is in a clipboard format called **"Object Descriptor"**. To retrieve it, you'll need the corresponding **CLIPFORMAT** value, which you get with a call to **RegisterClipboardFormat()**. This may seem a strange call - we're not registering a new format, after all - but the reason for it is that if the name you pass belongs to an existing format, then you'll get that **CLIPFORMAT** returned.

We can then obtain a global memory handle by calling **COleDataObject::GetGlobalData()** on the value returned, like this:

```
DROPEFFECT CContView::OnDragEnter(COleDataObject* pDataObject,
                                  DWORD dwKeyState, CPoint point)
{
    // Get the existing clipboard format
    CLIPFORMAT fm = (CLIPFORMAT)::RegisterClipboardFormat(
                                        _T("Object Descriptor"));
    // Get the data
    HGLOBAL hg = pDataObject->GetGlobalData(fm);
    ASSERT(hg != NULL);
```

The global memory block contains an **OBJECTDESCRIPTOR** structure that contains the size and offset we require in **MM_HIMETRIC** coordinates. We can cast the block to get a pointer to an **OBJECTDESCRIPTOR**, then extract the values:

```
    LPOBJECTDESCRIPTOR lpDesc = (LPOBJECTDESCRIPTOR)GlobalLock(hg);
    ASSERT(lpDesc != NULL);
```

```
// Get the size and offset
m_dragItemSize.cx = (int)lpDesc->sizel.cx;
m_dragItemSize.cy = (int)lpDesc->sizel.cy;


m_dragOffset.cx = (int)lpDesc->pointl.x;
m_dragOffset.cy = (int)lpDesc->pointl.y;
```

Since these values are supplied in **HIMETRIC** coordinates, we need to convert them to device coordinates:

```
// Convert from HIMETRIC
CClientDC aDC(this);
aDC.HIMETRICtoDP(&m_dragItemSize);
aDC.HIMETRICtoDP(&m_dragOffset);
```

Finally, we need to dispose of the global memory we allocated:

```
// Dispose of global memory
GlobalUnlock(hg);
GlobalFree(hg);
```

```
   return CView::OnDragEnter(pDataObject, dwKeyState, point);
}
```

3   That's got the data; now we need to use it to draw the feedback rectangle. The place to do this is **OnDragOver()**, and it's made easy by the way **CDC::DrawFocusRect()** works. Because it's doing XOR'd drawing, all we need to do is to draw the previous rectangle (thus erasing it) and then draw the new one. This will take care of drawing the focus rectangle while the drag is occurring, and the only special cases we need to concern ourselves with are drawing the first and last ones.

Another problem we have to deal with is that **OnDragEnter()** must return a **DROPEFFECT** value - but how do we know what to return? A handy solution presents itself: as well being the place to do the drawing, **OnDragOver()** also calculates the **DROPEFFECT**. If we call **OnDragOver()** from **OnDragEnter()**, we can get it to draw the rectangle for us, and also provide a **DROPEFFECT** to use as the function's return value. All we need to do is to amend the last line of **OnDragEnter()**:

```
   return OnDragOver(pDataObject, dwKeyState, point);
}
```

Now for the modifications to **OnDragOver()**. We're going to redraw the previous rectangle to erase it, and then draw the new one; the problem is that when the function is called for the very first time (from **OnDragEnter()**), we haven't got a previous rectangle to redraw. This is quickly solved by adding a flag to the class, which is set **TRUE** when we're in the middle of a drag, and **FALSE** otherwise. We also need a second data member to store the origin of the previous rectangle we drew:

```
class CContView : public CView
{
   COleDropTarget m_dropTarget;

   CSize m_dragItemSize;
   CSize m_dragOffset;
```

```
    BOOL m_doRedraw;
    CPoint m_lastOrigin;

    // Rest of class definition omitted...
};
```

Set **m_doRedraw** to **FALSE** in the constructor so we start in the right state; here's the code to add to **OnDragOver()**:

```
DROPEFFECT CContView::OnDragOver(COleDataObject* pDataObject,
                                 DWORD dwKeyState, CPoint point)
{
    // Get a device context
    CClientDC aDC(this);

    // Clear the last rectangle, if necessary
    if (m_doRedraw)
    {
        CRect rc(m_lastOrigin, m_dragItemSize);
        aDC.DrawFocusRect(rc);
    }

    // And draw the new one
    point -= m_dragOffset;
    CRect rc(point, m_dragItemSize);
    aDC.DrawFocusRect(rc);

    m_lastOrigin = point;
    m_doRedraw = TRUE;

    // Decide what action to report
    DROPEFFECT dr;

    DWORD state = dwKeyState & (MK_CONTROL | MK_ALT | MK_SHIFT);

    if (state == (MK_CONTROL | MK_SHIFT))
        dr = DROPEFFECT_LINK;
    else if (state == MK_CONTROL)
        dr = DROPEFFECT_COPY;
    else if (state == 0 || state == MK_SHIFT)
        dr = DROPEFFECT_MOVE;
    else
        dr = DROPEFFECT_NONE;

    return dr;
}
```

If we're in the middle of a drag, we construct a rectangle based on the saved origin, and then draw it to erase the existing rectangle. We don't want the new rectangle to have its origin at the mouse point, so we offset the origin accordingly and draw the new rectangle, before setting the flag and saving the origin for next time round.

4   The only bit of tidying up left to do is to get rid of the focus rectangle by drawing it one last time in **OnDragLeave()**:

```
void CContView::OnDragLeave()
{
    // Redraw the focus rectangle to erase it
    CClientDC aDC(this);

    CRect rc(m_lastOrigin, m_dragItemSize);
    aDC.DrawFocusRect(rc);

    // Reset the flag
    m_doRedraw = FALSE;
}
```

The call to the base class **OnDragLeave()** which ClassWizard puts in for you does nothing, so it can be removed.

5   That leaves us with a correctly functioning focus rectangle, but we need to make a minor alteration to placing the item in **OnDrop()**, so that it's placed correctly relative to the mouse position:

```
    // Let the object get its data, depending on the type
    // of drop operation
    if (dropEffect == DROPEFFECT_LINK)
    {
        if (!pItem->CreateLinkFromData(pDataObject))
            AfxThrowMemoryException();
    }
    else
    {
        if (!pItem->CreateFromData(pDataObject))
            AfxThrowMemoryException();
    }

    // Clear the focus rectangle
    OnDragLeave();

    // Set the item's position and size in the container
    pItem->SetPosition(point - m_dragOffset);
    pItem->UpdateSize();

    // Make this the selected item
    SetSelected(pItem);
    Invalidate();

    // Tell the document it's been modified
    pDoc->SetModifiedFlag();
```

Now rebuild the application and test the drag and drop behavior. You should see the outline of the item being displayed as you drag the mouse pointer across the container's view.

Adding Clipboard Formats

As a final exercise, let's see how we can add another clipboard format to GraphServer. Why would we want to do this? Well, it enables a server application to put its data on the clipboard in a number of different ways, so that a variety of client applications can select the one that is most suitable for their needs.

As an example, a spreadsheet program might put its data on the clipboard in three formats:

- A native data format, for those who want to be able to in-place edit the item
- A graphical format, consisting of a bitmap or a metafile, for those who just want to display a picture of the item
- A text format, for those who want a textual representation of the data

Supplying a new clipboard format takes place in the server item class, and it's a two-stage process. Firstly, the new format needs to be set up so that we can use it; secondly, we need to supply the code to provide the item data in the new format.

If data is offered in different formats, it's supplied by the server item functions **OnRenderFileData()** or **OnRenderData()**, depending on whether the data is to be written to a file object or supplied in a more general way using the **FORMATETC** and **STGMEDIUM** structures.

What we'll do is add support for a textual representation of the data, which uses the **CF_TEXT** clipboard format. Since this is a standard format, we don't need to use **RegisterClipboardFormat()** to create a completely new one - we can use the **CF_TEXT** descriptor we already have.

Try It Out - Adding Support for the CF_TEXT Clipboard Format

1 Open the server item's source file, **SrvrItem.cpp**, and add a couple of lines to the item constructor:

```
CGraphSrvSrvrItem::CGraphSrvSrvrItem(CGraphSrvDoc* pContainerDoc)
    : COleServerItem(pContainerDoc, TRUE)
{
    // Tell the data source what to do with the new clipboard format
    COleDataSource* pDS = GetDataSource();
    pDS->DelayRenderFileData(CF_TEXT);

    // Set the item name for linking
    SetItemName("Graph1");
}
```

The **COleDataSource** object associated with the server item is used to store the clipboard formats that the item supports. We get a pointer to it, and then use its **DelayRenderFileData()** to register the **CF_TEXT** format. This means that when a request comes in for data in the **CF_TEXT** format, the data source will call **OnRenderFileData()** to get it, which we're just about to supply.

2   Add an override of **COleServerItem::OnRenderFileData()** as a public member of the **CGraphSrvSrvrItem** class. The prototype for the header file is:

```
BOOL OnRenderFileData(LPFORMATETC lpFormatEtc, CFile* pFile);
```

The function gets passed a pointer to a **FORMATETC** structure and a pointer to a **CFile**, into which it should write the data. We want to check the clipboard format – if it's **CF_TEXT**, then we'll handle it, otherwise we'll pass it on to the base class for default processing:

```
BOOL CGraphSrvSrvrItem::OnRenderFileData(LPFORMATETC lpFormatEtc, CFile* pFile)
{
   ASSERT(lpFormatEtc != NULL);

   if (lpFormatEtc->cfFormat == CF_TEXT)
   {
      CGraphSrvDoc* pDoc = GetDocument();
      ASSERT_VALID(pDoc);

      // Get the object's size...
      CSize size;
      OnGetExtent(DVASPECT_CONTENT, size);

      CString s;

      s.Format("GraphSrv object with %d data points, size %d by %d
               HIMETRIC units", pDoc->GetGraph()->Size(), size.cx, size.cy);
      LPTSTR pBuff = s.GetBuffer(80);

      // make sure to include the terminating NULL
      pFile->Write(pBuff, strlen(pBuff)+1);
      return TRUE;
   }
   else
      return COleServerItem::OnRenderFileData(lpFormatEtc, pFile);
}
```

3   As an illustration of how this works, we're writing out some information about the object: the number of data points on the graph, and its size. Rebuild the project, then start GraphServer and copy a graph to the clipboard. Start a container that can handle plain text, such as Microsoft Word; our container won't do this time, because we haven't made it handle this format.

Choose Word's Edit | Paste Special... menu item, and you'll get the Paste Special dialog displayed:

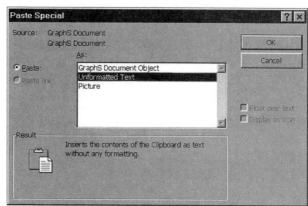

This time we have a new option, Unformatted Text, which corresponds to the **CF_TEXT** clipboard format. Select this format, press OK, and you'll get the text pasted into your document:

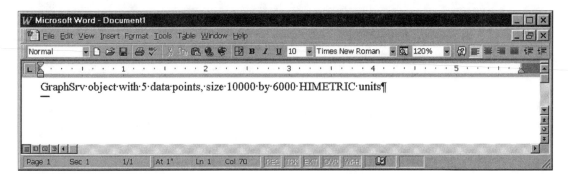

Summary

We've now come quite a way, and have seen how to develop OLE server and container applications. We started this chapter by looking briefly at the way in which servers and containers interact when objects are activated and deactivated, noting that it's quite a complex process!

We've also covered several important points about data transfer. COM has a data-transfer mechanism called UDT (Uniform Data Transfer), which provides a way for applications to exchange data in a variety of formats, using a standard COM interface called **IDataObject**.

Two existing Windows data transfer mechanisms - the clipboard, and drag and drop - have been re-engineered to use the UDT mechanism. MFC encapsulates both these mechanisms in classes; it is simple to add drag support to a server, and only slightly more complicated to add drop support to a container.

We've now covered the basic functionality required by 'traditional' servers and containers. In the next chapter, we'll take a look at a new type of server that has become available with ActiveX: the Active Document server.

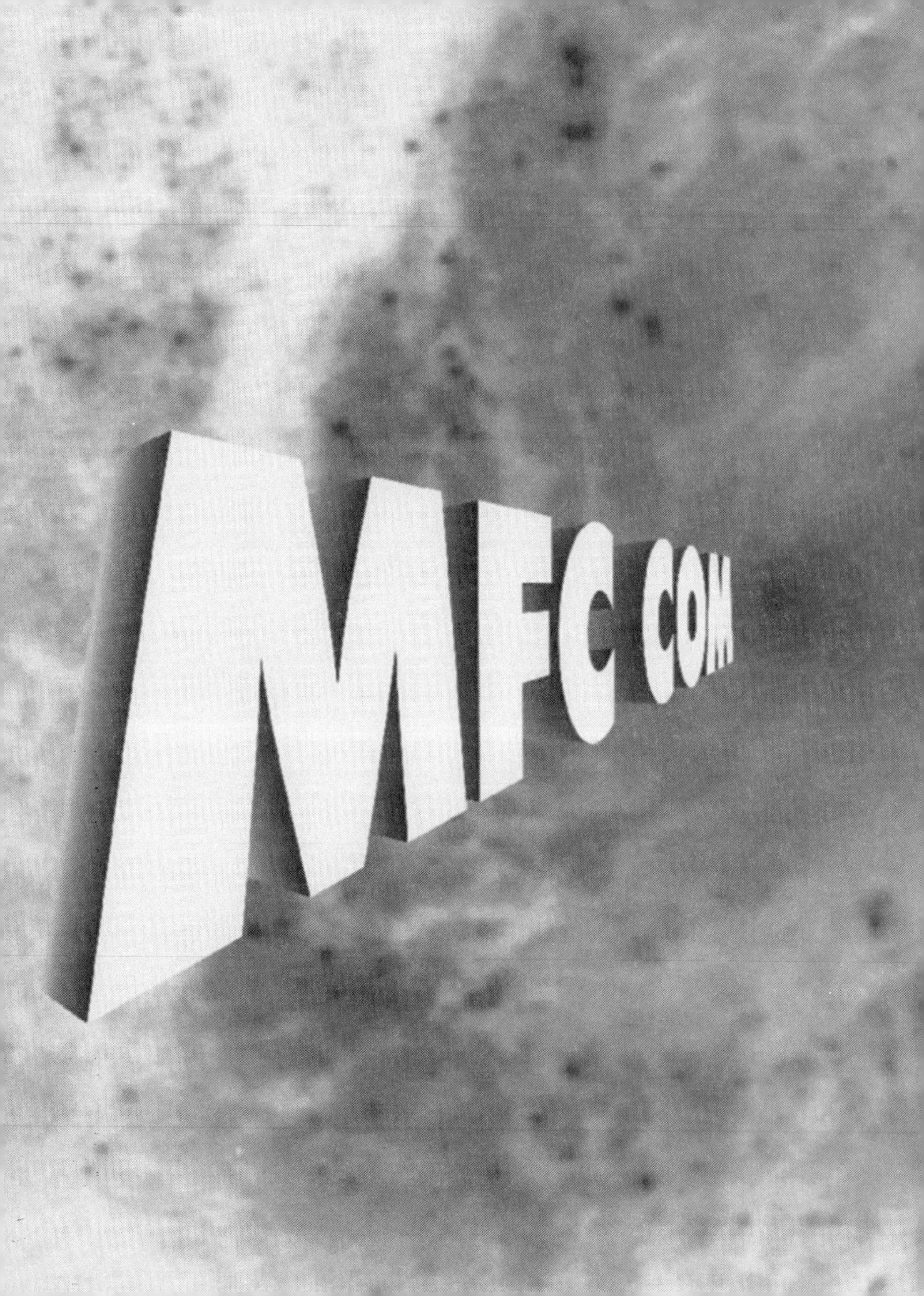
MFC COM

Active Documents

In this chapter we're going to take a look at one of the newer arrivals on the ActiveX scene: **Active documents**, or **DocObjects**, as they're called by the MFC classes which handle them. After investigating what they are and how they work, we'll see how to add some extra capability to our GraphSrv application.

What are Active Documents?

By now, you should be used to embedding objects in containers. The container gives the server a rectangle in its view within which to display the object, and to support in-place editing, but the container application is still firmly in control. The container may allow the embedded object's server to share the toolbar and menu bar, but the application in charge is still very definitely the container.

Active documents work at a higher level. Instead of being displayed within a rectangle in the view, they take over the *entire* client area of the container, they can play with the frame and its menus and toolbars, and they generally make the container look like the server application. This behavior needs to be implemented from both sides, so both the container and the server have to know about Active documents, and must be able to handle them correctly. Furthermore, if you try to display a document from an Active document server in a container that doesn't handle them, it should behave like an ordinary embedded object.

Active documents differ from traditional embedded objects in several ways:

- They display in the entire client area of the frame window
- There's no frame with a hatched border or resize handles
- They may have multiple pages
- They are *always* in-place active

It should be clear that the intention is not for Active documents to replace traditional embedded objects. Active documents add a useful new layer of functionality, but there will still be many occasions when you want to embed a small item as part of a larger document.

Active Document Servers and Containers

The implementation of Active documents requires special servers to produce them, and special container applications to use them. Active document servers are identified in the system by a key in their registry entries. If you look under the CLSID for an Active document server, it will have a key called DocObject to identify it as such.

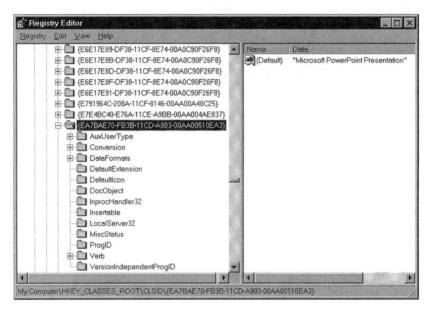

When you decide to add an Active document to a container, the container will search the registry for appropriate servers and present you with a list to choose from. At the time of writing there aren't too many Active document container applications, the only two of any note being Microsoft's Office Binder and Internet Explorer.

The concept of Active documents was originally designed to work with the Microsoft Office Binder, and developers could sign up with Microsoft in order to develop Active document server applications that would work with the Binder. It turned out, though, that this was a useful step in the evolution of compound documents in general, and so the interfaces that implemented Active documents have now been generalized and re-released as part of the ActiveX technologies.

Here's the Office 97 Binder with no documents open, showing its native interface:

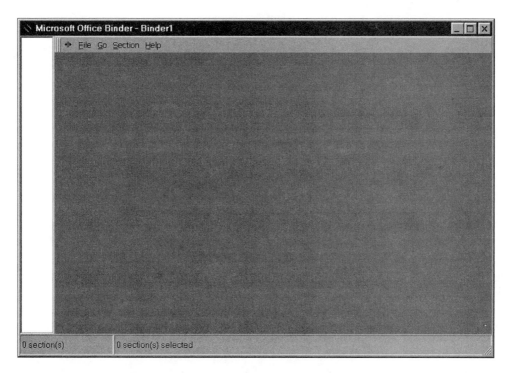

A Binder **Section** is a document belonging to an Active document server. On my system I have four such servers, which are shown in a dialog when I select **Section** | **Add**...:

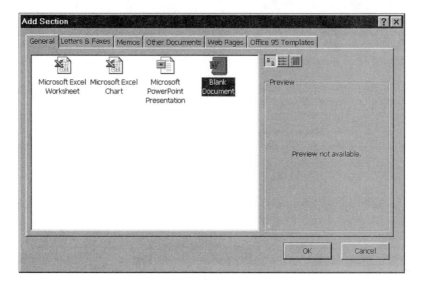

If I choose to insert a Word document, the Binder looks like this:

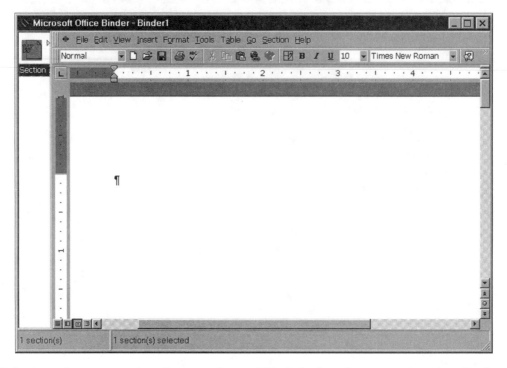

Notice how the menus and toolbars are those of Word. In fact, there are only a few details which tell us that it isn't Word we're looking at, such as the section pane on the left of the frame, the button at the left-hand end of the menu bar, and the Section menu.

As another example, let's look at Internet Explorer. If this is an Active document container, then we'd expect it to be able to open a Word document in the same way as the Binder... and it can! Here's the sort of thing you'll see if you try it:

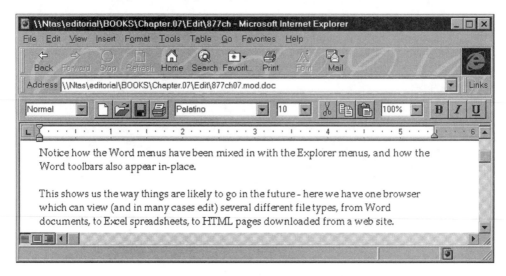

*How long before we see editable HTML pages? After all, users can now load a Word
document into Internet Explorer and edit it, but they can't do anything with HTML pages
except view them. When IE4 becomes the system browser for the next release of Windows,
quite a few people are going to start asking why there's one format of document they can't
edit in-place.*

Active Document Interfaces

Now we've seen what Active documents are, let's explore how they're implemented, starting with
the interfaces. On the server side, Active documents are supported by several interfaces:

> `IOleDocument`

> `IOleDocumentView`

> `IOleDocumentSite`

> `IOleCommandTarget`

> `IPrint`

> `IEnumOleDocumentViews`

> `IContinueCallback`

Most of these are documented in the Visual C++ 5.0 online help, although the explanation is
rather scattered around. What follows is a brief explanation of what each is, and what it does,
to help you get an overall understanding of how these things fit together.

The IOleDocument Interface

A server implements the `IOleDocument` interface to show that it can act as an Active document
server. An Active document container can then use the interface to perform any of three
operations, which are supported by the following functions:

> `CreateView()` creates and optionally initializes new views.

> `GetDocMiscStatus()` retrieves the `DOCMISC` bits which apply to an Active document.
> There are four status bits, showing whether the document supports multiple views,
> whether it supports complex rectangles, whether it can be opened for editing in a
> separate window, and whether it supports file I/O.

> `EnumViews()` enumerates the views by returning either an enumeration of the views, or
> a pointer to a single view if there's only one of them. The enumerator returned is a
> pointer to an implementation of `IEnumOleDocumentViews`, described below.

The IOleDocumentView Interface

`IOleDocumentView` implements a single instance of an Active document view, which is very
similar in concept to an MFC view. In fact, when it's used in a program with the MFC
document/view architecture, information sent to the `IOleDocumentView` interface will be passed
on to the server's view class, so that it can respond to changes in its environment. This interface
provides all the functionality necessary for a container to manage a document view object,
including activating it.

IOleDocumentView implements functions to set and get the **in-place site**. Server items and client items are particular cases of in-place sites, which represent in-place objects. Sites are implemented by the **IOleInPlaceSite** interface, which contains methods for interacting with, and controlling, in-place objects. Managing in-place objects includes such actions as activating and deactivating them, notifying the object when its borders have changed, and notifying the container when one of its objects has been activated.

The **IOleDocumentView** interface also implements several other important functions, including:

▶ **GetDocument()** returns a pointer to the view's document

▶ **SetRect()** and **GetRect()** set or get the viewport coordinates for the view

▶ **Show()** tells the view to show or hide itself

▶ **UIActivate()** activates or deactivates this view's user interface elements

▶ **Open()** opens the view for editing in a separate window, if that is supported

▶ **Close()** tells the view to close itself

▶ **Clone()** tells this view to duplicate itself in a different viewport

The IOleDocumentSite Interface

This interface has just one function, the interestingly-named **ActivateMe()**. Usually, activation of an in-place object follows the rather convoluted mechanism I outlined in flowchart form in the previous chapter. This interface provides a shortcut, allowing the Active document to tell its client site in the container to activate it. The client site implements this interface, and the Active document can then call its **ActivateMe()** function when it needs to be activated.

The IOleCommandTarget Interface

IOleCommandTarget provides a mechanism by which Active document servers and containers can send commands to each other. This could be done using Automation, but the demands of Active documents are simpler, and don't justify the whole **IDispatch** mechanism needed by Automation. We can therefore regard this as a simpler form of Automation for use by Active documents, and like Automation, it may or may not be used by a particular application.

IOleCommandTarget allows a container to receive commands that originate in an Active document's user interface, and to send the same commands (such as New, Open, Save As, and Print on the File menu; and Copy, Paste, Undo, and so forth on the Edit menu) to an Active document.

> *Support for this interface is optional, so you shouldn't rely on it being available.*

Simpler in use than Automation's **IDispatch** mechanism, **IOleCommandTarget** relies entirely on a standard set of commands that rarely have arguments, and no type information is involved either (type safety is diminished for command arguments as well). If you do need to dispatch commands with arguments, use **COleServerDoc::OnExecOleCmd()**, since the MFC default implementation of **IOleCommandTarget::Exec()** only routes the parameterless calls to the frame's **OnCmdMsg()** handler.

Suppose that the container wants to forward all print commands to the Active document server. We could arrange it so that the message handler for **ID_FILE_PRINT** in the container calls the corresponding handler in the server, but this is not a good solution because it requires the use of fixed menu IDs, and isn't easily extendible.

The method provided by **IOleCommandTarget** is similar to Automation, in that a caller can discover what commands are supported by an object, and then call them. The interface implements two functions:

▶ **QueryStatus()** says whether an object supports a given command

▶ **Exec()** actually executes a command

A client will use **QueryStatus()** by passing an array of **OLECMD** structures, which look like this:

```
typedef struct _tagOLECMD {
    ULONG cmdID;
    DWORD cmdf;
} OLECMD;
```

The **cmdID** member holds the ID of the command it wants to know about, and the object puts status information into the **cmdf** member, such as **OLECMDF_SUPPORTED** to show that the command is supported, **OLECMDF_ENABLED** to show that the command is available and enabled, and so on.

The **QueryStatus()** function can also return name and status string information for each supported command, so that the container can update its status lines appropriately. A number of common commands, such as New, Save, Print and Page Setup, are already defined for use with **QueryStatus()**. If you're interested, you'll find them in the **OLECMDID** enumeration, in **Docobj.h**.

Once you know that a command is supported, it can be called using the **Exec()** function. As well as input and output arguments, you can also supply a flag to instruct how the command should be executed. There are four execution options, all part of the **OLECMDEXECOPT** enumeration, and all of which have pretty self-explanatory names:

Option	Meaning
OLECMDEXECOPT_DODEFAULT	Perform the default action.
OLECMDEXECOPT_PROMPTUSER	Prompt the user first.
OLECMDEXECOPT_DONTPROMPTUSER	Don't prompt the user first.
OLECMDEXECOPT_SHOWHELP	Show help. Note that this one isn't supported by MFC's implementation of **Exec()**, so you'd have to override **COleServerDoc::OnExecOleCmd()** in order to handle it.

The IPrint Interface

`IPrint` (not `IOlePrint`!) is another optional interface. It supports printing the Active document, and contains three functions:

- ▶ `SetInitialPageNum()`, as its name implies, sets the initial page number for the print job
- ▶ `GetPageInfo()` retrieves information about the print job
- ▶ `Print()` tells the server object to print.

The IEnumOleDocumentViews Interface

Active documents may implement this interface if they support more than one view of their data. It has the usual functions supported by enumeration interfaces: `Next()`, `Skip()`, `Reset()` and `Clone()`. These functions enable a client to step through the views supported by the Active document.

The IContinueCallback Interface

`IContinueCallback` - for some reason they decided to omit '`Ole`' from the name - is an optional (and undocumented) interface which can be implemented by containers to help control long operations. Using the two functions in this interface, `FContinue()` and `FContinuePrinting()`, a server can ask the container whether it should continue with a lengthy operation or not.

MFC Support for Active Documents

Now that I've explained the basics about the interfaces that support Active documents, we'll discuss how MFC implements them. The first thing to note is that at present (VC++ version 5.0), MFC provides support for Active document servers, but not for containers. It is possible to get some of the functionality of Active document containers by roundabout means, but it isn't easy to create a complete container using MFC.

What you can do at present is use the Web Browser Control that implements most of Internet Explorer's functionality. You can use this control in a dialog or form view, just as you would use any other control, and you'll be able to view HTML files and even edit documents belonging to other Active document servers, like Word and Excel.

If you've installed Internet Explorer, you'll be able to find the Web Browser Control in the Components and Controls Gallery; choose the control, and you'll get a wrapper class, as usual. That's fine as far as it goes, but what you don't get is the menu and toolbar negotiation that's necessary for a server and container to work together. This means that you can edit a Word document, as long as you don't want to use any menu or toolbar items! Adding this menu negotiation using COM coding is one of the things that would make writing an Active document container from scratch a fairly daunting prospect.

Active document servers, on the other hand, are supported in MFC by three classes:

- **CDocObjectServer**
- **CDocObjectServerItem**, which takes the place of **COleServerItem**
- **COleDocIPFrameWnd**, which takes the place of **COleIPFrameWnd**

The CDocObjectServer Class

Four of the new interfaces I mentioned are implemented by **CDocObjectServer**, and they provide the extra functionality needed to make a **COleDocument** server into a full Active document server.

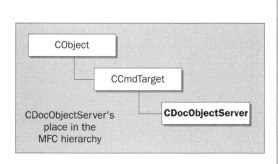

CDocObjectServer's place in the MFC hierarchy

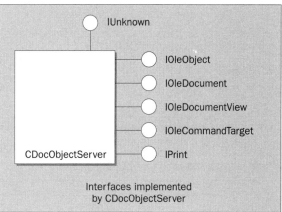

Interfaces implemented by CDocObjectServer

This class has four particularly interesting functions, which map some of the corresponding interface methods:

- **ActivateDocObject()** is called to activate the server, but not show the view.

- **OnActivateView()** is called in order to activate the view. This function creates an in-place frame window, draws scrollbars within the view, sets up the menus the server shares with its container, adds frame controls, sets the active object, and then finally shows the in-place frame window and sets the focus to it. It's called by the MFC framework in response to a **UIActivate()** with **TRUE** as first parameter. The method is virtual, but you shouldn't override it without taking a look at the MFC implementation of **CDocObjectServer::OnActivateView()** in **Oledocvw.cpp**. You'll find that the routine is complex, bearing a distinct similarity to the **COleClientItem::ActivateInPlace()** function that was mentioned at the start of the last chapter. Overriding this routine will be a non-trivial process!

- **OnSaveViewState()** is called in response to the **IOleDocumentView::SaveViewState()** interface method. It can be overridden in order to save state information, such as scrollbar and caret positions, zoom factors and so on. This function is called when the view is being deactivated, and saves the state information to a **CArchive** object.

▶ **OnApplyViewState()** is called in response to the **IOleDocumentView::ApplyViewState()** interface method. It is called when the view is being displayed for the first time. If you saved state information using **OnSaveViewState()**, you'll want to override this function in order to restore and act on the saved data.

Together, **ActivateDocObject()** and **OnActivateView()** activate and display the Active document view. Active document activation differs from other kinds of in-place activation, in that it bypasses displaying in-place hatched borders and object adornments (such as sizing handles), and ignores object extent functions. Also, scroll bars are drawn *within* the view rectangle as opposed to outside it (as would be the case in normal in-place activation).

The **COleServerDoc** document class uses **CDocObjectServer** to provide the extra functionality needed when it is representing an Active document. It contains a **CDocObjectServer** data member called **m_pDocObjectServer**, which is set to **NULL** initially, and has a new object assigned to it when the container calls the server's **IOleObject::SetClientSite()** function in order to pass it information about the container site. If the container is an Active document container, it will have implemented the **IOleDocumentSite** interface; **SetClientSite()** checks for this interface, and if it is present, creates a **CDocObjectServer** to manage the extra functionality, or calls its **SetDocSite()** method if it already exists.

The CDocObjectServerItem Class

This class is derived from **COleServerItem**, and implements the extra functionality needed by a server item belonging to an Active document server. Using it is simple: when a **COleServerDoc** (or derived class) is asked to return a server item using **OnGetEmbeddedItem()**, the function creates and returns a **CDocObjectServerItem** rather than a **COleServerItem**.

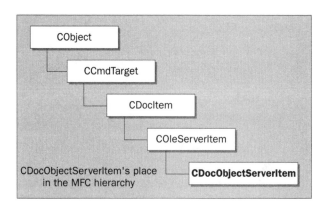

CDocObjectServerItem's place in the MFC hierarchy

The class implements three functions:

▶ **OnOpen()** is called to make the item in-place active, and can be overridden if you want to provide any special processing. If the item is not an Active document, the default code calls **COleServerItem::OnOpen()**.

▶ **OnShow()** does the same as **OnOpen()**.

▶ **OnHide()** is called by the framework to hide the item, but this isn't a valid operation for an Active document item, because they fill the entire view. The default action is therefore to throw an exception. If the item is not an Active document, the default code calls **COleServerItem::OnHide()**.

The COleDocIPFrameWnd Class

The **COleDocIPFrameWnd** class makes a few modifications to the basic in-place frame class, **COleIPFrameWnd**. These are mainly to cope with the fact that an Active document takes up the whole of the container's view, so calls such as **OnRequestPositionChange()** don't have any effect. Similarly, the **RecalcLayout()** function is modified for Active documents, because whereas ordinary in-place objects place their scrollbars on the outside, Active documents place them on the inside.

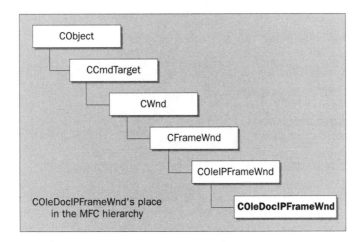

COleDocIPFrameWnd's place
in the MFC hierarchy

The COleCmdUI Class

COleCmdUI is, as its name implies, derived from **CCmdUI**, and implements the optional **IOleCommandTarget** interface for an Active document. This means that many servers may not implement it, but for those that do, it provides a way for MFC to update the state of user interface objects related to the **IOleCommandTarget**-driven features of the application.

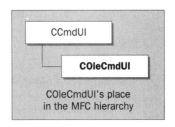

COleCmdUI's place
in the MFC hierarchy

In an application that doesn't support Active documents, you process **UPDATE_COMMAND_UI** notifications, which use **CCmdUI** objects; in an Active document-enabled application, you process **UPDATE_OLE_COMMAND_UI** notifications, which use **COleCmdUI** objects.

The **IOleCommandTarget** mechanism essentially lets a menu item on a container menu be routed so that it is handled by a handler in the Active document, and vice versa. This is done through **COleServerDoc**'s **OnExecOleCmd()** function which, by default, does nothing and returns **E_NOTIMPL**; you therefore need to override it if you want to do your own processing.

MFC implements **IOleCommandTarget**'s set of standard commands as a set of command macros, similar to those supplied to message maps. Examples include **ON_OLECMD_COPY()** to implement the Edit | Copy menu item, **ON_OLECMD_PASTESPECIAL()** to implement Edit | Paste Special..., and so on.

Commands coming into the server will be farmed out to the appropriate handler using a mapping mechanism similar to the normal **CCmdTarget** message maps. These command maps, and the macros used to implement them, are used in a very similar way to message maps. The **DECLARE_OLECMD_MAP()** macro is used in the class definition, and the class implementation uses **BEGIN_OLECMD_MAP()** and **END_OLECMD_MAP()** to define the map.

Creating New Active Document Server Applications

AppWizard supports the creation of Active document servers - just choose the right option in the dialog:

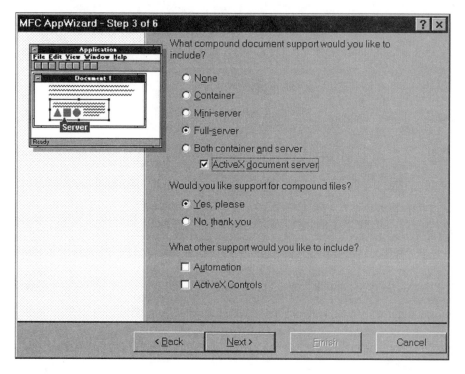

You get the ActiveX document server option when you select the mini-server, full-server or container-and-server options; note that when you select a server, you need to use the Advanced... button on the Step 4 dialog to select a file extension.

> *Don't be put off by the fact that the dialog refers to 'ActiveX documents'. During their brief existence so far, Active documents have already been known as 'DocObjects' and 'ActiveX documents', and this is just a case of the AppWizard dialogs falling slightly behind the times.*

If you look at the classes generated for an Active document server application, you'll find that there aren't very many differences from a normal server:

1 **StdAfx.h** includes the Active document header file:

```
#define VC_EXTRALEAN       // Exclude rarely-used stuff from Windows headers

#include <afxwin.h>        // MFC core and standard components
#include <afxext.h>        // MFC extensions
#include <afxole.h>        // MFC OLE classes
#include <afxdocob.h>
#ifndef _AFX_NO_AFXCMN_SUPPORT
#include <afxcmn.h>         // MFC support for Windows Common Controls
#endif // _AFX_NO_AFXCMN_SUPPORT
```

2 The server item class inherits from **CDocObjectServerItem**.

3 The in-place frame class inherits from **COleDocIPFrameWnd**.

4 The application's **InitInstance()** function registers the application as an Active document server:

```
m_server.UpdateRegistry(OAT_DOC_OBJECT_SERVER);
```

The document class still inherits from **COleServerDoc**, and the added Active document functionality is hidden from us.

Modifying Existing Server Applications

Since the difference in the code between Active document and ordinary servers is quite small, it's fairly easy to modify existing server applications so that they will work as Active document servers. Full details are given in the online help (in the section called *Upgrade to an Active Document Server*), and we'll see how it's done in practice here, as we modify GraphSrv to work as an Active document server.

Try It Out - Turning GraphSrv into an Active Document Server

1 Modifying GraphSrv to work as an Active document server isn't an onerous task. The first step is to edit **StdAfx.h** and add a line to include the MFC Active document header file:

```
#define VC_EXTRALEAN       // Exclude rarely-used stuff from Windows headers

#include <afxwin.h>        // MFC core and standard components
#include <afxext.h>        // MFC extensions
#include <afxole.h>        // MFC OLE classes
#include <afxdisp.h>       // MFC OLE automation classes
#ifndef _AFX_NO_AFXCMN_SUPPORT
#include <afxcmn.h>         // MFC support for Windows Common Controls
#endif // _AFX_NO_AFXCMN_SUPPORT
#include <afxdocob.h>       // MFC Active document support
```

2 Next, change the line in `CGraphSrvApp::InitInstance()` which updates the registry so that this is registered as an Active document server rather than an ordinary one:

```
// Check to see if launched as OLE server
if (cmdInfo.m_bRunEmbedded || cmdInfo.m_bRunAutomated)
{
   // Application was run with /Embedding or /Automation.  Don't show the
   //  main window in this case.
   return TRUE;
}

// When a server application is launched stand-alone, it is a good idea
//  to update the system registry in case it has been damaged.
m_server.UpdateRegistry(OAT_DOC_OBJECT_SERVER);
COleObjectFactory::UpdateRegistryAll();

// Dispatch commands specified on the command line
if (!ProcessShellCommand(cmdInfo))
   return FALSE;
```

3 Change the in-place frame class, `CInPlaceFrame`, so that it inherits from `COleDocIPFrameWnd` rather than `COleIPFrameWnd`. You'll first need to change it in the header file:

```
class CInPlaceFrame : public COleDocIPFrameWnd
{
   DECLARE_DYNCREATE(CInPlaceFrame)
public:
   CInPlaceFrame();

   // Rest of class definition omitted
};
```

You'll also need to use Edit | Replace... to edit the source file for the class so that all references to `COleIPFrameWnd` are replaced with `COleDocIPFrameWnd`.

4 In a similar way, change the server item class, `CGraphSrvSrvrItem`, so that it inherits from `CDocObjectServerItem` rather than `COleServerItem`. First of all, change it in the header file:

```
class CGraphSrvSrvrItem : public CDocObjectServerItem
{
   DECLARE_DYNAMIC(CGraphSrvSrvrItem)

   // Rest of class definition omitted
};
```

Once again, use search-and-replace to edit the class source code to replace all instances of `COleServerItem` with `CDocObjectServerItem`.

5 Adding a command map to your project is optional, depending on whether you want to support the `IOleCommandTarget` interface in your application. By including a command map and supporting `IOleCommandTarget` at this end, you allow the container to route certain of its menu commands through to your Active document server for processing. The container might, for instance, want the Active document server to handle printing the document when its Print menu command is chosen.

The command map goes in the document class and, like message maps, has to be added in two parts. First, add the declaration of the map to the document class definition; it can conveniently be placed after the message map definition, although it doesn't really matter where it goes:

```
class CGraphSrvDoc : public COleServerDoc
{
    // The class definition is the same up to here...
    DECLARE_MESSAGE_MAP()
```

```
    // OLE command map for Active document support
    DECLARE_OLECMD_MAP()
```

```
// This goes after all the AppWizard-generated code...
private:
    CGraph* m_pGraph;  // graph object for this document

public:
    CGraph* GetGraph()
        { return m_pGraph; }
};
```

Next, add the map itself to the document class source code, using the **BEGIN_OLECMD_MAP()** and **END_OLECMD_MAP()** macros. Like message maps, the **BEGIN** macro takes the names of the class and its base class as arguments, so we add the following:

```
IMPLEMENT_DYNCREATE(CGraphSrvDoc, COleServerDoc)

BEGIN_MESSAGE_MAP(CGraphSrvDoc, COleServerDoc)
    // Message map entries go in here...
END_MESSAGE_MAP()
```

```
BEGIN_OLECMD_MAP(CGraphSrvDoc, COleServerDoc)
END_OLECMD_MAP()
```

6 The next thing to do is to populate the map with entries. Because Active document support is still fairly new, there's no help from ClassWizard, so we have to do it manually. As with ordinary message maps, MFC provides some handy macros for use in command maps. These cover all the common menu items supported by **IOleCommandTarget**:

Macro	Command
ON_OLECMD_CLEARSELECTION()	Edit	Clear
ON_OLECMD_COPY()	Edit	Copy
ON_OLECMD_CUT()	Edit	Cut
ON_OLECMD_NEW()	File	New...
ON_OLECMD_OPEN()	File	Open...
ON_OLECMD_PAGESETUP()	File	Page Setup...
ON_OLECMD_PASTE()	Edit	Paste

Table Continued on Following Page

253

Macro	Command
ON_OLECMD_PASTESPECIAL()	Edit | Paste Special...
ON_OLECMD_PRINT()	File | Print...
ON_OLECMD_PRINTPREVIEW()	File | Print Preview
ON_OLECMD_REDO()	Edit | Redo
ON_OLECMD_SAVE()	File | Save
ON_OLECMD_SAVE_AS()	File | Save As...
ON_OLECMD_SAVE_COPY_AS()	File | Save Copy As...
ON_OLECMD_SELECTALL()	Edit | Select All
ON_OLECMD_UNDO()	Edit | Undo

There's also a general macro, **ON_OLECMD()**, which can be used to create map entries for other menu items; in fact, all the above are implemented in terms of **ON_OLECMD()**.

Note that none of these commands takes any arguments. If you want to use commands which take arguments, you'll need to use the **COleServerDoc::OnExecOleCmd()** function. The framework calls this before trying to dispatch OLE commands, and it's the place where you can put special processing for unusual or complex commands. Showing how to do that is (as they say) beyond the scope of this chapter.

If we wanted to let GraphSrv handle printing, we could structure our map like this:

```
BEGIN_OLECMD_MAP(CGraphSrvDoc, COleServerDoc)
    ON_OLECMD_PAGESETUP()
    ON_OLECMD_PRINT()
END_OLECMD_MAP()
```

Now, if the container so desires, it can ask us to handle the Print and Page Setup commands. What we have to ensure is that we have standard message map entries for these commands.

A rather frustrating aspect of all this is that the Visual C++ online help says that an AppWizard-generated application contains the following map:

```
BEGIN_OLECMD_MAP(CMyDoc, COleServerDoc)
  ON_OLECMD_PAGESETUP()
  ON_OLECMD_PRINT()
END_OLECMD_MAP()
```

Unfortunately, in Visual C++ versions 4.2 and 5.0, AppWizard doesn't do this! You need to add the code yourself, as we have here.

7 Lastly, we need to add a public function to the document class, called **GetDocObjectServer()**, as follows. Add this prototype to the header file:

```
CDocObjectServer* GetDocObjectServer(LPOLEDOCUMENTSITE pSite);
```

And then add the function itself to the document class source file:

```
CDocObjectServer* CGraphSrvDoc::GetDocObjectServer(LPOLEDOCUMENTSITE pSite)
{
   return new CDocObjectServer(this, pSite);
}
```

We've discussed how the **CDocObjectServer** class adds the extra functionality needed to turn a standard **COleServerDoc** into the super Active document model. When that functionality is required, the framework calls this function, which creates and returns a **CDocObjectServer** object.

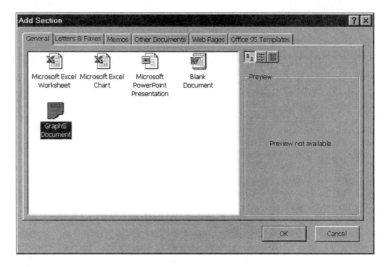

8 When you've modified the GraphSrv code, rebuild the project and then run it, so that it registers itself as an Active document server in the registry. Test it by running the Office Binder, and trying to add a GraphS Document as a new section.

GraphSrv is now recognized as an Active document server, so we can use its documents in Active document containers. Inserting a GraphSrv document into the Binder gives you a new section, as shown in the figure:

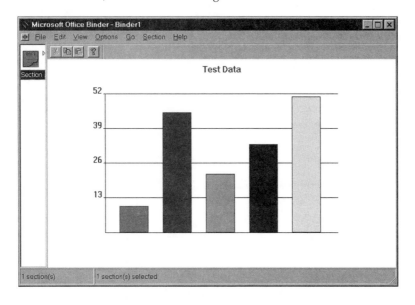

Notice that the Binder menu and toolbar now incorporate those of GraphSrv. The document is active, and can be edited immediately without the need to double-click on it first.

Summary

Active documents, or DocObjects (or indeed ActiveX documents), are an up-and-coming feature of the Windows environment, and one that Microsoft is very keen to promote.

Active document containers provide a 'frame' within which Active document servers can display their documents, allowing the server to take over the entire display area and user interface. This is done by adding several new COM interfaces that implement the extra functionality required.

There are many more Active document servers than there are containers, and it's a lot harder to write a container than a server. MFC provides rather rudimentary support for Active document servers, but none whatsoever for writing containers.

This chapter concludes our examination of servers and containers. Now we'll move on to look at one of the most widely used COM-based technologies: Automation.

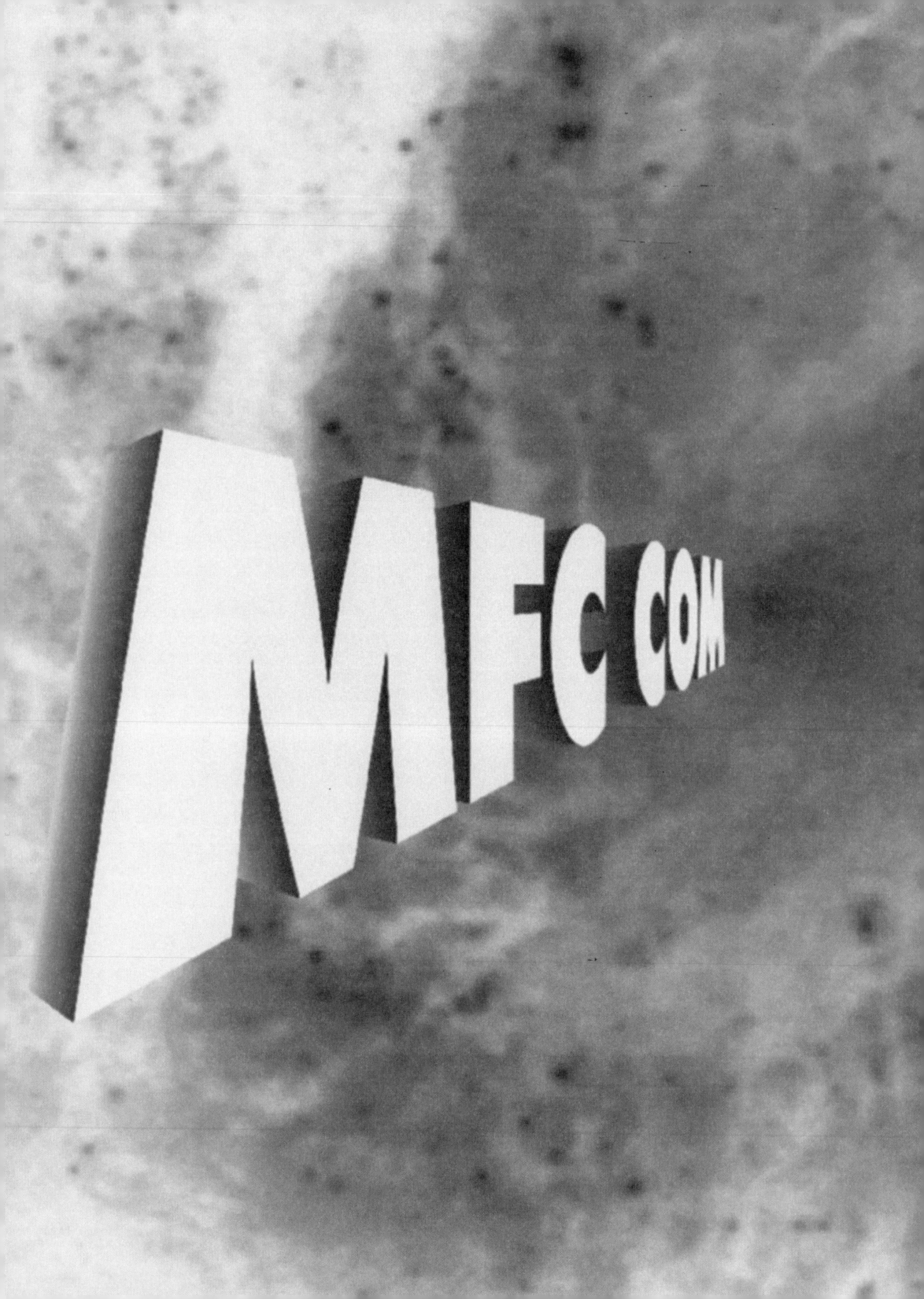
MFC COM

Automation

This chapter covers the important topic of Automation, which for many people is one of the most accessible and immediately useful of the COM-based technologies. Before we move ahead, though, let's take a moment to recap.

Automation provides a way for objects to make functions and items of data available to other objects, so components can drive one another. This can either be done directly, with one application calling functions in the other, or with the advent of **Active Scripting**, the user of an application can use a scripting language to write scripts which drive it. This is similar in concept to the way we can write Word macros to drive Microsoft Word. Applications can then be assembled from a selection of Automation-enabled components, driven by a main program.

How Automation Works

The old way to achieve this was to use **DDE**, which on this occasion stands for **Dynamic Data Exchange**; try not to get it confused with MFC's Dialog Data Exchange! Using DDE involves two programs sending Windows messages to one another, using a set protocol to communicate. It tends to be quick to use and reasonably efficient, but it's limited in scope and hard to get right, because the onus of setting up and maintaining the protocol falls squarely on the programmer.

COM provides us with a much more useful alternative. By exposing a COM interface, a program can define a set of functions that can be used to drive it externally. There is a problem here, however: it's easy enough for a program to define a custom interface, but how would it be used in practice? If *every* application defines its own custom interface, how can an application drive another about which it knows nothing?

Automation provides a 'one-stop shop' by using a single, universal method to allow programs to make themselves able to be driven by others. An application can find out if another supports Automation, and can discover what it can do dynamically, at runtime. This is done using a single interface called **IDispatch**, through which all an object's **Automation methods** and **properties** can be accessed, and which can be queried to find out what methods and properties are supported.

Automation is composed of three essential parts:

- Automation servers
- Automation clients
- Type libraries

Automation servers (also called **Automation components**) are the applications that expose the programmable objects in an Automation-enabled application; the Automation itself is done through the implementation of an **IDispatch** interface in the programmable object. A simple application may only expose a single object with a single interface, while complex applications may have several, all of which are used to perform different groups of Automation methods. Excel, for example, possesses over a dozen groups of Automation methods that enable you to drive different aspects of the program. Note the nomenclature here: **IDispatch** is a COM interface, while the functions and properties that are accessed through a particular implementation of **IDispatch** are called a **dispatch interface**. We'll talk more about these shortly.

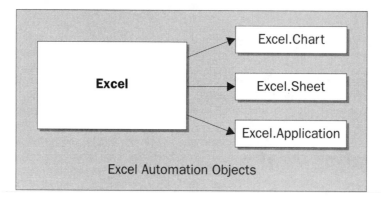

In the figure above, the names of the Automation objects are given as progIDs, just as they appear in the registry. We can see three Excel Automation objects: one to access Excel's charting functionality, one to manipulate a worksheet, and one to talk to the Excel application itself.

Automation clients (also called **Automation controllers**) are the applications that access the objects within an Automation server. They may or may not be COM-enabled applications themselves.

The final essential component of the Automation system is the **type library**, a set of data which defines the objects that a server supports, and the methods and properties that each of the objects exposes. Clients can discover this information at runtime. This type information can exist either as part of the Automation object itself, or as a separate file, which usually has a **.tlb** or **.olb** extension.

Type library data is described by constructing a file in the **Object Description Language** (**ODL**), which is then compiled into a type library by the ODL compiler, **MIDL**. Microsoft has now merged ODL with the IDL language used to describe COM interfaces, and it is possible to describe ordinary COM interfaces and type library data using IDL alone, although MFC Wizard-produced projects still use ODL.

MIDL, the Microsoft Interface Definition Language compiler, is used to compile both ODL and IDL.

Methods, Properties and Events

Automation supposes that an object is going to expose its functionality as a series of properties, methods and events.

▶ **Properties** are attributes, such as color or font size. We can choose to let the user access them directly, or via get/set methods.

▶ **Methods** are requests to an object to perform an action. These are the functions within the object which can be called from outside.

▶ **Events** are notifications from the object that something has happened. They are similar to methods, except that the call is *from* the object *to* the client. Events are described to the client in the object's type library.

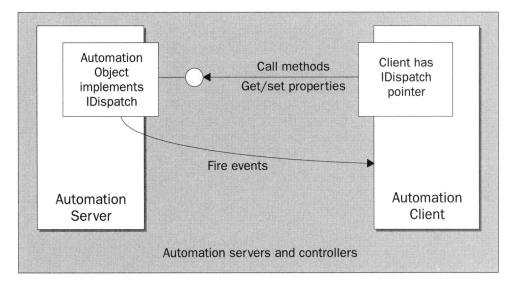

Although I said above that we can access Automation properties directly, remember that COM interfaces only expose functions, so even though we may appear to be accessing a variable directly, it isn't actually so. The illusion is there only as a convenience for the programmer.

How COM Implements Automation

We saw an example of this back in Chapter 2, when we put together some COM code to start Word and run it by Automation. You might care to refer back to that code for reference during the discussion that follows.

The IDispatch Interface

IDispatch is the interface through which Automation is implemented, and this means by definition that anything which implements **IDispatch** is automated. We can therefore add Automation to *any* MFC class, regardless of whether it is part of the user interface code or not (subject to one condition, which I'll come back to later).

The interface exposes four functions in addition to the **IUnknown** triplet:

- **GetTypeInfoCount()**
- **GetTypeInfo()**
- **GetIDsOfNames()**
- **Invoke()**

This doesn't seem much to allow us to automate any program, does it? Nevertheless, it provides all the functionality needed for the job.

Dispatch Interfaces

Each Automation method and property that **IDispatch** exposes is given a unique ID, called a **dispatch ID**, or **dispID**, and it is this that's passed to **Invoke()** in order to access a particular property or invoke a method. If you're familiar with programming using Windows DLLs, it's rather similar to referring to functions in a DLL by ordinal number, rather than by name. In addition to the dispID, **Invoke()** is passed a structure which defines the number and types of method parameters.

The set of dispIDs that an object's **IDispatch** interface responds to defines a **dispatch interface**, also known as a **dispinterface**. These dispID values are only unique within a particular implementation of **IDispatch**, and may change if methods and properties are added to, or removed from the dispatch interface.

The **GetIDsOfNames()** function is used by a client to retrieve the dispID corresponding to a given method or property name, as shown in the following diagram:

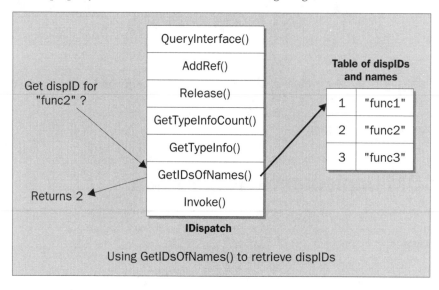

Here's an example showing how this is done in practice:

```
DISPID disp;
OLECHAR FAR* szFunction = OLESTR("func2");

hr = pDisp->GetIDsOfNames(
                IID_NULL,               // Reserved - must be NULL
                &szFunction,            // Array of function names
                1,                      // Number of names
                LOCALE_SYSTEM_DEFAULT,  // Locale information
                &disp);                 // Address for dispIDs returned
```

The **szFunction** variable holds the name of the method as an OLE string; this is passed to **GetIDsOfNames()**, which returns the dispID in **disp**.

The Invoke() Function

Invoke() is arguably the most important of **IDispatch**'s functions, as it's the one that actually 'does' the Automation. As its name implies, **Invoke()** is used to invoke, or execute, Automation methods which are passed to it by dispID. In fact, it does more than that, because it also allows us access to Automation properties.

Invoke() is quite a complex function, taking a number of arguments:

```
HRESULT IDispatch::Invoke(
            DISPID            dispIdMember, // Dispid of member to invoke
            REFIID            riid,         // Unused - must be IID_NULL
            LCID              lcid,         // Locale context
            WORD              wFlags,       // Invocation flags
            DISPPARAMS FAR*   pDispParams,  // Argument array
            VARIANT FAR*      pVarResult,   // Result
            EXCEPINFO FAR*    pExcepInfo,   // Error information
            unsigned int FAR* puArgErr);    // Index of first argument
                                            // that has an error
```

The most important of these are:

- **dispIdMember**, the dispID of the method or property being accessed

- **wFlags**, which describe what sort of call is being made

- **pDispParams**, a pointer to the array of arguments to be passed

- **pVarResult**, a pointer to the location at which to store the result, if any

- **pExcepInfo**, a pointer to an **EXCEPINFO** structure

The following diagram shows how **Invoke()** works. Instead of each function in the dispatch interface having its own entry in the vtable, **IDispatch** maintains a table of dispIDs versus function pointers. When **Invoke()** is called with a dispID, it uses the table to call the appropriate function.

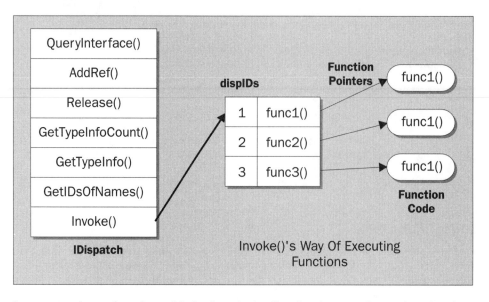

Invoke()'s Way Of Executing Functions

Here's an example to show how this is done in 'real' code. Assume that we've already retrieved the dispID for **func2()**, that the function takes no arguments, and that **pDisp** is a pointer to the object's **IDispatch** interface. The following call will tell **Invoke()** to call the method whose dispID is held in the **disp** variable:

```
HRESULT hr = pDisp->Invoke(
                    disp,                   // Dispatch ID for func2()
                    IID_NULL,               // Reserved
                    LOCALE_SYSTEM_DEFAULT,  // Locale info
                    DISPATCH_METHOD,        // We're invoking a method
                                            // (as opposed to getting
                                            // a property or whatever)
                    &dispNoArgs,            // Null parameter block
                    NULL, NULL, NULL);      // Nulls for result (there
                                            // isn't one), exception
                                            // info (not bothered) and
                                            // argument error return
```

Passing Data

Data is passed through to and returned from **Invoke()** using structures called **VARIANT**s and **VARIANTARG**s, both of which are data types we've met before. **VARIANT**s are used for data that cannot be passed by reference, such as returning values from a method call, or a property 'get' function, while **VARIANTARG**s are used for the arguments of method calls and property 'set' functions. In fact, **VARIANT** and **VARIANTARG** are **typedef**s of the same structure, the difference between them being that the **VARIANT** cannot have its **VT_BYREF** (pass by reference) bit set.

Why do we need to use a new data type for Automation? Well, the whole point of the **IDispatch** interface is that it defines a standard way of accessing Automation methods and properties, and this standardization must extend to method arguments and return types. For this reason, the only data type used in Automation is the **VARIANT** (and its close cousin the **VARIANTARG**), so that methods take arrays of **VARIANTARG**s as arguments, and return **VARIANT**s as results.

The ability of a **VARIANT** to contain any type of data is accomplished through the use of a data type flag, and a union carrying the data. Here's the definition from the Visual C++ 5.0 version of the **oaidl.h** include file:

```
typedef struct tagVARIANT VARIANT;

struct tagVARIANT
{
    union
    {
        struct __tagVARIANT
        {
            VARTYPE vt;
            WORD wReserved1;
            WORD wReserved2;
            WORD wReserved3;
            union
            {
                LONG lVal;
                BYTE bVal;
                SHORT iVal;
                FLOAT fltVal;
                DOUBLE dblVal;
                VARIANT_BOOL boolVal;
                _VARIANT_BOOL bool;
                SCODE scode;
                CY cyVal;
                DATE date;
                BSTR bstrVal;
                IUnknown __RPC_FAR *punkVal;
                IDispatch __RPC_FAR *pdispVal;
                SAFEARRAY __RPC_FAR *parray;
                BYTE __RPC_FAR *pbVal;
                SHORT __RPC_FAR *piVal;
                LONG __RPC_FAR *plVal;
                FLOAT __RPC_FAR *pfltVal;
                DOUBLE __RPC_FAR *pdblVal;
                VARIANT_BOOL __RPC_FAR *pboolVal;
                _VARIANT_BOOL __RPC_FAR *pbool;
                SCODE __RPC_FAR *pscode;
                CY __RPC_FAR *pcyVal;
                DATE __RPC_FAR *pdate;
                BSTR __RPC_FAR *pbstrVal;
                IUnknown __RPC_FAR *__RPC_FAR *ppunkVal;
                IDispatch __RPC_FAR *__RPC_FAR *ppdispVal;
                SAFEARRAY __RPC_FAR *__RPC_FAR *pparray;
                VARIANT __RPC_FAR *pvarVal;
                PVOID byref;
                CHAR cVal;
                USHORT uiVal;
                ULONG ulVal;
                INT intVal;
                UINT uintVal;
                DECIMAL __RPC_FAR *pdecVal;
                CHAR __RPC_FAR *pcVal;
                USHORT __RPC_FAR *puiVal;
                ULONG __RPC_FAR *pulVal;
                INT __RPC_FAR *pintVal;
```

265

```
        UINT __RPC_FAR *puintVal;
      } __VARIANT_NAME_3;
    } __VARIANT_NAME_2;
    DECIMAL decVal;
  } __VARIANT_NAME_1;
};
```

```
typedef VARIANT __RPC_FAR *LPVARIANT;
typedef VARIANT VARIANTARG;
typedef VARIANT __RPC_FAR *LPVARIANTARG;
```

The **VARTYPE** flag, **vt**, determines what is stored in the union, and as you can see, a wide variety of data types is available. We could declare and use a **VARIANT** containing an integer like this:

```
// Declare a VARIANT
VARIANT v;


v.vt = VT_I2;        // Hold a two-byte integer
v.iVal = 6;          // Set the 'iVal' member
```

The types are members of an enumeration called **VARENUM**, defined in **wtypes.h**, which describes values that can appear in **VARIANT**s and certain other COM data structures. For example:

Type	Description
VT_I2	Two-byte integer
VT_I4	Four-byte integer
VT_R4	Four-byte real
VT_R8	Eight-byte real
VT_BSTR	OLE string
VT_BOOL	Boolean type (True = -1, False = 0)

There are a bunch of macros available which can make working with **VARIANT**s easier and more portable, so the above example could be written as:

```
// Declare a VARIANT
VARIANT v;


V_VT(v) = VT_I2;     // Hold a two-byte integer
V_I2(v) = 6;         // Set the 'iVal' member
```

You'll find these and other related macros in the **oleauto.h** header file.

Functions are available to coerce **VARIANT**s into other types, such as converting a **short** integer to a **float**. These can either be called directly (as in **VarR4FromI2()**), or via the more general **VariantChangeType()** function. Note that although **VARIANT**s are provided in COM for use with Automation, they can also be used as a general type conversion API. In fact, they can be very useful in this role, and require only a call to **CoInitialize()** to ensure that COM is loaded, because the **BSTR** and **SAFEARRAY** data types use COM's memory management.

*If you want more information, **BSTR**s and **SAFEARRAY**s are covered in many of the books mentioned in Appendix F, including 'Inside OLE' and 'Inside COM'.*

Data is actually passed to **Invoke()** using a **DISPPARAMS** structure, which contains an array of **VARIANTARG**s.

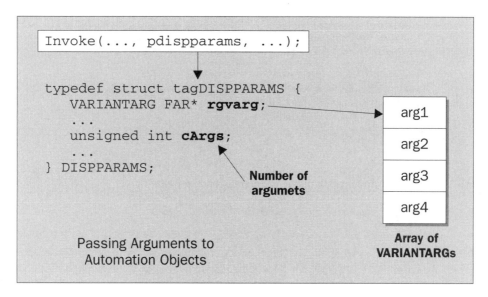

```
Invoke(..., pdispparams, ...);

typedef struct tagDISPPARAMS {
    VARIANTARG FAR* rgvarg;
    ...
    unsigned int cArgs;
    ...
} DISPPARAMS;
```

Number of argumets

| arg1 |
| arg2 |
| arg3 |
| arg4 |

Array of VARIANTARGs

Passing Arguments to
Automation Objects

The other members of the **DISPPARAMS** structure handle the passing of named arguments. These can also used in the setting of properties, as we did back in Chapter 2 when we set Word 97's **Visible** property.

Exception Handling

There are many errors that can occur during a call to **Invoke()**, and they all result in an **HRESULT** of the form **DISP_E_xxx** being returned, as shown in the following table:

HRESULT	Description
DISP_E_BADPARAMCOUNT	The number of parameters is wrong
DISP_E_BADVARTYPE	An argument is not a valid **VARIANT** type
DISP_E_EXCEPTION	The application needs to raise an exception
DISP_E_MEMBERNOTFOUND	The requested member does not exist, or you're trying to set a read-only property
DISP_E_NONAMEDARGS	Named arguments not supported by this interface
DISP_E_OVERFLOW	An argument couldn't be coerced to the requested type
DISP_E_PARAMNOTFOUND	A parameter dispID was invalid
DISP_E_TYPEMISMATCH	One or more arguments could not be coerced
DISP_E_UNKNOWNINTERFACE	The interface ID passed in **riid** is not **IID_NULL**
DISP_E_UNKNOWNLCID	The locale ID is not recognized
DISP_E_PARAMNOTOPTIONAL	A required parameter was omitted

In the case of **DISP_E_EXCEPTION**, **Invoke()** will fill in an **EXCEPINFO** structure, which looks like this:

```
typedef struct FARSTRUCT tagEXCEPINFO {
    unsigned short wCode;            // An error code describing the error
    unsigned short wReserved;
    BSTR           bstrSource;       // Source of the exception
    BSTR           bstrDescription;  // Textual description of the error
    BSTR           bstrHelpFile;     // Help file path
    unsigned long  dwHelpContext;    // Help context ID
    void FAR*      pvReserved;

    // Pointer to function that fills in Help and description info
    HRESULT (STDAPICALLTYPE FAR* pfnDeferredFillIn)
          (struct tagEXCEPINFO FAR*);
    RETURN VALUE return value;       // A return value describing the error
} EXCEPINFO, FAR* LPEXCEPINFO;
```

This structure contains enough information to allow the error to be handled meaningfully in the context of a scripting language. Among the items returned are:

- A meaningful error string, provided by the object itself
- A WinHelp filename and context ID, so that help can be provided in a familiar form
- An error number, so that 'On Error' or its equivalent can be used in Visual Basic and related languages

> *An Automation 'exception' is not the same as a C++ exception: there is no need to use **try/catch** blocks, and there is no non-local transfer of control.*

Using IDispatch

There are two ways in which an Automation client can use an object's **IDispatch** interface: dynamically or statically. Let's take a look at each of these in turn.

Dynamic Use of IDispatch

When an Automation object is used dynamically, clients use the **IDispatch** methods at runtime to query the object for details of its Automation properties and methods. Clients don't need to know anything at all about the Automation object in advance, so the system is truly dynamic. VBA and Excel 3 use this method, and while it gives the flexibility needed by interpreted languages, it's slower than the static access we'll look at shortly.

To see how it works, consider the following simple piece of Visual Basic code:

```
' Create an object
Dim myObj as Object
Set myObj = CreateObject("anObj.Document")

' Invoke one of its methods, SetX, which takes a single integer argument
myObj.SetX 3
```

An Automation server has an entry in the registry under **anObj.Document**, so the Visual Basic **CreateObject()** function can be used to create an Automation object of this type.

Once we've got an object, we want to do something with it, which in this case is to invoke its **SetX** method. Visual Basic will use the **GetIDsOfNames()** function to retrieve the dispID of the function, and then use that dispID in a call to **Invoke()**.

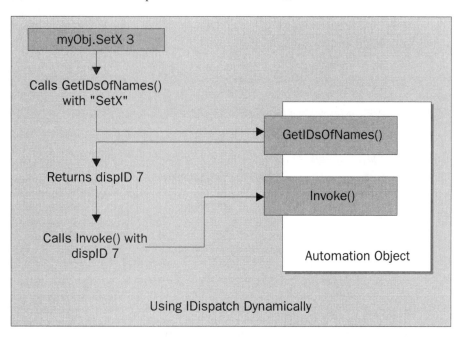

This process is slow because the client will end up calling **GetIDsOfNames()** at least once for each property or method it wants to **Invoke()**. Note also that the call to **GetIDsOfNames()** contains no information about the number or types of the arguments needed for the call to **Invoke()**. Visual Basic will make up a suitable set of arguments for **Invoke()** using what we supply in the Visual Basic code, but no-one will know until the actual call is made whether or not the arguments were valid. This can make using Automation objects from Visual Basic a rather hit-or-miss affair, and is one reason why we need good error reporting via the **EXCEPINFO** structure!

Static Use of IDispatch Using Type Libraries

Static use of **IDispatch** is equivalent to using DLLs with an import library, in that information on what the Automation server (or DLL) can do is available before it is used. This ensures that calls to the server are correct when the code is written, rather than leaving it until runtime. The client or development tool reads the server's type library information, which gives details of all the IDs, names and type information for the Automation methods and properties. Type library information can either be stored in a separate type library file (which usually has a **.tlb** or **.olb** extension), or may be included in the server itself.

This method of getting type information is evidently faster and safer than dynamic **IDispatch** use. It is used by Excel 5 and 7, as well as by Visual C++'s ClassWizard and the Component Gallery, and can be used by Visual Basic 4.0 too. The problem is that it may result in the creation of a very large class for complex Automation clients, such as Word or Excel.

Type Libraries and ODL

MFC uses ODL, the Object Description Language, to describe dispatch interfaces. The ODL scripting language is provided as a convenient way to define dispatch interfaces, and the MIDL tool is provided to convert these details into type library information. We'll see what ODL looks like, and what it does for us, when we come to look at how Visual C++ implements Automation in practice.

Clients can get at Automation type information using API functions such as **LoadRegTypeLib()**, which loads a type library from information in the registry, and **LoadTypeLib()**, which loads one from a file path. As you've probably come to expect, type information is manipulated using interface pointers, so opening a type library returns a pointer to an **ITypeLib** interface, which can be used to query the type information held in the library. This information is itself accessed using **ITypeInfo** pointers, which can be obtained using functions supported by the **ITypeLib** interface.

> *Microsoft have merged ODL's functionality into the Interface Definition Language, IDL, so that all interface definitions can be compiled with a single tool.*

Dual Interfaces

Dual interfaces are an advanced feature of Automation, and they aren't yet directly supported by MFC. However, they're a useful device, and there's a strong chance that they will be supported in a future release, so they're certainly worthy of mention here.

A **dual interface** is an extension to **IDispatch**, the standard interface for Automation, and it lets an Automation client bind to a vtable instead of having to use **Invoke()**. What this means is that each Automation method has its own entry in the COM interface; Automation clients which know how to use dual interfaces can thus get to the methods directly, without having to go through **Invoke()**. Controllers which can't work in this way will still use **Invoke()**, which now simply makes use of the new vtable entries.

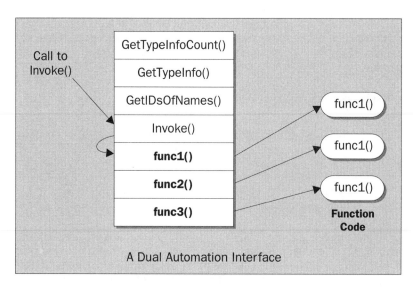

A Dual Automation Interface

Using vtable entries directly is clearly going to be quicker than going through **Invoke()**, and there's another advantage: using **Invoke()** requires the controller to package each argument as an element in the **VARIANTARG** array, while with a dual interface the controller can call the method directly.

As I noted in Chapter 2, 'dual interface' isn't a rigid definition like **IUnknown** or **IDispatch**, but is a convention followed when creating a custom interface. You create an interface class that is *derived* from **IDispatch**, so that it has the same methods as **IDispatch**, together with one or more custom methods that are compatible with Automation. A 'compatible' method is one whose argument types will fit into a **VARIANT**, and this limitation is the main disadvantage of using a dual interface.

Using Dual Interfaces With MFC

There's no support built into MFC yet (as of version 4.21), so you have to code your own dual interfaces. Support for dual interfaces *has* been added for COM objects created using ATL, and may conceivably be added for MFC, but in the meantime you'll find details on how to add both dual interface and collection support to MFC applications in Appendix C.

You may also like to consult the following sources about how to support dual interfaces in MFC applications:

- *OLE Q&A* by Don Box, Microsoft Systems Journal, vol.4 no.11, Dec.1995
- *OLE's Dual Nature* by Brett Foster, Windows Tech Journal, vol.5 no.4, April 1996
- Technical Note TN065: Dual-Interface Support for OLE Automation Servers
- The **Acdual** sample on the Visual C++ 5.0 CD

How MFC Implements Automation

Automation support is built into MFC's **CCmdTarget** class, so that any derived class can use Automation through a mechanism called a **dispatch map**. This is similar in concept to both the message maps that all MFC programmers know, and the interface maps we looked at earlier.

We've already seen that **CCmdTarget** supports the basic **IUnknown** interface, and in order for it to support **IDispatch**, we might expect to be able to look at the MFC source code and find the interface defined using the **BEGIN_INTERFACE_PART()** and **END_INTERFACE_PART()** macros. If you try, though, you won't find them... because they aren't there!

CCmdTarget uses a special helper class called **COleDispatchImpl**, which implements its **IUnknown** and **IDispatch** interfaces. This class is designed for use *only* with **CCmdTarget**, and won't work in other contexts. Why does **CCmdTarget** do this? The answer will become a little clearer as we see how Automation is added to classes.

CCmdTarget's **EnableAutomation()** function is used to enable Automation for a class; it essentially sets **CCmdTarget**'s **m_xDispatch** variable to hold a pointer to the vtable of a **COleDispatchImpl** object. This variable is initialized to **NULL**, so if this function isn't called to enable Automation, there won't be a dispatch interface pointer stored in **m_xDispatch**. Anyone using **QueryInterface()** will be told that the class doesn't support **IDispatch**. If **EnableAutomation()** is called, **m_xDispatch** will point to the dispatch interface object, and calls to **QueryInterface()** will succeed. Using a separate class is therefore an easy way to signal whether this class supports Automation or not.

```
const AFX_INTERFACEMAP_ENTRY CCmdTarget::_interfaceEntries[] =
{
#ifndef _AFX_NO_OLE_SUPPORT
   INTERFACE_PART(CCmdTarget, _IID_IDispatch, Dispatch)
#endif
   { NULL, (size_t)-1 }     // end of entries
};
```

If we look at the interface map for **CCmdTarget**, we see that the **Dispatch** entry is turned into **m_xDispatch** in the macro, and will either have a value or be **NULL**, depending on whether Automation has been enabled.

Dispatch Maps

Dispatch maps are like message maps, but instead of associating a message ID with a function, they associate dispIDs with methods and properties. Dispatch maps are used to provide support for the **IDispatch** interface in MFC classes that are derived from **CCmdTarget**.

The map gives a simple way to associate class member functions with the Automation methods and properties which are accessed via the **IDispatch::Invoke()** function, similar to the way in which Windows message IDs are matched with handler functions in message maps.

As you'd expect with MFC, these maps are implemented using macros, so you start off by using the **DECLARE_DISPATCH_MAP()** macro in a class definition to add a dispatch table to the class. In the class implementation, you then use the **BEGIN_** and **END_DISPATCH_MAP()** macros to define the map, and a number of other macros to define the different types of entry that are supported.

Let's take a look at how these work. Note, though, that in Visual C++ these maps are created and maintained for you by ClassWizard; the explanation here is so that you understand what is going on, and it isn't (normally!) necessary for you to do any work to make Automation work in MFC programs.

The DECLARE_DISPATCH_MAP Macro

The **DECLARE_DISPATCH_MAP()** macro adds an Automation dispatch map to a **CCmdTarget**-derived class:

```
class CSomeClass : public CCmdTarget
{
...
protected:
...
   DECLARE_DISPATCH_MAP()
};
```

Here's the MFC code for **DECLARE_DISPATCH_MAP()**:

```
#define DECLARE_DISPATCH_MAP() \
private: \
```

```
    static const AFX_DISPMAP_ENTRY _dispatchEntries[]; \
    static UINT _dispatchEntryCount; \
    static DWORD _dwStockPropMask; \
protected: \
    static AFX_DATA const AFX_DISPMAP dispatchMap; \
    virtual const AFX_DISPMAP* GetDispatchMap() const; \
```

We can see that the macro basically adds an **AFX_DISPMAP** and array of **AFX_DISPMAP_ENTRY** items (plus a count) to the class, together with a function to retrieve the dispatch map. Like interface maps, dispatch maps contain a pointer to their list of entries and another pointer to the dispatch map in their base class, which we can see in the definition of **AFX_DISPMAP**:

```
struct AFX_DISPMAP
{
    const AFX_DISPMAP* pBaseMap;        // pointer to map in base class
    const AFX_DISPMAP_ENTRY* lpEntries;  // pointer to entries
    UINT* lpEntryCount;
    DWORD* lpStockPropMask;
};
```

Each **AFX_DISPMAP_ENTRY** contains the data for an individual entry in the map, including the method or property name, its dispID, and details of its arguments and the way in which properties are accessed (either directly or via get/set methods). The same structure is used for both methods and properties:

```
struct AFX_DISPMAP_ENTRY
{
    LPCTSTR lpszName;         // member/property name
    long lDispID;             // DISPID (may be DISPID_UNKNOWN)
    LPCSTR lpszParams;        // member parameter description
    WORD vt;                  // return value type or type of property
    AFX_PMSG pfn;             // normal member On<membercall> or OnGet<property>
    AFX_PMSG pfnSet;          // special member for OnSet<property>
    size_t nPropOffset;       // property offset
    AFX_DISPMAP_FLAGS flags;  // flags (e.g. stock/custom)
};
```

In fact, MFC always assigns a value of **DISPID_UNKNOWN** (which is -1) to the dispID in an **AFX_DISPMAP_ENTRY**. Since the dispatch map for a class is chained to that of its parent, a given method or property may not be found in the class itself, but further up the chain.

When **GetIDsOfNames()** is called to retrieve a dispID, the run-time code walks through the chain of dispatch maps, and calculates a dispID based on where it found the method or property in the chain. The top word of the dispID shows which map the entry was found in; values start at 0 for the most-derived class, and are incremented by one each time we move one map up the chain. The bottom word of the dispID shows the position of the method or property in the map.

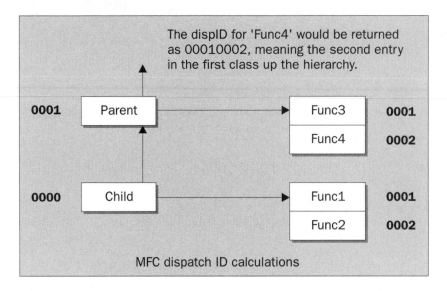

The dispID for 'Func4' would be returned as 00010002, meaning the second entry in the first class up the hierarchy.

MFC dispatch ID calculations

This mechanism is explained in more detail in Technical Note TN039: MFC/OLE Automation Implementation.

The BEGIN_ and END_DISPATCH_MAP Macros

The dispatch map is constructed using the **BEGIN_** and **END_DISPATCH_MAP** macros:

```
#define BEGIN_DISPATCH_MAP(theClass, baseClass) \
   const AFX_DISPMAP* theClass::GetDispatchMap() const \
      { return &theClass::dispatchMap; } \
   const AFX_DISPMAP theClass::dispatchMap = \
      { &baseClass::dispatchMap, &theClass::_dispatchEntries[0], \
        &theClass::_dispatchEntryCount, &theClass::_dwStockPropMask }; \
   UINT theClass::_dispatchEntryCount = (UINT)-1; \
   DWORD theClass::_dwStockPropMask = (DWORD)-1; \
   const AFX_DISPMAP_ENTRY theClass::_dispatchEntries[] = \
   { \

#define END_DISPATCH_MAP() \
   { VTS_NONE, DISPID_UNKNOWN, VTS_NONE, VT_VOID, \
     (AFX_PMSG)NULL, (AFX_PMSG)NULL, (size_t)-1, afxDispCustom } }; \
```

The **BEGIN_DISPATCH_MAP** code defines a function to return a pointer to the map, the map itself, and the start of the array of entries. The corresponding **END_** macro simply defines a dummy entry to signal the end of the array.

The actual entries themselves are declared using a variety of macros, each of which fills in the appropriate entries in an **AFX_DISPMAP_ENTRY** structure:

▶ **DISP_DEFVALUE()** defines the default property for the class. This is the one that's returned when the Automation object is referenced without specifying a method or a property.

▶ **DISP_FUNCTION()** defines an Automation method.

▶ **DISP_PROPERTY()** defines an Automation property, to be accessed directly.

▶ **DISP_PROPERTY_EX()** defines an Automation property that is to be accessed via get/set methods.

▶ **DISP_PROPERTY_NOTIFY()** defines an Automation property along with a notification function in the server which will be called whenever the property has been modified.

▶ **DISP_PROPERTY_PARAM()** is similar to **DISP_PROPERTY_EX()**, and allows you to specify parameters to be passed to the get/set methods.

When you construct a dispatch map using the macros, you'll end up with something like this:

```
BEGIN_DISPATCH_MAP(CSomeClass, CCmdTarget)
    DISP_FUNCTION(CSomeClass, "TryMe", TryMe, VT_EMPTY, VTS_NONE)
    DISP_PROPERTY(CSomeClass, "value", m_value, VT_I2)
END_DISPATCH_MAP()
```

The map has two entries: the first defines a method called **TryMe**, which maps onto a function also called **TryMe()**. This function has no return type (**VT_EMPTY**), and takes no arguments (**VTS_NONE**). The second entry defines a property called **value**, which maps onto a two-byte integer member of the class called **m_value**. Don't use the **_T()** macro when passing the method names, as this is done for you at a lower level.

DispID Assignment

I've already mentioned that assignment of dispIDs is done dynamically when **GetIDsOfNames()** is called. It's worth emphasizing this: you can't rely on hard-coding dispIDs into your programs, because they might have changed next time you come to use them.

Creating an Application with Automation Support

Now that we've covered the theory, let's look at how to include Automation in a Visual C++ application. Creating an application with Automation support is easy: it's simply a matter of checking the right option in AppWizard. You'll find the option at the bottom of step 3 of the AppWizard dialog:

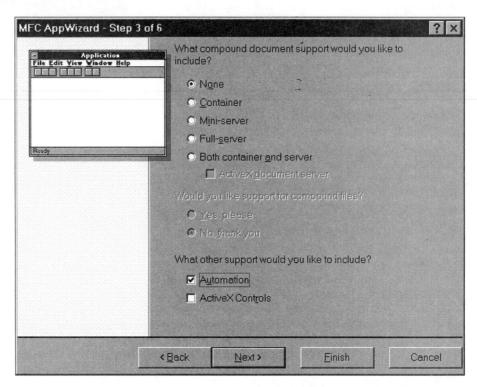

Checking the A<u>u</u>tomation option adds appropriate initialization code to the application's **InitInstance()** function, and provides skeleton Automation for the document class by adding an empty dispatch map. Note that AppWizard doesn't actually add any Automation itself, it just sets up the skeleton. You go on to add the functionality yourself, using ClassWizard.

Adding Automation Support to Classes

What do you do if you already have an application, and wish to add Automation to a class? If it is to be a new class, you can create a class using ClassWizard and make it automated in the creation dialog, as we'll see in the next section. If the class already exists, you'll have to add the support manually, which we'll show how to do later in the chapter. Visual C++ 4.*x* had an Automation tool in the Component Gallery, whose purpose in life was to add Automation to a class, but this has disappeared in version 5.0, depriving us of a useful facility.

> *You may need to add OLE support to the application yourself if it isn't there already. This is simply a case of adding a call to* **AfxOleInit()** *in* **InitInstance()***, and checking that it returns* **TRUE***.*

Adding a New Class with Automation Support

Let's suppose that we have a project which has been built Automation-enabled, so that it has Automation support added to the document class, and we want to add another Automation-enabled class.

Start ClassWizard and press the Add Class... button, then select New... from the drop-down menu that appears. This will bring up the class creation dialog, as shown below. The class I'm creating, **CAuto**, doesn't play any part in the user interface, as it's only accessed via Automation. This means we can derive it from the most general of the suitable classes, **CCmdTarget**. Selecting **CCmdTarget** from the Base class combo box automatically enables the Automation radio buttons, of which there are three:

▶ None, as you might expect, results in a non-automated class.

▶ Automation results in Automation code being added to the class.

▶ Creatable by type ID means that an entry for this class will be placed in the registry, so that objects of this class can be created in their own right. You don't always want to do this, the most usual choice is the Automation button.

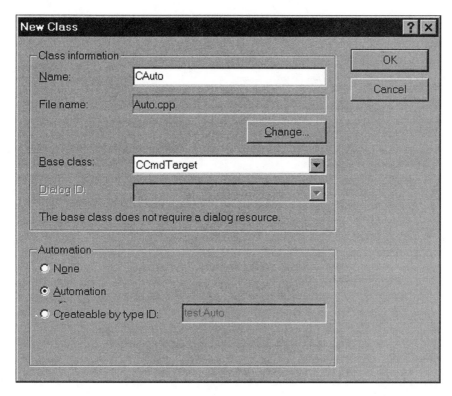

In this case, the default type ID suggested by ClassWizard is **test.Auto**, constructed from the names of the application (**test**) and the class (**CAuto**). You're free to change this to something more suitable, if you require.

When ClassWizard has built the class and added it to the project, you can open the ODL file to check that the new class has been added to the information that will be placed in the type library:

```
// test.odl : type library source for test.exe

// This file will be processed by the MIDL compiler to produce the
// type library (test.tlb).
```

```
[ uuid(FEFD1E27-D8F6-11D0-9257-00201834E2A3), version(1.0) ]
library Test
{
   importlib("stdole32.tlb");


   //  Primary dispatch interface for CTestDoc

   [ uuid(FEFD1E28-D8F6-11D0-9257-00201834E2A3) ]
   dispinterface ITest
   {
      properties:
         // NOTE - ClassWizard will maintain property information here.
         //    Use extreme caution when editing this section.
         //{{AFX_ODL_PROP(CTestDoc)
         //}}AFX_ODL_PROP

      methods:
         // NOTE - ClassWizard will maintain method information here.
         //    Use extreme caution when editing this section.
         //{{AFX_ODL_METHOD(CTestDoc)
         //}}AFX_ODL_METHOD

   };

   //  Class information for CTestDoc

   [ uuid(FEFD1E26-D8F6-11D0-9257-00201834E2A3) ]
   coclass Document
   {
      [default] dispinterface ITest;
   };


   //  Primary dispatch interface for CAuto

   [ uuid(FEFD1E3F-D8F6-11D0-9257-00201834E2A3) ]
   dispinterface IAuto
   {
      properties:
         // NOTE - ClassWizard will maintain property information here.
         //    Use extreme caution when editing this section.
         //{{AFX_ODL_PROP(CAuto)
         //}}AFX_ODL_PROP

      methods:
         // NOTE - ClassWizard will maintain method information here.
         //    Use extreme caution when editing this section.
         //{{AFX_ODL_METHOD(CAuto)
         //}}AFX_ODL_METHOD

   };

   //  Class information for CAuto
```

```
[ uuid(FEFD1E41-D8F6-11D0-9257-00201834E2A3) ]
coclass Auto
{
    [default] dispinterface IAuto;
};
```

```
//{{AFX_APPEND_ODL}}
//}}AFX_APPEND_ODL}}
};
```

Filling in the Interface

Methods and properties can be added to this interface in the same way as they can be added to the default document Automation interface. As an example, we can add a simple method called **TryMe**, which is just going to display a message box to show that it has been called. Bring up ClassWizard, choose the Automation tab, and press the Add Method... button, which brings up the following dialog:

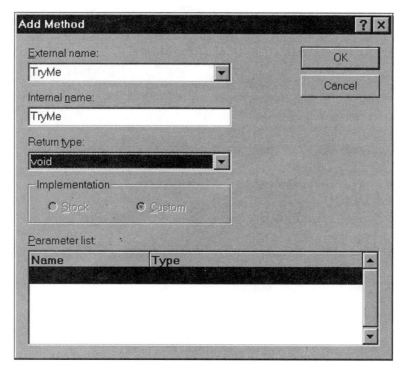

The method takes no parameters, returns nothing, and has the same internal and external names. The **external name** is that by which an Automation client will invoke the method, while the **internal name** is the function in the class that implements the method. You can make them different, if for instance you want to map an Automation method onto an existing member function, but often they'll be the same. Pressing OK gets you back to ClassWizard:

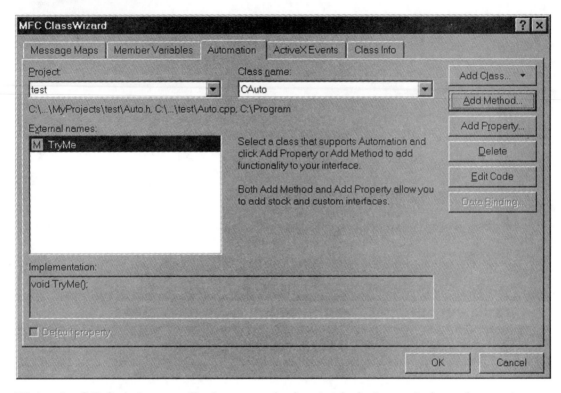

Hitting the Edit Code button will take you to the function body, just as it does when you're adding message handlers. We can then provide a trivial body for the function:

```
void CAuto::TryMe()
{
    AfxMessageBox("New Automation object successfully called");
}
```

If you look at the ODL file, you'll see that an entry has been added in the **methods:** section. Although it's tagged with a dispID of 1, remember that this may not be the number which is dynamically assigned to it when **GetIDsOfNames()** is called.

```
// Primary dispatch interface for CAuto

[ uuid(FEFD1E3F-D8F6-11D0-9257-00201834E2A3) ]
dispinterface IAuto
{
    properties:
        // NOTE - ClassWizard will maintain property information here.
        //     Use extreme caution when editing this section.
        //{{AFX_ODL_PROP(CAuto)
        //}}AFX_ODL_PROP

    methods:
        // NOTE - ClassWizard will maintain method information here.
        //     Use extreme caution when editing this section.
        //{{AFX_ODL_METHOD(CAuto)
        [id(1)] void TryMe();
```

```
        //}}AFX_ODL_METHOD

    };
```

Lastly, if you look in the source code for the **CAuto** class, you'll see that a dispatch map entry has been added for the **TryMe()** function:

```
BEGIN_DISPATCH_MAP(CAuto, CCmdTarget)
    //{{AFX_DISPATCH_MAP(CAuto)
    DISP_FUNCTION(CAuto, "TryMe", TryMe, VT_EMPTY, VTS_NONE)
    //}}AFX_DISPATCH_MAP
END_DISPATCH_MAP()
```

The use of **DISP_FUNCTION()** tells us that it's a method we're adding here. The method is called **TryMe** and maps onto function **TryMe()**, which has a void return type (**VT_EMPTY**) and takes no parameters.

Making Objects Creatable by Type ID

In the New Class dialog, you get a choice of pure Automation support, or of making the class createable by type ID (or progID, if you prefer). In the latter case, you get a registry entry for the class, so that in languages such as VBA, you can create objects by name:

```
Dim myObj as Object
Set myObj = CreateObject("test.Auto")
```

We don't tend to want to do this for MFC document objects, because the document is properly created by the document template, which creates a document/view/frame set, and it would seldom be useful to create a document object on its own.

Support for Automation Clients

We've covered the support given by MFC in providing Automation servers, but what about Automation clients? There are two main classes involved in client support: **COleDispatchDriver** and **COleDispatchException**.

The key to client support in MFC is the **COleDispatchDriver** class. When ClassWizard reads the type library for an Automation server, it will create classes to represent Automation objects; these classes are derived from **COleDispatchDriver**, which does all the heavy-duty COM work. You seldom need to have anything to do with **COleDispatchDriver** itself - it's designed to be a tool for use by ClassWizard.

COleDispatchDriver manages the **IDispatch** interface for us. It has a number of methods for creating and communicating with the server, some of the most important of which are outlined below:

▶ **CreateDispatch()** is used to set up the server. It takes a progID or CLSID, calls **CoCreateInstance()** to start a server, and retrieves a pointer to its **IDispatch** interface. This pointer is then attached to the MFC object so that methods and properties can be used.

▶ **InvokeHelper()** is used to make up calls to **IDispatch::Invoke()**, taking the parameters in C++ form and making them into **VARIANT**s for use with **Invoke()**.

➧ **GetProperty()** and its fellow, **SetProperty()**, are used in the manipulation of properties.

The second class I mentioned, **COleDispatchException**, is used to handle exceptions resulting from an error during Automation operations. It contains more information than the basic **COleException** class, and this information tends to be needed by Automation clients such as Visual Basic. This information includes:

➧ An application-specific error code

➧ An error description, such as 'Disk full'

➧ A help context that can be used to provide additional information

➧ The name of the help file

➧ The name of the application that generated the exception

These exceptions are thrown using the **AfxThrowOleDispatchException()** MFC helper call.

Error Handling

We learned earlier how error information is passed back from calls to **Invoke()** using the **EXCEPINFO** structure. When we use the MFC-provided mechanisms for implementing Automation, we don't get access to the **Invoke()** call itself, so how do we get to pass information back from our Automation servers, and how do we receive error information in our clients?

The answer is to use the **COleDispatchException** class I described in the preceding section; if an error occurs when you're dealing with a method or property, use **AfxThrowOleDispatchException()** to throw an exception. This means, of course, that the programmer will have to enclose potentially troublesome calls in **try/catch** blocks.

Here's an example: suppose an Automation server has a **Calculate()** method, and that it's possible that it might attempt a divide by zero. We might code up the method like this:

```
void CAuto::Calculate()
{
    // Check divisor
    if (div == 0)
        AfxThrowOleDispatchException(100, "Divide by zero");

    // OK to continue...
}
```

The first argument is an error number, and the second is the error string. You'd invoke the method in the usual way:

```
// IAuto is the wrapper class generated by ClassWizard to let us
// talk to CAuto Automation objects
IAuto myObj;
...
try
{
    myObj.Calculate();
```

```
    }
    catch(COleDispatchException* pCE)
    {
        // Report the error code and string
        CString s;
        s.Format("Error %d: %s", pCE->m_wCode, pCE->m_strDescription);
        AfxMessageBox(s);

        pCE->Delete();
    }
```

Dialog-based Applications

In Visual C++ 5.0, AppWizard can add Automation to the dialog class in dialog-based applications if required. If you generate a dialog-based application and choose Automation support, you'll find that you get a 'proxy' class generated, so that an application called 'Test' would consist of the following classes:

▶ **CAboutDlg**, the standard About box class

▶ **CTestApp**, the application class, which inherits from **CWinApp**

▶ **CTestDlg**, the main dialog class, which inherits from **CDialog**

▶ **CTestDlgAutoProxy**, which inherits from **CCmdTarget**

The purpose of the proxy class, as its name suggests, is to handle Automation for the dialog class. In a 'normal' automated application, the Automation is added to the document class, but here we don't have such a thing. The proxy class adds Automation capability to the dialog class when required; the support wasn't added to the base **CDialog** class because the majority of dialogs are not created to be automated, and it would add an unnecessary overhead. As you might expect, it's the proxy class that implements the dispatch and interface maps on behalf of the dialog.

The application and proxy classes maintain pointers to one another, so that they can communicate. The pointer to the proxy will be initialized to **NULL** in the dialog object, and if the dialog isn't being automated, that's how it will stay:

```
    CTestDlg::CTestDlg(CWnd* pParent /*=NULL*/)
       : CDialog(CTestDlg::IDD, pParent)
    {
       //{{AFX_DATA_INIT(CTestDlg)
          // NOTE: the ClassWizard will add member initialization here
       //}}AFX_DATA_INIT
       // Note that LoadIcon does not require a subsequent DestroyIcon in Win32
       m_hIcon = AfxGetApp()->LoadIcon(IDR_MAINFRAME);
       m_pAutoProxy = NULL;
    }
```

If the dialog is to be automated, the pointers are set up when the proxy object is constructed:

```
    CTestDlgAutoProxy::CTestDlgAutoProxy()
    {
       EnableAutomation();
```

```
    // To keep the application running as long as an OLE automation
    //  object is active, the constructor calls AfxOleLockApp.
    AfxOleLockApp();

    // Get access to the dialog through the application's
    //  main window pointer.  Set the proxy's internal pointer
    //  to point to the dialog, and set the dialog's back pointer to
    //  this proxy.
    ASSERT (AfxGetApp()->m_pMainWnd != NULL);
    ASSERT_VALID (AfxGetApp()->m_pMainWnd);
    ASSERT_KINDOF(CTestDlg, AfxGetApp()->m_pMainWnd);
    m_pDialog = (CTestDlg*) AfxGetApp()->m_pMainWnd;
    m_pDialog->m_pAutoProxy = this;
}
```

It's possible that the client may still be using the application when a user decide to close down the dialog, in which case the application needs to remain running. The dialog's **OnClose()**, **OnOK()** and **OnCancel()** members are overridden so they all call **CanExit()**, which checks whether the proxy object is still alive:

```
void CTestDlg::OnClose()
{
    if (CanExit())
        CDialog::OnClose();
}

BOOL CTestDlg::CanExit()
{
    // If the proxy object is still around, then the automation
    //  controller is still holding on to this application.  Leave
    //  the dialog around, but hide its UI.
    if (m_pAutoProxy != NULL)
    {
        ShowWindow(SW_HIDE);
        return FALSE;
    }

    return TRUE;
}
```

If the dialog object's destructor gets called, it sets its proxy pointer to **NULL**, which tells the proxy that the dialog has gone.

Automation methods and properties get added to the proxy class, and it is up to the programmer to make them work with corresponding functions and data members in the dialog class. The proxy class is made a **friend** of the dialog class in order to make this easier.

Adding Automation Support to GraphSrv

We've already got basic OLE support in GraphSrv, so now we'll add simple Automation support, giving us the ability to create a new graph, add points to it, change the graph style, stuff like that. We could get a lot more complex, such as adding whole datasets at a time, but the things I've mentioned so far should be more than enough to keep us occupied. The steps that follow are generic, right up to the point where we start adding GraphSrv's own methods and properties to the dispatch interface, and can be modified to work with just about any application.

Adding the Basic Structure

Before we do any real work, the very first step involves adding **<afxdisp.h>** to **stdafx.h**, to get access to the Automation functions:

```
#include <afxwin.h>         // MFC core and standard components
#include <afxext.h>         // MFC extensions
#include <afxole.h>         // MFC OLE classes
#include <afxdisp.h>        // MFC OLE automation classes
#ifndef _AFX_NO_AFXCMN_SUPPORT
#include <afxcmn.h>         // MFC support for Windows Common Controls
#endif // _AFX_NO_AFXCMN_SUPPORT
#include <afxdocob.h>       // MFC OLE DocObject support
```

Next, we need to add a line to the application's **InitInstance()** function, which calls **UpdateRegistryAll()** to ensure that all the class factories in the application get registered:

```
if (cmdInfo.m_bRunEmbedded || cmdInfo.m_bRunAutomated)
{
    // Application was run with /Embedding or /Automation. Don't show the
    //   main window in this case.
    return TRUE;
}

// When a server application is launched stand-alone, it is a good idea
//   to update the system registry in case it has been damaged.
m_server.UpdateRegistry(OAT_DOC_OBJECT_SERVER);
COleObjectFactory::UpdateRegistryAll();

// Dispatch commands specified on the command line
if (!ProcessShellCommand(cmdInfo))
    return FALSE;
```

Note that if our application hadn't already been an Active document server, we'd need to insert a call to **UpdateRegistry(OAT_DISPATCH_OBJECT)**, to add the entries for an object with a dispatch interface. It turns out that these are included in the **OAT_DOC_OBJECT_SERVER** type, so in this case we don't need to modify the code.

Try It Out - Adding Automation to the Document Class

It would be nice to have a tool in the Component Gallery to add Automation code for us, but there's no such thing in Visual C++ 5.0. There *was* one in Visual C++ 4.*x*, but it was limited, and wouldn't have done the job we require. So, unless we want to write a custom Component Gallery mini-Wizard to do this for us, we'll have to work out what to do ourselves, and add the code by hand. It's just as well this book is supposed to be a learning process.

1 We're creating an Automation server, so if we hadn't had any OLE support before, we'd need to add a GUID for the server. However, we already have one for GraphSrv, which we'll continue to use:

```
/////////////////////////////////////////////////////////////////////////
// The one and only CGraphSrvApp object

CGraphSrvApp theApp;
```

```
// This identifier was generated to be statistically unique for your app.
// You may change it if you prefer to choose a specific identifier.

// {9A1C8724-96CC-11D0-9257-00201834E2A3}
static const CLSID clsid =
{ 0x9a1c8724, 0x96cc, 0x11d0, { 0x92, 0x57, 0x0, 0x20, 0x18, 0x34, 0xe2, 0xa3 } };
```

2 Now, add dispatch and interface map declarations to the document class header file:

```
// Generated message map functions
protected:
    //{{AFX_MSG(CGraphSrvDoc)
        // Lots of message map functions omitted
    //}}AFX_MSG
    DECLARE_MESSAGE_MAP()

    // OLE command map for DocObject support
    DECLARE_OLECMD_MAP()

    // Dispatch map implementation
    //{{AFX_DISPATCH(CGraphSrvDoc)
    //}}AFX_DISPATCH

    DECLARE_DISPATCH_MAP();
    DECLARE_INTERFACE_MAP();

private:
    CGraph* m_pGraph;  // graph object for this document

public:
    CGraph* GetGraph()
        { return m_pGraph; }
    CDocObjectServer* GetDocObjectServer(LPOLEDOCUMENTSITE pSite);
};
```

3 At this stage, the only modification to the document class source file is to add the dispatch map declaration. You can add it anywhere you like - I usually do it near the top of the file, where all the other maps are declared:

```
BEGIN_MESSAGE_MAP(CGraphSrvDoc, COleServerDoc)
    // Message map contents go here...
END_MESSAGE_MAP()

BEGIN_OLECMD_MAP(CGraphSrvDoc, COleServerDoc)
END_OLECMD_MAP()

BEGIN_DISPATCH_MAP(CGraphSrvDoc,COleServerDoc)
    //{{AFX_DISPATCH_MAP(CGraphSrvDoc)
    //}}AFX_DISPATCH_MAP
END_DISPATCH_MAP()
```

Make sure you put in the **AFX_DISPATCH_MAP** markers, so that ClassWizard will have somewhere to put its Automation code later on.

Try It Out - Creating a Type Library

We want to be able to generate a type library for GraphSrv, so we need to provide an ODL file. This contains details of the Automation methods supported by the application; in this case, the document class is the only one with any Automation capability.

1 Start by generating a GUID to use for the dispinterface. Choose the GUID Generator from Developer Studio's Components and Controls Gallery:

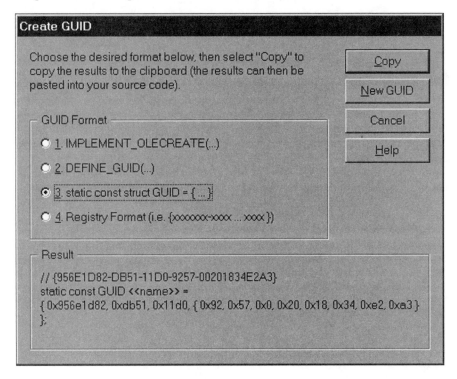

Choose the third radio button, which produces a GUID in a form suitable for pasting straight into the application code, and then hit the Copy button to put it onto the clipboard.

2 Paste the GUID into the code for the document class; the location isn't significant, but it is useful to put it along with all the other maps at the top of the file. We need to add in the name of the dispinterface; these are usually generated by AppWizard by prepending an **I** to the class name, so in this case it will be **IGraphSrv**. The identifier in the source code file has an **IID_** prefix, so the whole name will be **IID_IGraphSrv**:

```
BEGIN_DISPATCH_MAP(CGraphSrvDoc,COleServerDoc)
 //{{AFX_DISPATCH_MAP(CGraphSrvDoc)
 //}}AFX_DISPATCH_MAP
END_DISPATCH_MAP()
```

```
// GUID for dispatch interface
// {9B4E19E0-11d0-904A-444553540000}
static const IID IID_IGraphSrv =
{ 0x9b4e19e0, 0x4ab4, 0x11d0, {0x90, 0x4a, 0x44, 0x45, 0x53, 0x54, 0x0, 0x0}};
```

3 Now we've added the IID, we need to think about adding an interface map to support the dispinterface:

```
// GUID for dispatch interface
// {9B4E19E0-11d0-904A-444553540000}
static const GUID IID_IGraphSrv =
{ 0x9b4e19e0, 0x4ab4, 0x11d0, {0x90, 0x4a, 0x44, 0x45, 0x53, 0x54, 0x0, 0x0}};
```

```
BEGIN_INTERFACE_MAP(CGraphSrvDoc, COleServerDoc)
  INTERFACE_PART(CGraphSrvDoc, IID_IGraphSrv, Dispatch)
END_INTERFACE_MAP()
```

```
/////////////////////////////////////////////////////////////////
// CGraphSrvDoc construction/destruction
```

The **BEGIN_INTERFACE_MAP()** macro shows that this is an interface map for **CGraphSrvDoc**, whose base class is **COleServerDoc**. The **INTERFACE_PART()** macro again needs the class name, plus the interface ID, and a partial name which will be used to form the name of the pointer variable which accesses the interface (in this case, **m_xDispatch**).

4 The last step is to create the ODL file itself. You can use the code below as a pattern, and edit it to fit your version of GraphSrv. Remember that you'll have to plug in your own GUIDs in place of the ones given here. Generate a new one for the first one in the listing (the library).

```
// GraphSrv.odl : type library source for GraphSrv.exe, which
// will be used to produce the type library (GraphSrv.tlb).

[ uuid(<<insert your library GUID here>>), version(1.0) ]
library GraphSrv
{
   importlib("stdole32.tlb");

   // Primary dispatch interface for CGraphSrvDoc

   [ uuid(<<insert your dispinterface GUID here>>) ]
   dispinterface IGraphSrv
   {
      properties:
         // NOTE - ClassWizard will maintain property information here.
         //    Use extreme caution when editing this section.
         //{{AFX_ODL_PROP(CGraphSrvDoc)
         //}}AFX_ODL_PROP

      methods:
         // NOTE - ClassWizard will maintain method information here.
         //    Use extreme caution when editing this section.
         //{{AFX_ODL_METHOD(CGraphSrvDoc)
         //}}AFX_ODL_METHOD

   };
```

```
// Class information for CGraphSrvDoc

[ uuid(<<insert your document GUID here>>) ]
coclass Document
{
    [default] dispinterface IGraphSrv;
};

//{{AFX_APPEND_ODL}}
//}}AFX_APPEND_ODL}}
};
```

There's no need to adjust anything in the build process, as processing an ODL file is built-in.

Adding Automation Functionality

Now we have the structure in place, we can start to add some Automation. What we'll do is to add the same functionality we already have in the GraphSrv Options menu.

If an application is started as an Automation server, its default behavior is to start up invisibly in the background, without showing a main window. We can see this from looking at the code in **InitInstance()**:

```
// Check to see if launched as OLE server
if (cmdInfo.m_bRunEmbedded || cmdInfo.m_bRunAutomated)
{
    // Application was run with /Embedding or /Automation. Don't show the
    // main window in this case.
    return TRUE;
}
```

The idea is that when the application is started as a server - either an Automation server, or to handle an embedded object - it will be passed either the **/Automation** or the **/Embedding** flag on the command line. This is not the most elegant method of doing it – in this day and age we might expect Microsoft to have implemented some registry-based solution.

MDI and SDI applications both behave like this, although there is an exception if there's already an instance of an MDI server running. In that case, all that happens is that the server gains another child window when it is requested to create a new document.

As far as we're concerned, it's never going to be very useful to have an invisible graphing server, so the first thing we'll do is modify the code so that the server always starts up visibly in Automation mode. You might expect that this would be easy - just check for the **/Automation** flag, and if we find it, display the main window. The problem is that it simply doesn't work! Even when you start up an Automation server from one of Microsoft's own controllers, such as Visual Basic, you won't see the **/Automation** command line flag being used. Instead, the **/Embedding** flag seems to be used as a catch-all way of telling an application that it has been started as a server of either variety.

How then are we to ensure that our application gets displayed when started as an Automation server? The easiest way will be to add an Automation method to tell the application to make itself visible; this doesn't involve hacking the source code too much, and fits in well with making the application automated.

Try It Out - Adding Methods

As we've already discovered, the default behavior of an Automation server is not to appear. The server itself will start up in the background, and even if you're already running an MDI server, the new frame associated with the Automation document you create will also be invisible!

What we need to do is to add a couple of Automation methods, which we'll call **ShowApp()** and **ShowWindow()**, to persuade the server to show its main window, and to show the new document window. We'll look in detail at the first one, showing how to add it and what impact it has on the code; the other Automation methods will follow in a similar vein.

1 To add a **ShowApp()** Automation method, bring up ClassWizard, select the document class, and move to the **Automation** tab:

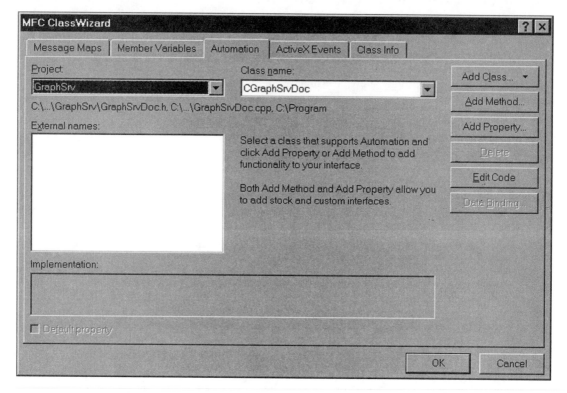

Choose the **Add Method...** button, and the method dialog will appear. Fill in the names and return type, as shown on the following page:

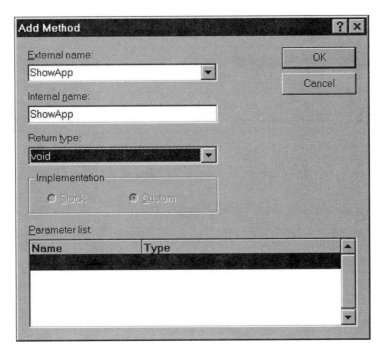

Remember that the *external* name is the one that clients will use to invoke this method; the *internal* name is the name of the C++ routine that contains the code. In most cases they will be the same, but they can be different. In fact, you can sometimes use the name of an existing member function in your class; what you'll find you can't do is to use functions which are already defined in other maps, such as message maps.

Once you've completed the screen and pressed OK, your class has an Automation method defined. What difference has this made to the application code? You'll find changes in three places:

▶ In the document header file

▶ In the document class source code

▶ In the ODL file

The header file has had a new entry added to the dispatch map definition:

```
// Dispatch map implementation
//{{AFX_DISPATCH(CGraphSrvDoc)
afx_msg void ShowApp();
//}}AFX_DISPATCH
```

This is matched in the source for the class, where we have the entry in the dispatch map, and the source for the routine itself:

```
BEGIN_DISPATCH_MAP(CGraphSrvDoc,COleServerDoc)
    //{{AFX_DISPATCH_MAP(CGraphSrvDoc)
```

```
    DISP_FUNCTION(CGraphSrvDoc, "ShowApp", ShowApp, VT_EMPTY, VTS_NONE)
  //}}AFX_DISPATCH_MAP
END_DISPATCH_MAP()

// And further on...
```

```
void CGraphSrvDoc::ShowApp()
{

   // TODO: Add your dispatch handler code here

}
```

2 While we're here, we may as well add the functionality to the routine:

```
void CGraphSrvDoc::ShowApp()
{
   // Get the application to show its main window
   CGraphSrvApp* pApp = (CGraphSrvApp*)AfxGetApp();
   pApp->ShowApp(SW_SHOW);
}
```

3 I could have called **ShowWindow()** for the application's main window from this function directly, but instead I've delegated the actual displaying to a helper function in the application class:

```
void CGraphSrvApp::ShowApp(int nShow)
{
   m_pMainWnd->ShowWindow(nShow);
}
```

The reasons for this are twofold. Firstly, it gives me a more general-purpose routine, which I can reuse to hide or iconize the main window if I so desire. Secondly, I know that MFC is proud of its public member variables, but it isn't good OO practice to use them, so I won't use the application's **m_pMainWnd** variable outside the class.

The third place we'll see a difference is in the ODL file, where a method has been added to the dispatch interface:

```
[ uuid(A4299100-4AE8-11d0-904A-444553540000) ]
dispinterface IGraphSrv
{
   properties:
      // NOTE - ClassWizard will maintain property information here.
      //    Use extreme caution when editing this section.
      //{{AFX_ODL_PROP(CGraphSrvDoc)
      //}}AFX_ODL_PROP

   methods:
      // NOTE - ClassWizard will maintain method information here.
      //    Use extreme caution when editing this section.
      //{{AFX_ODL_METHOD(CGraphSrvDoc)
      [id(1)] void ShowApp();
      //}}AFX_ODL_METHOD

};
```

Try It Out - Making the View Visible

GraphSrv is an MDI server, and as such, even if we have the server itself visible, new child windows opened as Automation objects won't themselves be visible. The **ShowWindow()** Automation method tells the child window to make itself visible; you should add it in exactly the same way as you did **ShowApp()**, using ClassWizard and the Add Method dialog. Like **ShowApp()**, the function has no arguments and returns **void**. Once you've added the skeleton to the code, we can fill in the body:

```
void CGraphSrvDoc::ShowWindow()
{
    // Display the view
    POSITION pos = GetFirstViewPosition();
    CView* pV = GetNextView(pos);

    if (pV != NULL)
    {
        CFrameWnd* pFrame = pV->GetParentFrame();
        if (pFrame != NULL)
            pFrame->ActivateFrame(SW_SHOW);
    }
}
```

Reading through the code, you'll see that this routine simply finds the first view associated with the document, and tells it to make itself visible. Since the document has just been created as part of the Automation process, we'd only expect it to have one view.

Try It Out - Adding Other Methods

We now want to add some functions which are supported by the document class, namely setting the frame type (to none, partial or full), setting the graph type (to line, bar or pie), and the **Redraw()** function. Some other functions are actually supported by the **CGraph** object, but will be accessed through the document class - namely **Add()** (to add an item to the dataset), and a function to set the title of the dataset.

1 We'll start by constructing the **Redraw()** method. Once again, it's an Automation method that takes no parameters and has a **void** return type. While we're here, we may as well add the functionality to the routine in order to ensure that the graph redraws itself:

```
void CGraphSrvDoc::Redraw()
{
    // Redraw the graph
    UpdateAllViews(NULL);
    UpdateAllItems(NULL);
}
```

You'll be familiar with **UpdateAllViews()** from your MFC programming; **UpdateAllItems()** does a similar job for OLE servers, ensuring that all embedded items update themselves.

2 Now we'll write the methods which will give us some basic control over the graph: `Clear()`, `Add()`, and `SetTitle()` will allow us to clear the dataset, add a new datum to it, and to give it a title respectively. Let's start with `Add()`. Once again, use ClassWizard to add a new Automation method to the document class, this time giving it two parameters, as shown in this figure:

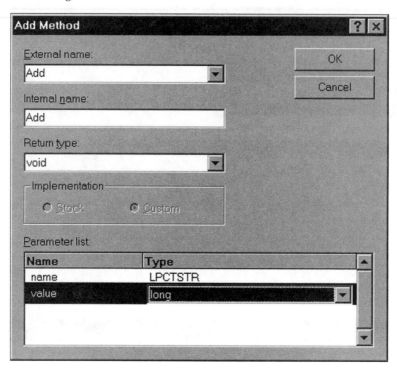

The routine is simply going to add the data point represented by the name/value pair to the graph object's list of data items:

```
void CGraphSrvDoc::Add(LPCTSTR name, long value)
{
    // Add the item to the graph item
    ASSERT(m_pGraph);

    m_pGraph->Add(name, (int)value);
    SetModifiedFlag(TRUE);
    Redraw();
}
```

3 The `SetTitle()` method is added in the same way, taking a string called `title` as the single argument, and passing it to the graph object:

```
void CGraphSrvDoc::SetTitle(LPCTSTR title)
{
    // Set the title for the dataset
    ASSERT(m_pGraph);

    m_pGraph->SetTitle(title);
    SetModifiedFlag(TRUE);
```

```
    Redraw();
}
```

4 Finally, `Clear()` takes no parameters, and calls the corresponding function in the graph object:

```
void CGraphSrvDoc::Clear()
{
    // Clear data from the graph object
    ASSERT(m_pGraph);

    m_pGraph->Clear();
    Redraw();
}
```

Adding More Automation Methods

We can add other Automation methods to allow full control of the style and appearance of the graph, and can also add query methods to return the graph, axis and frame types too.

As an example, let's add the option to change the graph to a pie chart. We've already got a function - a menu item handler - to do this, and you might think that the obvious way forward would be to reuse this function as an Automation method. Unfortunately, ClassWizard won't let you use a handler function for Automation, presumably because it would then be a part of two maps (the message map and the dispatch map), and this is not allowed.

The solution, however, is not difficult: just take the body out of the menu handler, make it into an Automation method, and then call this from the menu handler. Our original menu handler code looks like this:

```
void CGraphSrvDoc::OnOptionsGraphtypePie()
{
    if (!m_pGraph->IsPieChart())
    {
        m_pGraph->SetPieChart();
        SetModifiedFlag(TRUE);
        UpdateAllViews(NULL);
        UpdateAllItems(NULL);
    }
}
```

Having created an Automation method called **DoPie()**, and taking advantage of the **Redraw()** function we created recently, we now have:

```
void CGraphSrvDoc::OnOptionsGraphtypePie()
{
    DoPie();
}

void CGraphSrvDoc::DoPie()
{
    if (!m_pGraph->IsPieChart())
    {
```

295

```
        m_pGraph->SetPieChart();
        SetModifiedFlag(TRUE);
        Redraw();
    }
}
```

We could also add some query methods - for instance, **IsLineGraph()** - which will return
TRUE if the graph is currently displayed as a line graph:

```
BOOL CGraphSrvDoc::IsLineGraph()
{
    return m_pGraph->IsLineGraph();
}
```

The Automation method queries the graph object for its Boolean return value. You could also
add the other graph query functions (**IsBarGraph()** and **IsPieChart()**), and the axis query
functions (**IsNoFrame()**, **IsAxisFrame()** and **IsFullFrame()**).

The rest of the methods are just as simple, and you shouldn't have any difficulty adding them
all to GraphSrv. You'll end up with a list of Automation methods that includes the following:

- **ShowWindow()** and **ShowApp()**
- **Add()**
- **Redraw()** and **Clear()**
- **SetTitle()**
- **DoPie()**, **DoLine()** and **DoBar()**
- **IsPieChart()**, **IsLineGraph()** and **IsBarGraph()**
- **SetNoFrame()**, **SetAxisFrame()** and **SetFullFrame()**
- **IsNoFrame()**, **IsAxisFrame()** and **IsFullFrame()**

You should now be able to appreciate the power of Automation: a data-gathering application
could start a copy of GraphSrv to display its output, passing over data points as they are
acquired. It would be quite easy to extend the example to open more than one graph at a time,
and to add methods to 'tile' the graphs.

Testing Automation from Visual C++

Now we've added Automation to the server, the next task ought to be to write an Automation
client in Visual C++ to test it. With the help given to us by ClassWizard, you'll find that the job
is not too difficult at all.

Try It Out - A Visual C++ Automation Client

1 The first step involves creating a skeleton application - call it **VCTest**, or something
similarly original. In our case, this might as well be a dialog-based application. In Step 2
of the AppWizard dialog, remember to check the A̲utomation box:

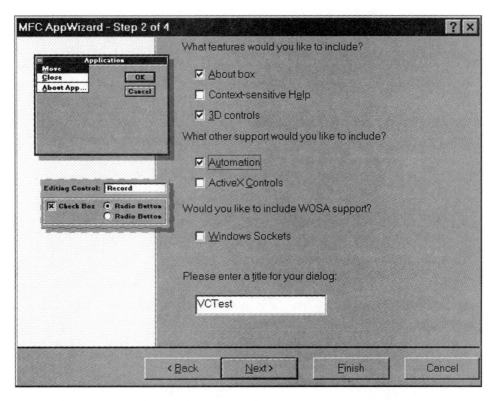

Selecting this option will add a **#include** for **<afxdisp.h>** into **stdafx.h**, and add a call to **AfxOleInit()** to the application's **InitInstance()** function.

2 Now we need to read the type library for our Automation server, GraphSrv. ClassWizard can read type library files and use the information to construct a C++ class whose member functions are wrappers for the methods and properties of an Automation object, so start up ClassWizard and select the Add Class... button.

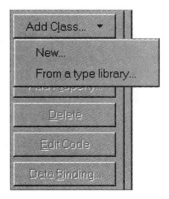

Adding a class 'from a type library' will, as it suggests, create a class from a type library. Choose this option and browse for GraphSrv's type library, which you'll find in the **Debug** directory, along with the GraphSrv executable:

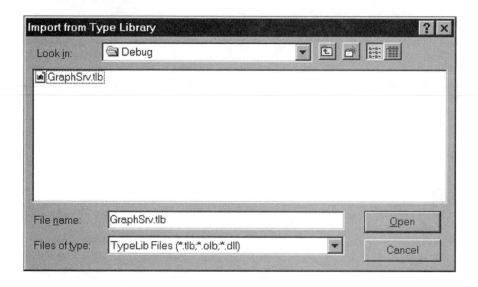

Type library files usually come with the extensions **.tlb** or **.olb**. Type libraries created with Visual C++ are given a **.tlb** extension (for 'type library'); other type libraries, especially those which come with products such as Excel and PowerPoint, tend to have **.olb** extensions (for 'object library'), but they both contain essentially the same information.

When you select the library and press **O**pen, ClassWizard will then read the library file and show you a list of the classes it proposes to create to wrap the Automation objects found in the library:

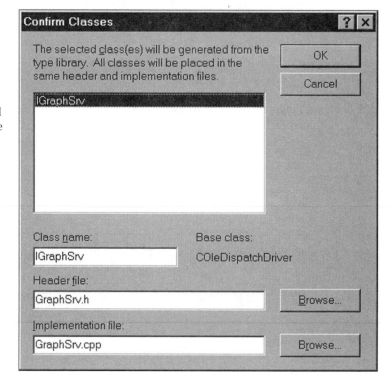

In our case, there's only one Automation object – the **GraphSrv.Document** object – which will be wrapped in a class called **IGraphSrv**. Once you've pressed OK and dismissed ClassWizard, take a look at the **GraphSrv.h** header file:

```
// Machine generated IDispatch wrapper class(es) created with ClassWizard
////////////////////////////////////////////////////////////////////////////
// IGraphSrv wrapper class

class IGraphSrv : public COleDispatchDriver
{
public:
    IGraphSrv() {}          // Calls COleDispatchDriver default constructor
    IGraphSrv(LPDISPATCH pDispatch) : COleDispatchDriver(pDispatch) {}
    IGraphSrv(const IGraphSrv& dispatchSrc) : COleDispatchDriver(dispatchSrc) {}

// Attributes
public:

// Operations
public:
    void ShowApp();
    void ShowWindow();
    void Redraw();
    void Add(LPCTSTR name, long value);
    void SetTitle(LPCTSTR title);
    void Clear();
    void DoLine();
    void DoBar();
    void DoPie();
    BOOL IsLineGraph();
    BOOL IsBarGraph();
    BOOL IsPieChart();
    BOOL IsNoFrame();
    BOOL IsAxisFrame();
    BOOL IsFullFrame();
    void SetNoFrame();
    void SetAxisFrame();
    void SetFullFrame();
};
```

Let's take a look at what we've got in here. The first thing that should strike you is that the class name, **IGraphSrv**, starts with an **I** rather than the usual MFC **C**; this is to show that the class is a wrapper for a COM interface, and follows the usual interface naming convention.

After a few constructors, you can see a bunch of member functions that exactly match the definitions of all the methods we defined for GraphSrv. If we'd added any Automation properties to GraphSrv, they'd have appeared as member variables in the 'Attributes' section.

Here's an extract from the source code for **IGraphSrv**:

```
void IGraphSrv::ShowApp()
{
    InvokeHelper(0x1, DISPATCH_METHOD, VT_EMPTY, NULL, NULL);
}

void IGraphSrv::ShowWindow()
{
```

```
        InvokeHelper(0x2, DISPATCH_METHOD, VT_EMPTY, NULL, NULL);
    }

    void IGraphSrv::Redraw()
    {
        InvokeHelper(0x3, DISPATCH_METHOD, VT_EMPTY, NULL, NULL);
    }

    void IGraphSrv::Add(LPCTSTR name, long value)
    {
        static BYTE parms[] =
            VTS_BSTR VTS_I4;
        InvokeHelper(0x4, DISPATCH_METHOD, VT_EMPTY, NULL, parms,
            name, value);
    }
```

We've already met **InvokeHelper()** in our discussion of how MFC implements Automation clients; its job is basically to help in converting the data to and from the **VARIANT**s needed by calls to **Invoke()**. The first argument in each call is the dispID of the method, as read from the type library; note that the dispIDs in your code may be different from those here, depending on the order in which you added the methods and properties.

The second argument says that we're invoking a method (as opposed to getting or setting a property). The third and fourth arguments give the type of the return value and the address of the variable that will hold it. In our case, we don't have a return value, so the type is **VT_EMPTY**, and the address is **NULL**.

Subsequent arguments detail the arguments passed to the Automation method, and take the form of a **BYTE** array that describes the number and types of the arguments, and then the arguments themselves. In the case of the **Add()** method, we have two arguments, so the **parms[]** array contains two descriptors: **VTS_BSTR** to denote a string, and **VTS_I4** to denote a **long**.

> *The fact that the dispIDs are hard-coded means that C++'s early binding to dispIDs has a significant drawback when compared to Visual Basic's dynamic, late binding. If we change GraphSrv's dispatch interface in any way that changes the relative order or numbering of the methods and properties in the ODL file, then our hard-coded dispIDs may no longer be correct, and we would need to regenerate this class in every application which uses GraphSrv.*

3   Using this class, running GraphSrv is simplicity itself. We simply need to create an **IGraphSrv** object, make sure the Automation server starts up properly, and then use its member functions to call the Automation methods. Start by adding an **IGraphSrv** object to the dialog class header file, remembering to include the appropriate header:

```
#include "graphsrv.h"

class CVCTestDlgAutoProxy;

//////////////////////////////////////////////////////////////////////////
// CVCTestDlg dialog

class CVCTestDlg : public CDialog
{
```

```
    DECLARE_DYNAMIC(CVCTestDlg);
    friend class CVCTestDlgAutoProxy;
    IGraphSrv m_graphObject;

// Construction
public:
    CVCTestDlg(CWnd* pParent = NULL);   // standard constructor
    virtual ~CVCTestDlg();
```

Why put the object in this class? Well, most of the communication is going to be between controls in the dialog and the Automation object, so it seems a sensible place to store it.

4 When the application starts up, we want to launch GraphSrv. This means using the Automation object's **CreateDispatch()** function to start the Automation server and create an object, as shown in the code below:

```
BOOL CVCTestDlg::OnInitDialog()
{
    CDialog::OnInitDialog();

    // Add "About..." menu item to system menu.

    // IDM_ABOUTBOX must be in the system command range.
    ASSERT((IDM_ABOUTBOX & 0xFFF0) == IDM_ABOUTBOX);
    ASSERT(IDM_ABOUTBOX < 0xF000);

    CMenu* pSysMenu = GetSystemMenu(FALSE);
    if (pSysMenu != NULL)
    {
        CString strAboutMenu;
        strAboutMenu.LoadString(IDS_ABOUTBOX);
        if (!strAboutMenu.IsEmpty())
        {
            pSysMenu->AppendMenu(MF_SEPARATOR);
            pSysMenu->AppendMenu(MF_STRING, IDM_ABOUTBOX, strAboutMenu);
        }
    }

    // Set the icon for this dialog.  The framework does this automatically
    //  when the application's main window is not a dialog
    SetIcon(m_hIcon, TRUE);          // Set big icon
    SetIcon(m_hIcon, FALSE);         // Set small icon

    // Start the Automation server
    if (!m_graphObject.CreateDispatch(_T("GraphSrv.Document")))
    {
        AfxMessageBox("Cannot start GraphSrv");
        EndDialog(-1);  // fail
    }
    m_graphObject.ShowApp();
    m_graphObject.ShowWindow();

    return TRUE;  // return TRUE  unless you set the focus to a control
}
```

The call to **CreateDispatch()** takes the progID of the Automation object as an argument, which tells the function where to look in the registry to get the server information. Assuming that the server is started successfully, the routine will return **TRUE** and we can continue. If the function returns **FALSE**, the server wasn't started, and we exit from the application.

Once the server is started, we can call the object's **ShowApp()** and **ShowWindow()** methods to make GraphSrv visible. The **IGraphSrv** class which ClassWizard constructed for us converts our calls into ones to **IDispatch::Invoke()** using its inherited **InvokeHelper()** function, although this is transparent to us.

5 The final step is to add some user interface elements to the dialog and demonstrate the Automation methods being used. First, use the dialog editor to add some buttons and edit controls: one to clear the dataset, one to set the title, and one to add a new point to the dataset. You can see the kind of thing I'm getting at in the next diagram.

Adding the code is very simple to do, so I'll just show you how to handle the **AddPoint()** method as an example. Use ClassWizard to add a handler for the Add Data Item button; you need to get the text from the name and value edit controls, which is simply done using **GetDlgItemText()**. Convert the value to a number and call the graph's **Add()** method - that's all there is to it!

```
void CVCTestDlg::OnAdddataitem()
{
    // Add a point to the dataset - get the data from the edit controls
    CString sName, sVal;
    GetDlgItemText(IDC_NAME, sName);
    GetDlgItemText(IDC_VALUE, sVal);
    long lVal = atol(sVal);

    // Add the point
    m_graphObject.Add(sName, lVal);
}
```

The following figure shows the completed application running:

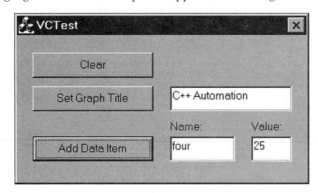

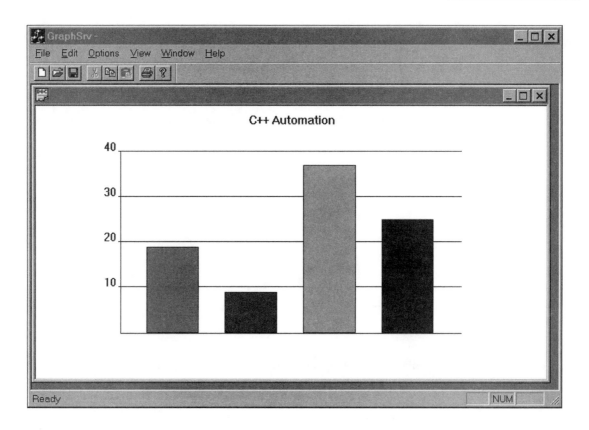

Testing Automation from Visual Basic

We've tested our server from C++, and found that it performs as required. Remember, though, that Automation servers can be used from many other languages apart from C++, and if you can, you really ought to test your server from as many as possible. Not all environments are perfect, and you may find some problem in using your server from a particular language; it is better to catch that sort of thing at an early stage. As an example, we'll use Visual Basic to write a simple Automation client application to drive GraphSrv, and test all the methods we've added so far.

As we'll see shortly, Visual Basic implements all the functionality needed by an Automation client, hiding it from the sight of the Visual Basic programmer. In fact, the average Visual Basic programmer probably knows very little (and cares even less!) about what's actually going on when they use Automation to start up an application and interact with it.

Try It Out - A Visual Basic Automation Client

1 Kicking off an Automation server and creating a new Automation object is very simple in Visual Basic. Start up Visual Basic, create a new project, place a button on the form, and give it a suitable caption, like so:

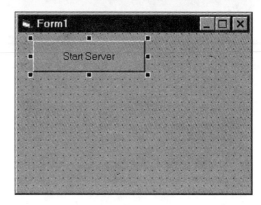

2 Double-click on the button to bring up the form's code editing window; use the combo boxes at the top to select (General) as the Object, and (Declarations) as the Procedure, and enter the following declaration:

```
Dim myGraph as Object
```

3 Now select the button Command1 as the Object, and Click as the Procedure, and fill in the button's **Click** procedure:

```
Private Sub Command1_Click()
    Set myGraph = CreateObject("GraphSrv.Document")
End Sub
```

That's actually all that's needed to start the Automation server. The **Dim** statement creates a variable of type **Object**; in Visual Basic, these are variables that are used to refer to Automation objects. We've created our object as a global variable - if we'd created it *inside* the **Command1_Click** procedure, our Automation object would have disappeared as soon as the button-click operation completed, which isn't what we want at all.

Objects like this can't be used until they've been attached to an actual COM object using the **Set** statement. The **CreateObject()** function is what actually does the work of creating a new graph object for us.

Where do we get the **GraphSrv.Document** from? Way back, when we originally created the application, we had a chance in AppWizard to specify the name by which our document object would be entered in the registry. In case you don't remember, it happens in Step 4 of AppWizard, in the File type ID field of the dialog that appears when you press the Advanced... button. We didn't change it, so we got the default name, formed by tacking **.Document** onto the application name.

If you think back to the discussion of how Automation works at the start of the chapter, and the earlier discussions on how OLE servers work in general, you'll quickly realize that **CreateObject()** is doing an awful lot of work behind the scenes.

4 When these two lines of code have been executed, GraphSrv will be executing in the background with a new graph document open, but it will be doing this invisibly. It's a good idea at this stage to add some error handling to the client. There's quite a lot that can go wrong when you're trying to start up an Automation server: registry entries can get corrupted or mislaid, server executables can disappear - and it's always good to do some intelligent checking before the user finds out via a Visual Basic run-time error!

```
Private Sub Command1_Click()
    On Error GoTo handler
    Set myGraph = CreateObject("GraphSrv.Document")
    Exit Sub

handler:
    Dim Msg As String
    If Err.Number <> 0 Then
        Msg = "Runtime error # " & Str(Err.Number) & Chr(13) & Err.Description
        MsgBox Msg, , "Error", Err.HelpFile, Err.HelpContext
    End If
End Sub
```

In typical Visual Basic fashion, when a run-time error is detected, the error handler located at the label **handler:** will be executed. In our case, all this will do is show a message box giving details of the error that has occurred. The global Visual Basic **Err** object has properties that enable us to get at the error number and description, among other details. In the case of using **CreateObject()** to start an Automation server, the error we're most likely to encounter is number 429: 'ActiveX component can't create object or return reference to this object'.

5 We now need to tell the server to make itself visible, and to show the new document which has been created for us. Insert calls to the **ShowApp()** and **ShowWindow()** methods, like this:

```
Private Sub Command1_Click()
    On Error GoTo handler
    Set myGraph = CreateObject("GraphSrv.Document")

    ' Get server to show itself and the document
    myGraph.ShowApp
    myGraph.ShowWindow

    Exit Sub

handler:
    Dim Msg As String
    If Err.Number <> 0 Then
        Msg = "Runtime error # " & Str(Err.Number) & Chr(13) & Err.Description
        MsgBox Msg, , "Error", Err.HelpFile, Err.HelpContext
    End If
End Sub
```

Once you've done this, run the project, and if all has gone to plan, you should see GraphSrv appear, with a new graph window.

6 We're going to add some data to the graph, but first we'll add a button to clear the graph and reset the data. This is simply a push button whose action is to call the document's **Clear()** Automation method, like this:

```
Private Sub Command2_Click()
    myGraph.Clear
End Sub
```

7 Setting the graph's title is also easy: add an edit control to hold a title string, and a button which takes the text from the edit control and passes it to the Automation object. Tidy up the form a bit, and you should have something like this:

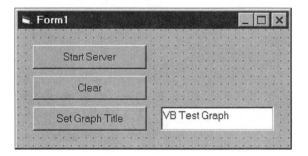

The code behind the button is pretty simple:

```
Private Sub Command3_Click()
    myGraph.SetTitle(Text1.Text)
End Sub
```

8 Now for adding a data item to the graph. We could get fancy and use grid controls, but we'll do it the simple way, one point at a time. Add edit controls for the item's name and value, and a button that will add them to the graph:

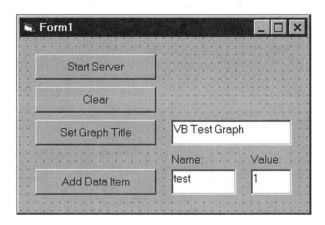

The code takes the data out of the edit controls, and uses the values as parameters for the **Add()** Automation method:

```
Private Sub Command4_Click()
    ' Add a new data point to the graph. First, check the entries
    ' in the edit controls are valid
    Dim value As Integer
    Dim name As String

    name = Text2.Text
    value = Val(Text3.Text)

    myGraph.Add name, value
End Sub
```

9 Run the application, and you should be able to create a custom graph, setting the title and adding as many data points as you should wish:

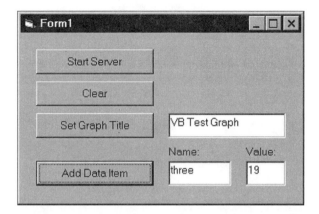

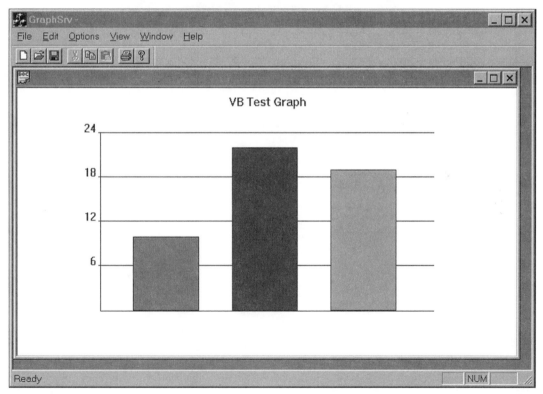

Summary

In this chapter we have looked at Automation, formerly known as OLE Automation, which is one of the major COM based technologies.

Automation provides a standard way for applications to drive one another, via the **IDispatch** interface. Automation servers implement **IDispatch**, while Automation clients (or 'controllers') use the functionality provided by **IDispatch** to drive the server.

IDispatch provides a standard way by which applications can expose functions and data for clients to use. Functions exposed via **IDispatch** are called **methods**, while data items are called **properties**. The collection of properties and methods accessible through a particular implementation of **IDispatch** form a **dispatch interface**, or **dispinterface**. Every method and property in a dispatch interface has a unique numeric ID, called a **dispatch ID**, or **dispID**.

IDispatch consists of four functions, of which **GetIDsOfNames()** and **Invoke()** are the most important. **GetIDsOfNames()** takes the name of a method or property, and returns its dispID. **Invoke()** takes the dispID plus any arguments, and invokes the method, sets a property value, or returns a property value. Automation servers can also use events to provide a notification service for clients.

MFC implements Automation using **dispatch maps**, which are analogous to message maps, in that they map a function in an MFC class to an Automation method. ClassWizard is normally used to maintain the dispatch interface for MFC classes.

In the next chapter we'll move on to discuss ActiveX controls, which make heavy use of Automation, as well as introducing a few new tricks of their own.

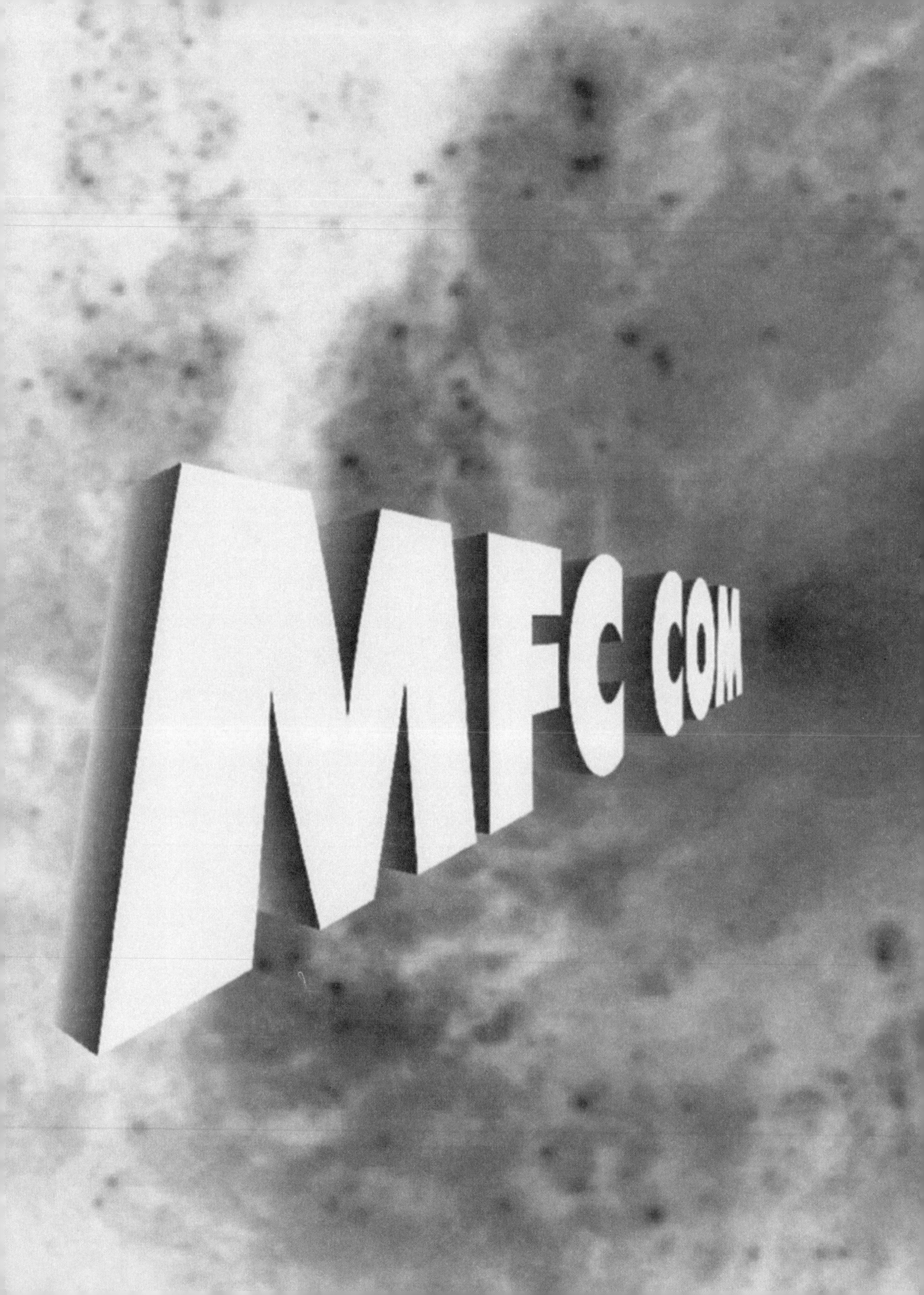
MFC COM

ActiveX Controls

In this chapter, we're going to look at the last, and possibly the most impressive, of the major COM-based technologies supported by MFC. ActiveX controls are the direct descendants of Visual Basic's VBX controls, and make use of many of the features we've discussed in preceding chapters, especially Automation. They are now an important part of building many sorts of applications in the Windows environment, from simple Visual Basic programs to Active Server Pages running on web servers, and there are few major tools and applications that cannot use ActiveX controls.

We'll look at the COM technology that underlies these controls, explore how MFC supports them, and then show how to create and use ActiveX controls.

Control Specifications

Before we start on the technical stuff, a word about specifications. There have been three specifications governing what are now called ActiveX controls, and it's useful to be aware of them.

The original specification was released in 1994, and is often known as **OCX94**. It provided the initial design for **OLE controls** as the successors to VBXs, and the specification could be used for both 16- and 32-bit controls. The main problem was that these controls were not optimized for performance at all, so for applications that had a number of OLE controls loaded, the memory use and performance could be poor. This led to OCXs gaining a reputation for being large, slow and memory hogging.

Because of this, several groups in Microsoft started to work on improving things. The MFC team set about improving performance for Visual C++ 4.0, while the Visual Basic team set about creating a framework which provided for faster, smaller controls that didn't need the hand-holding (and associated overheads) of using MFC. This resulted in the BaseCtl framework, which was included with the ActiveX SDK. The new specification for these leaner, faster controls was published in 1996 as **OCX96**, which improved control performance in several areas, for example:

▶ **Activation**. There are considerable overheads associated with every control being active (i.e. having a window open on the screen), and many controls can get away without this for at least part of the time. Inactive controls can get certain mouse messages forwarded to them by the container, so that they can do a limited amount of processing.

▶ **Windowless controls**. Some controls may not ever need a window. This will decrease loading time, and allows for neat effects like non-rectangular and transparent controls (because windows have to be rectangular, but a windowless control can just paint what it likes on the screen). The container window acts as the display area for the control, which can draw onto the container, as well as perform operations such as accepting dropped objects.

▶ **Drawing optimizations**. These include flicker-free activation, which means that when the active and inactive states of the control are the same, the control isn't redrawn; and flicker-free drawing, which allows a container to draw overlapping objects in an optimized manner.

For OLE controls to work properly on the Internet, some more changes were needed, and these resulted in the **ActiveX control** specification. To start with, the set of interfaces that a control needed to support to conform to the specification was cut down to just one: **IUnknown**. Most controls will tend to provide more interfaces than just this one, but the point is that they don't *have* to provide all the 20-odd interfaces needed for a full-blown OCX96 control. This makes it possible to write small, fast, specialized controls that are still 'standard'.

So, all your old OLE controls are now ActiveX controls, but not all the ActiveX controls you'll write would have qualified as OLE controls. Still, even the simplest ActiveX control will need to implement a little more than **IUnknown** to be truly useful.

Also among these changes are a couple of new dispatch IDs for a 'ready' property (which can be used to find whether a control has finished loading all it needs), and a way of telling the container when this ready state changes. There are also additions to allow asynchronous downloading of properties, which may be needed when large bitmaps or sound clips need to be accessed over an Internet link.

These changes mean that any OCX can be 'upgraded' to work with the Internet, and that small, fast controls can also be built to take advantage of the new cut-down specification.

Tools for Creating ActiveX Controls

ActiveX controls are increasing in functionality and importance all the time, and it's worth spending just a little while to consider the options available when you want to create one. At present, there are three Microsoft tools that are able to create controls:

> Visual C++
> Visual Basic 5/Control Creation Edition
> Visual J++

Visual C++

Visual C++ is the traditional way to build ActiveX controls, and it's what we'll be concentrating on in the remainder of this chapter. There are now several ways to build controls within the Visual C++ environment, depending on your priorities, and we'll discuss them shortly.

Visual Basic

Visual Basic 5.0 is the first version of Visual Basic that has had the ability to *create* controls as well as simply to use them. Microsoft has prepared a cut-down version of Visual Basic 5.0, specifically designed for control creation, and made it freely available. This **Control Creation Edition** (CCE) is as capable as the full version of Visual Basic 5.0 when it comes to creating controls, but it can't create executables, and it doesn't have other advanced Visual Basic functionality. Given the ease of programming with Visual Basic, and the fact that the CCE is free, I think we can expect to see quite a few new ActiveX controls being produced in the near future.

Visual J++

It's also possible to write ActiveX controls using Microsoft's J++ Java development tool. Java is a very good language for writing COM code, because Java's interfaces fit the concept of COM interfaces even better than C++ classes. Java, however, is not a Windows-specific development environment, so how can it be used to write ActiveX controls without violating its system-independent principles?

Control creation is possible because support for COM is built into the **Microsoft Java Virtual Machine** (JVM), the run-time engine responsible for executing Java applets and applications. The JVM makes Java objects look like COM objects to the outside world, and also implements the class factory needed to make them work as proper COM objects. In addition, the JVM gives Java objects transparent access to COM, so that Java programmers can use Automation objects and controls in the same way we do in C++.

At present, though, the support in J++ isn't as mature as you might like, with two main drawbacks. Firstly, there's no Wizard support, so if you want to implement all the features a control can have, you'll have to write a lot of code on your own. The second drawback is more significant: the Java language doesn't provide a way of firing the events that we need in controls. Microsoft will doubtless work on this for a future release of J++, and it will then become a really useful tool for writing COM code.

Tools for Testing ActiveX Controls

When developing a control, it's useful to be able to test its functionality. As well as the Registry Editor and the OLE/COM Object Viewer, Microsoft provides two tools specifically to help test controls: the ActiveX Control Test Container, and the ActiveX Control Pad.

The Test Container

The Test Container application came as part of your Visual C++ installation, and is accessible from the Tools menu. The application provides an ActiveX control container, with specialized functionality to allow you to interact with all aspects of your control, so that you can:

▶ Check that it sizes and positions itself correctly

▶ Check its run-time appearance

▶ List its methods, and invoke them

▶ List its properties, and change them

▶ Display its property sheets

▶ Cause it to fire events

The Test Container is an indispensable tool for the control developer, and you are strongly recommended to use it for testing your controls thoroughly as you're developing them. I'll explain in detail how to use this tool later in the chapter.

The ActiveX Control Pad

Nowadays, many controls are being developed for use in web pages. Hand-crafting HTML pages to contain controls is time-consuming, and Microsoft's ActiveX Control Pad utility is available to help automate the task. We'll look at the use of this tool at the end of the chapter.

Control Architecture

An ActiveX control can be thought of as an Automation server with extra features, and with many additions that make it easy for a developer to use.

Communication between the control and its container uses Automation, and we'll see that **IDispatch** is implemented on both sides. Since the control is embedded in its container, a lot of the user interface functionality can be provided by the normal interfaces used by embedded objects and in-place activation. A consequence of this is that controls end up with a large collection of interfaces that they can implement, depending on precisely what functionality they need to support.

Control Interfaces

A control that matches the OCX96 specification needs to implement a large number of interfaces. The next figure shows the major ones:

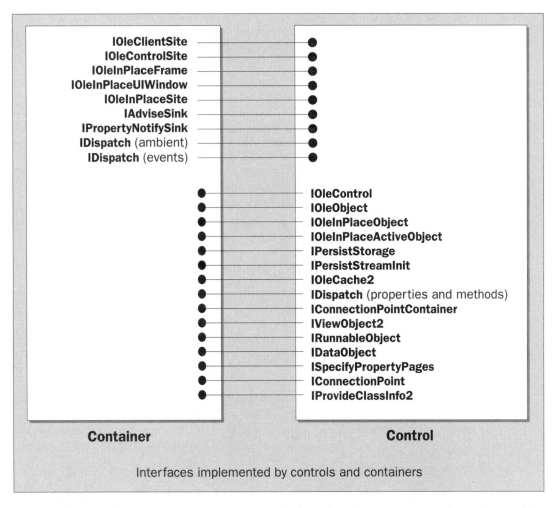

Interfaces implemented by controls and containers

Many of these, such as **IPersistStorage**, are for housekeeping purposes, and are also used in other places, such as OLE servers and containers. Others are used for very specialised purposes, and need not concern us here. However, it is worth just briefly noting some of those that are of special importance to controls, such as **IOleControl**, whose main purpose is to manage the interaction between the control and its container, including the area of keyboard input.

IOleInPlaceObject is supported by controls so that they can be activated and deactivated in-place within the container. It also provides a function to return a handle to the control's window (**GetWindow()**), and another for the client to tell the control when its size or position has been changed (**SetObjectRects()**).

IOleInPlaceActiveObject must be provided if a control wants to be able to process accelerator keys.

IOleObject is used as part of the compound document architecture, and we looked at it in Chapter 4 when we discussed servers. Controls use it to help the container and control communicate.

315

Bear in mind that for an ActiveX control, the interfaces shown here form the complete set, and they may or may not be implemented. If an ActiveX control doesn't support a particular feature, such as being able to store its properties, then it can choose not to implement those interfaces that would support the feature.

Control Clients

On the client side, the container provides a **client site** for each control, the site being the object in the client that implements all the interfaces for talking to a control. As we've already mentioned, there are usually a number of interfaces involved in the communication between the control and its container, some implemented on the control side, and others on the container side.

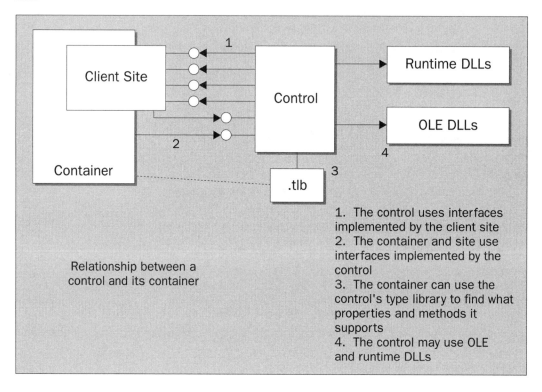

Relationship between a control and its container

1. The control uses interfaces implemented by the client site
2. The container and site use interfaces implemented by the control
3. The container can use the control's type library to find what properties and methods it supports
4. The control may use OLE and runtime DLLs

The control implements a dispatch interface, which the client site uses to access the control's methods and properties. On the container side, the client site implements two dispatch interfaces: one for access to extended and ambient properties, and the other to allow the control to call event handlers, as shown in the following diagram:

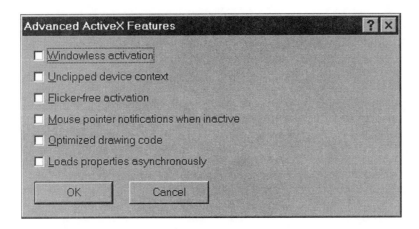

Properties, Methods and Events

As an Automation server, we'd expect a control to have properties, methods and events. Some of these, such as a **Font** property or a **Click** event, are regarded as being standard, and are called **stock** properties and events.

The Automation properties for a control are slightly more complex than those for Automation servers that aren't controls. Because of the interaction between a control and its container, control properties come in three flavors:

▶ **Control properties**, which are unique to, and managed by, the control itself, such as the text in an edit control, or the position of the needle in a meter control.

▶ **Extended properties**, which might appear to the user to be managed by the control, but are actually specified by the container. For example, the container is responsible for a control's size and position, so although it may look to the user as though these properties logically belong to the control, they actually belong to the container. Extended properties apply on a per-control basis; there are also extended methods and events.

▶ **Ambient properties**, which are specified by the container in order to set the environment for all the controls it manages. There is one set of ambient properties, which are used by all controls. Controls ought to take notice of these properties when they load, and adjust themselves accordingly, although this cannot be enforced. Examples could include a background color, or a text font and size.

Ambient properties are given a standard dispID, and it's this that's actually the standard, *not* the name. The following table shows a few common ambient properties:

Name	DispID	Symbolic Name
BackColor	-701	DISPID_AMBIENT_BACKCOLOR
Font	-703	DISPID_AMBIENT_FONT
ForeColor	-704	DISPID_AMBIENT_FORECOLOR
UserMode	-709	DISPID_AMBIENT_USERMODE

It is, however, recommended that you should always use the symbolic name in code; the dispIDs could change in future, and non-English versions may not use the same names. Notice also that the dispID's are negative. This is common to all standard properties, events and methods, and we'll meet negative dispIDs again later.

Ambient properties are like Windows messages, in that there's a standard set which are known to everyone, but applications can also define their own. A container can define its own ambient properties that controls can use, provided that they know about them.

I keep mentioning events in passing, without going into any detail. I hope you've got some sort of idea of what events are for - they're a fairly self-evident concept - but we need to take a closer look at what they are and how they work. The following discussion is at a pretty high level, since the workings of the event mechanism are well hidden from you in both Visual Basic and MFC, so we don't need to know every detail here.

So far, we've thought of Automation as being a one-way process, with the client using the methods and properties exposed by the server. This may be fine for out-of-process servers, but the whole purpose of a control is to communicate with its container, and that requires a way for the control to call back to the container.

COM objects that can do this are called **connectable objects**.do This functionality isn't limited to controls - indeed, if you want to do the programming, you can add it to any Automation server - but controls are the only place where MFC provides any support, so that's why we're discussing it here.

Connectable objects support outgoing interfaces, known as **connection points**, which are used to specify which events the object can originate (or 'fire'). A client can look at the definition of this interface, and decide if it wants to implement it. In effect, the control uses its outgoing interface to say, "If you want to be notified of a particular event, then here's the handler function you need to implement, and I'll call it when the event occurs."

You can see that outgoing interfaces differ from normal (i.e. incoming) interfaces in two respects:

- The server doesn't implement the interface itself, it just provides the definition
- The server knows how to act as a client for the outgoing interface, so it can call its functions

We've seen how the control can specify what events are available, and that the container can examine the interface and decide whether to implement it. How does the container tell the control that it wants to be notified?

The event mechanism is supported through two interfaces: **IConnectionPointContainer** and **IConnectionPoint**. A connectable object, such as a control, implements one **IConnectionPointContainer** interface, and an **IConnectionPoint** for each outgoing interface it supports. A client can get a pointer to the **IConnectionPointContainer** interface, and use its two functions to find out information about what the connectable object can do:

- **FindConnectionPoint()** enables the client to determine whether a particular outgoing interface is supported
- **EnumConnectionPoints()** retrieves a list of all the outgoing interfaces from the server

Once the client has the **IConnectionPoint** it wants, it can establish a connection with the connectable object, using **IConnectionPoint::Advise()** to pass a pointer to its implementation of the interface. Once the connectable object has this pointer, it is able to call the event handler.

The outgoing interface definition is part of the connectable object's type library, so a client can read the type library to obtain information on the events it wants to use.

Property Pages

ActiveX controls are Automation servers, and as such often have properties that can be accessed by clients. Some containers provide a way to display and modify control properties; in the case of Visual Basic, we have the Properties window:

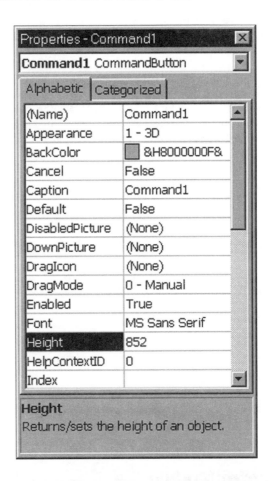

Visual C++, on the other hand, displays control properties using the popular tabbed dialog presentation:

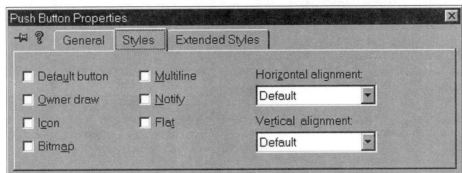

Property pages provide a container-independent way to display and/or modify a control's properties. They use the familiar tabbed dialog to present the properties, and for a container which doesn't support its own scheme (like Visual Basic's Properties window), this interface may be the only way to get at the control's properties.

Property pages are implemented using the **IPropertyPage** interface, and each of the tabs in the dialog above represents a separate COM object that has its own GUID and implements **IPropertyPage**. This means that a control can divide up its properties as it wishes among property pages, and because each page is a COM object in its own right, it's possible to share common pages with other controls. MFC provides several common property page objects, and we'll see later how these can be added to the custom pages provided by a control.

A control implements the **ISpecifyPropertyPages** interface, which supports a single function called **GetPages()**. A container can call **GetPages()** in order to retrieve a list of the property page objects supported by the control. When the container wants to display the property pages, it creates a property frame, and then creates an instance of each of the page objects it wants to display; each page object then presents its page to the property frame, which assembles them into a tabbed dialog box.

Any changes to the properties are communicated from the property frame to the property page object, and the property page object then uses Automation to pass them on to the control.

MFC Support for ActiveX Controls

ActiveX controls are comprehensively supported in MFC versions 4.0 and above by a deceptively simple set of classes, which has four main members:

- **COleControlModule**
- **COleControl**
- **COlePropertyPage**
- **COleDispatchDriver**

The services that they're providing are complex - in fact, there are 25 source code files implementing ActiveX control material in the MFC source - but our interaction with them is usually relatively simple. Let's take a look at each of these four in turn.

COleControlModule

COleControlModule is the **CWinApp**-derived class that's used as base class for control applications. It is a simple class, having just two overridable member functions: **InitInstance()** and **ExitInstance()**. It doesn't implement any COM interfaces.

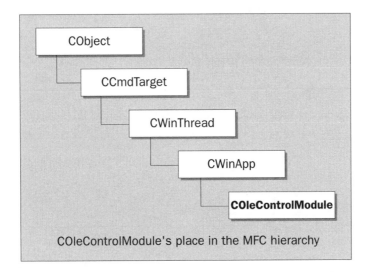

COleControlModule's place in the MFC hierarchy

In a normal application, the application class provides the basic Windows services, including startup routines (**InitInstance()**) and a message loop, while the rest of the application functionality is provided by the document/view architecture. In the same way, **COleControlModule** provides the Windows services for a control, and the next class, **COleControl**, provides the functionality which makes the application into a control.

COleControl

This **CWnd**-derived class is used as base class for 'full' ActiveX controls, and encapsulates a large amount of functionality. It possesses all the functionality of a window, plus Automation and event handling mechanisms, and implements 18 COM interfaces.

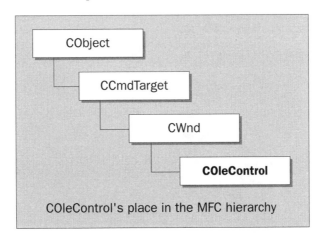

COleControl's place in the MFC hierarchy

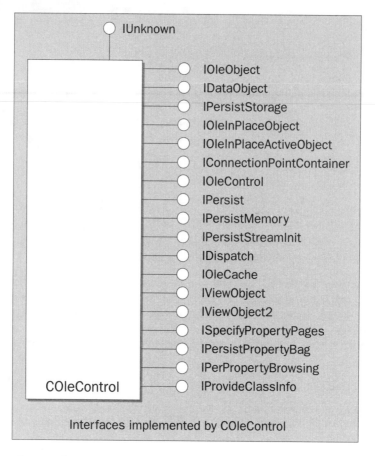

Interfaces implemented by COleControl

COleControl has mechanisms for communicating with the client site that represents the control in the container:

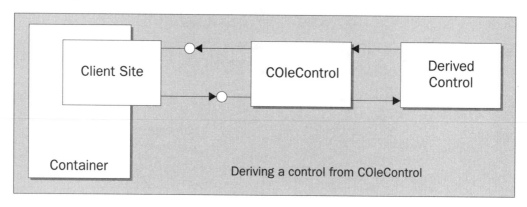

Deriving a control from COleControl

The **COleControl** class has a very large number of member functions - over 150 - which goes to show how much work it has to do to implement the functionality of a 'full' ActiveX control. You can find a full list of the functions, with descriptions, in the online help, and we'll discuss the essential ones as we come across them. In the meantime, this table lists some of the more important of them:

Member Function	Description
SetInitialSize()	Set the size when the control is first displayed
SetControlSize()	Set the control's size (also **GetControlSize()**)
SetRectInContainer()	Set the position in the container (also **GetRectInContainer()**)
OnResetState()	Reset the control's properties
InvalidateControl()	Force a redraw
OnDraw()	Called when the control needs to draw itself
OnDrawMetafile()	Called to get the control to draw into a metafile, typically at design time
DoSuperclassPaint()	Called by a control in **OnDraw()** when the control has been subclassed from a Windows control
ThrowError()	Throw an exception
FireError()	Fire an error event
AmbientBackColor()	Get value of ambient **BackColor** property. There are several similar calls
FireClick()	Fire the click event. There are several more stock events
FireEvent()	Fire a custom event
SetBackColor()	Set background color (also **GetBackColor()**)

Managing Control State

At this point it's worth giving a brief mention to the notion of **control state**. Many ActiveX controls will be used in two modes: in **design mode**, by a programmer working with the Visual C++ dialog editor or the Visual Basic toolbox, and in **user mode**, when the control is active in a program. It is quite possible that you'll want a control to react or display itself differently depending on the mode it is operating in. For instance, you probably won't want the control to respond to key or mouse input in design mode in the same way that it would react in user mode.

Two stock ambient properties, **UserMode** and **UIDead**, both of which are Boolean, can be used by the control to respond correctly in these (and other) circumstances. **UserMode** will be set depending on whether the control is in run-mode (**TRUE**) or design mode (**FALSE**). **UIDead** can be checked by the control to determine whether the container wants it to respond to user-interface operations (in which case it will be **TRUE**).

COlePropertyPage

COlePropertyPage is derived from **CDialog**, and provides a simple way to create and use property pages with MFC and the Developer Studio. This includes visual dialog editing, and DDX for getting property data into and out of the page. Although the **COlePropertyPage** class has member functions of its own, property page objects are frequently used as if they were dialogs.

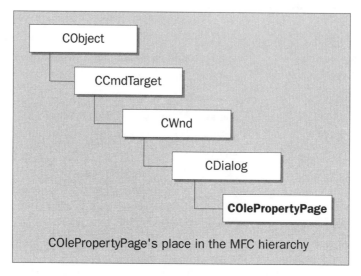

COlePropertyPage's place in the MFC hierarchy

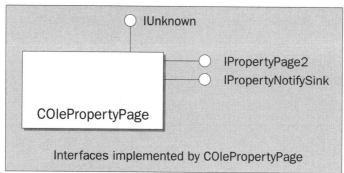

Interfaces implemented by COlePropertyPage

When you create a control using the ActiveX ControlWizard, it will be given a single property page class; if you want your control to have more property pages, you can easily add more by creating more property page classes. We'll see how to add extra property pages into the application when we build a control later in the chapter.

COleDispatchDriver

The three classes we've talked about so far are involved with *implementing* controls in MFC; this last one helps with *using* controls in MFC programs, by providing support for placing controls in control containers. As we discussed in the previous chapter, this class provides access to an Automation object by creating a wrapper class whose members represent the methods and properties of the object. When you use Component Gallery to insert a control into your project, it creates a **COleDispatchDriver**-derived class to represent the control.

You'll notice, though, that controls you insert from the Controls and Components Gallery derive from **CWnd**, because they often have a window to implement their user interface. In fact, **CWnd** contains a **COleControlSite** member, which in turn contains a **COleDispatchDriver**. **CWnd**'s control-related functions are, for the most part, similar to the ones we've already seen in **COleDispatchDriver**:

Function	Purpose
`GetProperty()`	Get a control property value
`SetProperty()`	Set a control property value
`InvokeHelper()`	Invoke a control method or property
`OnAmbientProperty()`	Called to get an ambient property from a container window
`GetControlUnknown()`	Gets a pointer to the **IUnknown** interface of the control represented by the **CWnd** object

Before leaving **COleDispatchDriver**, let me re-emphasize the pitfalls inherent in using control wrapper classes in MFC. The dispIDs for the control's properties and methods are hard-coded into the wrapper class, so if the control changes its properties or methods in any way, the class will need to be regenerated, and the project recompiled.

Events in MFC Controls

Support is provided in the **COleControl** class for two sorts of events: stock and custom. Stock events are those that **COleControl** will handle automatically, such as mouse clicks and key presses, while custom events are those you provide for your control.

As you might expect, MFC support for events is handled by yet another type of map: an **event map**. This operates much like a message map, and in this case the mapping is between a function that you call in your control code to fire an event, and the actual COM event which gets fired. As with message maps, the name of the function you call is usually related to the name of the event (e.g. **FireClick()** for firing the stock **Click** event), but for custom events you can make them as different as you like.

Using an event map involves having a **DECLARE_EVENT_MAP()** macro in the class header, with matching **BEGIN_** and **END_EVENT_MAP()** macros in the class implementation. ClassWizard helps you maintain the event map via its ActiveX Events tab, which you can use to add and remove events. Support for stock events is provided by a number of **COleControl** member functions:

Member	Description
`FireClick()`	Fire the stock **Click** event
`FireDblClick()`	Fire the stock **DblClick** event
`FireError()`	Fire the stock **Error** event (discussed in the next section)
`FireKeyDown()`	Fire the stock **KeyDown** event
`FireKeyUp()`	Fire the stock **KeyUp** event
`FireKeyPress()`	Fire the stock **KeyPress** event

Table Continued on Following Page

Member	Description
FireMouseDown()	Fire the stock **MouseDown** event
FireMouseMove()	Fire the stock **MouseMove** event
FireMouseUp()	Fire the stock **MouseUp** event
FireReadyStateChange()	Fires an event when the control's ready state changes

Firing a stock event just involves adding the appropriate event to the control's event map using ClassWizard, and then calling the appropriate function. If we added a stock **Click** event, the event map would look like this:

```
BEGIN_EVENT_MAP(CGraph1Ctrl, COleControl)
//{{AFX_EVENT_MAP(CGraph1Ctrl)
   EVENT_STOCK_CLICK()
   //}}AFX_EVENT_MAP
END_EVENT_MAP()
```

Custom events are a little more complicated, and are handled by the **FireEvent()** function:

```
void FireEvent(DISPID dispID, BYTE FAR* pbParams, ...);
```

The first argument is the dispID of the event, while the second points to an array of bytes representing the arguments for the event. In practice, this is represented as a space-separated list of **VTS_** constants representing the argument types, such as **VTS_HWND** to represent an **HWND**, or **VTS_XPOS_HIMETRIC** to represent an *x*-coordinate in HIMETRIC units; the full list of these can be found in **afxdisp.h**, in case you need them. This list is followed by the argument values themselves; if you have no arguments, use **VTS_NONE** as the argument type.

The following code fragments assume that we have a custom event called **MyEvent**, which has a dispID of 3 and takes a single short as a parameter:

```
short* val;
...
long disp = 3L;
FireEvent(disp, (BYTE*) VTS_PI2, val);
```

The call to **FireEvent()** takes the dispID, one argument specifier of type **VTS_PI2** (pointer to a two-byte integer), and the pointer itself.

When you add a custom event, ClassWizard provides a function that wraps the call to **FireEvent()**. For the example above, the following code might be generated in the class header file:

```
// Event maps
   //{{AFX_EVENT(CGraph1Ctrl)
   void FireMyEvent(short FAR* val)
      {FireEvent(DISPID_CUSTOM_EVENT, EVENT_PARAM(VTS_PI2), val);}
   //}}AFX_EVENT
   DECLARE_EVENT_MAP()
```

And an entry is placed in the event map:

```
BEGIN_EVENT_MAP(CGraph1Ctrl, COleControl)
//{{AFX_EVENT_MAP(CGraph1Ctrl)
   EVENT_STOCK_CLICK()
   EVENT_CUSTOM_ID("MyEvent", DISPID_KEYPRESS, FireMyEvent, VTS_PI2)
//}}AFX_EVENT_MAP
END_EVENT_MAP()
```

The event can now be fired by calling **FireMyEvent()**.

On the client side, events are handled by yet another map type: the event sink map. ClassWizard adds an entry to this map for each handler provided by the container, so that at runtime the correct handler routine can be found for a particular event:

```
BEGIN_EVENTSINK_MAP(CCtlTestDlg, CDialog)
   //{{AFX_EVENTSINK_MAP(CCtlTestDlg)
   ON_EVENT(CCtlTestDlg, IDC_GRAPH1CTRL1, -600 /* Click */, OnClickGraph1ctrl1,
VTS_NONE)
   //}}AFX_EVENTSINK_MAP
END_EVENTSINK_MAP()
```

This map contains a single entry, showing that if an event with a dispID of -600 (the stock **Click** event) is fired by the control **IDC_GRAPHCTRL1**, the function **OnClickGraphctrl1()** should be called.

Error Handling in Controls

What happens when an error occurs in an MFC program that either implements or uses ActiveX controls? In 'pure' Automation code, when we aren't using MFC, we use the **EXCEPINFO** structure to pass back information about errors that have occurred during Automation operations. Using the MFC classes, we don't have access to the **Invoke()** function itself, so we need some other method.

The **COleControl** class provides us with two ways in which we can signal errors from controls: **FireError()** and **ThrowError()**. The first of these fires the standard **Error** event. This event is never fired by the framework, and is only used for user errors.

```
void FireError(SCODE   scode,              // Status code
              LPCTSTR lpszDescription,     // Error message text
              UINT    nHelpID = 0);        // Optional help context ID
```

There are about 40 standard error status codes defined in the **Olectl.h** header file, or you can define your own by using the **CUSTOM_CTL_SCODE** macro (which is defined in the same file), like this:

```
#define MYCTL_E_SPECIALERROR CUSTOM_CTL_SCODE(1000)
```

The last parameter to **FireError()** can be used to pass the context ID of a help file page.

ThrowError() throws an exception of type **COleDispatchException**, and has a similar parameter list to **FireError()**:

```
void ThrowError(
   SCODE   sc,                    // Status code
   PCTSTR pszDescription = NULL,  // Error message text, this time optional
   UINT    nHelpID = 0);          // Optional help context ID
```

327

When should you use one, and when the other? If you have to signal an error from within a method or a property handling function, then use **ThrowError()**. Otherwise, use **FireError()**. In other words, don't fire an event from within a handler.

Licensing

The way ActiveX controls work is both a blessing and a curse for the programmer. The former is true because the flexibility provided by **IDispatch** and the other standard interfaces makes it easy to use controls in development tools. Unfortunately, the latter is also true because this very flexibility makes it easy for an unscrupulous programmer to take an ActiveX control, find out how it works (by looking at its type information to discover its properties and methods), and then pirate it for use in their own applications.

How, then, can ActiveX controls be protected? We need a safeguard, so that when controls have been distributed with applications or web pages, they don't get pirated, and will only work with the application they're supposed to.

Microsoft has implemented a **licensing** scheme by altering the way in which the class factory interface creates objects. In finest COM style, they did this by creating a new interface - **IClassFactory2** - which adds licensing functions to the existing functionality supported by the original **IClassFactory**.

Two sorts of license can be provided. A license file, typically containing a known, unique text string, can be placed in the same directory as the control; this is a **global license**, and will allow the control to be used with any container on the machine, which is just what you want when you're developing. The alternative is for a container itself to possess the license string, which it will provide to the control on request, and this is what happens when a control is distributed with an application.

When a container wants to create an instance of a control, it can use **IClassFactory2**'s **GetLicInfo()** function to see whether there is a license file available. If there is, then the container can call **CreateInstance()** as usual; the control will see the global license, and create the file. If there isn't a license file, then the container has to provide the license string. It does this using **IClassFactory2**'s **CreateInstanceLic()** function, which takes the key string as an additional parameter.

How does the container get the license string in the first place? It uses the **IClassFactory2** function **RequestLicKey()** to get a string from the control, which it can then save away. An MFC program which uses ActiveX controls will use **RequestLicKey()** to get keys for its controls at compilation time, so that the finished application can be distributed. Note that the control will only give a license key away if it can find a license file, which indicates that it is running on a licensed machine.

We'll see in the next section how MFC implements licensing, when we walk through a typical control's skeleton code.

Creating Controls with Visual C++

Let's move on from the theoretical to the practical, and look at how we can create controls with Visual C++. We're actually rather spoilt for choice, in that there are three ways we can do this:

-   The MFC ActiveX ControlWizard
-   The ActiveX SDK
-   The Active Template Library (ATL)

The **ActiveX ControlWizard** produces full, MFC-based ActiveX controls. It's very easy to produce controls using this Wizard (as we'll see), and you get access to all of MFC's functionality, with the additional benefit of not having to deal with the underlying COM code. The downside of creating controls in this way is that they aren't optimized for speed or size, and in addition need the MFC run-time libraries. This may not be the best way to create controls if you want to make very small, fast controls for Internet use.

> *This isn't necessarily the problem it first appears. Many users now have the MFC libraries installed, as they ship with Internet Explorer (MFC 4.0 with Internet Explorer 3, and MFC 4.2 with Internet Explorer 4). Providing your control uses the same version of MFC as the user has installed, the need to download them disappears.*

The **ActiveX SDK** provides a sample skeleton for a control, called the **BaseCtl** control framework. It provides lighter and faster controls than the MFC Wizard, but requires considerably more knowledge of COM. Also, there's no Wizard support within the Visual C++ environment.

The **Active Template Library**, currently at version 2.*x*, is designed, among other things, to allow the production of the smallest, fastest ActiveX controls possible. A Wizard for building ATL controls is included with Visual C++ 5.0, and will generate code both for controls that use MFC, and for controls which use only 'standard' C++. It can also generate code for special-purpose controls, such as those for use only in Internet Explorer.

> *If you wish to know more about producing ATL controls, you may want to take a look at another Wrox Press title,* Beginning ATL Programming. *ISBN 1-861000-11-1.*

Which of these methods you choose will depend on the features you need to support, and how easy you want the job to be! In this book we're concentrating on programming with MFC, so we're only going to look at the first one in detail.

The MFC ActiveX ControlWizard

Creating a control with the ActiveX ControlWizard involves two steps, the first of which is shown on the following page:

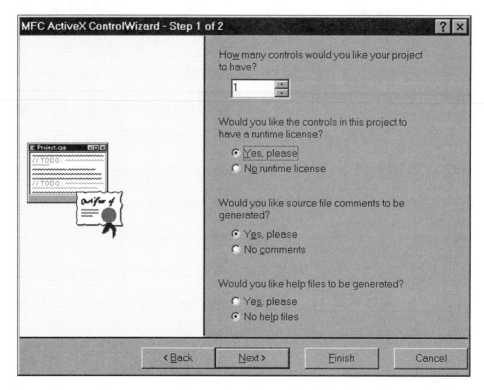

The first option on this screen sets the number of controls the project will contain. You can include any number you wish, and having more than one control per project cuts down on the number of DLLs that have to be distributed with your application (and loaded at runtime), but most people tend to stick to one control per project, in the interests of modularity.

If selected, the second option will add code to support control licensing. We'll look at how this works shortly.

The third option will include the usual MFC **// TODO:** comments in the code, and should be left selected until you ascend to guru level and don't need them any more!

The last option determines whether you want the usual MFC-style help files generated for the control. We'll see how to use this later on, as well.

The second screen has some rather more interesting options:

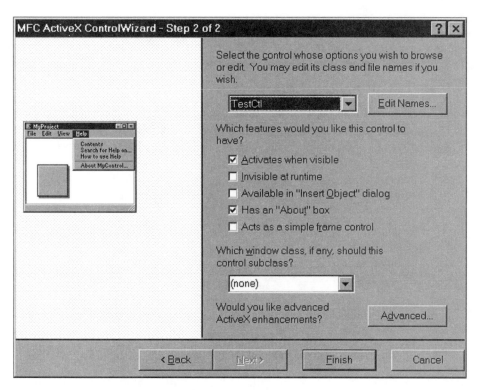

If you have more than one control in the project, you use the combo box at the top to select the one whose properties you want to display. The button next to the combo box can be used to modify the object and file names associated with the control if necessary.

The block of check boxes is used to set various options for the control:

Option	Description
Activates when visible	The control should be activated whenever it is visible
Invisible at runtime	For a control which doesn't need a user interface at runtime, such as a timer control, this option removes the drawing functionality
Available in "Insert Object" dialog	Adds the **Insertable** key to the control's registry entry, so that the Insert Object dialog will include it
Has an "About" box	Adds an About box to the control
Acts as a simple frame control	Check this if your control is going to include other standard Windows controls, such as edit controls and buttons

The combo box below this block allows you to make your control subclass an existing Windows control, thus gaining the built-in functionality of the base control.

The Advanced... button takes you to another dialog, which allows you to set a number of advanced ActiveX features. That dialog, and a table explaining the options it contains, is given here:

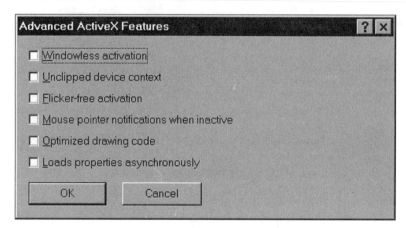

Option	Description
Windowless activation	The control will not create its own window, but will draw directly onto the container. If this option is chosen, the next two are irrelevant.
Unclipped device context	If you *know* your control won't draw outside its bounding rectangle, this option can speed up drawing by omitting clipping checks.
Flicker-free activation	If your control looks the same in its active and inactive states, this option will prevent it being redrawn when the state changes.
Mouse pointer notifications when inactive	The control will track the mouse even when it is inactive.
Optimized drawing code	Some containers will cache the drawing tools for the control's device context, so that the control doesn't have to reload them each time it draws. This option requests the container to cache if it can.
Loads properties asynchronously	Useful for Internet controls, this option lets the control load some property data asynchronously in the background.

The MFC Control Skeleton

The skeleton code generated by the ActiveX ControlWizard for an MFC control is deceptively simple, mainly because of the large amount of processing power being supplied by the base classes. I ran the Wizard to generate a project consisting of a single control called **TestCtl**, with licensing. The skeleton produced consists of three classes:

▶ **CTestCtlApp**, the **COleControlModule**-derived class that implements the equivalent of an MFC application's **CWinApp** object

▶ **CTestCtlCtrl**, which implements the control's functionality

▶ **CTestCtlPropPage**, the default property page for the control

Along with two interfaces:

▶ **_DTestCtl**, which is the main dispatch interface for the control

▶ **_DTestCtlEvents**, which is used to specify events

The Application Class

This is a very simple class indeed, consisting of just two functions:

```
class CTestCtlApp : public COleControlModule
{
public:
   BOOL InitInstance();
   int ExitInstance();
};
```

These functions call their base class equivalents, but if you need to do any initialization or resource allocation and deallocation, you can modify them.

The header file for the application class also defines three constants: the GUID for the control's type library, and the control's major and minor version numbers:

```
extern const GUID CDECL _tlid;
extern const WORD _wVerMajor;
extern const WORD _wVerMinor;
```

DLL Functions

Our control will build into a DLL, and the application class source file also declares two global functions, **DLLRegisterServer()** and **DLLUnregisterServer()**, which are used to handle registering and de-registering the control DLL:

```
//////////////////////////////////////////////////////////////////////
// DllRegisterServer - Adds entries to the system registry

STDAPI DllRegisterServer(void)
{
   AFX_MANAGE_STATE(_afxModuleAddrThis);

   if (!AfxOleRegisterTypeLib(AfxGetInstanceHandle(), _tlid))
      return ResultFromScode(SELFREG_E_TYPELIB);

   if (!COleObjectFactoryEx::UpdateRegistryAll(TRUE))
      return ResultFromScode(SELFREG_E_CLASS);

   return NOERROR;
}
```

```
///////////////////////////////////////////////////////////////////////
// DllUnregisterServer - Removes entries from the system registry

STDAPI DllUnregisterServer(void)
{
   AFX_MANAGE_STATE(_afxModuleAddrThis);

   if (!AfxOleUnregisterTypeLib(_tlid, _wVerMajor, _wVerMinor))
      return ResultFromScode(SELFREG_E_TYPELIB);

   if (!COleObjectFactoryEx::UpdateRegistryAll(FALSE))
      return ResultFromScode(SELFREG_E_CLASS);

   return NOERROR;
}
```

These functions are used when the control's data is to be added to or removed from the system registry, and they are typically used by applications such as installers or the **Regsvr32.exe** utility. When you build an ActiveX control project, the build process will register the control for you, and will call the **DLLRegisterServer()** function in the process.

The Control Class

The control class itself is slightly more complex, but not by much. We learned earlier how **COleControl** has over 150 member functions; this class overrides precisely three of them!

The start of the implementation file defines the various maps used. As ActiveX controls make use of Automation, we have dispatch and event maps as well as the more familiar message map:

```
///////////////////////////////////////////////////////////////////////
// Message map

BEGIN_MESSAGE_MAP(CTestCtlCtrl, COleControl)
   //{{AFX_MSG_MAP(CTestCtlCtrl)
   // NOTE - ClassWizard will add and remove message map entries
   //    DO NOT EDIT what you see in these blocks of generated code !
   //}}AFX_MSG_MAP
   ON_OLEVERB(AFX_IDS_VERB_PROPERTIES, OnProperties)
END_MESSAGE_MAP()


///////////////////////////////////////////////////////////////////////
// Dispatch map

BEGIN_DISPATCH_MAP(CTestCtlCtrl, COleControl)
   //{{AFX_DISPATCH_MAP(CTestCtlCtrl)
   // NOTE - ClassWizard will add and remove dispatch map entries
   //    DO NOT EDIT what you see in these blocks of generated code !
   //}}AFX_DISPATCH_MAP
   DISP_FUNCTION_ID(CTestCtlCtrl, "AboutBox",
                            DISPID_ABOUTBOX, AboutBox, VT_EMPTY, VTS_NONE)
END_DISPATCH_MAP()


///////////////////////////////////////////////////////////////////////
// Event map
```

```
BEGIN_EVENT_MAP(CTestCtlCtrl, COleControl)
   //{{AFX_EVENT_MAP(CTestCtlCtrl)
   // NOTE - ClassWizard will add and remove event map entries
   //    DO NOT EDIT what you see in these blocks of generated code !
   //}}AFX_EVENT_MAP
END_EVENT_MAP()
```

The maps are followed by a property page block. The **PROPPAGEID()** macros are used inside a **BEGIN_/END_PROPPAGEIDS** block to define the GUIDs of the property pages that are associated with this control:

```
/////////////////////////////////////////////////////////////////////
// Property pages

// TODO: Add more property pages as needed.  Remember to increase the count!
BEGIN_PROPPAGEIDS(CTestCtlCtrl, 1)
   PROPPAGEID(CTestCtlPropPage::guid)
END_PROPPAGEIDS(CTestCtlCtrl)
```

The **IMPLEMENT_OLECREATE_EX()** macro implements the class factory functions for the control. The '**_EX**' version adds a virtual function to return the CLSID of our control:

```
/////////////////////////////////////////////////////////////////////
// Initialize class factory and guid

IMPLEMENT_OLECREATE_EX(CTestCtlCtrl, "TESTCTL.TestCtlCtrl.1",
    0xb5a84f65, 0xe311, 0x11d0, 0x92, 0x57, 0, 0x20, 0x18, 0x34, 0xe2, 0xa3)
```

The **IMPLEMENT_OLETYPELIB()** macro defines static functions to get the type library information for the control:

```
/////////////////////////////////////////////////////////////////////
// Type library ID and version

IMPLEMENT_OLETYPELIB(CTestCtlCtrl, _tlid, _wVerMajor, _wVerMinor)
```

Next in line are the definitions for the GUIDs of the two dispatch interfaces our control supports: the incoming interface for Automation properties and methods, and the outgoing interface for events:

```
/////////////////////////////////////////////////////////////////////
// Interface IDs

const IID BASED_CODE IID_DTestCtl =
     { 0xb5a84f63, 0xe311, 0x11d0, { 0x92, 0x57, 0, 0x20, 0x18, 0x34, 0xe2, 0xa3
} };
const IID BASED_CODE IID_DTestCtlEvents =
     { 0xb5a84f64, 0xe311, 0x11d0, { 0x92, 0x57, 0, 0x20, 0x18, 0x34, 0xe2, 0xa3
} };
```

The next section sets up the 'MiscStatus' bits, which are used to set various options for the object. The settings are held in the **_dwTestctlOleMisc** variable, while the **IMPLEMENT_OLECTLTYPE** macro implements two functions: one to return the status bits, and the other to return the type name string, which is a user-friendly string describing the object, such as "Word document":

```
//////////////////////////////////////////////////////////////////////////
// Control type information

static const DWORD BASED_CODE _dwTestCtlOleMisc =
    OLEMISC_ACTIVATEWHENVISIBLE |
    OLEMISC_SETCLIENTSITEFIRST |
    OLEMISC_INSIDEOUT |
    OLEMISC_CANTLINKINSIDE |
    OLEMISC_RECOMPOSEONRESIZE;

IMPLEMENT_OLECTLTYPE(CTestCtlCtrl, IDS_TESTCTL, _dwTestCtlOleMisc)
```

The next function in the file implements the class factory **UpdateRegistry()** function, which is called to register our control. Then, after the licensing functions (which I'll come back to), is the constructor, which calls the base class **InitializeIIDs()** function, in order to pass through the GUIDs for our dispatch and event interfaces:

```
//////////////////////////////////////////////////////////////////////////
// CTestCtlCtrl::CTestCtlCtrl - Constructor

CTestCtlCtrl::CTestCtlCtrl()
{
    InitializeIIDs(&IID_DTestCtl, &IID_DTestCtlEvents);

    // TODO: Initialize your control's instance data here.
}
```

The first of the overridden **COleControl** methods is **OnDraw()**, where the control does its drawing. The default action is to draw a white rectangle with an ellipse inside, just so you'll have something to display when you test the control. Note that unlike a normal MFC **OnDraw()** function, we get passed a pointer to a device context, plus **CRect**s defining the clipping rectangle and the invalid rectangle:

```
//////////////////////////////////////////////////////////////////////////
// CTestCtlCtrl::OnDraw - Drawing function

void CTestCtlCtrl::OnDraw(
        CDC* pdc, const CRect& rcBounds, const CRect& rcInvalid)
{
    // TODO: Replace the following code with your own drawing code.
    pdc->FillRect(rcBounds,
CBrush::FromHandle((HBRUSH)GetStockObject(WHITE_BRUSH)));
    pdc->Ellipse(rcBounds);
}
```

DoPropExchange() is used to implement property persistence. A container may ask the controls it contains to store their property data, in the same way that an embedded object will store its data into a stream provided by the container. Like Dialog Data Exchange, **DoPropExchange()** is called both to store and restore the property values. It is overridden here so that we can add our own properties if necessary, and also to ensure that the right version number gets used:

```
//////////////////////////////////////////////////////////////////////////
// CTestCtlCtrl::DoPropExchange - Persistence support

void CTestCtlCtrl::DoPropExchange(CPropExchange* pPX)
```

```
{
    ExchangeVersion(pPX, MAKELONG(_wVerMinor, _wVerMajor));
    COleControl::DoPropExchange(pPX);

    // TODO: Call PX_ functions for each persistent custom property.

}
```

The last of the overridden functions is **OnResetState()**, which is provided so that we can add code to reset our control to its default state:

```
//////////////////////////////////////////////////////////////////////
// CTestCtlCtrl::OnResetState - Reset control to default state

void CTestCtlCtrl::OnResetState()
{
    COleControl::OnResetState();  // Resets defaults found in DoPropExchange

    // TODO: Reset any other control state here.
}
```

Licensing

The control code also contains the licensing implementation code, if you've chosen to include it. The **COleObjectFactory** class implements the **IClassFactory2** interface with its licensing functionality. If you choose to add licensing to a control, several routines are overridden in the class factory in order to give you control over how the license is implemented and checked. The control's header file defines the class factory as a nested class, and when licensing is included, provides the definitions of two licensing functions:

```
class CTestCtlCtrl : public COleControl
{
    DECLARE_DYNCREATE(CTestCtlCtrl)

// Constructor
public:
    CTestCtlCtrl();

// Overrides
    // ClassWizard generated virtual function overrides
    //{{AFX_VIRTUAL(CTestCtlCtrl)
    public:
    virtual void OnDraw(CDC* pdc, const CRect& rcBounds, const CRect& rcInvalid);
    virtual void DoPropExchange(CPropExchange* pPX);
    virtual void OnResetState();
    //}}AFX_VIRTUAL

// Implementation
protected:
    ~CTestCtlCtrl();

    BEGIN_OLEFACTORY(CTestCtlCtrl)          // Class factory and guid
        virtual BOOL VerifyUserLicense();
        virtual BOOL GetLicenseKey(DWORD, BSTR FAR*);
    END_OLEFACTORY(CTestCtlCtrl)
};
```

The licensing scheme itself is implemented in the source code. Two constants give the name of the license file, and the actual license string itself. By default, the license string is the first line out of the **.lic** file.

```
//////////////////////////////////////////////////////////////////////
// Licensing strings

static const TCHAR BASED_CODE _szLicFileName[] = _T("TestCtl.lic");

static const WCHAR BASED_CODE _szLicString[] =
   L"Copyright (c) 1997 Wrox Press";
```

The two class factory functions are used to verify the presence of the license file, and to return the license string. **VerifyUserLicense()** is used by a container to check that a control is licensed. The control uses **AfxVerifyLicFile()** to check that the file exists, and that the license string matches the first line in the file:

```
//////////////////////////////////////////////////////////////////////
// CTestCtlCtrl::CTestCtlCtrlFactory::VerifyUserLicense -
// Checks for existence of a user license

BOOL CTestCtlCtrl::CTestCtlCtrlFactory::VerifyUserLicense()
{
   return AfxVerifyLicFile(AfxGetInstanceHandle(), _szLicFileName,
      _szLicString);
}
```

GetLicenseKey() is used to get the key from the control. A tool such as Developer Studio will use this to embed a key into an application that's using a control.

```
//////////////////////////////////////////////////////////////////////
// CTestCtlCtrl::CTestCtlCtrlFactory::GetLicenseKey -
// Returns a runtime licensing key

BOOL CTestCtlCtrl::CTestCtlCtrlFactory::GetLicenseKey(DWORD dwReserved,
   BSTR FAR* pbstrKey)
{
   if (pbstrKey == NULL)
      return FALSE;

   *pbstrKey = SysAllocString(_szLicString);
   return (*pbstrKey != NULL);
}
```

You would override these two functions if you wanted to implement a more secure licensing strategy. There's a third function, **VerifyLicenseKey()**, which isn't provided for you by AppWizard, but which you can also override if you want to customise the licensing procedure. You may, for instance, want to adjust which properties and methods are available to the client, based on the license information returned. For more information, see the topic 'ActiveX Controls: Licensing an ActiveX Control' in Books Online.

The Property Page Class

The property page class derives from **COlePropertyPage**, which in turn derives from **CDialog**. The class contains all the members you'd expect for a dialog class, and in addition has some special code related to its function as a property page.

As the property page is a COM object in its own right, the class implementation contains an **IMPLEMENT_OLECREATE_EX()** macro to implement the class factory functions for the object, as well as an **UpdateRegistry()** function for registration. The GUID used in the arguments to **IMPLEMENT_OLECREATE_EX()** is used to set the **guid** static data member, which is then used in the control's **PROPPAGEID()** macro:

```
//////////////////////////////////////////////////////////////////////
// Initialize class factory and guid

IMPLEMENT_OLECREATE_EX(CTestCtlPropPage, "TESTCTL.TestCtlPropPage.1",
    0xb5a84f66, 0xe311, 0x11d0, 0x92, 0x57, 0, 0x20, 0x18, 0x34, 0xe2, 0xa3)


//////////////////////////////////////////////////////////////////////
// CTestCtlPropPage::CTestCtlPropPageFactory::UpdateRegistry -
// Adds or removes system registry entries for CTestCtlPropPage

BOOL CTestCtlPropPage::CTestCtlPropPageFactory::UpdateRegistry(BOOL bRegister)
{
    if (bRegister)
        return AfxOleRegisterPropertyPageClass(AfxGetInstanceHandle(),
            m_clsid, IDS_TESTCTL_PPG);
    else
        return AfxOleUnregisterClass(m_clsid, NULL);
}
```

The only other functions in the class are a constructor and an empty **DoDataExchange()** function.

Making GraphSrv into a Control

Let's see how we can turn our graphing program into a control that we can use in programs and on web pages.

The first step is to create a basic control project. Start a new project, and choose the ActiveX ControlWizard; call it 'Graph1'. The options for our control project are very simple: we're only going to have one control, we want to include licensing and help files, and there are no special options to set. Once you've visited both pages of the Wizard, press OK to create the project files.

Creating the Basis of the Control

Since we built all the graphing functionality of GraphSrv into the **CGraph** class, most of the groundwork we have to do involves simply importing the **CGraph** files from the GraphSrv project, and linking them in.

Try It Out - Your First Control

1 Copy the **CGraph** files, **Graph.cpp** and **Graph.h**, from the GraphSrv project to your new Graph1 project. Next, add a private **CGraph*** member variable to the control class definition, remembering to include the required header files as well:

```
// Graph1Ctl.h : Declaration of the CGraph1Ctrl ActiveX Control class.

/////////////////////////////////////////////////////////////////////////////
// CGraph1Ctrl : See Graph1Ctl.cpp for implementation.
#include <fstream.h>
#include "graph.h"

class CGraph1Ctrl : public COleControl
{
   DECLARE_DYNCREATE(CGraph1Ctrl)

// Constructor
public:
   CGraph1Ctrl();

// ...

// Dispatch and event IDs
public:
   enum {
   //{{AFX_DISP_ID(CGraph1Ctrl)
      // NOTE: ClassWizard will add and remove enumeration elements here.
      //    DO NOT EDIT what you see in these blocks of generated code !
   //}}AFX_DISP_ID
   };

private:
   CGraph* m_pGraph;    // graph object for this document
};
```

2 Create a new **CGraph** object in the control's constructor:

```
CGraph1Ctrl::CGraph1Ctrl()
{
   InitializeIIDs(&IID_DGraph1, &IID_DGraph1Events);

   // Create the graph object
   m_pGraph = new CGraph();
}
```

3 Many controls, such as buttons, are pretty small, but we expect our graphs to be a little larger, so it makes sense to set a reasonable initial size, say 300 by 200 pixels. We can do this with a call to **SetInitialSize()** in the control constructor:

```
CGraph1Ctrl::CGraph1Ctrl()
{
   InitializeIIDs(&IID_DGraph1, &IID_DGraph1Events);

   // Create the graph object
```

```
    m_pGraph = new CGraph();
    SetInitialSize(300,200);
}
```

Note that **SetInitialSize()** is used in the *constructor*. If you want to set the size of your control at another time, use the **SetControlSize()** function instead. This function calls the **SetExtent()** method of the interface, and if you forget to call it you'll get the default values of (100, 50).

4 Now is quite a good time to add some default data to the graph object, so we see something at design- and run-time:

```
CGraph1Ctrl::CGraph1Ctrl()
{
    InitializeIIDs(&IID_DGraph1, &IID_DGraph1Events);

    // Create the graph object
    m_pGraph = new CGraph();

    // Test only - give it some data to use, while we're developing
    m_pGraph->SetTitle("Test Data");
    m_pGraph->Add("One", 10);
    m_pGraph->Add("Two", 45);
    m_pGraph->Add("Three", 22);
    m_pGraph->Add("Four", 33);
    m_pGraph->Add("Five", 51);

    SetInitialSize(300,200);
}
```

5 Getting the control to draw itself is simple: we replace the default drawing code in **OnDraw()** with a call to the graph object's **Display()** function, like this:

```
void CGraph1Ctrl::OnDraw(
        CDC* pdc, const CRect& rcBounds, const CRect& rcInvalid)
{
    // Get the control to display itself within the given rectangle
    // using the DC we've been given
    m_pGraph->Display(rcBounds, pdc);
}
```

6 There are a couple of minor housekeeping tasks that need to be done before we build and test our first version of the control. The first is to edit the control's toolbar bitmap so that it will look OK in toolboxes. This is the bitmap **IDB_GRAPH1**, which is initially a gray square containing the word 'OCX' in purple. Edit it to make it look a little more graph-like:

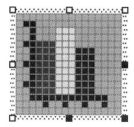

The other job is to change the entries in the control's string table for IDs 1 and 2 to Graphing Control and Graphing Control Property Page respectively. This will give slightly more useful and descriptive names when the object's name is listed in various tools and dialogs.

Testing the Control

Now we can build the control and test it in the Test Container. Start the container from the **T**ools menu, then press the far-left toolbar button (or choose the **E**dit | **I**nsert OLE Control... menu item) to bring up the control insertion dialog:

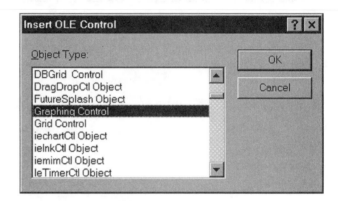

Select a Graphing Control, press OK, and after a few seconds you should see a graph control appear in the container window, like this:

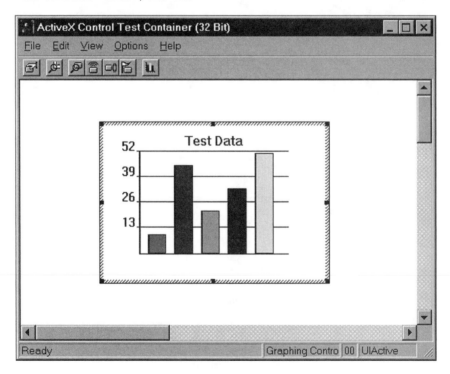

Check that the control works as expected; you can't do too much right now, but you can check that clicking on the control selects it, and that you can drag and resize it. You'll find that there are some problems with the window redrawing properly at this stage, but we'll fix those in a short while...

You can also check the **AboutBox()** method that was added for us by AppWizard: use either the Methods button on the toolbar (the third button from the right), or the Edit | Invoke Methods... menu item to bring up the Invoke Control Method dialog box:

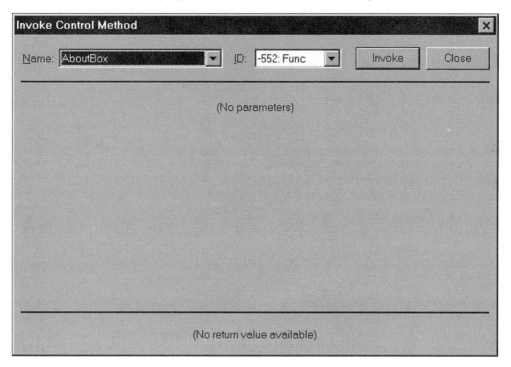

We've only got one method, which has a stock dispID of -552. If you press the Invoke button, you'll see the About box displayed for the control.

Everything seems to work so far; now let's use RegEdit to examine the control's registry entries. In the registry, look at the **HKEY_CLASSES_ROOT** key and find the entry under **GRAPH1.Graph1Ctrl.1**:

Then, look up the CLSID you've discovered under the **CLSID** key:

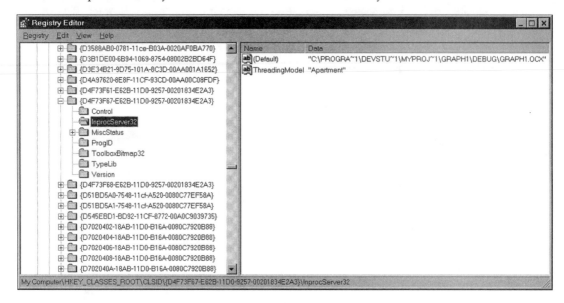

We can see that the CLSID is marked as being a control by the presence of the **Control** key, and that it has the correct server. A pointer to the control's type information is found under the **TypeLib** key.

We can look at the type information using the OLE/COM Object Viewer that comes with Visual C++. Open the viewer, find the Graphing Control entry, and expand it:

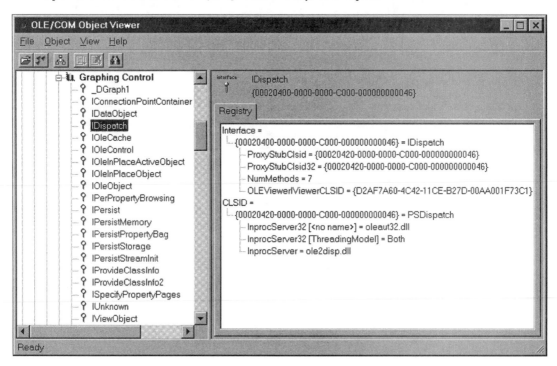

Double-clicking on the **IDispatch** entry will give you the option of opening the type information viewer:

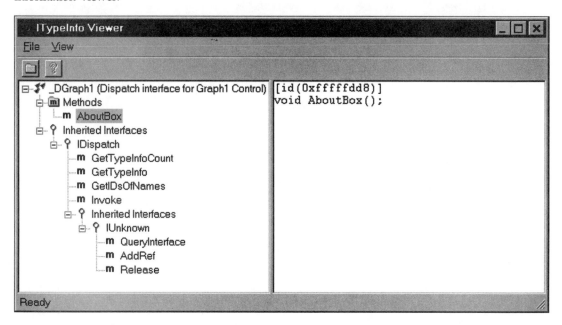

We can see that so far there's no Automation supported by the control, apart from the default About box supplied by AppWizard. We can use this tool later on to check that the type information has been added correctly to the control.

Adding Graphing Control

In order that the control container can use the control to graph data, we need to add the same Automation methods we added to the GraphSrv Automation server. In the simplest case, we need to add three methods to clear the dataset, set the graph title, and add points to the dataset. We'll also set the axis and graph types using methods, as we did for the Automation server, but in addition we'll make properties available to set these, which we'll come to in the next section.

Try It Out - Adding Automation Methods

1 Adding methods involves exactly the same process as we used to add Automation to GraphSrv in the previous chapter. Use the Automation tab in ClassWizard to add the methods to the control class according to the following prototypes:

```
void Clear();
void SetGraphTitle(LPCTSTR pszTitle);
void AddPoint(LPCTSTR pszName, short nVal);
```

The internal and external names can be the same, as there's no need for them to be different in this case. The methods need to call the appropriate functions in **CGraph**, and then tell the control to update itself. This is done by a call to the control's **InvalidateControl()** function, as shown in this example for the **Clear()** method:

```
void CGraph1Ctrl::Clear()
{
    // Clear the graph object and refresh the control
    m_pGraph->Clear();
    InvalidateControl();
}
```

You should remember to add the same call to other methods that need to update the control.

2 Now use ClassWizard to add methods to set the graph and axis types, according to the following prototypes:

```
void SetPieChart();
void SetLineChart();
void SetBarChart();
void SetNoFrame();
void SetAxisFrame();
void SetFullFrame();
```

3 Remember that you'll need to call **InvalidateControl()** in order to get the control to refresh itself. We should also add the inquiry methods, too, like this. Note that they query the graph object to get the information:

```
BOOL CGraph1Ctrl::IsBarChart()
{
    // Query the graph object
    return m_pGraph->IsBarGraph();
}
```

```
short CGraph1Ctrl::ChartType()
{
    short type;

    if (m_pGraph->IsPieChart())
        type = 0;
    else if (m_pGraph->IsLineGraph())
        type = 1;
    else if (m_pGraph->IsBarGraph())
        type = 2;

    return type;
}
```

Here's the full list of the inquiry methods you should add:

```
BOOL IsPieChart();
BOOL IsLineChart();
BOOL IsBarChart();
short ChartType();        // 0=pie, 1=line, 2=bar
BOOL IsNoFrame();
BOOL IsAxisFrame();
BOOL IsFullFrame();
short FrameType();        // 0=none, 1=axis, 2=full
```

Testing the Control

We can now once again test the control in the Test Container, using the Invoke Control Method dialog to test the Automation methods. As you can see, the dialog allows you to set the parameters for the method, and then invoke it:

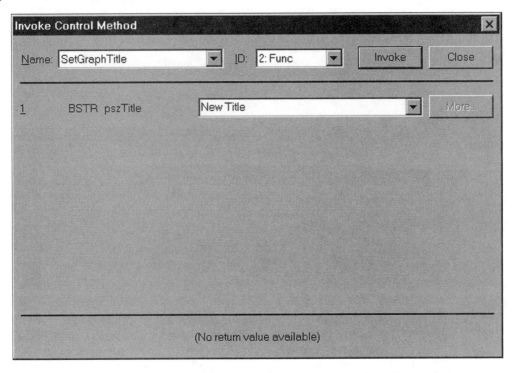

When press Invoke and dismiss the dialog, you'll see your control displayed with the new title, New Title.

Working with Properties

Now that we've added some methods, we need to add some properties to the control. We'll start by adding the title and the graph and axis types as properties, to complement the methods we already have, and then add some of the stock properties that every control should support.

Why would we want to add items as properties when we've already added methods that can be used to control them? Two reasons are apparent: first, we can give the user the choice of using a method or a property; and second, the properties we define can be included in a property page, so that they can be set at design time. With that in mind, I'll also show you how to use the control's property page class for design-time property modification.

Try It Out - Adding Custom Properties

1   Custom properties are added using ClassWizard, in just the same way as they are added for an Automation server. Move to the Automation tab on the ClassWizard dialog, and use the Add Property... button to bring up the property dialog:

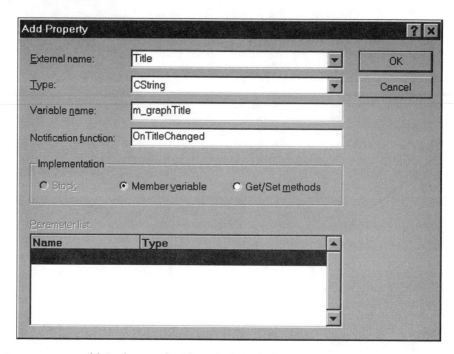

The first property to add is the graph title, which I shall imaginatively call **Title**. It's obviously a **CString**, and I've changed its name to **m_graphTitle** in order to make it slightly more descriptive. ClassWizard also offers to generate a notification function for us, which will be called whenever a client modifies the property. If you aren't going to want notification, just delete the function name and it won't get generated. In this case, leave the notification functions in place, as we'll need to use them later.

As you can see, there are three choices for property implementation: Stock, Member variable, and Get/Set methods. If you're defining your own properties, you have a choice - you can have the property handled in two ways. The Member variable button adds a data member to the class, and gives you an optional notification function that will be called when something has changed its value. The other option provides a pair of methods that are used to get and set theproperty.

> *The user of the control just sees a property - all that's different is how the property is handled in the control code. You can choose to have properties handled by whichever method you prefer, but be aware that the notification function will only get called* after *the property has been modified.*
>
> *The Stock button will become enabled if you drop down the* External Name *combo box and choose one of the stock properties, such as* **BackColor**. *In that case, you can choose to add your own implementation, or choose the* Stock *button, which enables you to call built-in functions, such as* **GetBackColor()**, *to work with the property.*

2 Next, add two more properties to represent the frame and graph types:

```
short AxisType;      // 0=none, 1= axis, 2=full
short GraphType;     // 0=pie, 1=line, 2=bar
```

It would have been useful to use the name **FrameType**, but that conflicts with the **FrameType()** method, and ClassWizard won't let us do it.

3 We want the graph to update itself whenever a client changes one of the properties. In this simple case, all we need to do is to add a call to the notification function that will set the underlying property of the **CGraph** object, and then cause the control to refresh itself:

```
void CGraph1Ctrl::OnTitleChanged()
{
    // The m_graphTitle variable has been changed by this time, so tell
    // the CGraph object, and refresh the control
    SetGraphTitle(m_graphTitle);
    SetModifiedFlag();
}
```

4 The other two functions use the value of the integer that represents the combo box selection to call the requisite function in the **CGraph** object:

```
void CGraph1Ctrl::OnAxisTypeChanged()
{
    if (m_axisType == 0)
        SetNoFrame();
    else if (m_axisType == 1)
        SetAxisFrame();
    else if (m_axisType == 2)
        SetFullFrame();
    SetModifiedFlag();
}
```

```
void CGraph1Ctrl::OnGraphTypeChanged()
{
    if (m_graphType == 0)
        SetPieChart();
    else if (m_graphType == 1)
        SetLineChart();
    else if (m_graphType == 2)
        SetBarChart();
    SetModifiedFlag();
}
```

Try It Out - Using the Property Page

1 The control's property page has a class to represent the property page object, plus a dialog template that's used to design the page itself. We can use the dialog editor to produce a suitable property page, as shown in the figure below. The page has three controls: a simple edit control to hold the graph title, and two combo boxes for the style settings.

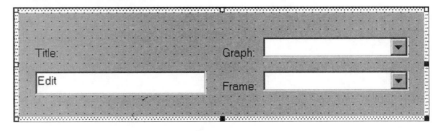

> *Property page dialogs ought to be one of two standard sizes: 250x62, or 250x100 pixels. If you make your dialog any other size, you'll get complaints at compile time in a Debug build.*

2   When you've added the combo boxes, you can add their initial data using the Data tab on the combo property sheet. The picture below shows the data for the Graph combo box, and you should add the 'None', 'Partial' and 'Full' entries to the Frame combo box. Don't forget to turn off sorting in the Styles tab.

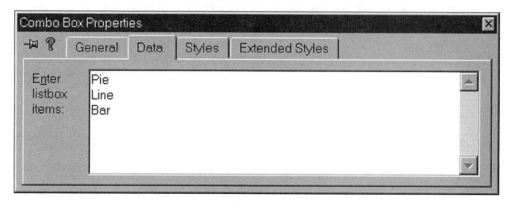

3   The next step is to hook up the controls to their corresponding Automation properties. We'll need to add a little code to the **DoDataExchange()** function for the property sheet manually, as in this case ClassWizard doesn't handle the **DDP_** function calls that exchange data between the property sheet variables and their corresponding Automation properties.

The **DDP_** functions are similar in functionality to their corresponding **DDX_** functions. The only difference from our point of view is that they take a final parameter that represents a property name, and we therefore get a three-way mapping. The dialog control is mapped onto a data member, and this in turn is mapped to a property in the control that this property sheet is representing.

For the graph title, use ClassWizard to add a **CString** member variable called **m_graphTitle** to the class, then manually add a **DDP_Text()** function call to link it to the **Title** property:

```
void CGraph1PropPage::DoDataExchange(CDataExchange* pDX)
{
    //{{AFX_DATA_MAP(CGraph1PropPage)
    DDP_Text(pDX, IDC_TITLE, m_graphTitle, _T("Title"));
    DDX_Text(pDX, IDC_TITLE, m_graphTitle);
    //}}AFX_DATA_MAP
    DDP_PostProcessing(pDX);
}
```

4   For the two combo boxes, add two **int** data members to the class, called **m_nAxisType** and **m_nGraphType**. You'll need to do this manually, since ClassWizard doesn't let you use anything but a **CString** as the member variable for a combo box. This isn't very helpful, since the 'CBIndex' **DDX_** and **DDP_** functions can be used to link the index of a combo box to an integer variable, as shown:

```
void CGraph1PropPage::DoDataExchange(CDataExchange* pDX)
{
    //{{AFX_DATA_MAP(CGraph1PropPage)
    DDP_CBIndex(pDX, IDC_GRAPHTYPE, m_nGraphType, _T("GraphType") );
    DDX_CBIndex(pDX, IDC_GRAPHTYPE, m_nGraphType);
    DDP_CBIndex(pDX, IDC_FRAMETYPE, m_nAxisType, _T("AxisType") );
    DDX_CBIndex(pDX, IDC_FRAMETYPE, m_nAxisType);
    DDP_Text(pDX, IDC_TITLE, m_graphTitle, _T("Title") );
    DDX_Text(pDX, IDC_TITLE, m_graphTitle);
    //}}AFX_DATA_MAP
    DDP_PostProcessing(pDX);
}
```

If you now look in the dispatch map, you'll see that three property entries have been added. Each is of type **DISP_PROPERTY_NOTIFY**, showing that these properties have a notification function associated with them:

```
BEGIN_DISPATCH_MAP(CGraph1Ctrl, COleControl)
    //{{AFX_DISPATCH_MAP(CGraph1Ctrl)
    DISP_PROPERTY_NOTIFY(CGraph1Ctrl, "Title", m_graphTitle, OnTitleChanged,
        VT_BSTR)
    DISP_PROPERTY_NOTIFY(CGraph1Ctrl, "AxisType", m_axisType, OnAxisTypeChanged,
        VT_I2)
    DISP_PROPERTY_NOTIFY(CGraph1Ctrl, "GraphType", m_graphType, OnGraphTypeChanged,
        VT_I2)
    DISP_FUNCTION(CGraph1Ctrl, "Clear", Clear, VT_EMPTY, VTS_NONE)
    // ...
    DISP_FUNCTION(CGraph1Ctrl, "FrameType", FrameType, VT_I2, VTS_NONE)
    //}}AFX_DISPATCH_MAP
    DISP_FUNCTION_ID(CGraph1Ctrl, "AboutBox", DISPID_ABOUTBOX, AboutBox, VT_EMPTY,
VTS_NONE)
END_DISPATCH_MAP()
```

Testing the Control

It's time to test the control again! Build it, and open up the ActiveX Control Test Container. Insert a control, and use the View | Properties... menu item to bring up the Properties dialog:

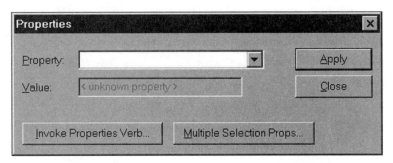

The Invoke Properties Verb... button, as its legend suggests, invokes the control's **Properties** verb, which tells it to display its property dialog. Press this button, and you should see a dialog like the one shown here. Note that the property sheet has only a single tab, because so far we only have one property page object associated with the control:

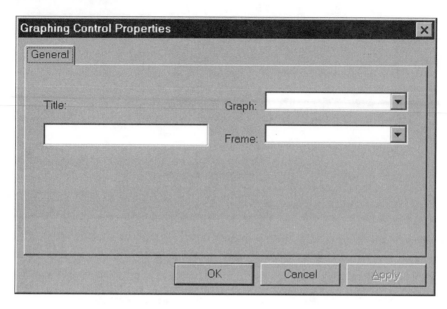

Set the properties you require, press **Apply**, and you should see the control's appearance change.

Try It Out - Using Stock Properties

The table below shows the list of stock properties that we can use with our controls. If we add any of these, they'll be handled automatically by the framework. The table below shows those stock properties that are implemented in MFC 4.2:

Property	Description
Appearance	Determines the appearance of a control
BackColor	The background color for the control
BorderStyle	Determines the style of the control's border: single, double or none
Caption	The caption for a control with a title bar. This is the same as the **Text** property
Enabled	Determines whether the control is enabled or disabled
Font	The font used by the control
ForeColor	The color used for text and drawing
hWnd	The handle to the control's main window
ReadyState	The readiness of the control during a download process
Text	The text in a control

Note that the **Caption** and **Text** properties are 'the same'; this means that they are used to pass a string to a control, which may be used as the caption on the title bar, or as text within the control itself, so you can use whichever of these you wish.

1 As an example, and to fix those annoying refresh problems I promised to do something about, let's add the **BackColor** stock property. Use ClassWizard to add a new property, but this time use the button on the External name combo box to drop down a list of the stock properties supported by the control. Select BackColor from the list, and the dialog should change, as shown:

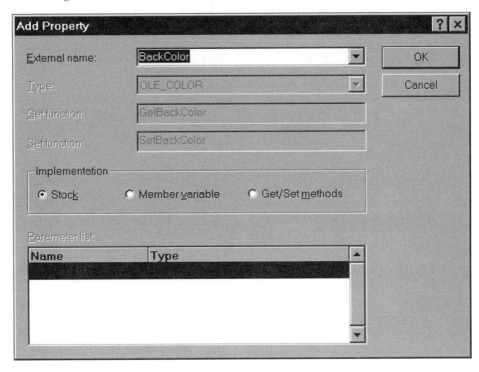

Leave the implementation as Stock. If you look in the dispatch map at this stage, you'll see that a standard stock property entry has been added:

```
BEGIN_DISPATCH_MAP(CGraph1Ctrl, COleControl)
    //{{AFX_DISPATCH_MAP(CGraph1Ctrl)
    DISP_PROPERTY_NOTIFY(CGraph1Ctrl, "Title", m_graphTitle, OnTitleChanged,
        VT_BSTR)
    DISP_PROPERTY_NOTIFY(CGraph1Ctrl, "AxisType", m_axisType, OnAxisTypeChanged,
        VT_I2)
    DISP_PROPERTY_NOTIFY(CGraph1Ctrl, "GraphType", m_graphType, OnGraphTypeChanged,
        VT_I2)
    DISP_FUNCTION(CGraph1Ctrl, "Clear", Clear, VT_EMPTY, VTS_NONE)
    // ...
    DISP_FUNCTION(CGraph1Ctrl, "FrameType", FrameType, VT_I2, VTS_NONE)
    DISP_STOCKPROP_BACKCOLOR()
    //}}AFX_DISPATCH_MAP
    DISP_FUNCTION_ID(CGraph1Ctrl, "AboutBox", DISPID_ABOUTBOX, AboutBox, VT_EMPTY,
VTS_NONE)
END_DISPATCH_MAP()
```

2 The values of stock properties such as **BackColor** are maintained by the **COleControl** class. **COleControl**'s **SetBackColor()** member function automatically calls the **OnBackColorChanged()** member function after setting the **BackColor** value. It also invalidates the control, causing the **OnDraw()** function to be called, so that the control gets a chance to redraw itself using the new background color, as I do here:

```
void CGraph1Ctrl::OnDraw(
            CDC* pdc, const CRect& rcBounds, const CRect& rcInvalid)
{
    // Set the background colour from stock properties
    CBrush cb;
    cb.CreateSolidBrush(TranslateColor(GetBackColor()));
    pdc->FillRect(rcBounds, &cb);

    // Get the control to display itself within the given rectangle
    // using the DC we've been given
    m_pGraph->Display(rcBounds, pdc);
}
```

3 We ought to make a couple of changes to the **CGraph** class itself at this point. First, we need to set the background mode of the device context to transparent when the graph draws itself, so that the text is overlaid properly onto the background:

```
void CGraph::Display(CRect area, CDC* pDC)
{
    int oldBkMode = pDC->SetBkMode(TRANSPARENT);

    ASSERT(pDC);

// And the rest of the function...

    default:
        AfxMessageBox("Bad graph type in CGraph::Display");
        ASSERT(0);
    }

    pDC->SetBkMode(oldBkMode);
}
```

Second, we need to made a little adjustment to the **DrawFrame()** function so that when we draw the graph with a 'full' frame, the background color of the control isn't overwritten. This wasn't a problem before, but it certainly is now:

```
    if (m_frame == FULL)
    {
        CBrush* pOldBrush = (CBrush*)pDC->SelectStockObject(NULL_BRUSH);
        pDC->Rectangle(&m_rcBnd);
        pDC->SelectObject(pOldBrush);
    }
```

Selecting a null brush into the device context at this point makes sure that the rectangle is drawn only as an outline.

Try It Out - Adding Stock Property Pages

Microsoft provides several stock property pages, which are there to help you use the stock **Font**, **Color** and **Picture** data types that are supported by ActiveX controls. It's fairly obvious what **Font** and **Color** are for; the **Picture** type allows you to use bitmaps, metafiles and icons in a control, and to give the user control over the image at runtime.

In MFC, these property pages are implemented by a set of classes that don't appear in the online help, all of which derive from **CStockPropPage**:

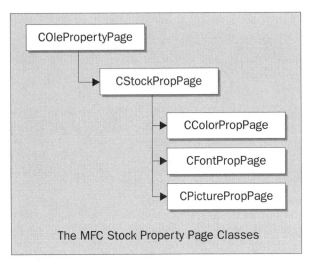

The MFC Stock Property Page Classes

It isn't really necessary to know too much about what these classes do, because they're simple enough to use. Let's start by looking at the existing code. The association between a control and its property pages is done in the control's source file, using the **BEGIN_** and **END_PROPPAGEIDS()** macros. The first argument to **BEGIN_PROPPAGEIDS()** gives the control class name, while the second argument determines the number of pages:

```
BEGIN_PROPPAGEIDS(CGraph1Ctrl, 1)
    PROPPAGEID(CGraph1PropPage::guid)
END_PROPPAGEIDS(CGraph1Ctrl)
```

1 We can include as many property pages for our control as we like, by modifying the count in the **BEGIN_PROPPAGEIDS()** macro, and adding extra **PROPPAGEID()** entries. The **PROPPAGEID()** macro takes the GUID of a property page class as its argument; in the case of our existing class, the GUID is given by the static **guid** member of the class. For stock pages, the GUIDs can be referenced via the constants **CLSID_CColorPropPage**, **CLSID_CFontPropPage** and **CLSID_CPicturePropPage**.

Here's what the code will look like with all three stock pages added:

```
BEGIN_PROPPAGEIDS(CGraph1Ctrl, 4)
    PROPPAGEID(CGraph1PropPage::guid)
    PROPPAGEID(CLSID_CColorPropPage)
    PROPPAGEID(CLSID_CFontPropPage)
    PROPPAGEID(CLSID_CPicturePropPage)
END_PROPPAGEIDS(CGraph1Ctrl)
```

2   Rebuild the project and start up the Test Container. Choose <u>E</u>dit | Properties, and you'll see that the dialog now has four property pages:

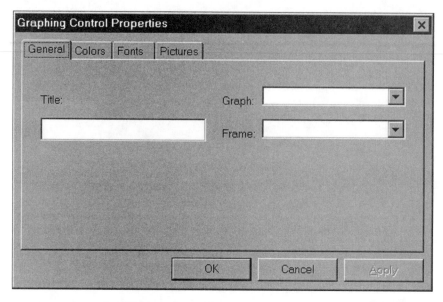

The Colors page contains a list of properties and an array of buttons that can be used to set the colors. The dialog will fill the Property <u>N</u>ame combo with any properties whose type is **OLE_COLOR**, and will automatically manage setting the property and invalidating the control:

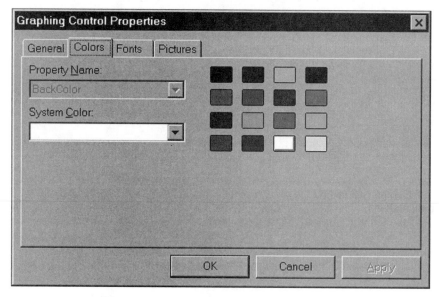

3   We can also usefully add a **Font** property, which will determine the font used to draw the axis labels and the title. Use ClassWizard to add the stock **Font** property, and then modify the control's **OnDraw()** function so that the stock font is selected into the device context before the graph is drawn:

```
void CGraph1Ctrl::OnDraw(
            CDC* pdc, const CRect& rcBounds, const CRect& rcInvalid)
{
    // Select the font from the stock font
    CFont* pOldFont = SelectStockFont(pdc);

    // Set the background colour from stock properties
    CBrush cb;
    cb.CreateSolidBrush(TranslateColor(GetBackColor()));
    pdc->FillRect(rcBounds, &cb);

    // Get the control to display itself within the given rectangle
    // using the DC we've been given
    m_pGraph->Display(rcBounds, pdc);

    pdc->SelectObject(pOldFont);
}
```

The ActiveX control and property page classes will work together so that the font selected in the property page will be available through the **SelectStockFont()** member function of the control; you can call **GetStockTextMetrics()** to get information about the font metrics. The figure below shows the Fonts property page being used to change the graph's font:

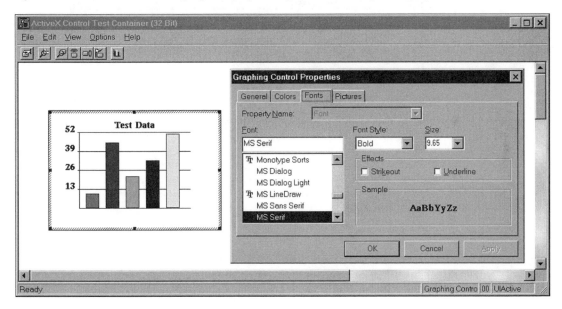

Adding Events

Adding events to a control is not difficult, and in the case of stock events, it is almost trivial. The graph control is perhaps not a natural candidate for events, as it is really for display and doesn't have too much to communicate back to the container, but let's add support for firing an event when the user clicks on the control.

Try It Out - Firing an Event

1 Bring up ClassWizard, and select the control class, then click on the ActiveX Events tab. This tab looks like the Automation tab, and is used in a similar way. Click on the Add Event... button to bring up this dialog:

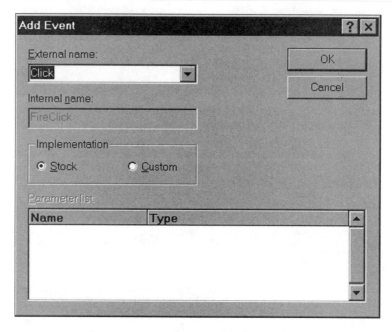

You can create a custom event by typing a name into the External name box; if you drop the combo box down, you'll see a list of the stock events, from which you can select Click.

We get a choice of two implementation methods. Stock means that we'll use the standard **FireClick()** function provided by **COleControl**, while Custom allows us to define our own function. The difference is that **FireClick()** will fire the event automatically, whereas a custom implementation gives us a routine that we can fire ourselves.

> *You might use a custom implementation of a stock event if, for example, you didn't want the event to be fired when the stock **Click** event would be fired, but at a time of your choosing instead.*

Leave the implementation as Stock, and press OK till you're out of ClassWizard. If you look at the event map, you'll see that we have an entry for a stock Click event:

```
BEGIN_EVENT_MAP(CGraph1Ctrl, COleControl)
    //{{AFX_EVENT_MAP(CGraph1Ctrl)
    EVENT_STOCK_CLICK()
    //}}AFX_EVENT_MAP
END_EVENT_MAP()
```

2 How do we use the event? We want to trigger the event when the user has clicked on the control, so define a **WM_LBUTTONDOWN** handler for the control, and use it to fire the click event:

```
void CGraph1Ctrl::OnLButtonDown(UINT nFlags, CPoint point)
{
  // Generate a click event
  FireClick();

  COleControl::OnLButtonDown(nFlags, point);
}
```

3 How about a custom event? Open ClassWizard as before, and add another event. This time, don't choose one of the stock events, but type a name of your choosing - **MyEvent** will do. You'll see that in the figure below, I've chosen to give the event a single **short** parameter:

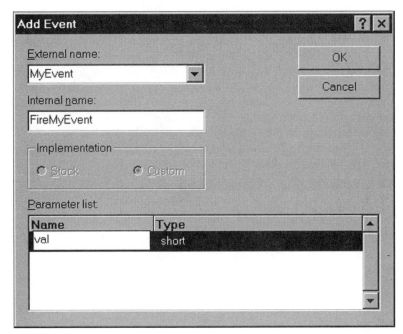

Exit from ClassWizard, and look at the event map. You'll see that it now contains two events, one of which is a custom event:

```
BEGIN_EVENT_MAP(CGraph1Ctrl, COleControl)
    //{{AFX_EVENT_MAP(CGraph1Ctrl)
    EVENT_CUSTOM("MyEvent", FireMyEvent, VTS_I2)
    EVENT_STOCK_CLICK()
    //}}AFX_EVENT_MAP
END_EVENT_MAP()
```

The **EVENT_CUSTOM()** macro tells us that **MyEvent** is implemented by the **FireMyEvent()** function. If you look in the class header, you'll see that the function is implemented inline, wrapping a call to **FireEvent()**:

```
    //{{AFX_EVENT(CGraph1Ctrl)
    void FireMyEvent(short val)
        {FireEvent(eventidMyEvent,EVENT_PARAM(VTS_I2), val);}
    //}}AFX_EVENT
```

We'd fire this custom event in the same way as we fired the click event, by calling the **FireMyEvent()** method with an appropriate argument. You can see how the outgoing event interface is constructed by looking in the ODL file, where you'll see an entry like this:

```
[ uuid(AE220342-8427-11D0-904A-444553540000),
  helpstring("Event interface for Graph1 Control") ]
dispinterface _DGraph1Events
{
    properties:
        //  Event interface has no properties

    methods:
        // NOTE - ClassWizard will maintain event information here.
        //     Use extreme caution when editing this section.
        //{{AFX_ODL_EVENT(CGraph1Ctrl)
            [id(DISPID_CLICK)] void Click();
            [id(1)] void MyEvent(short val);
        //}}AFX_ODL_EVENT
};
```

The entries in the event interface have their own dispIDs. Those for stock events have stock values and are usually referenced by constants (**DISPID_CLICK** here), while custom events are given positive dispIDs, starting from 1. This information becomes part of the type library, and will be available to containers so that they can construct a dispatch interface to implement event handlers.

Adding Online Help

AppWizard has created a basic help file for us, but we need to fill in the appropriate information and make it usable. There are several different sorts of help we can supply for a control, such as context-sensitive help to be displayed when the user clicks on parts of the graph, but here we'll add help of a different kind. When you open the Components and Controls Gallery and display the ActiveX controls, there is a button with the caption More Info at the bottom of the window. When you've selected a control, pressing this button will attempt to display the control's help file.

> *The Gallery searches for the help files in the SharedIDE directory of the Visual C++ installation, so if the file isn't in that directory (which it won't be by default), you'll have to browse to where the file is located. This can make it difficult to know whether the control doesn't have a help file, or whether you just can't find it!*

We need to provide information on which help file the control is using, and on the context ID that should be displayed on pressing the More Info button. This information is provided as part of the control's type information, in the type library, so we'll need to modify the ODL file in order to provide it.

First, though, we ought to modify the default help file provided for us by AppWizard. Unlike applications, the build process for controls doesn't include automatically making the help file, so you have two choices. You can either modify the build process, inserting a custom build step for generating the help file, or you can run Help Workshop manually to generate (and indeed regenerate) the file. As we're not going to be modifying the help file very much, we'll take the easy way out for this example and run Help Workshop manually; in a real development project, you'd probably use a custom build step if you were going to need to rebuild the help file often.

Try It Out - Online Help

1 Open the help source file of the control for editing by double-clicking on the **graph1.rtf** file in the Resource Files section of FileView. This will either open it in Visual Studio itself, or else spawn an instance of whatever program you have registered for handling **.rtf** files. If you prefer, you can use a suitable word processor or help-writing tool, in which case you'll find the file in the **Hlp** project subdirectory, with a **.rtf** extension.

The first page in the file is the main help screen for the control, and if you look at the footnotes, you'll see that its context ID is **main_index**.

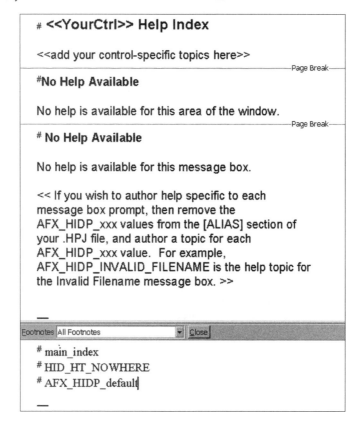

2   This is a good time to edit the text to provide something suitable for your control. I'm not about to provide a tutorial on help file writing, but here's an example of the sort of thing you might supply for a control, to get you started. Remember that your control may have methods, properties and events, and you need to document them.

> *If you've never written a help file before, here's a basic survival kit:*
>
> *Each help screen (or topic) is a page, so introduce a new topic with a page break.*
>
> *A topic needs a context ID to identify it in hypertext jumps. The ID is given as the text to a footnote with a '#' symbol, and can be any string you like.*
>
> *To put a jump in your help file, double-underline the text that will trigger the jump (this usually appears in green in help files). Immediately afterwards, put the context ID of the page you wish to jump to, and make it hidden text. This attribute can be selected from Word's* **Format | Font...** *dialog.*

Basic help for a control might look like this:

Graphing Control Help Index

Get help on
<u>Control Methods</u>Methods
<u>Control Properties</u>Properties

···Page Break·······················

Methods
Help on control methods

···Page Break·······················

Properties
Help on control properties

···Page Break·······················

#No Help Available

No help is available for this area of the window.

···Page Break·······················

No Help Available

No help is available for this message box.|

Save the file again, making sure that it remains in RTF format.

3   The first step in generating the help file is to run the **makehelp.bat** file which resides in the project directory. The purpose of this file is to generate a Help Map file, **graph1.hm**, which gives IDs for all the resources in the project. Open an MS-DOS prompt window, change to the project directory, and type **makehelp**. When the command has finished executing, you should find the **graph1.hm** file in the **Hlp** subdirectory.

4 Now open the help project file, **Graph1.hpj**, in Help Workshop, either by double-clicking on the file, or by starting Help Workshop and opening the file from there:

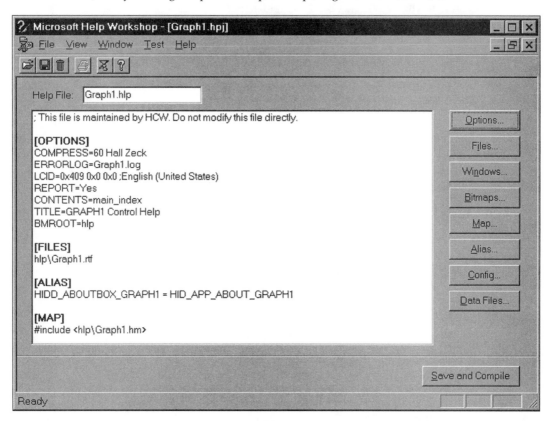

5 To add a new map entry, click on the <u>M</u>ap... button, and press <u>A</u>dd... in the dialog that appears. Completing the dialog as shown will ensure that references to a numeric topic ID of 10 will get mapped to the context ID **main_index**.

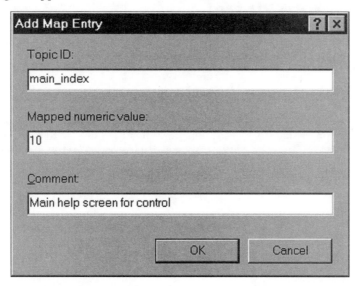

6 Press OK to exit from these screens, then use the <u>S</u>ave and Compile button in the main Help Workshop window to generate the help file. You'll find that **Graph1.odl** already has an entry for the help file, which was added by AppWizard:

```
[ uuid(AE220340-8427-11D0-904A-444553540000), version(1.0),
  helpstring("Graph1 OLE Control module"),
  helpfile("graph1.hlp"),
  control ]
library GRAPH1Lib
{
```

We need to add the numeric topic ID for the main help screen to the class information entry:

```
// Class information for CGraph1Ctrl

[ uuid(AE220343-8427-11D0-904A-444553540000), licensed,
  helpstring("Graphing Control"),
  helpcontext(10),
  control ]
coclass Graph1
```

You'll remember that when we built the help file using Help Workshop, we assigned an ID of 10 to the context ID **main_index**. In this rather roundabout way, we're saying that when help is needed for the control, context ID 10 should be used, and we've mapped 10 on to the **main_index** topic.

7 If you rebuild the project, bring up Components and Controls Gallery, and select the Graphing Control, you can press the <u>M</u>ore Info button to display your help file.

For information on other ways to add context-sensitive help and tooltips to your controls, see the TestHelp sample and the section entitled 'ActiveX Controls: Adding Context-Sensitive Help' in the Visual C++ online documentation.

Using the Graph Control

In the final section of this chapter, we'll take a look at how our graph control can be used, using Visual C++ and Internet Explorer as examples.

Using the Control from Visual C++

Until version 4.0 of Visual C++, it was hard to use ActiveX controls in C++ projects. There was nothing *technically* impossible to prevent you from doing so, but there was no support built into the Wizards or MFC for ActiveX controls, so you'd have had to write a control container for yourself, coding up the interface code by hand. Unsurprisingly, this was not a task that many people felt like undertaking.

Try It Out - ActiveX Controls in Visual C++

1 In order to use an ActiveX control in a Visual C++ MFC project, you must first be sure to check the ActiveX Controls option in the appropriate step of the AppWizard dialog. I've chosen to create a dialog-based application called **CtlTest**, so step 2 of the AppWizard looks like this:

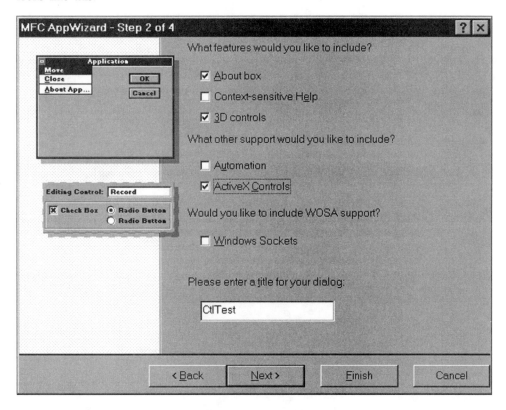

In fact, it isn't terribly serious if you miss this out, as it only adds one line to the project's **InitInstance()** function. It follows that if you want to use ActiveX controls in an existing project, all you need to do is to add this one line:

```
BOOL CCtlTestApp::InitInstance()
{
    AfxEnableControlContainer();

    // Standard initialization
    // If you are not using these features and wish to reduce the size
    //  of your final executable, you should remove from the following
    //  the specific initialization routines you do not need.

#ifdef _AFXDLL
    Enable3dControls();          // Call this when using MFC in a shared DLL
#else
    Enable3dControlsStatic();    // Call this when linking to MFC statically
#endif
```

2 Now you're set up to use ActiveX controls. Open the Components and Controls Gallery, choose **Registered ActiveX Controls**, and select the Graphing Control.

Inserting a control into a project involves two operations:

▶ Adding the control to the dialog editor palette

▶ Creating a wrapper class for the control's Automation interface

When you press the In**s**ert button, the Gallery code will examine the type information for the control, in order to decide what classes it has to create for you. You'll get one based on the name of your control's dispatch interface, and you may get others (such as **COleFont** and **COlePicture**) if your control uses stock **Font** or **Picture** types. In this case, the Gallery wants to create two classes, because the control makes use of a **Font** property; you can omit this class if you wish, as we're not going to require it.

> **Fonts** *and* **Pictures** *are COM types that provide a uniform mechanism for creating and using font and picture information in ActiveX controls. For more information, see 'ActiveX Controls Inside Out', referenced in Appendix F.*

3 Press OK, and the Gallery will create the class code and add the files to your project. It will also add the graph control icon to the dialog editor palette. The figure below shows the main dialog window with a graph control inserted; note the control icon in the palette, and the fact that the control has adjusted its background color to that of the dialog.

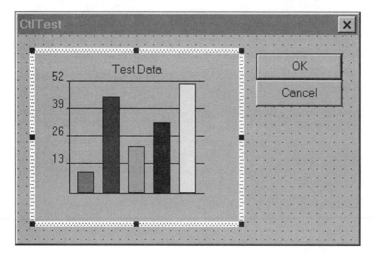

As a test that the licensing is working, try removing the **Graph1.lic** file from the debug directory, and then create a new control. You should get a message box telling you that a control cannot be created because a design-time license cannot be found.

4 Once you have the control on the dialog, right-clicking on it and selecting **P**roperties from the context menu will bring up its property sheet. You'll see that it contains all the pages we added, including our custom page:

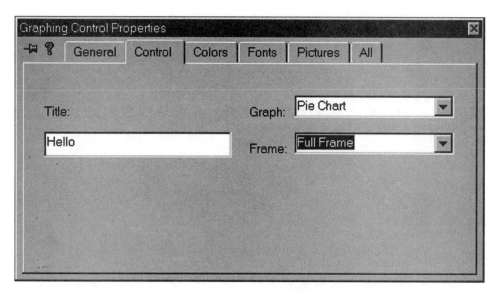

5 Modify each of the properties in turn, and you'll see the control respond to the changes you make. To interact with the control in the program, we need to add a data member of the appropriate type to the dialog class. This can be most easily done using ClassWizard, which will automatically assign a variable of the right type:

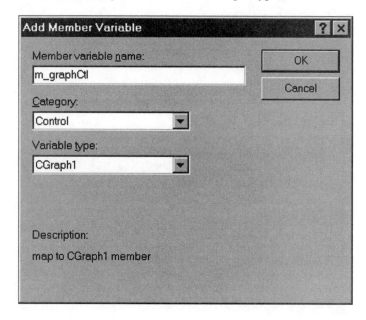

6 We've already explored how to manipulate the graph class in our initial development of GraphSrv. In order to save time here, let's check out the control functionality by adding a button to the dialog that will display a new dataset as a pie chart. Add a button with the legend Change Data, and code up the handler for the **BN_CLICKED** event like this:

```
void CCtlTestDlg::OnChangedata()
{
    // Set some new data into the control, to show that it works!
    m_graphCtl.Clear();
    m_graphCtl.SetTitle("New Data");
    m_graphCtl.AddPoint("First", 37);
    m_graphCtl.AddPoint("Second", 9);
    m_graphCtl.AddPoint("Third", 44);
    m_graphCtl.AddPoint("Fourth", 23);
    m_graphCtl.AddPoint("Fifth", 15);

    m_graphCtl.SetPieChart();
}
```

7 Build and run the application. Before pressing the button, the window looks like this:

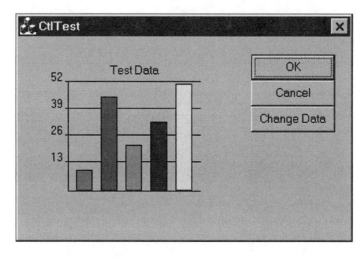

Press the Change Data button, and the control changes to display the new data:

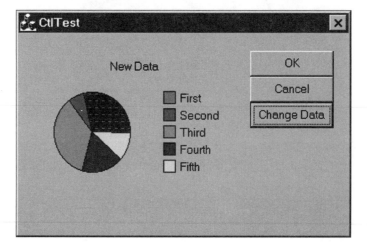

Try It Out - Testing Control Events

We added two events to our control - how do we use them in the container? It turns out that the work has been done for us.

Start ClassWizard and select the **Message Maps** tab; if you select the dialog class and click on **IDC_GRAPH1CTRL1**, the graph object ID, you should see that the **Messages** pane has two entries: one for **Click** and one for **MyEvent**.

ClassWizard has provided the infrastructure for implementing event handlers in the container. All we need to do is to double-click on the event we require, and a handler will be added to the dialog class. Try adding a handler for the **Click** event, and you'll end up with code like this:

```
BEGIN_EVENTSINK_MAP(CCtlTestDlg, CDialog)
    //{{AFX_EVENTSINK_MAP(CCtlTestDlg)
    ON_EVENT(CCtlTestDlg, IDC_GRAPH1CTRL1, -600 /* Click */, OnClickGraph1ctrl1,
VTS_NONE)
    //}}AFX_EVENTSINK_MAP
END_EVENTSINK_MAP()

void CCtlTestDlg::OnClickGraph1ctrl1()
{
    // TODO: Add your control notification handler code here

}
```

You can see that an entry has been added to the event sink map, to show that the **OnClickGraphctrl1()** function is the handler that should be called whenever the control fires the stock **Click** event, which has a dispID of -600. Obviously, what gets done in the handler is entirely up to you!

Using the Control from a Web Page

When it created ActiveX controls, one of the main uses Microsoft envisaged them being put to was to enhance the content of web pages. Our second test, therefore, will show how the Graphing Control can be used in a web page viewed in Internet Explorer 3.

This isn't the place to discuss all the basics of web page construction - if you aren't familiar with the way in which web pages are constructed using HTML, you might want to consult one of the many good books available on the topic.

VBScript

Until recently, web pages were relatively dull affairs, with little opportunity for interaction with the user. What interaction there was had to be provided by CGI scripts running at the server end, and not only are CGI scripts tricky to program, but they can also place a severe strain on the web server. Furthermore, every bit of interaction needs communication from the client page back the server.

This situation changed with the advent of **scripting languages**. The idea is that small scripts can be embedded in the HTML of a web page, and that these scripts can perform some client-side operations, such as, for instance, checking the legitimacy of input fields on a form. There are now two major scripting languages: Microsoft's VBScript and Netscape's JavaScript. Both can be used to perform the same tasks, and both are supported by their respective browsers.

VBScript is a lightweight version of Visual Basic, implementing much of Visual Basic's functionality. In addition, it can easily work with the object model provided by IE3, which makes it easy to write scripts that communicate with the browser. The following example shows a simple script in an HTML document:

```
<HTML>

<HEAD>
<TITLE>A VBScript Demo</TITLE>
</HEAD>

<BODY>
<HR>

<SCRIPT LANGUAGE="VBScript">
<!--
document.write "This is a sample script<br>"
-->
</SCRIPT>

<HR>

</BODY>
</HTML>
```

The script itself is written between the **<SCRIPT>** and **</SCRIPT>** tags. The HTML comment markers are used to hide the script from browsers that don't support scripting, so that all they'll see is the comment.

The script itself uses the **document** object, one of the objects supported by IE3, and which refers to the page currently loaded into Explorer. The object's **write** method is used here to construct a simple piece of HTML, which is displayed on the screen between two ruled lines, as shown here.

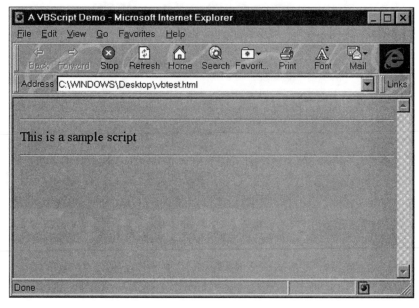

The ActiveX Control Pad

HTML provides a way to include objects, such as ActiveX controls or Java applets, in a Web page, using the **<OBJECT>** tag. Scripting languages then provide a way for us to communicate with these controls once they're on the page.

Although it's possible to code up the HTML and the scripts manually, Microsoft provides a useful tool - the ActiveX Control Pad - which will do a lot of the donkey work for us. Furthermore, it's free, so there's really very little reason not to use it.

The Control Pad, as well as appearing on numerous CDs from Microsoft (including the MSDN), can be downloaded from the SiteBuilder page on the Microsoft web site at **http://www.microsoft.com**. The precise URL you have to access may well change from time to time - it has changed twice in the time I've been writing this book - so you're best advised to start at the top and use the search engines to find the right page.

When you start up the Control Pad, you're presented with a simple HTML editor:

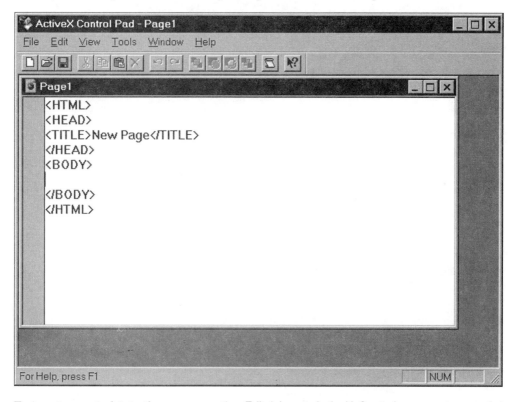

To insert a control into the page, use the Edit | Insert ActiveX Control... menu item to bring up the insertion dialog:

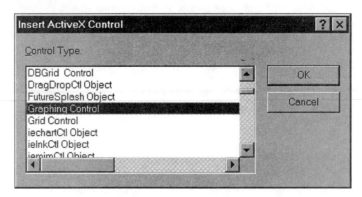

Pressing OK inserts a Graphing Control into the HTML of the page, and displays you a pair of control editing screens:

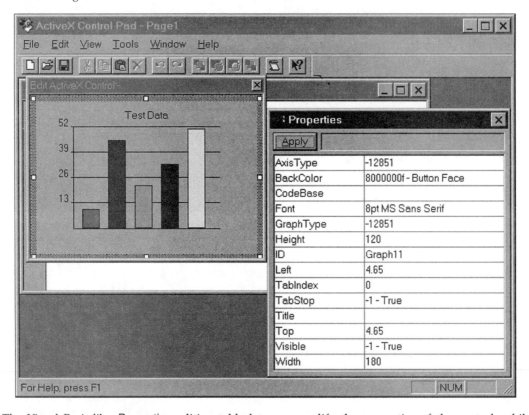

The Visual Basic-like Properties editing table lets you modify the properties of the control, while the Edit ActiveX Control window shows you what the control looks like, and will reflect changes you make in the properties. When you've finished setting the initial properties of your control, close the Edit window and you'll see the HTML entry for the control in the editing window. The standard entry gives the ID of the object, its width and height on the page, its CLSID, and the values of various parameters:

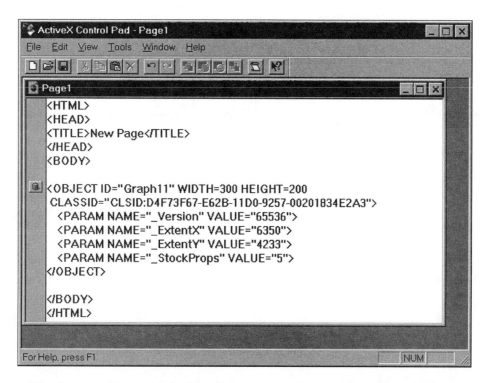

Next, add a Command Button, which we'll script to interact with the graph object. (You'll find the Command Button listed as Microsoft Forms 2.0 CommandButton in the insertion dialog.)

Bring up the ScriptWizard (the button with the scroll on the toolbar), select CommandButton1, expand its list of events, and select the Click event. We can now use the actions listed in the right-hand list box; in this case, we want to interact with the graph control, so expand the actions under the Graph11 icon. We want to do the same as we did in the C++ example: clear the graph, set the title, add some data, and display a pie chart. Start by double clicking on the Title property, which will add one action to the code:

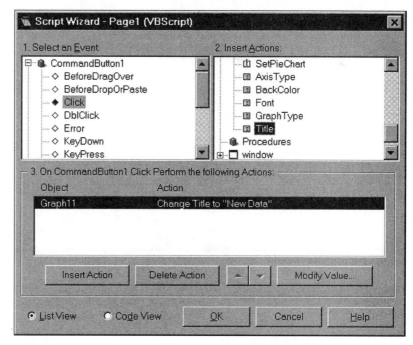

This will add a script, which will be run when the button is pressed:

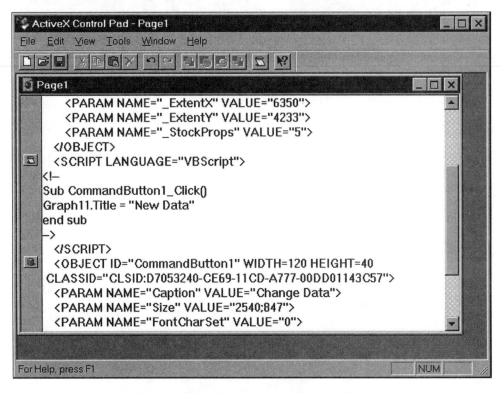

```
    <PARAM NAME="_ExtentX" VALUE="6350">
    <PARAM NAME="_ExtentY" VALUE="4233">
    <PARAM NAME="_StockProps" VALUE="5">
</OBJECT>
<SCRIPT LANGUAGE="VBScript">
<!--
Sub CommandButton1_Click()
Graph11.Title = "New Data"
end sub
-->
</SCRIPT>
<OBJECT ID="CommandButton1" WIDTH=120 HEIGHT=40
CLASSID="CLSID:D7053240-CE69-11CD-A777-00DD01143C57">
    <PARAM NAME="Caption" VALUE="Change Data">
    <PARAM NAME="Size" VALUE="2540;847">
    <PARAM NAME="FontCharSet" VALUE="0">
```

Test this by saving away the HTML file, and then opening it up in Internet Explorer:

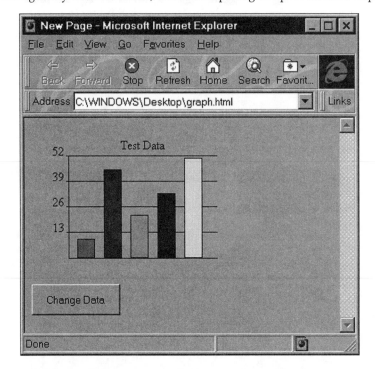

Press the Change Data button, and the title changes:

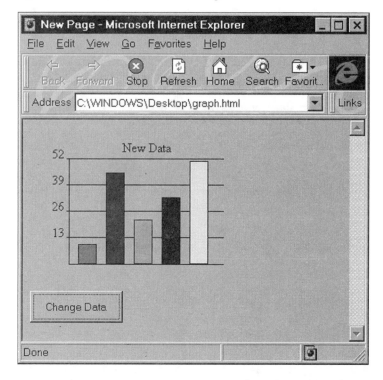

> *You may need to alter the security settings of Internet Explorer in order for this demo to run. In order to protect users from potentially malicious controls, web browsers use various methods in order to test controls' authenticity and safety. We haven't provided these in this simple example, so Explorer won't be happy to let our control be used with any scripting. In order to test the script, you'll need to bring up the Explorer options with the View | Options... menu command, and then use the Security tab to turn off all checking. Remember to turn it back on once you've finished the test!*

Now we can add the other commands to change the dataset and display it as a pie chart, as shown below. You can't use the ScriptWizard to add some of the commands, because it doesn't list all the control methods and properties in its action list, but in all truth it's probably quicker to add the commands manually anyway. Type them into the HTML editor window, to create the following script:

```
<SCRIPT LANGUAGE="VBScript">
<!--
Sub CommandButton1_Click()
Graph11.Clear
Graph11.title = "Monthly Data"
Graph11.AddPoint "Jan",  9
Graph11.AddPoint "Feb",  22
Graph11.AddPoint "Mar",  12
Graph11.AddPoint "Apr",  27
```

```
Graph11.AddPoint "May",  17
Graph11.SetPieChart
end sub
-->
   </SCRIPT>
```

If you test this page in Internet Explorer, you should be able to change the graph by clicking on the button:

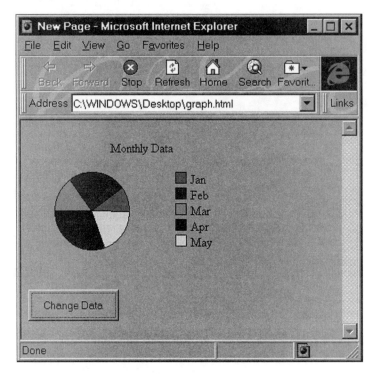

Summary

In this chapter, we've covered one of the biggest, and most exciting of the COM-based technologies: ActiveX controls.

These controls make sophisticated use of many of the COM technologies we've covered in preceding chapters. They are 'inside-out' OLE servers, and they use Automation to communicate with their containers. Controls don't involve many new interfaces of their own, but because of all the things they bring together, a full control implementation can require the provision of nearly two dozen interfaces.

Licensing provides security for controls, and their properties can be modified through the use of property sheet objects.

ActiveX controls are useful in many environments, from programming languages to the Internet, and much of the impetus for their development has come from the need to produce efficient controls for use on web pages.

In the next and final chapter, we'll put some of these technologies to work, building a small-scale COM-based system, consisting of a server and two clients.

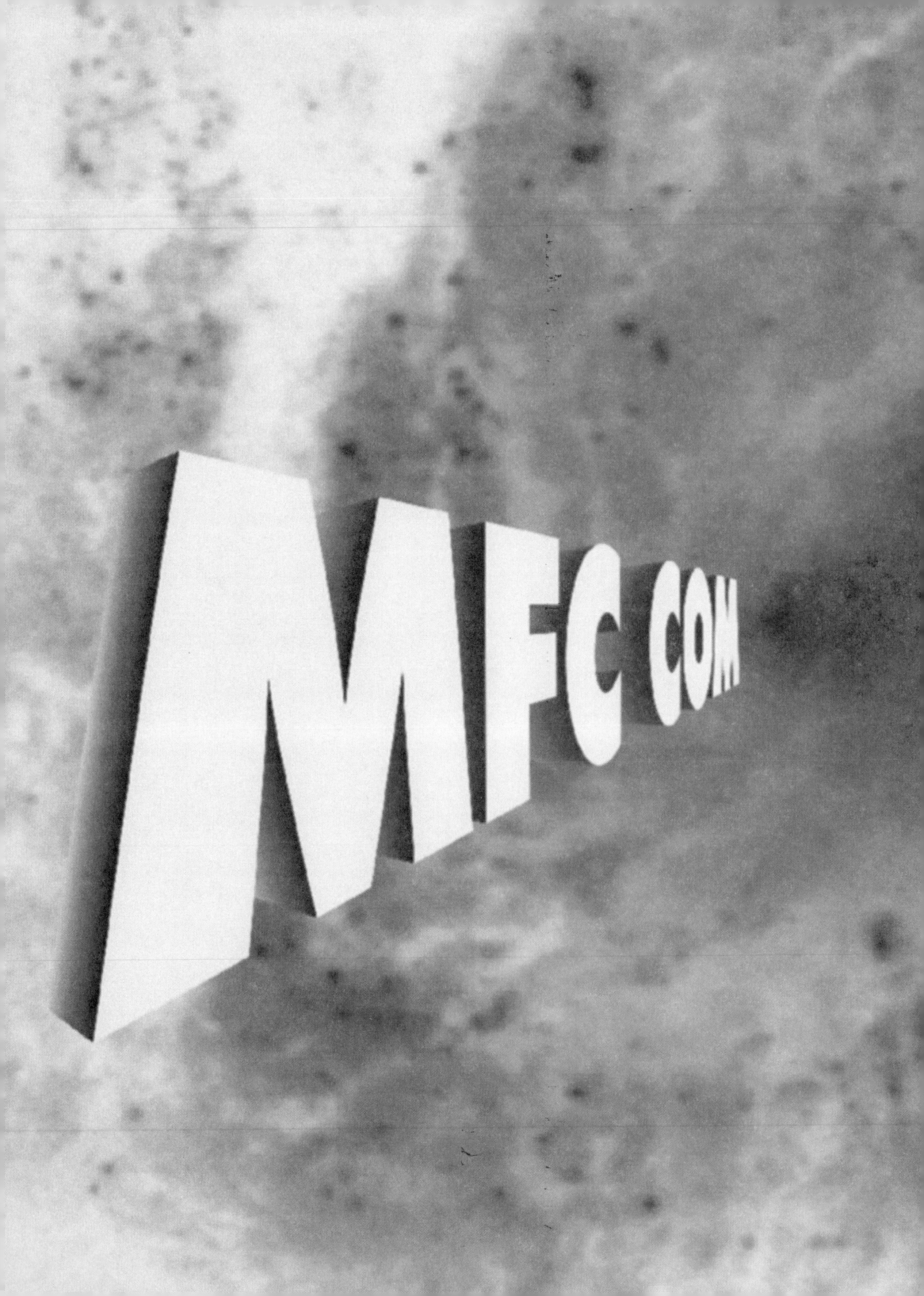
MFC COM

Putting It All Together

In this final chapter, we're going to build a simple system which makes use of all the things we've been talking about (and building) during the course of the book, to show how to make use of the COM-based technologies to build a real program.

The Application

We're going to write three programs that will cooperate with one another. The main application will be a 'data repository' application - an Automation server that sits in the background and stores datasets (which, for ease of programming, will be the same as the ones as we used in the GraphSrv application). Client programs will talk to the data server via Automation, and will perform the following operations

▶ Creating, opening and deleting datasets

▶ Adding data to a dataset

▶ Searching for a named dataset

▶ Retrieving items from a dataset

We'll develop two client applications to work with the Automation server. The first, written using Visual Basic, will create and store datasets; the second, written with Visual C++, will plot the datasets using (surprise!) the Graphing Control.

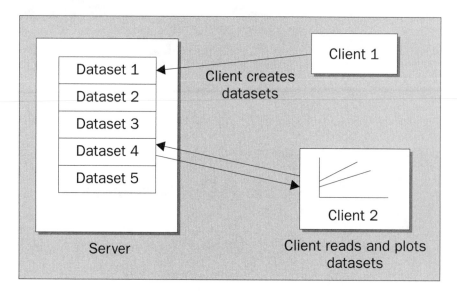

Like the other programs in this book, those presented here are simplified, designed to show the essentials of a COM-based system in operation. In a real application you'd do some things differently, for reasons such as speed or robustness, but these programs are still useful in their own right.

The Server

The dataset server, called RPO (short for 'repository'), will be an MFC application, with Automation access provided by the document class. In order to handle multiple clients reasonably simply, we'll code it as an MDI application, with each new document representing a connection to a client program. The server will therefore work like Word 95, where each new request for an Automation object opens a new document.

The dataset collection will be held as a single static object - an MFC collection object - that each document can reference. The application will use MFC's serialization mechanism to load and save the datasets it is currently holding; it will automatically load its data when it starts up, and save it when it exits. The server will also implement a simple locking scheme, to ensure that clients don't use a dataset that someone else has open.

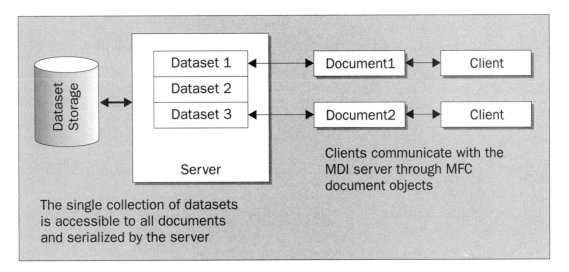

Clients communicate with the MDI server through MFC document objects

The single collection of datasets is accessible to all documents and serialized by the server

Let's begin by creating a new workspace. Choose the MFC AppWizard (exe) option, and give it the name **RPO**. When AppWizard appears, make it produce an MDI application. Most of the options can keep their default values, but make sure that you enable Automation in step 3; you can also turn off the ActiveX Controls option, as we won't be using any in this project. In step 4, use the Advanced... button to provide a suitable file extension, such as **.rpo**. While you're in the Advanced Options dialog, use the Window Styles tab and check the Minimized box for the main frame, so that the application will start up minimized.

Adding the Dataset Classes

The first step in implementing the server's functionality is to add the **CDataset** and **CDatum** classes. We've met **CDatum** before, at the beginning of Chapter 4, and its definition here is exactly the same as it was then. **CDataset** holds a dataset; it's similar in structure to the **CGraph** class, in that it holds a list of **CDatum** objects, but it doesn't have the graph-specific stuff, and it does have some locking capability. In real life, you'd probably end up deriving **CDataset** and **CGraph** from a common base class. **CDataset** derives from **CObject**, so that it can be held in a **CTypedPtrList** and take part in serialization.

Here, to save you the trouble of finding it again, is the definition of **CDatum** and its one member function:

```
class CDatum : public CObject
{
public:
    char name[12];
    long value;

    DECLARE_SERIAL(CDatum);
    void Serialize(CArchive& ca);
};
```

```
void CDatum::Serialize(CArchive& ca)
{
    if (ca.IsStoring())
    {
        ca.Write(name,12);
        ca << (DWORD)value;
    }
    else
    {
        ca.Read(name,12);
        ca >> (DWORD&)value;
    }
}
```

We'll do exactly as we did for the GraphSrv application, and include the above code in the source files of the **CDataset** class, which we'll look at next. The definition of **CDataset** joins the **CDatum** definition in a file called **Dataset.h**, which looks like this:

```
// Insert definition of CDatum here

class CDataset : public CObject
{
    // Serialization
    DECLARE_SERIAL(CDataset);
    void Serialize(CArchive& ca);

    long m_lock;           // lock value
    CObList m_data;        // data item list
    CString m_sTitle;      // Dataset title

public:
    CDataset();
    virtual ~CDataset();

    BOOL Open(long& lck);
    BOOL Release(long lck);
    BOOL IsLocked();
    BOOL VerifyLock(long lck);

    void SetTitle(const char* cs);
    const char* GetTitle() const;

    void Add(const char* n, long d);
    int Size();
    void Clear();
    BOOL GetItem(int index, char* name, long& value);
    BOOL SetItem(int index, const char* name, long value);
};
```

General Dataset Functions

Let's have a quick look at these functions, starting with the constructor and destructor. The data storage uses a simple MFC **CObList** object, the contents of which ought to be freed up when the dataset is destroyed:

```
CDataset::CDataset()
{
   m_sTitle = "";
   m_lock = 0L;      // zero means unlocked
}

CDataset::~CDataset()
{
   // Clear the data out of the list
   while (!m_data.IsEmpty())
      delete m_data.RemoveHead();
}
```

Setting and retrieving the title present no problems; the functions are so small that you may as well declare them as **inline** and put them in the header file:

```
inline void CDataset::SetTitle(const char* cs)
{
   m_sTitle = cs;
}

inline const char* CDataset::GetTitle() const
{
   return m_sTitle;
}
```

The **Size()** function returns the number of items in the dataset, and it can be **inline**, too:

```
inline int CDataset::Size()
{
   return m_data.GetCount();
}
```

Since the only persistent data in the dataset comprises the **CObList** and the name, serialization is pretty easy:

```
void CDataset::Serialize(CArchive& ca)
{
   // Store the title...
   if (ca.IsStoring())
      ca << m_sTitle;
   else
      ca >> m_sTitle;

   // ...and get the data list to serialize itself
   m_data.Serialize(ca);
}
```

The **Clear()** function removes all the items from a dataset, and resets the title:

```
void CDataset::Clear()
{
   // Clear the data out of the list
   while (!m_data.IsEmpty())
      delete m_data.RemoveHead();
```

```
        m_sTitle = "";
}
```

Manipulating the items in a dataset is done using the **Add()**, **GetItem()** and **SetItem()** functions. **Add()** adds a **CDatum** object to the end of the list held by the dataset:

```
void CDataset::Add(const char* n, long d)
{
    CDatum *pd = new CDatum;
    ASSERT(pd);

    pd->value = d;
    strcpy(pd->name, n);

    m_data.AddTail(pd);
}
```

The **GetItem()** and **SetItem()** functions allow access to data items by zero-based index, allowing the retrieval and replacement of individual items:

```
BOOL CDataset::GetItem(int index, char* name, long& value)
{
    ASSERT(name);
    name[0] = '\0';
    value = 0;

    if (index < 0 || index > m_data.GetCount()-1)
        return FALSE;

    POSITION pos = m_data.FindIndex(index);
    if (pos == NULL)
        return FALSE;

    CDatum* pd = (CDatum*)m_data.GetAt(pos);
    ASSERT(pd);
    strcpy(name, pd->name);
    value = pd->value;
    return TRUE;
}

BOOL CDataset::SetItem(int index, const char* name, long value)
{
    if (index < 0 || index > m_data.GetCount()-1)
        return FALSE;

    POSITION pos = m_data.FindIndex(index);
    if (pos == NULL)
        return FALSE;

    CDatum* pd = new CDatum;
    ASSERT(pd);
    strcpy(pd->name, name);
    pd->value = value;
    m_data.SetAt(pos, pd);

    return TRUE;
}
```

Dataset Locking

Since we're dealing with the storage of datasets which can be written and read by multiple clients, we're going to need to provide some sort of locking mechanism, so that a client can be sure that the dataset it's reading isn't suddenly going to be rewritten. Providing this sort of functionality in a robust way can be pretty complicated; this example is about showing COM-based applications in use, so we'll stick to a simple (but hardly foolproof) implementation.

We will use the current time value, obtained as a number of seconds with the **time()** system call, as a simple way of getting a unique value for use as a lock. A lock is handed out when a dataset is opened or created, and must be specified in subsequent calls. The document functions must check that the dataset lock is valid before performing operations. The **Open()** function looks like this:

```
BOOL CDataset::Open(long& lck)
{
   if (m_lock != 0L)
      return FALSE;

   m_lock = lck = time(NULL);
   return TRUE;
}
```

A client can then signal that it has finished with a dataset by passing its lock to **Release()**. If the lock matches, it is reset to zero so that the dataset is available for use again:

```
BOOL CDataset::Release(long lck)
{
   if (m_lock == 0L || m_lock != lck)
      return FALSE;

   m_lock = 0L;
   return TRUE;
}
```

The only two functions we have yet to implement are internal functions, used for checking purposes. **IsLocked()** interrogates a dataset to see if there's a lock on it, while **VerifyLock()** checks whether a client has the right lock for a dataset:

```
BOOL CDataset::IsLocked()
{
   return (m_lock > 0L);
}

BOOL CDataset::VerifyLock(long lck)
{
   return lck == m_lock;
}
```

Here's how they work. Imagine that **pDS** points to a dataset that a client wants to use. The client has passed in a lock value, so we use a line like this to check whether the dataset is locked, and if so, whether the lock is the one handed in by the client:

```
if (!pDS->IsLocked() || !pDS->VerifyLock(*lck))
   // Error - that's the wrong lock!
```

Once you've added *all* the above functions to the **Dataset.cpp** file, there are four more lines to place at the beginning so that everything works properly:

```
#include <stdafx.h>
#include "Dataset.h"

IMPLEMENT_SERIAL(CDatum, CObject, 1)
IMPLEMENT_SERIAL(CDataset, CObject, 1)
```

The **#include**s are obvious; the **IMPLEMENT_SERIAL()** macros are simply the partners of the **DECLARE_SERIAL()** macros we had in the header file. This is just what we had in the GraphSrv application, all that time ago.

Document Data Storage

Since our server is going to hold a collection of datasets for all clients to access, this collection needs to be shareable by all documents, so the more usual per-document data storage we tend to use in typical document/view programs isn't suitable. What we'll do is to use a single MFC collection object to hold the datasets, which will be a **static** member of the document class, and thus accessible from all document objects.

Start by adding a **static** data member of type **CTypedPtrList<CObList, CDataset*>** to the document class declaration (and remember to add a **#include** for **afxtempl.h** to **StdAfx.h**):

```
class CRPODoc : public CDocument
{
    // The one dataset list used by all documents
    static CTypedPtrList<CObList, CDataset*> m_list;

protected: // create from serialization only
    CRPODoc();
    DECLARE_DYNCREATE(CRPODoc)
```

Then initialize the list in the document implementation file, **RPODoc.cpp**:

```
BEGIN_INTERFACE_MAP(CRPODoc, CDocument)
    INTERFACE_PART(CRPODoc, IID_IRPO, Dispatch)
END_INTERFACE_MAP()

// Static member initialization
CTypedPtrList<CObList, CDataset*> CRPODoc::m_list;

/////////////////////////////////////////////////////////////////////////////
// CRPODoc construction/destruction
```

So that everything will compile at this stage (although you can't actually do anything useful yet!), you need to make the RPO application, document and view classes aware of the **CDataset** class. To do this, add **#include** statements for **Dataset.h** to their source files.

Adding Automation Functions

Now we need to start providing the functions that RPO is going to use to manage its datasets. We'll provide these as Automation functions, and as such they'll form the basis for the communication between RPO and its clients.

Error Reporting

Before we go any further, though, let's add some very basic error reporting capability. You'll remember from our discussion on Automation that exceptions are used to pass back information about errors that occur during Automation operations. This makes it easy for us to signal errors, using the **AfxThrowOleDispatchException()** function.

The function is used to throw an exception from within an Automation function, and can take three parameters: a numeric error code, a string description, and a help context ID. We'll just use the first two, and we'll define eight possible error conditions, as listed below:

Code	Description
1	"Dataset name is blank"
2	"Dataset not found"
3	"Dataset already open"
4	"Invalid lock value"
5	"Dataset already exists"
6	"Dataset open failed"
7	"Dataset release failed"
8	"Index value out of range"

We can conveniently provide these as an array of structures at the top of the document class source file:

```
struct {
    unsigned short nCode;
    char* pMsg;
} rpoErr[] =
{
    {1, "Dataset name is blank"},
    {2, "Dataset not found"},
    {3, "Dataset already open"},
    {4, "Invalid lock value"},
    {5, "Dataset already exists"},
    {6, "Dataset open failed"},
    {7, "Dataset release failed"},
    {8, "Index value out of range"}
};
```

A typical error might then be signaled like this:

```
if (index < 0 || index > maxval)
    AfxThrowOleDispatchException(rpoErr[7].nCode, rpoErr[7].pMsg);
```

A C++ program will use this by enclosing the function call in a **try/catch** block, and catching a **COleDispatchException** object. The exception object has several data members; the interesting ones for us here are **m_wCode**, the error code, and **m_strDescription**, the error description:

```
try
{
   // Call function here
}

catch (COleDispatchException* pCE)
{
   CString s;
   s.Format("Error code: %d, %s", pCE->m_wCode, pCE->m_strDescription);
   AfxMessageBox(s);

   // Get rid of the exception object
   pCE->Delete();
}
```

Counting the Datasets

The simplest of all the member functions is **DatasetCount()**, which returns a count of the number of datasets held by the program. Use ClassWizard to add an Automation method with this name to the document class:

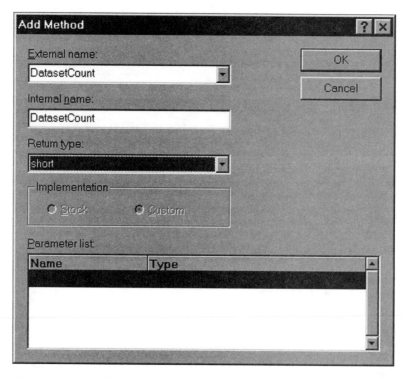

I've returned the count as a short, as it's pretty unlikely that we'll have more than thirty-odd thousand datasets per document. The body of the function simply returns the number of dataset items in the list, using **CObList**'s **GetCount()** function:

```
short CRPODoc::DatasetCount()
{
   return (short)m_list.GetCount();
}
```

> *Take particular notice of the cast. GetCount() returns an int, but that isn't an Automation data type, so we need to use one of the fixed-size integer types instead.*

At this point, we can usefully add a little help for prospective users of our server. Open the ODL file, find the entry for the **DatasetCount()** method, and add a **helpstring** attribute to the entry, like this:

```
[id(1), helpstring("Returns the number of datasets stored by the server")] short
DatasetCount();
```

You can add a string like this to many of the entries in an ODL file, and tools that use the type library can retrieve them and display them for users. We'll see this happening in the Visual Basic Object Browser later on, but for now, you can be kind to your users by adding help strings for the Automation methods as you add the methods themselves.

Finding Datasets

Knowing how many datasets there are is all well and good, but we also need to be able to find individual datasets, and we'll use three functions to help us do this. **GetDS()** is a private member function that searches the list for a dataset with a given title, and returns a pointer to it if such a dataset exists. It's here as a helper function for other methods in the class, and isn't an Automation method:

```
CDataset* CRPODoc::GetDS(const char* dsn)
{
    // Check the name isn't null
    if (!dsn[0])
        AfxThrowOleDispatchException(rpoErr[0].nCode, rpoErr[0].pMsg);

    // Look for the dataset
    POSITION pos = m_list.GetHeadPosition();

    while(pos)
    {
        CDataset* pDS = m_list.GetNext(pos);
        ASSERT(pDS);
        if (!strcmp(dsn, pDS->GetTitle()))
            return pDS;
    }

    return NULL;
}
```

FindDataset() should be added as an Automation method. It's a public member that can be used by clients to check whether a dataset with a given name exists:

```
BOOL CRPODoc::FindDataset(LPCTSTR dsn)
{
    return (GetDS(dsn)) ? TRUE : FALSE;
}
```

GetDatasetName() is related to **FindDataset()**, and is used to return the name of a dataset held by the server. If a client knows how many datasets the server currently has, it can use **GetDatasetName()** to enumerate them all in a simple manner. The routine uses **CObList**'s **FindIndex()** and **GetAt()** functions to get a pointer to the required dataset.

389

```
BSTR CRPODoc::GetDatasetName(short index)
{
    CString strResult;

    // Get the name of a dataset by index. First check the index
    int nSets = m_list.GetCount();
    if (index < 0 || index >= nSets)
      AfxThrowOleDispatchException(rpoErr[7].nCode, rpoErr[7].pMsg);

    POSITION pos = m_list.FindIndex(index);
    if (pos == NULL)
      AfxThrowOleDispatchException(rpoErr[1].nCode, rpoErr[1].pMsg);

    // Get the dataset name, and construct a BSTR to hold it
    CDataset* pDS = m_list.GetAt(pos);
    ASSERT(pDS);

    strResult = pDS->GetTitle();

    return strResult.AllocSysString();
}
```

Look at the help ClassWizard gives you when you're returning a string. As you know, all parameter passing in Automation is actually done using **VARIANT**s, and their string handling is done using **BSTR**s. However, the default code provided allows you to use C++-style strings in your function, and then converts the return string into a **BSTR** by using **AllocSysString()**.

Creating and Opening Datasets

The next thing we want is to be able to create datasets, and open existing ones. **CreateDataset()** creates and opens a dataset with a given name, returning a lock value for the newly opened dataset. The steps taken by this routine are as follows:

▶ Check whether the name is invalid (e.g. null), and signal an error if it is

▶ Check whether a dataset already exists with this name, and signal an error if it does

▶ If all is OK, create a new dataset

▶ Add it to the tail of the list

▶ Open it and return the lock value

To implement this function, create an Automation method with the following prototype:

```
void CreateDataset(LPCTSTR dsn, long FAR* lck);
```

Here's what the routine looks like:

```
void CRPODoc::CreateDataset(LPCTSTR dsn, long FAR* lck)
{
    // Check the name isn't null
    if (!dsn[0])
      AfxThrowOleDispatchException(rpoErr[0].nCode, rpoErr[0].pMsg);

    // Check the dataset doesn't already exist
    if (FindDataset(dsn))
      AfxThrowOleDispatchException(rpoErr[4].nCode, rpoErr[4].pMsg);
```

```
    // Create a new dataset and add it to the list
    CDataset* pDS = new CDataset;
    ASSERT(pDS);


    m_list.AddTail(pDS);

    // Open the dataset and get the lock
    pDS->SetTitle(dsn);
    BOOL bOK = pDS->Open(*lck);

    if (!bOK)
        AfxThrowOleDispatchException(rpoErr[5].nCode, rpoErr[5].pMsg);
}
```

Opening an existing dataset is pretty similar, although in this case the routine signals an error if the dataset doesn't exist, or if someone else has already locked it:

```
void CRPODoc::OpenDataset(LPCTSTR dsn, long FAR* lck)
{
    // Check the name isn't null
    if (!dsn[0])
        AfxThrowOleDispatchException(rpoErr[0].nCode, rpoErr[0].pMsg);

    // Get a pointer to the dataset
    CDataset* pDS = GetDS(dsn);
    if (pDS == NULL)
        AfxThrowOleDispatchException(rpoErr[1].nCode, rpoErr[1].pMsg);

    // Open the dataset and get the lock
    if (pDS->IsLocked())
        AfxThrowOleDispatchException(rpoErr[2].nCode, rpoErr[2].pMsg);

    if (!pDS->Open(*lck))
        AfxThrowOleDispatchException(rpoErr[5].nCode, rpoErr[5].pMsg);
}
```

Closing and Deleting Datasets

Alongside creating and opening datasets come closing and deleting them. **CloseDataset()** is used to close a named dataset and clear its lock. The lock value is used to verify that the caller is the one who opened the dataset, and the function signals an error if the lock is invalid, if the dataset doesn't exist, or if it isn't already open:

```
void CRPODoc::CloseDataset(LPCTSTR dsn, long FAR* lck)
{
    if (!dsn[0])
        AfxThrowOleDispatchException(rpoErr[0].nCode, rpoErr[0].pMsg);

    // Get a pointer to the dataset
    CDataset* pDS = GetDS(dsn);
    if (pDS == NULL)
        AfxThrowOleDispatchException(rpoErr[1].nCode, rpoErr[1].pMsg);

    // The dataset's Release() function checks the lock
    BOOL bOK = pDS->Release(*lck);

    if (!bOK)
        AfxThrowOleDispatchException(rpoErr[6].nCode, rpoErr[6].pMsg);
}
```

DeleteDataset() closes and deletes an open dataset, and fails if the dataset doesn't exist, or if the caller didn't lock it. Due to the way that MFC iterates over its containers, we have to be very careful how we delete the item from the list. Because **GetNext()** updates the **POSITION** variable to point to the following item, by the time we find the item we want, the **POSITION** has been set to point to the following one, so we have to arrange to delete the item at the previous position:

```
void CRPODoc::DeleteDataset(LPCTSTR dsn, long FAR* lck)
{
    // Check the name isn't null
    if (!dsn[0])
        AfxThrowOleDispatchException(rpoErr[0].nCode, rpoErr[0].pMsg);

    // Find the item in the list. We won't use GetDS() here, as we need
    // the position variable.
    CDataset* pDS = NULL;
    POSITION pos1 = m_list.GetHeadPosition();
    POSITION pos2;   // for saving previous position

    while(pos1)
    {
        // Save previous position
        pos2 = pos1;

        pDS = m_list.GetNext(pos1);
        ASSERT(pDS);
        if (!strcmp(dsn, pDS->GetTitle()))
            break;
    }

    if (pDS == NULL)
        AfxThrowOleDispatchException(rpoErr[1].nCode, rpoErr[1].pMsg);

    // Check the lock
    if (!pDS->IsLocked() || !pDS->VerifyLock(*lck))
        AfxThrowOleDispatchException(rpoErr[3].nCode, rpoErr[3].pMsg);

    // Remove the item at the saved position, and delete the dataset
    m_list.RemoveAt(pos2);
    delete pDS;
}
```

Adding Values to the Dataset

Obviously, we need to be able to add data to the datasets we've created. In this simple example we're not going to implement any fancy dataset editing; instead we're just going to stick to adding items to datasets and retrieving them.

AddDatasetValue() adds a new datum to the dataset. As usual, it takes the dataset name and lock, along with the name and value for the new item:

```
void CRPODoc::AddDatasetValue(LPCTSTR dsn, long FAR* lck,
                                            LPCTSTR name, long value)
{
    // Check the name isn't null
    if (!dsn[0])
        AfxThrowOleDispatchException(rpoErr[0].nCode, rpoErr[0].pMsg);
```

```
   // Get a pointer to the dataset
   CDataset* pDS = GetDS(dsn);
   if (pDS == NULL)
     AfxThrowOleDispatchException(rpoErr[1].nCode, rpoErr[1].pMsg);

   // Check the lock
   if (!pDS->IsLocked() || !pDS->VerifyLock(*lck))
     AfxThrowOleDispatchException(rpoErr[3].nCode, rpoErr[3].pMsg);

   // Add the item to the dataset
   pDS->Add(name, value);
}
```

Retrieving Data

We'll provide a couple of functions for retrieving data. The first one will find the number of items in a given dataset, while the second will actually retrieve data items by index. Getting the size of a dataset is easy, and simply uses the **CDataset::Size()** member function:

```
short CRPODoc::DatasetValCount(LPCTSTR dsn)
{
   // Return the number of values in the specified dataset
   // Check the name isn't null
   if (!dsn[0])
     AfxThrowOleDispatchException(rpoErr[0].nCode, rpoErr[0].pMsg);

   // Get a pointer to the dataset. No lock checking, because we aren't
   // trying to use it or open it.
   CDataset* pDS = GetDS(dsn);
   if (pDS == NULL)
     AfxThrowOleDispatchException(rpoErr[1].nCode, rpoErr[1].pMsg);

   // Find number of values in the dataset
   return (short)pDS->Size();
}
```

There are numerous ways in which we could retrieve items from the dataset - you could imagine using an iterator variable, like MFC's **POSITION**, or implementing a **GetFirst()**/ **GetNext()** pair of methods. Here, we'll choose the simplest, in which we retrieve a value by index. The routine, **GetItem()** will fail for the usual reasons: the dataset doesn't exist, or the lock is wrong, or the index is out of range.

GetItem() uses **CDataset::GetItem()** to retrieve the string and value for an indexed item. We need to use a **BSTR*** to return the string in an Automation-compatible manner, and so we need to construct one of these from the C++ string:

```
void CRPODoc::GetItem(LPCTSTR dsn, long FAR* lck, short index,
                                BSTR FAR* name, long FAR* value)
{
   // Check the name isn't null
   if (!dsn[0])
     AfxThrowOleDispatchException(rpoErr[0].nCode, rpoErr[0].pMsg);

   // Get a pointer to the dataset
   CDataset* pDS = GetDS(dsn);
   if (pDS == NULL)
     AfxThrowOleDispatchException(rpoErr[1].nCode, rpoErr[1].pMsg);
```

```
   // Check the lock
   if (!pDS->IsLocked() || !pDS->VerifyLock(*lck))
      AfxThrowOleDispatchException(rpoErr[3].nCode, rpoErr[3].pMsg);

   // The dataset GetItem() will zero out the string and value
   // if the index is invalid
   char s[80];
   BOOL bOK = pDS->GetItem(index, s, *value);

   if (!bOK)
      AfxThrowOleDispatchException(rpoErr[7].nCode, rpoErr[7].pMsg);

   // Make a BSTR out of the character string
   CString cs(s);
   cs.SetSysString(name);
}
```

Dataset Persistence

This application is designed to provide a server for datasets, and those datasets are supposed to persist between invocations of the server. This is a natural use for MFC's serialization abilities, but AppWizard-generated applications add support for serialization on a per-document basis, which isn't what we want here. The default behavior is to call the document's **Serialize()** function when the user wants to open or save a file, but in our case we only have a single, global, persistent data item in the document class, which we want to be loaded when the application starts, and saved when it terminates.

We'll therefore scrap the normal serialization method, and arrange to have it performed on startup and exit, in the application's **InitInstance()** and **ExitInstance()** functions. One consequence of doing this is that you need to start the server as a stand-alone program in order for it to work; if you don't, and allow clients to create objects without a preloaded server, the **InitInstance()** and **ExitInstance()** functions won't get called in the way you'd expect. Since we aren't going to use files in the normal way, it also makes sense to remove from both File menus the items for New, Open..., Save and Save As..., which you can do straight away.

Add a call to our data-handling routine at the end of **InitInstance()**:

```
   // Dispatch commands specified on the command line
   if (!ProcessShellCommand(cmdInfo))
      return FALSE;

   // Load the data in from file
   SerializeData(FALSE);

   // The main window has been initialized, so show and update it.
   pMainFrame->ShowWindow(SW_SHOWMINIMIZED);
   pMainFrame->UpdateWindow();

   return TRUE;
}
```

An override of **ExitInstance()** provides the place for saving the data:

```
int CRPOApp::ExitInstance()
{
```

```
      // Automatically save the dataset on exit...
      SerializeData(TRUE);

   return CWinApp::ExitInstance();
}
```

The **SerializeData()** function is where the work is actually done:

```
BOOL CRPOApp::SerializeData(BOOL bSave)
{
   // Set the archive and file opening flags, depending on the mode.
   UINT uFileFlags, uArchFlags;
   if (bSave)
   {
      uFileFlags = CFile::modeCreate | CFile::modeWrite |
                   CFile::shareDenyNone;
      uArchFlags = CArchive::store;
   }
   else
   {
      uFileFlags = CFile::modeRead | CFile::shareDenyNone;
      uArchFlags = CArchive::load;
   }

   CFile cf;
   CFileException exc;
   LPCTSTR fileName = "data.rpo";
   BOOL bOK = cf.Open(fileName, uFileFlags, &exc);
   if (!bOK)
   {
      CString s;
      if (exc.m_cause == CFileException::fileNotFound)
         s = "Repository file 'data.rpo' not found";
      else
         s.Format("Error opening data.rpo: %d", exc.m_cause);

      AfxMessageBox(s);
      return FALSE;
   }

   CArchive ar(&cf, uArchFlags);

   // Tell the document to serialize itself on this archive...
   CRPODoc::SerializeData(ar);

   // Close the archive and the file...
   ar.Close();
   cf.Close();

   return TRUE;
}
```

You may never have played with **CArchive** like this before, but the process is pretty simple, and we're basically just doing manually what AppWizard applications do for us when we serialize data. After setting the access flags for the file and archive, we open the file, checking the error return if necessary.

For simplicity, the file is kept in the project directory, and is always truncated when opened for saving, because we're going to write out all the data each time. Next, we create the archive and attach it to the file, and then get the document class to serialize its data; since the list of datasets is a static member of the document class, we can use a static member function to do the work.

This serialization function, **SerializeData()**, is very simply declared as a public member function in **RPODoc.h**:

```
static void SerializeData(CArchive& ar);
```

The function itself is also about as simple as it can get:

```
void CRPODoc::SerializeData(CArchive& ar)
{
    m_list.Serialize(ar);
}
```

Things to Try at Home

That's all the functionality I'm going to add to the server in this example, but at the moment it really only provides a very basic set of facilities. There were a few places where I chose methods that were easy, and not necessarily optimal. What modifications could you make in order to make this an industrial-strength system?

Firstly, and most obviously, you'd probably use a proper database behind the server instead of an MFC collection. It could also be a good idea to replace the ad-hoc locking code with proper Win32 synchronization. Implementing decent locking, especially if you want to use multithreading, is a far-from-trivial matter, and beyond the scope of this chapter.

Another improvement would be to add better dataset finding facilities, such as the ability to enumerate all the datasets, or to find those whose names matched a pattern.

If you implemented some events, client programs could be notified of changes to datasets in which they're interested. Unfortunately, MFC only supports event handling for ActiveX controls, so to add it to an Automation class that wasn't a control, you'd have to do the low-level COM coding yourself, which is rather more than I want to attempt here.

As a final suggestion, it might be interesting to code an Automation 'collection', so that Visual Basic and VBA programmers could use the **for each** syntax:

```
dim aSet as DataSet
for each aSet in dataServer.Datasets
    ' aSet points to each document (dataset) in turn
next aDoc
```

I haven't done this here because it isn't directly supported by MFC and the Wizards, and requires a certain amount of low-level COM coding. If you're interested in trying it, details of collections can be found in Appendix C.

The Visual Basic Client: Manipulating Datasets

Discussing what the server might do is all very well, but we've come this far and it's about time we tested the one we've got. In order to do this, we'll write a simple client in Visual Basic that allows us to save datasets and test the basic server functionality. Coding in Visual Basic will help us test our Automation server from a popular language other than C++, and it's always useful for a C++ Automation programmer to see how the objects they produce will work in another environment.

> *I'm not going to supply a tutorial to Visual Basic here. It's actually pretty easy to write a simple application like this, but if you haven't used Visual Basic before, you may wish to consult an appropriate book, such as 'Peter Wright's Beginning Visual Basic 5' (ISBN 1-861000-39-1).*

Before starting on this client application, make sure that you've built and run the server application at least once, so that it has been able to make the appropriate registry entries. Then, start up Visual Basic 5.0, and create a Standard EXE project called **RPOTest**; in this application, we don't need any ActiveX functionality.

Accessing Type Information

Add RPO to Visual Basic's list of references using the Project | References... menu item. A **reference** in Visual Basic is a link to another application's objects, so that you can use them in your code.

When the References dialog appears, use the Browse... button to look for RPO's type library, and select it in order to add it to the list of objects that Visual Basic knows about. Before you close the References dialog, ensure that the entry for RPO in the list of objects is checked:

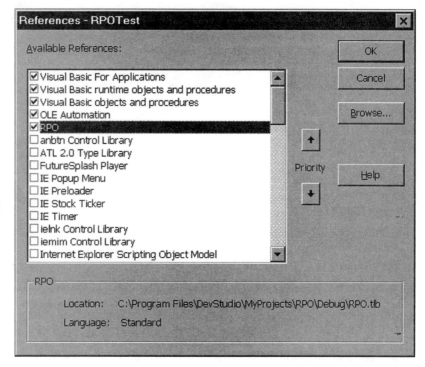

Once the reference has been set up, you can start the Object Browser by pressing *F2*, and look at the Automation methods for RPO:

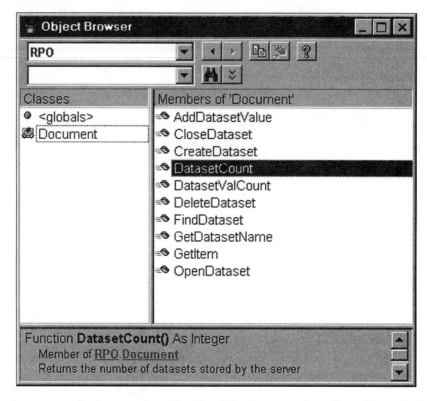

Notice that the pane at the bottom gives the Visual Basic syntax for calling the method, plus the help string that we added to the ODL file.

Adding Functionality

Add some basic Visual Basic controls to the form, as shown in the figure below. The rows of controls are as follows:

- The first row, consisting of a button and edit control, allows us to specify a name and create a new dataset

- The second row (button and static text item) gets and displays the number of datasets currently stored by the server

- The next row allows you to use a button to select a dataset from the list of datasets held by the server, which is displayed in a combo box

- The fourth row lets you delete a dataset that you have previously created or opened

- The fifth row, below the line, lets you add a value to the dataset you have open, using values taken from two edit controls

- The final row contains a list box that displays status information about the operations

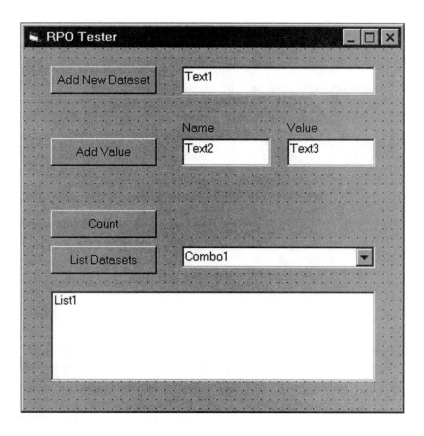

Creating the Object

An RPO object needs to be created when the application starts, so we'll take care of this in the form loading procedure. We need an object variable to hold the reference to the Automation object, so add the following declaration to the (General) (Declarations) section of the form's Code window:

```
Dim RPO as Object
```

Create the object in the form's **Load()** procedure:

```
Private Sub Form_Load()
    On Error GoTo ErrLbl

    ' Create the dataset object
    Set RPO = CreateObject("rpo.document")
    Exit Sub

ErrLbl:
    MsgBox Err.Description, vbOKOnly, "Create RPO"
End Sub
```

The routine will try to create an Automation object of type **rpo.document**; this is the default progID that was defined by AppWizard when we created the application. If the call doesn't succeed, a message box will be displayed showing the error, using the description found in the global **Err** object. This behavior - setting the **Err** object when there's an error - is Visual Basic's way of responding to the exception thrown by our server.

We can also load the list of datasets held by the server at this point. This is most usefully done via a helper function, because we'll want to do it from several places, so add a function to the (General) section of the form's code window:

```
Private Sub FillDatasetCombo()
    'Clear and fill the combo with the list of datasets
    DatasetCombo.Clear

    nsets = RPO.DatasetCount

    ' Get name for each one
    Dim name As String
    For i = 0 To nsets - 1
        name = RPO.GetDatasetName(i)

        ' Add to combo
        DatasetCombo.AddItem (name)
    Next i
End Sub
```

We're using a loop to call **GetDatasetName()** once for each dataset the server contains. In a real-life application though, as I mentioned earlier, this method of getting the names would be replaced by implementing a proper collection object in the server, and then using Visual Basic's **for each** construct.

Once you've added the function, call it from the form's **Load()** procedure:

```
Private Sub Form_Load()
    On Error GoTo errLbl

    ' Create the dataset object
    Set RPO = CreateObject("rpo.document")

    ' Fill in the list of datasets
    FillDatasetCombo
    Exit Sub

errLbl:
    MsgBox Err.Description, vbOKOnly, "Create RPO"
End Sub
```

Getting Dataset Details

The Count Datasets button displays the number of datasets held by the server in a static text control:

```
Private Sub CountBtn_Click()
    ' Get the number of datasets held by RPO
    CountLbl.Caption = Str(RPO.DatasetCount) + " datasets"
End Sub
```

In fact, this doesn't tell us anything terribly useful, because we can already get this information indirectly by counting the entries in the dataset combo box, but it does provide a useful test of this Automation function.

Adding and Opening Datasets

Once we've done this, we can start to add the rest of the functionality. Datasets are added by entering a name in the edit control and pressing the Add New Dataset button. If the action worked (the call to **CreateDataset()** returned **TRUE**), we add a line to the status combo box telling us the lock value which was returned. If it didn't work, we display a message box, and log the fact.

We need to add a couple more variables to the (General) section, to hold the name and lock value for the current dataset:

```
Dim dsn As String      ' name for current dataset
Dim lck1 As Long       ' lock value
```

The code to create a dataset goes in the button's **Click()** routine. As before, we need to use Visual Basic's **On Error** statement to set up an error handler, and we can access the error string through the **Description** member of the **Err** object. We get the text for the name of the new dataset from the edit control, and use that as input to **CreateDataset**:

```
Private Sub AddDatasetBtn_Click()
    On Error GoTo errLbl

    'If there's already a dataset, close it
    If Trim(dsn) <> "" Then
        RPO.CloseDataset dsn, lck1
        dsn = ""
    End If

    ' Tell RPO to create a dataset... first get the dataset name
    dsn = DSName.Text
    If Trim(dsn) = "" Then
        MsgBox "No name!"
        Exit Sub
    End If

    RPO.CreateDataset dsn, lck1
    List1.AddItem ("Dataset " + dsn + " has lock (" + Str(lck1) + ")")

    ' If that was OK, update the dataset combobox
    FillDatasetCombo
    Exit Sub

errLbl:
    MsgBox Err.Description, vbOKOnly, "Create Dataset"
    List1.AddItem ("Error creating Dataset " + dsn + " (" +
                                        Err.Description + ")")
    ' Throw away the name which didn't work
    dsn = ""
End Sub
```

If the call works, we'll have the lock value stored in **lck1**. This simple application only works with a single dataset at a time, so that adding or opening a new dataset means we have to close the existing one. This is especially important, since other clients may be using RPO, and may want to use this dataset after we've finished with it.

Once we're sure that the creation has succeeded, **FillDatasetCombo** is used to update the combo box so it reflects our new control. Remember that RPO is designed to be a multi-user application, and it is possible that other datasets may have been added or deleted by other applications since we last updated the list. This means we're better off asking the server for the new dataset list, rather than just adding our new one to the combo box.

Opening an existing dataset is a similar process, the only real difference being the call to **OpenDataset** rather than **CreateDataset**:

```
Private Sub OpenDatasetBtn_Click()
    On Error GoTo errLbl

    ' If there's already a dataset, close it
    If Trim(dsn) <> "" Then
       RPO.CloseDataset dsn, lck1
       dsn = ""
    End If

    ' Tell RPO to create a dataset... first get the dataset name
    dsn = DatasetCombo.Text
    If Trim(dsn) = "" Then
       MsgBox "No name!"
       Exit Sub
    End If

    RPO.OpenDataset dsn, lck1
    List1.AddItem ("Opened dataset " + dsn + " with lock " + Str(lck1))
    Exit Sub

errLbl:
    MsgBox Err.Description, vbOKOnly, "Open Dataset"
    List1.AddItem ("Error opening Dataset " + dsn + Err.Description)

    ' Throw away the name which didn't work
    dsn = ""
End Sub
```

Deleting Datasets

We can delete a dataset held by the server, provided we have opened it. Since the name of the current dataset is held in **dsn**, we can use this to check whether a dataset is open:

```
Private Sub DeleteDatasetBtn_Click()
    ' Delete the currently open dataset
    On Error GoTo errLbl

    If Trim(dsn) = "" Then
       MsgBox "You must have opened a dataset before you can delete it"
       Exit Sub
    End If
```

```
      RPO.DeleteDataset dsn, lck1
      List1.AddItem ("Dataset " + dsn + " deleted")
      dsn = ""

      ' If that was OK, update the dataset combobox
      FillDatasetCombo
      Exit Sub

   errLbl:
      MsgBox Err.Description, vbOKOnly, "Delete Dataset"
      List1.AddItem ("Error deleting Dataset " + dsn + Err.Description)
   End Sub
```

Once we've deleted the dataset, we blank out the dataset name and then refresh the list of dataset names in the combo box.

Adding Values

Adding values is done using the **Click()** method for the appropriate button:

```
Private Sub ValueBtn_Click()
   On Error GoTo errLbl

   ' Check we have a dataset open
   If Trim(dsn) = "" Then
      MsgBox "You must have opened a dataset before you can add data"
      Exit Sub
   End If

   ' Add a data item to the current dataset. First get the data from the
   ' edit controls
   Dim name As String
   Dim value As Integer

   If Trim(ValueName.Text) = "" Or Trim(ValueVal.Text) = "" Then
      MsgBox "Can't add a value without proper data!"
      Exit Sub
   End If

   name = ValueName.Text
   value = Val(ValueVal.Text)

   RPO.AddDatasetValue dsn, lck1, name, value
   List1.AddItem ("Added value OK")
   Exit Sub

errLbl:
   MsgBox Err.Description, vbOKOnly, "Create Dataset"
   List1.AddItem ("Error adding value (" + Err.Description + ")")
End Sub
```

Before trying to add a value, we check that we have a dataset open, and that there is some data in the edit controls. The checking here is very basic (if you'll pardon the pun), and only determines that there is something in the edit controls; it doesn't try to validate it apart from passing the value through **Val()** to convert it from a string. Assuming that all is OK, a call to **AddDatasetValue** adds the new value to the current dataset.

Tidying Up

We need to close any open datasets when the application exits, so that the server doesn't think they're still locked. We can do this in the form's **Unload()** procedure:

```
Private Sub Form_Unload(Cancel As Integer)
   ' When unloading the form, close any open dataset
   If Trim(dsn) <> "" Then
      RPO.CloseDataset dsn, lck1
   End If
End Sub
```

As you can see from this code, using Visual Basic as a client for RPO isn't hard, because Visual Basic's built-in support for talking to Automation servers is designed to be easy to use.

The Visual C++ Client: Graphing

Our second application will use the graphing control we developed in Chapter 9 to retrieve and plot a dataset from the server. We'll write this one in Visual C++, to test that the server works OK from there. The application is going to require us to use two Automation objects - one to access the server and the other to plot the data - and in a sense the only purpose of the application is to provide a link between these two objects.

Creating the Project

Create a Visual C++ project, using the MFC AppWizard (exe) to create a standard executable, **RpoCli**. We may as well make it a dialog-based application, since we're only interested in using it to demonstrate the use of an ActiveX control. All the other options in AppWizard can be left with their default values, except for making sure that the Automation checkbox is checked in step 2, which will ensure that all the COM libraries are initialized.

Adding a Graph Control

Open the dialog resource **IDD_RPOCLI_DIALOG**. Delete the static text item and the Cancel button, and rename the OK button to Done. Now, add the following controls to the dialog:

▶ A combo box to hold the dataset names, called **IDC_NAMES**, plus a static text item to label it.

▶ Another button, **IDC_PLOTBTN**, labeled Plot, which will be used to plot the dataset chosen.

▶ A group of three radio buttons, **IDC_BAR**, **IDC_LINE** and **IDC_PIE**, used to select the graph type.

Use ClassWizard to add member variables to represent the controls, as follows:

▶ The combo box **IDC_NAMES**, by **CComboBox m_nameList**.

▶ The radio button **IDC_BAR**, by **CButton m_bar**. This is the only one of the three that needs to have a control variable, as it's the only one we manipulate from this program.

To add the graph control, bring up the Components and Controls Gallery by selecting the
Project | Add To Project | Components and Controls... menu item. When the gallery dialog
appears, double click on the Registered ActiveX Controls entry, and select the graphing control
from the selection that appears:

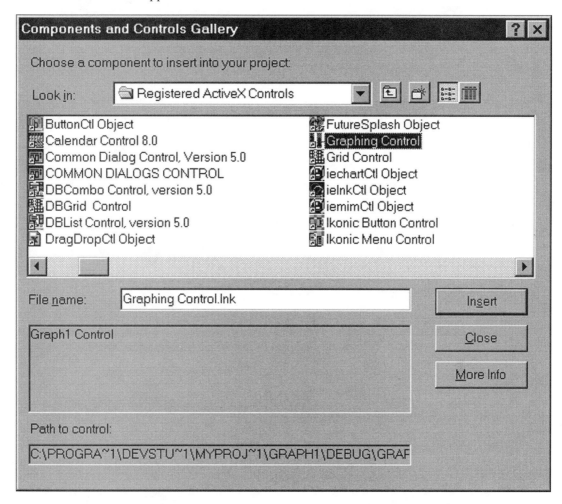

Press Insert to insert the control into the project, and confirm the class that you want added.
The Gallery will offer to add a **COleFont** class, but we don't require this, so it can be
unchecked.

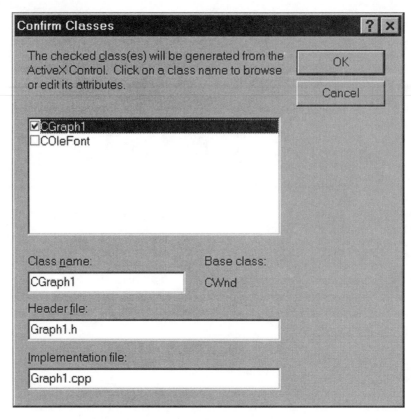

Add a graph control to your dialog, giving it an ID of **IDC_GRAPH**, and sizing it appropriately. You should end up with a dialog looking something like this:

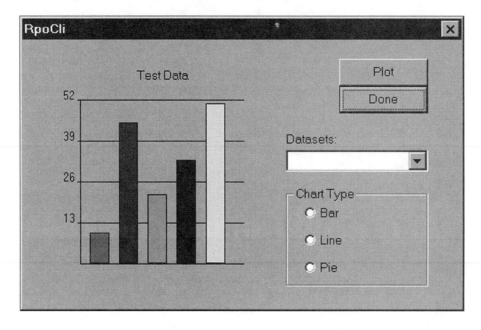

Finally, use ClassWizard's Member Variables tab to add a control variable called **m_graph** to represent the graph to the dialog class.

Adding Server Access

To add the class that will allow us to access the server, start ClassWizard and choose to add a new class from a type library. Browse till you find the RPO type library **rpo.tlb** (it should be in the RPO project's **Debug** directory) and select it. You should then see the class confirmation dialog:

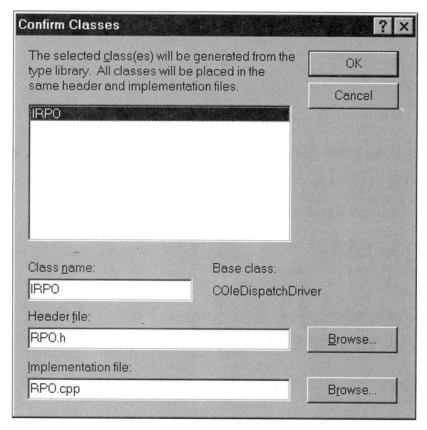

Having added the class code, we now need to create the server object. Start by adding a variable to the dialog class definition (remembering to include a reference to **rpo.h**!):

```
private:
    IRPO* m_pServer;
```

Use the dialog class constructor to set this to **NULL**. It will also be useful later to provide an inline member function to return this pointer to other classes that may want to use it:

```
const IRPO* Server() { return m_pServer; }
```

We want to create the object and attach its dispatch interface when the dialog starts, so add this code to the **OnInitDialog()** function:

```
// Set the icon for this dialog. The framework does this automatically
//   when the application's main window is not a dialog
SetIcon(m_hIcon, TRUE);          // Set big icon
SetIcon(m_hIcon, FALSE);         // Set small icon
```

```
// Start the dataset server
m_pServer = new IRPO;
if (!m_pServer->CreateDispatch(_T("rpo.document")))
{
   AfxMessageBox("Unable to create server object");
   return FALSE;
}
```

```
   return TRUE;  // return TRUE  unless you set the focus to a control
}
```

We create a new C++ server object (remember that this in itself doesn't do any of the COM work), and we then call **CreateDispatch()** in order to create the object. This routine gets a pointer to the object's dispatch interface, which is stored and used by the **IRPO** class. If that call succeeds we're all ready to go. If not, we return **FALSE** to show that initialization failed.

Selecting the Dataset

Selecting the dataset to plot involves getting a list of the datasets held by the server, and displaying them so that the user can select one. We'll do this in the dialog's **WM_INITDIALOG** handler by calling an appropriate function, as shown here:

```
// Start the dataset server
m_pServer = new IRPO;
if (!m_pServer->CreateDispatch(_T("rpo.document")))
{
   AfxMessageBox("Unable to create server object");
   return FALSE;
}
```

```
// Fill the combo with the dataset names
GetDSNames();

// Set bar chart as default type
m_bar.SetCheck(1);
```

```
   return TRUE;  // return TRUE  unless you set the focus to a control
}
```

Here's the **GetDSNames()** function. Notice how I'm using exception handling to check for errors returned by the server:

```
void CRpoCliDlg::GetDSNames()
{
   // Get the list of names from the server
   ASSERT(m_pServer);

   short nDS = m_pServer->DatasetCount();
   short i;
```

```
    for (i=0; i<nDS; i++)
    {
        CString s;
        try
        {
            s = m_pServer->GetDatasetName(i);
        }

        catch(COleDispatchException* pCE)
        {
            // Couldn't get name
            MessageBox(pCE->m_strDescription, "Error");
            pCE->Delete();
            return;
        }

        m_nameList.AddString(s);
    }

    // Set the selection to the first one
    if (nDS > 0)
        m_nameList.SetCurSel(0);
}
```

Plotting the Data

Now for the main event. Plotting the data is done in the **BN_CLICKED** handler for the
IDC_PLOTBTN button. The **OnPlotbtn()** function is responsible for opening the dataset, reading
the data, plotting the data and then closing the dataset. Before coding the function, add a couple
of private members to the dialog class - one to hold the dataset name, and the other to hold a
lock value:

```
private:
    CString m_dsn;
    long m_lock;
```

Here's the code for the **IDC_PLOTBTN** handler:

```
void CRpoCliDlg::OnPlotbtn()
{
    int nItem = m_nameList.GetCurSel();

    if (nItem >= 0)
        m_nameList.GetLBText(nItem, m_dsn);

    // Plot a dataset. The name is in m_dsn
    if (m_dsn == "")
    {
        AfxMessageBox("No dataset name!");
        return;
    }

    // Open the dataset
    ASSERT(m_pServer);
    try
```

```
   {
      m_pServer->OpenDataset(m_dsn, &m_lock);
   }

   catch(COleDispatchException* pCE)
   {
      // Couldn't open dataset
      MessageBox(pCE->m_strDescription, "Error");
      pCE->Delete();
      return;
   }

   // Clear the graph, and set the title to the dataset name
   m_graph.Clear();
   m_graph.SetGraphTitle(m_dsn);

   // Get the points one-by-one, and add them to the control
   short nvals = m_pServer->DatasetValCount(m_dsn);
   if (nvals == 0)
   {
      MessageBox("Dataset contains no data values");
   }

   for (short i=0; i<nvals; i++)
   {
      CString name;
      long val;

      try
      {
         BSTR bs = NULL;
         m_pServer->GetItem(m_dsn, &m_lock, i, &bs, &val);

         // The name comes back as a BSTR, which is a wide
         // char type. We need to convert it to an ordinary
         // string, and an easy way to do it is to use a CString
         // as an intermediary, as it is set up to deal with wide
         // chars
         name = bs;
         SysFreeString(bs);
      }

      catch(COleDispatchException* pCE)
      {
         // Couldn't get item
         MessageBox(pCE->m_strDescription, "Error");
         pCE->Delete();
         return;
      }

      m_graph.AddPoint(name, (short)val);
   }
```

410

```
    // Close the dataset
    try
    {
       m_pServer->CloseDataset(m_dsn, &m_lock);
    }

    catch(COleDispatchException* pCE)
    {
       // Couldn't close dataset
       MessageBox(pCE->m_strDescription, "Error");
       pCE->Delete();
       return;
    }
}
```

The function gets the dataset name from the combo box, and then tries to open it. If the open succeeds, we clear the graph and set the title from the dataset name. The server is then queried for the number of items in the dataset, and each item is retrieved via a call to **GetItem()**. Note the use of a **CString** as a simple way to convert the **BSTR** returned by **GetItem()** into a type that's easier for us to use. Each data item is added to the graph's collection as it is retrieved, and once we're done, we close the dataset. Note that I use exception handling to check for errors all the way through this example.

Controlling the Graph Type

The final step is to add the code to change the graph type in response to a radio button selection. All we need to do is to add handlers for the radio button **BN_CLICKED** events, and call the appropriate function in the graph control, like this:

```
void CRpoCliDlg::OnBar()
{
    m_graph.SetBarChart();
}

void CRpoCliDlg::OnLine()
{
    m_graph.SetLineChart();
}

void CRpoCliDlg::OnPie()
{
    m_graph.SetPieChart();
}
```

411

Start up the server, add a couple of datasets with the Visual Basic client, and you should be able to produce behavior something like this:

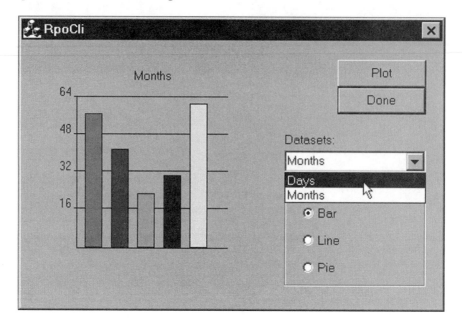

Summary

In this final chapter, you've seen how to use the COM-based technologies to build a simple system. We created an Automation server using Visual C++, and showed how it could be accessed from both Visual C++ and Visual Basic.

The server and client applications which we created are quite simplistic and could be improved in many ways, but they do show how these technologies can be used to provide component-based systems, and how using Automation for component communication is simple to implement.

The very last thing I hope this chapter shows is what I set out to demonstrate right at the start: that MFC makes COM programming a much less difficult prospect than it would otherwise be. The COM-based technologies are versatile and wide-ranging, and if you've come with me this far, you'll be well equipped to utilize them in your own applications. You might just be surprised at what you can achieve.

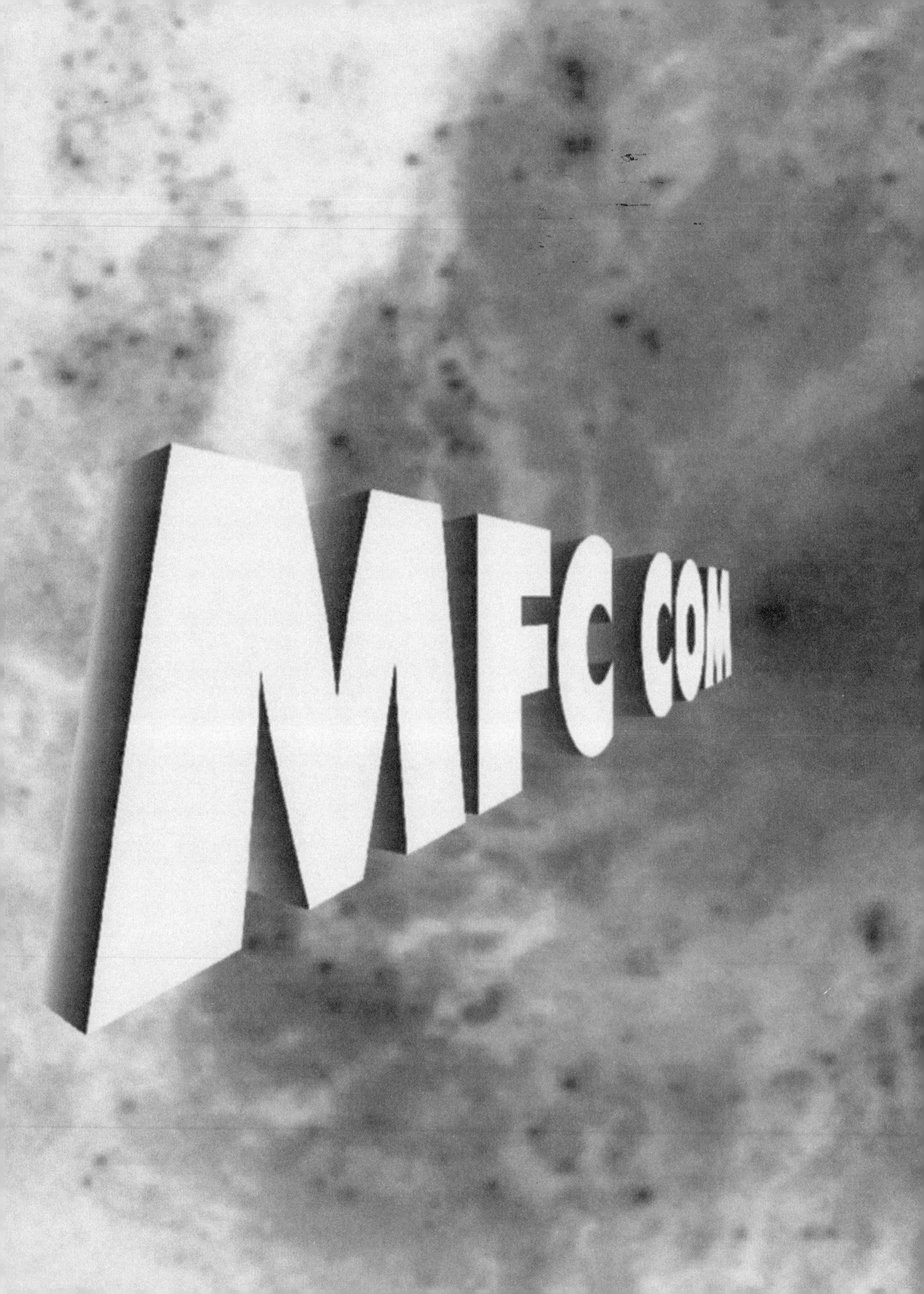
MFC COM

MFC COM-Related Classes

What follows is a brief guide to all the COM-related classes in MFC version 4.21. They're grouped together by topic, although some classes may well fit into more than one category. While not giving an exhaustive reference, this should give you a good idea of where each class fits into the grand scheme of things, what it's used for, and where you're likely to encounter it.

Base Classes

CCmdTarget

CObject → CCmdTarget

CCmdTarget is the base class for MFC's message-handling mechanism. Any MFC class which wishes to handle Windows messages must inherit from **CCmdTarget**; such classes include **CWinApp**, **CView**, **CDocument** and **CWnd**. By the same token, *any* class that inherits from **CCmdTarget** can handle messages, regardless of whether it has anything to do with the user interface of the application.

CCmdTarget provides mapping mechanisms for Windows messages, COM interfaces and Automation events, via message maps, interface maps and event maps respectively.

CDocItem

CObject → CCmdTarget → CDocItem

Documents in COM-enabled MFC applications can contain linked or embedded OLE objects. The document saves these as objects of classes derived from **CDocItem**. The two main derived classes are **COleClientItem**, representing client objects, and **COleServerItem**, which represents server objects.

CDocItem has only two member functions: **GetDocument()**, which returns a pointer to the document in which the object resides, and **IsBlank()**, which can be called to test whether the object contains any data. Why isn't it called **COleDocItem**? I have no idea!

See also: **COleDocument**, **COleServerItem**, **COleClientItem**

COccManager

MFC has a single, global instance of this class, called **afxOccManager**. Its job is to manage the display of ActiveX controls in dialog boxes, and to route events to their proper destinations.

COleControl

CObject → **CCmdTarget** → **CWnd** → **COleControl**

COleControl is the base class from which ActiveX controls are built. It inherits from **CWnd**, and thus gains all the abilities of a window, but it also has added COM functionality, such as the ability to support Automation methods and properties, and to fire events.

Since **COleControl** implements all the functionality needed by ActiveX controls (including the eighteen COM interfaces needed by a 'full' ActiveX control), it is a large and complex class, with over 150 member functions.

See also: **COleControlModule**, **COleControlSite**

COleControlModule

CObject → **CCmdTarget** → **CWinThread** → **CWinApp** → **COleControlModule**

COleControlModule takes the place of **CWinApp** in an ActiveX control project; as a result, each control contains exactly one **COleControlModule** object, declared as a global object within the project.

The class defines two member functions, **InitInstance()** and **ExitInstance()**, which override the corresponding base class member functions, and whose purpose is to register and de-register the class factory for the control.

See also: **COleControlSite**, **COleControl**

COleControlSite

CObject → **CCmdTarget** → **COleControlSite**

COleControlSite is an officially undocumented MFC class, but one which is important to the operation of ActiveX controls in MFC applications. A container document maintains one **COleControlSite** object for each ActiveX control it contains, and the class enables the control and container to communicate. These objects are handled by MFC as part of its control support, and it's very unlikely that you will ever have to deal with this class directly.

See also: **COleControlModule**, **COleControl**

COleDialog

`CWnd` → `CDialog` → `CCommonDialog` → `COleDialog`

COleDialog provides the base class for all the OLE-specific dialogs supported by MFC. The class itself only implements one member function: **GetLastError()**.

See also: **COleBusyDialog**, **COleChangeIconDialog**, **COleChangeSourceDialog**, **COleConvertDialog**, **COleInsertDialog**, **COleLinksDialog**, **COlePasteSpecialDialog**, **COlePropertiesDialog**, **COleUpdateDialog**

COleDispatchDriver

COleDispatchDriver implements the controller (client) side of Automation. The class greatly simplifies the task of talking to a dispatch interface on an Automation object.

COleDispatchDriver objects are used by attaching them to a dispatch interface. This can be done in one of two ways: if you already have a pointer to a dispatch interface, you can use **AttachDispatch()** to attach to it. Alternatively, if you know the CLSID or progID of the Automation object you want to use, you can use **CreateDispatch()** to create an Automation object and attach to it.

When you've finished with the dispatch interface, you can call **ReleaseDispatch()**, which will call the Automation object's **IDispatch::Release()** function. If, for some reason, you wish to disconnect but not to release the interface, you can call **DetachDispatch()** instead.

Three functions are provided to assist in using the dispatch interface: **GetProperty()**, **SetProperty()** and **InvokeHelper()**. The first two use the dispID to get or set the value of a property. **InvokeHelper()** provides a fairly direct interface to **IDispatch::Invoke()**, but gives some help in packing method parameters into an argument block.

Although you can use this class yourself, it's most commonly used as a base class for Automation classes created by ClassWizard. When you use ClassWizard to read a type library, a class is created which derives from **COleDispatchDriver**, and which contains custom member functions corresponding to the methods and properties of the Automation object.

These custom functions provide a simple, high-level interface which makes use of **GetProperty()**, **SetProperty()** and **InvokeHelper()** to interact with the Automation object.

COleDocument

`CObject` → `CCmdTarget` → `CDocument` → `COleDocument`

COleDocument is derived from MFC's standard **CDocument** class, and is used for compound document implementation, as well as basic container support. It differs from **CDocument** in that it treats the document data as a list of **CDocItem** objects.

The class has a number of member functions for managing this list, including:

▶ **AddItem()** and **RemoveItem()**, for adding and removing items

▶ **GetStartPosition()**, **GetNextItem()**, **GetNextServerItem()** and **GetNextClientItem()**, for iterating through the list

▶ **GetInPlaceActiveItem()**, for retrieving the current in-place active item

This class can be used as the base class for container documents, and is the base class for **COleServerDoc** and **COleLinkingDoc**.

See also: **CDocItem**, **COleServerDoc**, **COleLinkingDoc**

COleObjectFactory

CObject → **CCmdTarget** → **COleObjectFactory**

COleObjectFactory is the class that implements the class factory for MFC COM objects. In an MFC application, you won't tend to deal directly with this class, but rather with its derived class, **COleTemplateServer**.

COleObjectFactory contains a number of important COM-related functions, such as:

▶ **Register()** and **RegisterAll()**, which register the class factory with the COM system DLLs

▶ **Revoke()** and **RevokeAll()**, which are called on shutdown and which de-register the class factory

▶ **UpdateRegistry()** and **UpdateRegistryAll()**, which update the application's entries in the system registry

It wasn't until MFC version 4.0 that the **IClassFactory2** interface was implemented in **COleObjectFactory** as well; prior to that, there were two classes: **COleObjectFactory** to implement **IClassFactory**, and **COleObjectFactoryEx** to implement **IClassFactory2**.

See also: **COleTemplateServer**

Container Classes

COleLinkingDoc

CObject → **CCmdTarget** → **CDocument** → **COleDocument** → **COleLinkingDoc**

Document classes that need to support links to embedded objects (in applications whose documents can contain linked objects) should be derived from **COleLinkingDoc** rather than **COleDocument**.

Applications that use **COleLinkingDoc** as the base for their document class also need to ensure that they use a **COleTemplateServer** object. This is because a link container may need to be started programmatically if a user wishes to edit a linked object that's an item embedded in another document. This will be done for you in applications created by AppWizard.

See also: **COleDocument**, **COleTemplateServer**

COleClientItem

CObject → **CCmdTarget** → **CDocItem** → **COleClientItem**

COleClientItem implements a client item class, which represents the client's side of the connection to an embedded or linked OLE item. The client item represents the data which is maintained by a server object, and which is seamlessly incorporated into a container document. The **COleClientItem** class has over 80 member functions, which represents the wide range of functionality and user interaction that OLE items may support.

Client items may be embedded or linked, and can be created in a number of ways, including creation from a data object, a file, the contents of the clipboard, or by starting up an OLE server in order to create a new item from scratch. Once created, there are a wide range of operations which can be performed on a client item, such as copying its data to the clipboard, using it in drag and drop, activating the item and directing it to perform an action, or querying its status.

See also: **CDocItem**, **COleServerItem**, **COleDocument**

Server Classes

COleTemplateServer

CObject → **CCmdTarget** → **COleObjectFactory** → **COleTemplateServer**

COleTemplateServer is the class used to create new documents in an OLE server, and is used in visual (in-place) editing servers, Automation servers, and linking containers (those which can contain linked objects). This class inherits from **COleObjectFactory**, and so has the ability to create new COM objects.

When you use AppWizard to create one of the application types mentioned above, a **COleTemplateServer** object is added to the **CWinApp**-derived application class.

This class introduces two documented functions of its own: **ConnectTemplate()**, which connects an MFC document template to the underlying **COleObjectFactory**, and **UpdateRegistry()**, which takes the information from the document template string and uses it to update the registry. **COleTemplateServer** also overrides the base class function **OnCreateObject()**.

See also: **COleObjectFactory**

COleIPFrameWnd

`CObject` → `CCmdTarget` → `CWnd` → `CFrameWnd` → `COleIPFrameWnd`

`COleIPFrameWnd` is the base class for the in-place frame, which surrounds an embedded or linked object when it's being edited in-place in a container. It has few significant member functions.

When you create a server application using AppWizard, a class will be derived from `COleIPFrameWnd` to represent your server's in-place frame. This class can be customized if necessary, although the default behavior is fine for many server applications. Information on the in-place frame is stored in the document template object using the **`SetServerInfo()`** function, and the template is then registered with the application's **`COleTemplateServer`** object.

See also: **`COleTemplateServer`**

COleServerDoc

`CDocument` → `COleDocument` → `COleLinkingDoc` → `COleServerDoc`

`COleServerDoc` is the base class for document classes in OLE server applications. Its base class, `COleLinkingDoc`, provides functionality for OLE container documents, and this class adds support for activating and managing the state of embedded server objects.

When you build an MFC server application, the document class will be derived from `COleServerDoc` rather than **`CDocument`**. A `COleServerDoc` usually contains one or more `COleServerItem` objects, although it can also contain client items represented by `COleClientItem` objects, thus allowing the application to be both a server and container.

If a server only supports embedding, then it will have a single **`COleServerItem`** object representing the whole of the document. If it also supports linking, a new **`COleServerItem`** object will need to be created each time a selection is copied to the clipboard.

See also: **`COleLinkingDoc`**, **`COleServerItem`**, **`COleClientItem`**

COleServerItem

`CObject` → `CCmdTarget` → `CDocItem` → `COleServerItem`

`COleServerItem` implements a server item class, which represents the server side of the connection to an embedded or linked OLE item. The document in an MFC server application, which will be derived from `COleServerDoc`, will be represented by one or more `COleServerItem` items, which provide the interface to its functionality.

`COleServerItem` represents a document (or a portion of a document) that can be placed in a container as an embedded or a linked item. Note that an embedded item always represents a complete document, whereas a link can reference part of a server document, such as a range of cells in a spreadsheet.

This class provides an extensive list of member functions, including:

- **OnGetExtent()**, **GetItemName()** and **IsLinkedItem**, which query the status of the item
- **OnDraw()**, **OnOpen()** and **OnShow()**, which handle displaying the item
- **OnDoVerb()**, which executes the item's functions
- **CopyToClipboard()** and **DoDragDrop()**, which retrieve the item's data

These functions are usually called by the container in which the object is embedded, in order to manipulate the object. An MFC server application which has been created by AppWizard will have its own server item class, derived from **COleServerItem**.

See also: **COleLinkingDoc**, **COleServerDoc**, **COleClientItem**

COleResizeBar

CObject → **CCmdTarget** → **CWnd** → **CControlBar** → **COleResizeBar**

A **COleResizeBar** is a type of control bar that's used in the resizing of in-place OLE objects. It appears as a **CRectTracker** with a hatched border and outside resize handles. **COleResizeBar** has only two functions: the constructor and the **Create()** function.

UDT Classes

COleDataObject

COleDataObject objects implement the destination side of a data transfer operation. They get created when data is dropped onto a target, when an application is asked to perform a paste from the clipboard, or when data needs to be retrieved from an embedded OLE object.

When accepting a dropped object, the receiving application is passed a pointer to a **COleDataObject**. The data can be extracted from the object using one of the data-handling member functions: **GetGlobalData()** (for data passed via global memory), **GetFileData()** (for data passed via a pointer to a **CFile**) or **GetData()** (for data passed via structured storage).

When pasting from the clipboard, the application needs to create a **COleDataObject** and call its **AttachClipboard()** member function. Once the clipboard has been attached, the application can search for the required data format using **IsDataAvailable()**, or by enumerating the available formats. Data retrieval is then the same as for dropped objects.

See also: **COleDataSource**

COleDataSource

`CObject` → `CCmdTarget` → `COleDataSource`

COleDataSource objects implement the source side of a data transfer operation. They get created when data is provided for a drag and drop operation, or copied to the clipboard. You can create them yourself if necessary, although in many applications they are automatically created by higher-level MFC classes, such as **COleClientItem** and **COleServerItem**, when they need to transfer data.

COleDataSource supports both immediate and delayed rendering of data. **Immediate rendering** means that the data is copied to the clipboard regardless of whether anyone is likely to retrieve it. **Delayed rendering**, on the other hand, means that the data is only copied when a client requests it, thus saving memory and time.

See also: **COleDataObject**

COleDropSource

`CObject` → `CCmdTarget` → `COleDropSource`

COleDropSource works together with **COleDropTarget** to implement OLE drag and drop. The **COleDropSource** object determines when a drag operation starts, provides feedback during the drag operation, and determines when the operation ends.

Many MFC programs will use the higher-level support provided by the **COleDataSource**, **COleClientItem** and **COleServerItem** classes, each of which provides a **DoDragDrop()** function.

See also: **COleDropTarget, COleDataSource, COleClientItem, COleServerItem**

COleDropTarget

`CObject` → `CCmdTarget` → `COleDropTarget`

COleDropTarget works together with **COleDropSource** to implement OLE drag and drop. A **COleDropTarget** object allows a window to accept data through the OLE drag and drop mechanism. In order to use this class with a window, create a **COleDropTarget** object, and then call its **Register()** function with a pointer to the **CWnd** object.

The class contains a number of functions which can be overridden to provide the desired behavior, including **OnDragEnter()**, **OnDragOver()**, **OnDragLeave()** and **OnDrop()**.

See also: **COleDropSource**

Structured Storage Classes

COleStreamFile

CObject → CFile → COleStreamFile

COleStreamFile encapsulates a stream within a structured storage file. A stream can be attached to a **COleStreamFile**, either at construction time or later via the **Attach()** member function. Once attached, the stream can be read and written in the same way as a **CFile**.

OLE Dialog Classes

COleBusyDialog

CDialog → CCommonDialog → COleDialog → COleBusyDialog

This class implements the dialogs displayed by a **COleMessageFilter** object when its application is busy. The class has a data member **m_bz**; this is a structure of type **OLEUIBUSY**, whose members can be modified in order to control the appearance and behavior of the dialog. The class is used by AppWizard-generated code.

See also: **COleMessageFilter**

COleInsertDialog

CDialog → CCommonDialog → COleDialog → COleInsertDialog

COleInsertDialog displays the dialog box when the user selects Insert Object from the Edit menu. It allows the user to choose the item to insert, and also whether the object should be displayed as an icon or not.

See also: **COleChangeIconDialog**

COleConvertDialog

CDialog → CCommonDialog → COleDialog → COleConvertDialog

The **COleConvertDialog** class provides the standard interface for converting OLE items from one type to another. For instance, the user may have embedded a metafile in a document, and now wish to change the application to use as the object's server.

COleChangeIconDialog

`CDialog` → `CCommonDialog` → `COleDialog` → `COleChangeIconDialog`

The Change Icon dialog is displayed when the icon for an embedded or linked object is to be changed. This dialog needs to be displayed when the user has selected Change Icon from the Edit menu, or the Change Icon button in the Paste Special or Convert dialog boxes, or has used the Insert Object dialog and chosen Display as Icon.

See also: `COleInsertDialog`

COleChangeSourceDialog

`CDialog` → `CCommonDialog` → `COleDialog` → `COleChangeSourceDialog`

The `COleChangeSourceDialog` class displays a dialog allowing the user to change the source or destination of a link. This dialog gets displayed when the user presses the Change Source button on the Edit Links dialog.

See also: `COleLinksDialog`

COlePasteSpecialDialog

`CDialog` → `CCommonDialog` → `COleDialog` → `COlePasteSpecialDialog`

This class displays the Paste Special dialog, which is the standard way of implementing the Edit menu's Paste Special command. The Display as Icon checkbox can be used to force the item to be displayed as an icon. When it's checked, a button is displayed which brings up the Change Icon dialog.

See also: `COleChangeIconDialog`

COlePropertiesDialog

`CDialog` → `CCommonDialog` → `COleDialog` → `COlePropertiesDialog`

This class encapsulates the Windows common OLE properties dialog box, and is used with document items (objects derived from `CDocItem`).

By default, the common ...Properties dialog box has up to three tabs. The General tab contains system information for the file represented by the selected document item. From this tab, the user can convert the selected item to another type. The View tab contains options for displaying the item, changing the icon, and changing the scaling of the image. If the object is linked, the Link page contains options for updating or changing the location of the linked item. From this tab, the user can break the link of the selected item.

COlePropertyPage

CWnd → CDialog → COlePropertyPage

COlePropertyPage provides a way to display an ActiveX control's properties in a way that looks similar to a page on a property sheet. Controls may have more than one property page object, and ActiveX provides several stock property pages, to handle common properties such as color and font selection.

COleLinksDialog

CDialog → CCommonDialog → COleDialog → COleLinksDialog

A **COleLinksDialog** item displays the Edit Links dialog box, which provides the standard way to modify information about linked items. The class has only two member functions: a constructor, and **DoModal()**. It also has a single data member **m_el**, a structure whose members can be modified in order to control the appearance and operation of the dialog.

See also: **COleChangeSourceDialog**

COleUpdateDialog

CDialog → CCommonDialog → COleDialog → COleLinksDialog → COleUpdateDialog

COleUpdateDialog is a special case of the **COleLinksDialog**. It verifies the links to all the items in the document, and displays the Edit Links dialog if necessary. If no user action is necessary, no dialog will appear. It's usually called when a compound document is first opened.

Exception Handling Classes
COleException

CObject → CCmdTarget → CException → COleException

COleException inherits directly from **CException**, and is used when an exception is generated by a COM operation. The class includes a public data member that holds the status code indicating the reason for the exception. In general, you don't create **COleException** objects directly, but instead call **AfxThrowOleException()**.

See also: **COleDispatchException**

COleDispatchException

`CObject` → `CCmdTarget` → `CException` → `COleDispatchException`

COleDispatchException is the exception class used by Automation. Although used in fundamentally the same way as **COleException**, a **COleDispatchException** object contains more information about the error, which gets used by Automation controllers such as Visual Basic. The information supplied by this exception class includes:

- An application-specific error code
- An error description, such as 'Disk full'
- A help context that your application can use to provide additional information for the user
- The name of your application's help file
- The name of the application that generated the exception

As with **COleException**, you don't create exception objects directly, but instead call **AfxThrowOleDispatchException()**.

See also: **COleException**

Miscellaneous Classes

COleCmdUI

`CCmdUI` → `COleCmdUI`

COleCmdUI performs the same function for Active documents that **CCmdUI** does for standard MFC view objects. It possesses the same member functions as **CCmdUI**. A standard MFC application processes **UPDATE_COMMAND_UI** notifications, and assigns a **CCmdUI** object to each one. When an application is enabled for Active documents, it works with **UPDATE_OLE_COMMAND_UI** notifications and **COleCmdUI** objects.

COleCmdUI allows an Active document to process commands that originate in its container, and allows the container to process commands that originate in the Active document.

COleCurrency

COleCurrency provides a class that encapsulates the **CURRENCY** type, an 8-byte, two's-complement integer, which is scaled by 10,000 to give a fixed-point number with 15 digits to the left of the decimal point and 4 digits to the right. As its name implies, this data type is useful for calculations involving currency, and is one of the types that can be used in a **VARIANT** object.

426

COleDateTime & COleDateTimeSpan

The **COleDateTime** and **COleDateTimeSpan** classes are used to manipulate dates and times, and are analogous to MFC's standard **CTime** and **CTimeSpan** classes. **COleDateTime** encapsulates the **DATE** type used by Automation, one of the types that may be stored in a **VARIANT**.

The main improvements these classes give you over the standard ones lie in the areas of range and localization. The range of a **COleDateTime** date is from 1 January 100AD to 31 December 9999AD, whereas that for a **CTime** date is 1 January 1970 to 18 January 2038.

COleDateTime has a **Format()** member function which constructs a **CString** containing a textual representation of the date and time, based upon the current localization settings. It's thus possible, quite easily, to ensure that a date/time string will print correctly for different internationalization settings.

COleMessageFilter

CObject → **CCmdTarget** → **COleMessageFilter**

COleMessageFilter is used to handle concurrency in server, container and Automation applications. It can be made to make an application appear 'busy', so that calls from other applications are either rejected or retried later.

The **BeginBusyState()** and **EndBusyState()** members are used to control the busy state of the application, and the reply to calling applications is set by passing the **SetBusyReply()** function one of **SERVERCALL_ISHANDLED** (calls are accepted but may fail in processing), **SERVERCALL_REJECTED** (can't process calls, and there's no point waiting), or **SERVERCALL_RETRYLATER** (can't process calls right now, but if you'd care to try again later...).

You can control the timeout period after which the busy response will be triggered, and whether a dialog box will be displayed to warn the user or not. A **COleMessageFilter** object is allocated when the application is initialised, and a pointer to it can be retrieved using **AfxOleGetMessageFilter()**, although you seldom need to interact directly with this class.

See also: **COleBusyDialog**

COleSafeArray

The **COleSafeArray** class encapsulates the Automation **SAFEARRAY** data type. **SAFEARRAY**s allow clients to work with arrays of arbitrary size and dimension; they're called 'safe' because they include information on the array dimensions and bounds. The member functions of **COleSafeArray** are mainly wrappers for the Win32 API **SAFEARRAY** manipulation functions.

COleVariant

The **COleVariant** class is used as a wrapper for the **VARIANT** data type, which is widely used in Automation and with the DAO classes. Member functions are available to create **COleVariant**s from scratch, or to attach them to existing **VARIANT** objects, as well as to assign and test the equality of **COleVariant**s.

Operator functions for **LPVARIANT** and **LPCVARIANT** are provided, so that a **COleVariant** object can be passed wherever a **VARIANT** is required.

See also: **COleCurrency**, **COleDateTime**

CRichEditDoc

CDocument → COleDocument → COleLinkingDoc → COleServerDoc → CRichEditDoc

Rich edit controls (and hence MFC's rich edit view) can contain embedded OLE objects as well as formatted text. A **CRichEditDoc** object is used to maintain the list of OLE client items that are in MFC's rich edit view.

CRichEditDoc works together with **CRichEditView** to provide the server-side access to the rich text control. **CRichEditView** contains the text and its formatting, while **CRichEditDoc** maintains the list of items in the view.

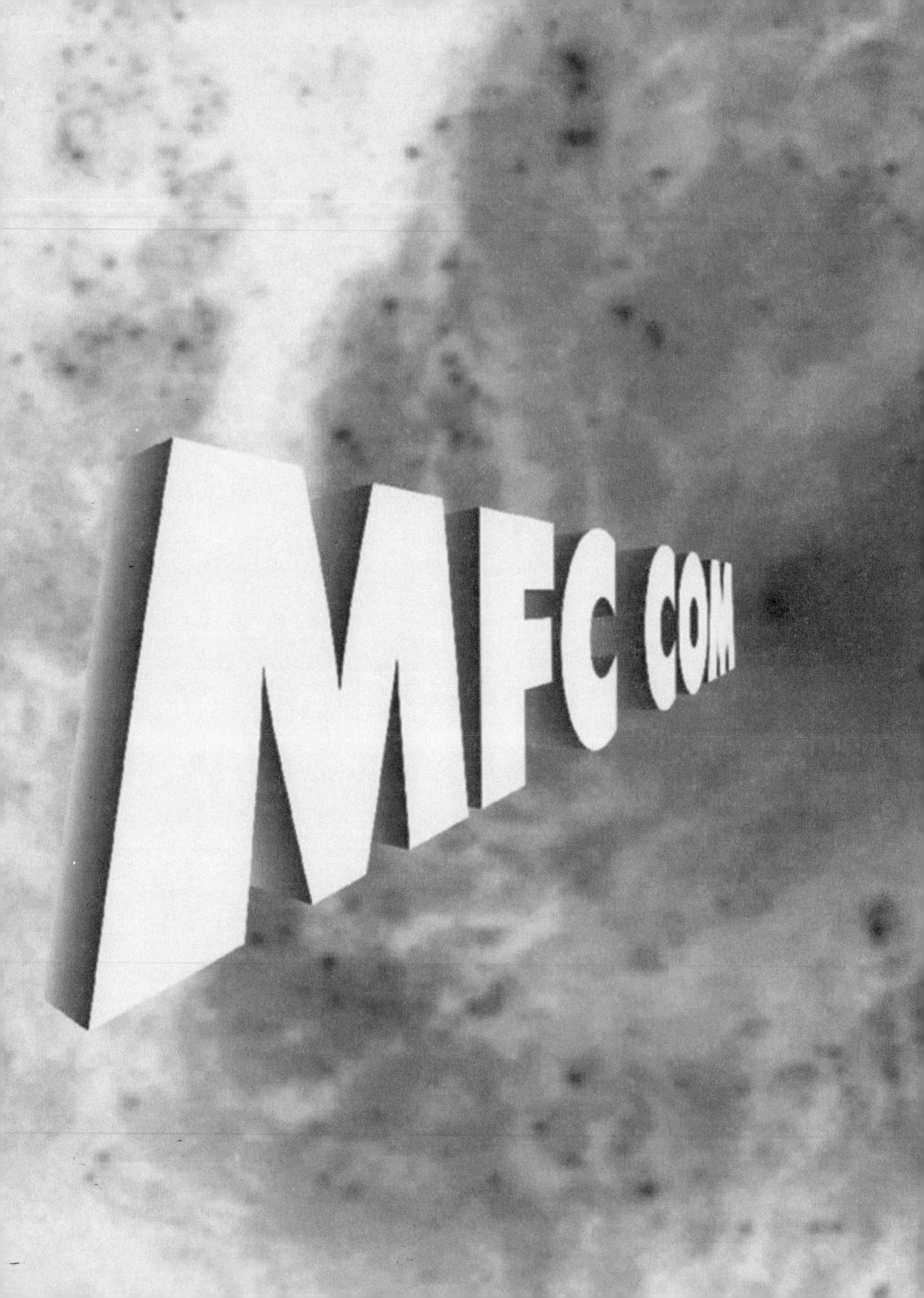
MFC COM

COM Data Types and Macros

Many of the macros and data types that support COM are defined in the **Objbase.h** header file, which gets included by many of the MFC COM and ActiveX header files, including **Afxconv.h** and **Afxdisp.h**. AppWizard includes these header files in your project's **Stdafx.h** file when you select COM-based options.

The **Objbase.h** file contains definitions for a number of different languages and platforms, so if you ever have cause to read it, make sure the sections you read are about C++ and Win32!

HRESULTs and SCODEs

We met the **HRESULT** data type in Chapter 2. In fact, despite what the **H** in its name might lead you to believe, it isn't actually a handle to anything. The best definition is probably the one Microsoft supplies in the **Winerror.h** header file:

```
// The return value of OLE APIs and methods is an HRESULT.
// This is not a handle to anything, but is merely a 32-bit value
// with several fields encoded in the value.  The parts of an
// HRESULT are shown below.
//
// Many of the macros and functions below were orginally defined to
// operate on SCODEs.  SCODEs are no longer used.  The macros are
// still present for compatibility and easy porting of Win16 code.
// Newly written code should use the HRESULT macros and functions.
```

So, the **HRESULT** is a 32-bit value that breaks down into four separate fields:

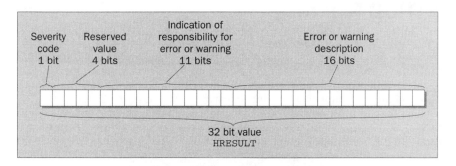

The comments about **SCODE** refer to a variable type of that name which is used for this same purpose on Win16 platforms; for compatibility's sake **HRESULT** and **SCODE** are synonymous under Win32, and so macros like **GetScode()** and **ResultFromScode()** do nothing on these systems.

All the **HRESULT** value definitions come later on in **Winerror.h**, and before them are the definitions of the macros used to test and manipulate **HRESULT** values, like **SUCCEEDED()**, **FAILED()**, and **IS_ERROR()**:

```
//
// Generic test for success on any status value (non-negative numbers
// indicate success).
//

#define SUCCEEDED(Status) ((HRESULT)(Status) >= 0)

//
// and the inverse
//

#define FAILED(Status) ((HRESULT)(Status)<0)

//
// Generic test for error on any status value.
//

#define IS_ERROR(Status) ((unsigned long)(Status) >> 31 == SEVERITY_ERROR)
```

While we're on the subject, there are several more useful macros that can be used to manipulate **HRESULT**s:

Macro	Purpose
HRESULT_CODE(hr)	Returns the code portion of the **HRESULT**
HRESULT_SEVERITY(hr)	Returns the severity portion of the **HRESULT**
HRESULT_FACILITY(hr)	Returns the facility portion of the **HRESULT**
HRESULT_FROM_NT(code)	Turns a Windows NT status code into an **HRESULT**
HRESULT_FROM_WIN32(code)	Turns a Win32 error code into an **HRESULT**

STDMETHOD Macros

Now I'll return to the theme of different languages and platforms that I broached before talking about **HRESULT**s, and consider the **STDMETHOD** macros: **STDMETHOD()**, **STDMETHOD_()**, **STDMETHODIMP()** and **STDMETHODIMP_()**. COM goes to some trouble to mask platform-dependent details (that's why there are so many definitions), and these macros are provided to help with declaring and implementing functions in COM classes in C++.

STDMETHOD() is a macro which declares a virtual function that returns an **HRESULT**. **STDMETHOD_()** does the same, except that it returns a type of your choosing. This means that the following declarations are equivalent:

```
STDMETHOD(Fred)(LPOLESTR pStr);
STDMETHOD_(HRESULT, Fred)(LPOLESTR pStr);
```

The **STDMETHODIMP()** and **STDMETHODIMP_()** macros are used when the functions are actually implemented, so we might code:

```
STDMETHODIMP CSomeClass::Fred(LPOLESTR pStr)
{
    // Body of function
}
```

Again, using the macro without a trailing underline character implies the return of an **HRESULT** value. If you look at the definitions in **Objbase.h**, you'll see exactly how this is achieved. Here are the relevant lines:

```
#define STDMETHODCALLTYPE          __stdcall
. . .
#define STDMETHODIMP               HRESULT STDMETHODCALLTYPE
#define STDMETHODIMP_(type)        type STDMETHODCALLTYPE
. . .
#define STDMETHOD(method)          virtual HRESULT STDMETHODCALLTYPE method
#define STDMETHOD_(type,method)    virtual type STDMETHODCALLTYPE method
#define PURE                       = 0
```

The **__stdcall** is simply the calling convention used for Win32 API calls, so

```
STDMETHOD(Fred)(LPOLESTR pStr);
```

expands to

```
virtual HRESULT __stdcall Fred(LPOLESTR pStr);
```

On other platforms and in other languages, this same declaration would be expanded quite differently; this is how platform-independence is achieved.

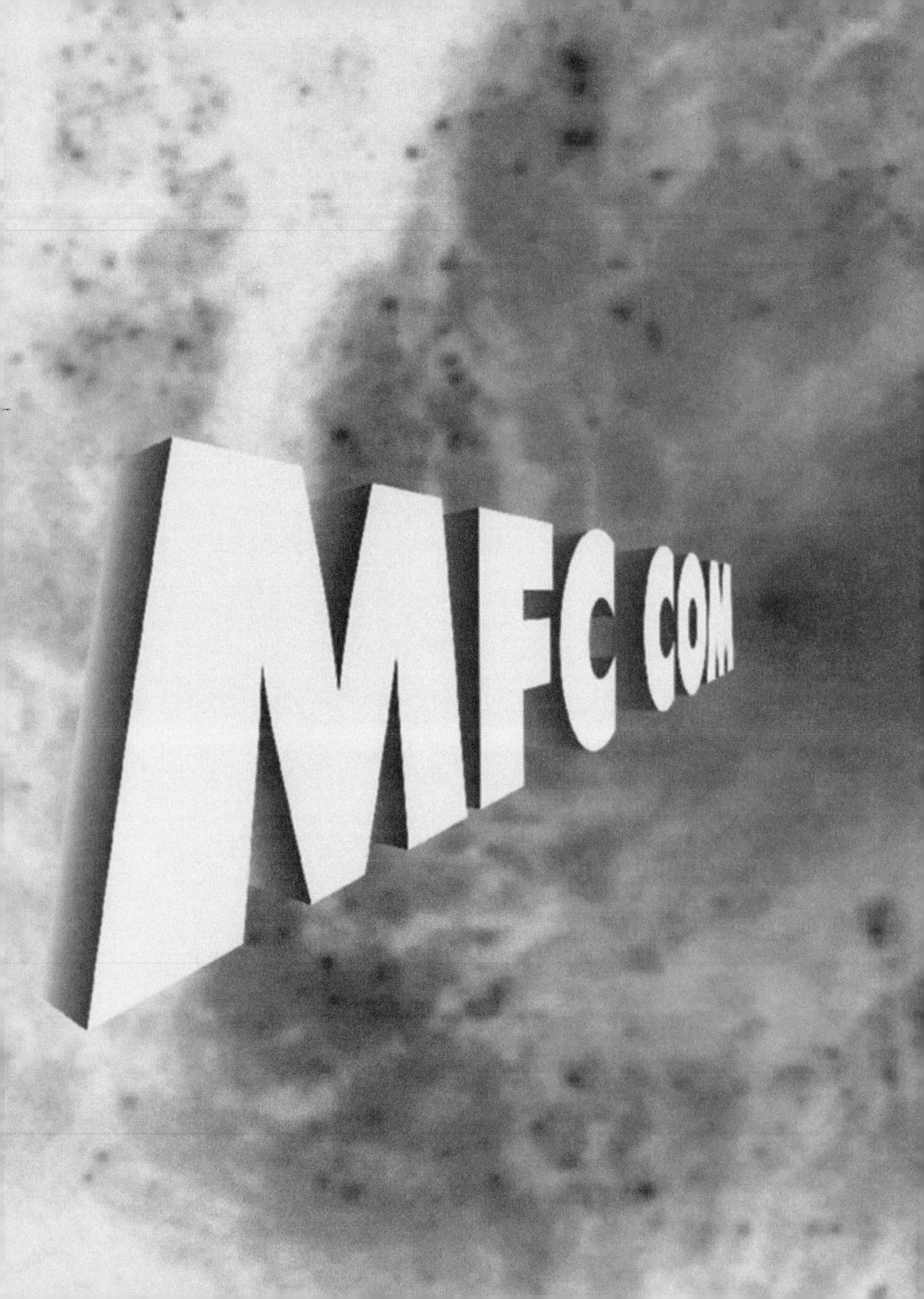
MFC COM

Advanced Automation Techniques

In this appendix I'm going to demonstrate how to implement two advanced features of Automation. These two features - dual interfaces and collections - are not supported by MFC, but it is often desirable to add them to Automation servers.

Since MFC and the Wizards don't support these features, we're going to have to plunge into COM coding in order to implement them. You'll need to have a basic understanding of how COM interfaces work and are implemented in MFC, so make sure you've read Chapters 2 and 3, and especially that you understand the sample applications, before going further - I'll be building on what you learned there.

If you're especially interested in collections, you'll need to read this appendix right through, as some concepts will be explained in the dual interfaces section and referred to when I come to talk about collections.

Dual Interfaces

Before we start, let's have a quick refresher: exactly what is a dual interface? The short answer is that it's an interface that supports both **IDispatch** and vtable binding, and Microsoft recommends that dual interface support be provided for all Automation objects. This rather begs the question why it hasn't been implemented in MFC, but I digress...

> *Although Microsoft provides a sample MFC project called* **Acdual** *on the Visual C++ CD, many people find the lack of explanation in the sample confusing. Dual interfaces can be used in ATL projects, but that doesn't help the MFC programmer who wants to use one.*

An Automation dispatch interface uses a two stage process to access a method: the client calls **IDispatch::Invoke()** using the dispID of the method, and **Invoke()** then performs the actual call. A standard interface, on the other hand, uses the vtable to access methods directly. Using dual interfaces has several advantages, including:

▶ Vtable information can appear in the type library, so tools can bind at compile time, as well as at runtime

▶ Accessing Automation methods using the vtable interface will be faster

▶ Controllers that use **IDispatch** will continue to work

▶ Dual interface support is required for compatibility with Visual Basic object support

With what you now know about COM and interfaces, most of what we need to do when adding the support should be at least *partly* familiar. Adding a dual interface will be longwinded, rather than difficult to understand.

Implementing a Dual Interface

The following sections show how to implement a dual interface, assuming you're using a normal AppWizard-generated project, with Automation added to the document class. The dual interface will end up delegating much of its functionality to the dispatch interface functions in the document class.

I'll assume for this discussion that we're using a project called **DA**, whose document class is called **CDADoc**, and that it implements some very simple Automation functionality:

▶ The class contains a **CString** data member called **m_str**, which is exposed as an Automation property called **String**

▶ The class implements an Automation method called **Square()**, which returns the square of its argument

Editing the ODL File

The first step is to edit the ODL file to add a new interface: the dual interface. You can actually get some of the work done for you by first entering your interface into the ODL file, and then letting MIDL create a header file, which will contain all the necessary GUIDs and interface descriptions.

Open the project's ODL file, and add a new interface statement that describes the dual interface:

```
[ uuid(your_uuid),
    oleautomation, dual
]
interface IMyDualInterface : IDispatch
{
};
```

There are a few things to note about this code:

▶ You'll need a new GUID for the new interface; you can use Guidgen to generate it, but it's best to wait until we start implementing the source code.

➤ You need to specify the **oleautomation** and **dual** attributes for the interface. The first attribute indicates that the interface is compatible with Automation, so the parameters and return types of its members will be of types that Automation recognizes (i.e. those which will fit into a **VARIANT**). The second indicates that this is a dual interface, and works together with a dispatch interface.

➤ The interface derives from **IDispatch**, because dual interfaces are a special case of dispatch interfaces. Note the inheritance in this case isn't like C++ inheritance, because we don't actually get access to any code at runtime. This is **interface inheritance**, in which we promise that we're going to implement all the methods and properties defined for **IDispatch**. It's very similar to Java's notion of interface inheritance.

We can now add methods and properties to the interface declaration. We'll inherit the **IDispatch** and **IUnknown** methods, so all we need to add are the custom ones. In the following example, I've added one property and one method to the interface, corresponding to the ones provided by the dispinterface:

```
[ uuid(your_uuid),
    oleautomation, dual
]
interface IMyDualInterface : IDispatch
{
    // Get and put for a single text property
    [propget, id(1)] HRESULT String([out,retval] BSTR* str);
    [propput, id(1)] HRESULT String([in] BSTR str);

    // A single method
    [id(2)] HRESULT Square([in]short val, [out,retval]long* result);
};
```

This isn't a standard ODL **dispinterface** description, so we have to enter things slightly differently. Note that we use get/put methods for the property, denoted by the **propget** and **propput** keywords. Input parameters are marked as **[in]**; output parameters are marked as **[out]**.

> All *interface properties and methods have to return an* **HRESULT**, *but by marking one of the parameters as* **[out,retval]** *we can indicate that the parameter should be treated like a return value by languages and tools that understand this attribute. This means that in Visual Basic we can say*
>
> ```
> Dim s As String
> s = myobj.String  ' Property get method
> ```
>
> *The* **[retval]** *parameter is used as Visual Basic's return value, while the* **HRESULT** *is used by Visual Basic to check that the operation worked.*

Once the interface has been defined, add it to the **coclass** definition, making it the default interface:

```
[ uuid(143D5390-DB27-11D0-90AE-00C0DF4A0272) ]
coclass Document
{
```

```
        dispinterface IDA;
        [default] interface IMyDualInterface;
};
```

This shows that our document class now has two interfaces, one of which (**IDA**) is a dispatch interface.

Generating a GUID for the Interface

We need to generate a GUID for the interface using Guidgen, and we need to insert it in two places. Start Guidgen, generate a GUID, and paste it into the ODL file:

```
[ uuid(C76C5F90-DC24-11d0-90AF-00C0DF4A0272),
    oleautomation, dual
]
interface IMyDualInterface : IDispatch
```

Generating the Header File

Running MIDL on the ODL file will generate the type library, and can also produce a header file with all the interface and GUID definitions, which will save us some programming later. You can get MIDL to produce a header file by selecting the ODL file in the Project Settings dialog, selecting the OLE Types tab and adding a filename to the Output header file name box. In this case, give the header file the name **Guids.h**.

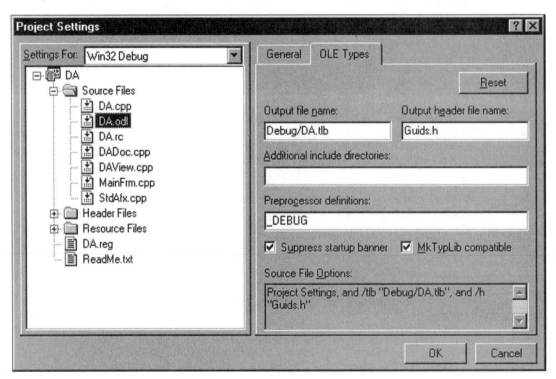

Once you dismiss this dialog, you can compile the ODL file and check that a new file called **Guids.h** has been created in the project directory. If you open this file, you'll see that the file contains all the interfaces and GUIDs necessary for the project. The code in the generated file may seem quite confusing because it includes a lot of things that you won't be used to (such as interface definitions that can be used from pure C). However, if you take a deep breath and take the time to examine its contents, you'll start to see some familiar features.

We're not too interested in manipulating this file directly, so just **#include** it in **StdAfx.h**. The GUID definitions in **Guids.h** are defined as **extern** to avoid multiple redefinitions, so we also need make sure that the GUIDs get defined without external linkage at least once. Fortunately, this is really easy to do. At the same time as MIDL produced the **Guids.h** file, it also produced another file called **DA_i.c**, which contains the definitions that we need. All we have to do is add this file to the project and change its project settings so that it doesn't use precompiled headers.

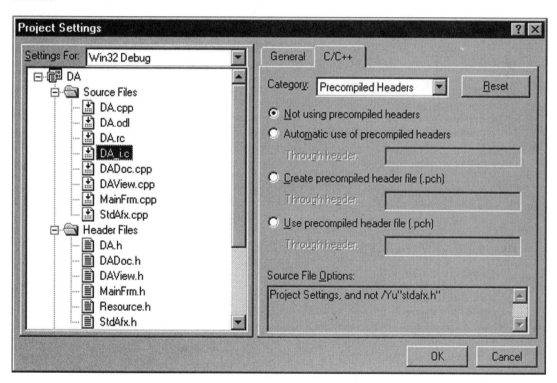

Adding the Interface Implementation

Now open the document class header file, and add a pair of **BEGIN** and **END_INTERFACE_PART()** macros to the class; it doesn't really matter where you put them, so I've put them after the **DECLARE_INTERFACE_MAP()** macro:

```
DECLARE_INTERFACE_MAP()
```

```
BEGIN_INTERFACE_PART(DualInt, IMyDualInterface)
END_INTERFACE_PART(DualInt)
};
```

The arguments to **BEGIN_INTERFACE_PART()** specify the name for the nested class (**DualInt**, which will give a nested class name of **XDualInt**), and the name of the interface which this is implementing (**IMyDualInterface**).

Now we need to add the declarations for the methods and properties that we're going to implement. Because we're inheriting from **IDispatch**, we have to declare all **IDispatch**'s methods; we don't have to declare those for **IUnknown**, because the macros provide those for us. In either case, when we come to implement these methods we can just delegate the hard work to the outer **CCmdTarget**-derived class.

Start with the definitions for the **IDispatch** methods. As usual, this will include **GetTypeInfoCount()**, **GetTypeInfo()**, **GetIDsOfNames()** and **Invoke()**:

```
DECLARE_INTERFACE_MAP()

BEGIN_INTERFACE_PART(DualInt, IMyDualInterface)
    // IDispatch's methods
    STDMETHOD(GetTypeInfoCount)(UINT FAR* pctinfo);
    STDMETHOD(GetTypeInfo)(UINT itinfo, LCID lcid,
                        ITypeInfo FAR* FAR* pptinfo);
    STDMETHOD(GetIDsOfNames)(REFIID riid,
                            OLECHAR FAR* FAR* rgszNames,
                            UINT cNames, LCID lcid,
                            DISPID FAR* rgdispid);
    STDMETHOD(Invoke)(DISPID dispidMember, REFIID riid,
                    LCID lcid, WORD wFlags,
                    DISPPARAMS FAR* pdispparams,
                    VARIANT FAR* pvarResult,
                    EXCEPINFO FAR* pexcepinfo,
                    UINT FAR* puArgErr);
END_INTERFACE_PART(DualInt)
};
```

We can then add declarations for our own Automation methods and properties. Note that every entry in the ODL file which has a **[propput]** or **[propget]** attribute needs to have a '**put_**' or '**get_**' function defined to implement it.

```
BEGIN_INTERFACE_PART(DualInt, IMyDualInterface)

    // IDispatch's methods as before

    // Automation properties and methods
    STDMETHOD(get_String) (BSTR* retstr);
    STDMETHOD(put_String) (BSTR str);
    STDMETHOD(Square) (short val, long* result);
END_INTERFACE_PART(DualInt)
```

Writing the Interface Code

Once the definition of the interface is complete, we then need to write the implementation code, adding it to the document class source file.

The first step is to provide the **IUnknown** methods for the implementation class:

```
STDMETHODIMP_(ULONG) CDADoc::XDualInt::AddRef()
```

```
{
   METHOD_PROLOGUE(CDADoc, DualInt)
   return pThis->ExternalAddRef();
}


STDMETHODIMP_(ULONG) CDADoc::XDualInt::Release()
{
   METHOD_PROLOGUE(CDADoc, DualInt)
   return pThis->ExternalRelease();
}


STDMETHODIMP CDADoc::XDualInt::QueryInterface(REFIID iid, LPVOID* ppvObj)
{
   METHOD_PROLOGUE(CDADoc, DualInt)
   return pThis->ExternalQueryInterface(&iid, ppvObj);
}
```

As we discussed in Chapter 3, classes derived from **CCmdTarget** can delegate their **IUnknown** functionality back to **CCmdTarget** using the 'External' functions. The **METHOD_PROLOGUE()** macro sets up the **pThis** pointer to point to the enclosing parent class object.

Once those are in place, we can provide the **IDispatch** functions. The parent class **CDADoc** has already implemented a dispatch interface, so we can delegate the dispatch interface functionality back to the enclosing class. This is done by using the **GetIDispatch()** function to get a pointer to the enclosing class' dispatch interface, and then calling the appropriate member:

```
STDMETHODIMP CDADoc::XDualInt::GetTypeInfoCount(UINT FAR* pctinfo)
{
   METHOD_PROLOGUE(CDADoc, DualInt)
   LPDISPATCH lpDispatch = pThis->GetIDispatch(FALSE);
   ASSERT(lpDispatch != NULL);
   return lpDispatch->GetTypeInfoCount(pctinfo);
}


STDMETHODIMP CDADoc::XDualInt::GetTypeInfo(UINT itinfo, LCID lcid,
                                           ITypeInfo FAR* FAR* pptinfo)
{
   METHOD_PROLOGUE(CDADoc, DualInt)
   LPDISPATCH lpDispatch = pThis->GetIDispatch(FALSE);
   ASSERT(lpDispatch != NULL);
   return lpDispatch->GetTypeInfo(itinfo, lcid, pptinfo);
}


STDMETHODIMP CDADoc::XDualInt::GetIDsOfNames(
   REFIID riid, OLECHAR FAR* FAR* rgszNames, UINT cNames,
   LCID lcid, DISPID FAR* rgdispid)
{
   METHOD_PROLOGUE(CDADoc, DualInt)
   LPDISPATCH lpDispatch = pThis->GetIDispatch(FALSE);
   ASSERT(lpDispatch != NULL);
   return lpDispatch->GetIDsOfNames(riid, rgszNames, cNames, lcid, rgdispid);
}


STDMETHODIMP CDADoc::XDualInt::Invoke(
   DISPID dispidMember, REFIID riid, LCID lcid, WORD wFlags,
   DISPPARAMS FAR* pdispparams, VARIANT FAR* pvarResult,
   EXCEPINFO FAR* pexcepinfo, UINT FAR* puArgErr)
```

```
{
    METHOD_PROLOGUE(CDADoc, DualInt)
    LPDISPATCH lpDispatch = pThis->GetIDispatch(FALSE);
    ASSERT(lpDispatch != NULL);
    return lpDispatch->Invoke(dispidMember, riid, lcid, wFlags,
                              pdispparams, pvarResult, pexcepinfo, puArgErr);
}
```

Finally, we can get around to implementing our own functions.

```
STDMETHODIMP CDADoc::XDualInt::get_String(BSTR* retstr)
{
    METHOD_PROLOGUE(CDADoc, DualInt)

    // Copy from a document data member, a CString called m_str, to the BSTR.
    *retstr = pThis->m_str.AllocSysString();

    // Set the HRESULT for the return code
    return NOERROR;
}

STDMETHODIMP CDADoc::XDualInt::put_String(BSTR str)
{
    METHOD_PROLOGUE(CDADoc, DualInt)

    // Copy BSTR to a document data member, a CString called m_str
    pThis->m_str = str;

    // Set the HRESULT for the return code
    return NOERROR;
}

STDMETHODIMP CDADoc::XDualInt::Square(short val, long* result)
{
    METHOD_PROLOGUE(CDADoc, DualInt)
    *result = pThis->Square(val);

    return NOERROR;
}
```

Updating the Interface Map

A standard automated MFC document class will only implement one interface - **IDispatch** - so there will only be one entry in the interface map:

```
BEGIN_INTERFACE_MAP(CDADoc, CDocument)
    INTERFACE_PART(CDADoc, IID_IDA, Dispatch)
END_INTERFACE_MAP()
```

We need to modify the map to include the new interface, and in order to do that, we add a new **INTERFACE_PART** macro to the interface map:

```
BEGIN_INTERFACE_MAP(CDADoc, CDocument)
    INTERFACE_PART(CDADoc, IID_IDA, Dispatch)
    INTERFACE_PART(CDADoc, IID_IMyDualInterface, DualInt)
END_INTERFACE_MAP()
```

Our document class now implements two interfaces, the first being a standard dispatch interface, and the second implementing **IMyDualInterface** via a nested class called **XDualInt**. The interface ID for **IMyDualInterface** is picked up from the **Guids.h** file.

Registering the Type Library

It would be useful if our application registered its type library automatically, but this isn't done by the default AppWizard-generated code. We can simply add code to the application's **InitInstance()** function, so that the type library will be registered each time the application runs.

We've already had a GUID for the library generated for us when we ran MIDL to generate the header file. If you look through the **Guids.h** file, you'll see the entry:

```
DEFINE_GUID(LIBID_DA,0x143D5391L,0xDB27,0x11D0,0x90,0xAE,0x00,0xC0,0xDF,0x4A,0x02,0x72);
```

Now modify **InitInstance()** to include a call to **AfxOleRegisterTypeLib()**. You'll need to include **<afxctl.h>** to get this function:

```
m_server.UpdateRegistry(OAT_DISPATCH_OBJECT);
COleObjectFactory::UpdateRegistryAll();
```

```
AfxOleRegisterTypeLib(AfxGetInstanceHandle(),   // Instance handle
                      LIBID_DA,                 // Type library ID
                      _T("DA.tlb"));            // Type library name
```

```
// Dispatch commands specified on the command line
if (!ProcessShellCommand(cmdInfo))
    return FALSE;
```

The function gets information about the filename and location of the library from the instance handle and name parameters, and registers it using the library ID.

Testing the Dual Interface

We've now added a dual interface to our application, but how should we test it? The best way to verify it is to write a test project:

▶ Create a standard MFC dialog-based application

▶ Add a call to **AfxOleInit()** in the application's **InitInstance()**

▶ Add a **#include** statement to **StdAfx.h** for the **Guids.h** file that we generated from the server

▶ Add the **DA_i.c** file to the client project, changing its settings so that it doesn't make use of precompiled headers.

With that done, you're all ready to write a bit of code to test the server. Here's the code that I wrote to test it:

```
void CClientDlg::OnDoit()
{
    // Declare a pointer to our dual interface
    IMyDualInterface* pInterface = NULL;
```

```
    // Now create the instance and get a pointer to the Document
    if (FAILED(CoCreateInstance(CLSID_Document, NULL, CLSCTX_SERVER,
                                IID_IMyDualInterface, (void**)&pInterface)))
    {
        AfxMessageBox(_T("CoCreateInstance() failed"));
        return;
    }

    CString str("Testing the dual interface");
    BSTR bstr = str.AllocSysString();
    pInterface->put_String(bstr);
    SysFreeString(bstr);

    long res = 0;
    pInterface->Square(2, &res);

    BSTR bstr2;
    pInterface->get_String(&bstr2);
    CString strRet = bstr2;
    SysFreeString(bstr2);

    AfxMessageBox(strRet);

    pInterface->Release();
}
```

Collections

And now on to our second topic: Automation collections. Collections are part of Microsoft's recommended structure for Automation-enabled applications. If a server holds a number of items of the same type (documents, strings, shapes or whatever), it should implement a collection to enable clients to work with them in a consistent way. This is a general mechanism, and is provided by adding certain standard Automation methods to the class that holds the objects:

- **Count()** returns the number of objects in the collection
- **Item()** provides access to elements in the collection
- **Add()** is an optional method to add a new item to the collection
- **Remove()** is an optional method to delete an object from the collection
- **_NewEnum()** is an optional method that returns an enumerator for your collection

The **Item()**, **Add()** and **Remove()** methods can take any parameters that you think are necessary to identify items in the collection. Commonly, collections allow items to be accessed by an integer value or a string value, but it's entirely up to you if you want to provide access to your items using both of these methods. **Item()** is usually the default method of the object. This allows Visual Basic programmers to refer to elements in your collection using array-style syntax, so **coll(1)** is equivalent to **coll.Item(1)**.

The **_NewEnum()** method is designed to allow Visual Basic programmers to iterate over a collection using the **For Each...Next** syntax:

```
Set People = Department.Employees
For Each Person in People
   Print Person.Name
Next
```

This provides the Visual Basic programmer with a friendlier and less error-prone way to iterate over a collection of objects than using array indices. The mechanism is implemented through the COM **IEnumVARIANT** interface. This interface *could* be implemented directly by the collection object, but it is invariably implemented using a separate class. This enables more than one enumerator object to be active at one time, which makes it unnecessary to add synchronization code to the enumerator, and simplifies the programming. Besides those inherited from **IUnknown**, **IEnumVARIANT** has the following methods:

> **Next()**
>
> **Skip()**
>
> **Reset()**
>
> **Clone()**

These are the same methods that you can find in any **IEnum*xxxx*** interface (such as **IEnumString** or **IEnumUnknown**), specialized to deal with **VARIANT**s. We'll examine this interface more closely a little later in the appendix when we implement it in one of our own objects.

In summary, to implement a full-featured collection mechanism for an MFC Automation server, we need to do three main things:

> ▶ Provide a class that implements the standard collection methods (our collection class)
>
> ▶ Provide a class that implements the **IEnumVARIANT** interface (our enumerator class)
>
> ▶ Implement **_NewEnum()** in the collection class so that it returns a new instance of the enumerator class on each call

The last two of these are of most use to Visual Basic clients, while the first is important to any client.

Creating a Sample Project

Let's create a new project to see how all this collection stuff works in practice. Start with a new project called **Coll**. This project should be created using the MFC AppWizard (exe) and you should create it as an SDI application with Automation support enabled.

We'll treat our document as a collection of strings. Since we're lying and cheating our way through this, we won't waste our time getting strings into our document through the user interface. Instead, we'll just add a **CStringArray** member to the document class and populate it in the constructor.

```
class CCollDoc : public CDocument
{
   //...
public:
   CStringArray m_strings;
```

```
    //...
};

CCollDoc::CCollDoc()
{
    // Save some strings
    m_strings.Add(_T("String One"));
    m_strings.Add(_T("String Two"));
    m_strings.Add(_T("Third String"));
    m_strings.Add(_T("Last One"));

    EnableAutomation();

    AfxOleLockApp();
}
```

Implementing IEnumVARIANT

Now we need to create a class that will implement the **IEnumVARIANT** interface for the strings
in the document class. Create a new header file called **EnumData.h** and add the following text
to it:

```
#if !defined(_ENUMDATA_H_)
#define _ENUMDATA_H_

#include "CollDoc.h"

///////////////////////////////////////////////////////////////////////////
// CEnumData command target

class CEnumData : public CCmdTarget
{
public:
    CEnumData(CCollDoc* pDoc);

// Implementation
protected:
    virtual ~CEnumData();
    CCollDoc* m_pOwner;
    int m_current;

    DECLARE_INTERFACE_MAP()

public:
    BEGIN_INTERFACE_PART(EnumVARIANT, IEnumVARIANT)
        STDMETHOD (Next) (unsigned long celt, VARIANT FAR* rgvar,
                          unsigned long FAR* pceltFetched);
        STDMETHOD (Skip) (unsigned long celt);
        STDMETHOD (Reset) ();
        STDMETHOD (Clone) (IEnumVARIANT FAR* FAR* ppenum);
    END_INTERFACE_PART(EnumVARIANT)

};

///////////////////////////////////////////////////////////////////////////
#endif // !defined(_ENUMDATA_H_)
```

The important things to note here are:

- The class constructor needs to take a pointer to its owning document and store it away in **m_pOwner**, so that it can use it to access the document data

- We need an integer data member, **m_current**, to point to the current entry as the client uses the class to iterate through the list

- The **IEnumVARIANT** interface is declared using the **_INTERFACE_PART** macros, so it will be implemented by a nested class called **XEnumVARIANT**

Now create a file called **EnumData.cpp**, save it and add it to the project. We'll use this file to store the implementation of **CEnumData**. Start by adding the following to the top of the file:

```
// EnumData.cpp : implementation file

#include "stdafx.h"
#include "Coll.h"
#include "EnumData.h"

/////////////////////////////////////////////////////////////////////////////
// CEnumData

CEnumData::CEnumData(CCollDoc* pDoc)
{
    m_pOwner = pDoc;
    m_current = -1;
    EnableAutomation();
    AfxOleLockApp();
}

CEnumData::~CEnumData()
{
    AfxOleUnlockApp();
}

BEGIN_INTERFACE_MAP(CEnumData, CCmdTarget)
    INTERFACE_PART(CEnumData, IID_IEnumVARIANT, EnumVARIANT)
END_INTERFACE_MAP()
```

Here we've just added the **#include** statements that you'll need, code for the constructor and destructor, and the interface map for the class. The calls to **AfxOleLockApp()** and **AfxOleUnlockApp()** in the constructor and destructor just ensure that the server stays around as long as any clients have outstanding references on these enumeration objects.

Implementing the IUnknown Functions

Now we have to provide the code for the interface functions including, of course, **IUnknown**. We'll start with the standard implementations of **AddRef()**, **Release()** and **QueryInterface()**:

```
STDMETHODIMP_(ULONG) CEnumData::XEnumVARIANT::AddRef()
{
    METHOD_PROLOGUE(CEnumData, EnumVARIANT)
    return pThis->ExternalAddRef();
}
```

```
STDMETHODIMP_(ULONG) CEnumData::XEnumVARIANT::Release()
{
    METHOD_PROLOGUE(CEnumData, EnumVARIANT)
    return pThis->ExternalRelease();
}

STDMETHODIMP CEnumData::XEnumVARIANT::QueryInterface(REFIID iid, LPVOID* ppvObj)
{
    METHOD_PROLOGUE(CEnumData, EnumVARIANT)
    return pThis->ExternalQueryInterface(&iid, ppvObj);
}
```

> *If you're going to implement several such interfaces, it would now be worth placing this code into a macro, since these functions are the same for all the interfaces you're likely to write. In fact, Microsoft does this in the* **Acdual** *sample, which you'll find on the Visual C++ CD, so you may wish to use or modify that one.*

Implementing the Interface Functions

Now we'll look at the four **IEnumVARIANT** functions themselves. We'll take them one by one, discussing what they're for, and showing how they might be coded up for this application.

The first, **IEnumVARIANT::Reset()**, is simply used to reset the object to point back at the start of the collection again. Note that the **IEnumxxxx**-type interfaces don't offer a **Previous()** function, so **Reset()** is particularly important, because we can't move backwards through the collection.

For our example, we set the current item pointer back to zero to point at the first string in the list, or to -1 if there are no strings currently stored. Note that since we're referring to a member of a class referenced by a pointer in the enclosing class, the syntax gets a little obscure.

```
STDMETHODIMP CEnumData::XEnumVARIANT::Reset()
{
    METHOD_PROLOGUE(CEnumData, EnumVARIANT)

    int nStrings = pThis->m_pOwner->m_strings.GetSize();
    if (nStrings == 0)
    {
        // No strings, so set to -1 and return error value
        pThis->m_current = -1;
        return S_FALSE;
    }

    pThis->m_current = 0;
    return NOERROR;
}
```

The second method, **IEnumVARIANT::Next()**, is used to retrieve an item. The function needs to get the item from the document, and package it up into a **VARIANT** for returning to the caller.

Here's the C++ prototype of the function, showing the argument types:

```
Next(unsigned long nElems, VARIANT FAR* rgvars, unsigned long FAR* pFetched);
```

The first argument, **nElems**, determines the number of items to be retrieved. In this case we will only allow retrieval of a single item at a time, although you should really return an array of values.

The second argument, **rgvars**, is a pointer to an array of **VARIANT**s in which the data is to be returned. This array must be at least **nElems** in size. The third argument, **pFetched**, returns the number of items returned, or **NULL**.

Here's the code for this function:

```
STDMETHODIMP CEnumData::XEnumVARIANT::Next(unsigned long nElems,
                     VARIANT FAR* rgvars, unsigned long FAR* pFetched)
{
    METHOD_PROLOGUE(CEnumData, EnumVARIANT)

    // Check the number of elements
    if (nElems != 1)
        return E_INVALIDARG;

    // Initialize count
    *pFetched = 0;

    // Get the item. Check the array has some strings, and that
    // we're within range
    int nStrings = pThis->m_pOwner->m_strings.GetSize();

    if (nStrings == 0 || pThis->m_current > nStrings-1)
    {
        pThis->m_current = -1;
        return S_FALSE;
    }

    // If the current pointer is -1, get the first item
    if (pThis->m_current == -1)
        pThis->m_current = 0;

    // Get the string
    CString s = pThis->m_pOwner->m_strings.GetAt(pThis->m_current++);

    // Make the return value. Initialize the VARIANT, then convert
    // the string to a BSTR, and store it in the return array
    VariantInit(&rgvars[0]);
    rgvars[0].vt = VT_BSTR;
    rgvars[0].bstrVal = s.AllocSysString();

    *pFetched = 1;
    return NOERROR;
}
```

The **m_current** variable keeps track of where we are in the array; if it's unset, we return the first item, and if it goes out of bounds, we reset it. Note that before returning the string, we first initialize the **VARIANT** by a call to the **VariantInit()** API function.

The **IEnumVARIANT::Skip()** function simply advances the **m_current** pointer by a number of elements.

```
STDMETHODIMP CEnumData::XEnumVARIANT::Skip(unsigned long nElems)
{
    METHOD_PROLOGUE(CEnumData, EnumVARIANT)

    if (pThis->m_current > -1)
        pThis->m_current += nElems;

    int nStrings = pThis->m_pOwner->m_strings.GetSize();
    if (pThis->m_current > nStrings)
    {
        pThis->m_current = nStrings;
        return S_FALSE;
    }

    return NOERROR;
}
```

Finally, the **IEnumVARIANT::Clone()** function creates a copy of the enumerator object, and returns a pointer to it.

```
STDMETHODIMP CEnumData::XEnumVARIANT::Clone(IEnumVARIANT FAR* FAR* ppenum)
{
    METHOD_PROLOGUE(CEnumData, EnumVARIANT)

    // Create a new CEnumData object, owned by the same document as
    // this one
    CEnumData* pNew = new CEnumData(pThis->m_pOwner);

    if (pNew == NULL)
        return E_OUTOFMEMORY;

    // Copy the current position
    pNew->m_current = pThis->m_current;

    return NOERROR;
}
```

Adding Document Functions

That completes our implementation of the **IEnumVARIANT** interface. In order to complete the application, we must add the standard collection functionality needed by a server. In this case, we'll limit ourselves to the **_NewEnum()** method, and the **Count** and **Item** properties.

Adding the Count Property

The **Count** property is very simple to implement. Just use ClassWizard to add a new Automation property that returns a **short** and set the property to use Get/Set methods. Since this property is read-only, delete the Set function from the dialog and then click OK, so you're left with a single function that you can implement like this:

```
short CCollDoc::GetCount()
{
    // Return the size of the string collection
    return m_strings.GetSize();
}
```

Adding the Item Property

Item is constructed similarly, as a read-only property. In this case, we return a **BSTR** to represent the string, and the property Get function takes an argument to specify the string that should be returned. The argument is, rather unhelpfully, passed in as a **VARIANT**, so we have to try to get the string index from the **VARIANT**. If we don't succeed, we pass back an empty string.

```
BSTR CCollDoc::GetItem(const VARIANT FAR& vtIdx)
{
    CString strResult;
    long index = -1L;

    // If the VARIANT is of the right type, extract the index, else
    // try to convert it
    if (vtIdx.vt == VT_I4)
        index = vtIdx.lVal;
    else
    {
        VARIANT vtTemp;
        VariantInit(&vtTemp);
        HRESULT hr = VariantChangeType(&vtTemp, (VARIANT FAR*)&vtIdx, 0, VT_I4);
        if (SUCCEEDED(hr))
            index = vtTemp.lVal;
    }

    // If we have a valid index, get the string
    if (index > -1L && index < m_strings.GetSize())
    {
        strResult = m_strings.GetAt(index);
    }

    return strResult.AllocSysString();
}
```

We can also usefully make **Item** the 'default property', meaning that this property will be used when no other is specified. You can do this by simply selecting the De̱fault property check box at the bottom of ClassWizard's Automation page.

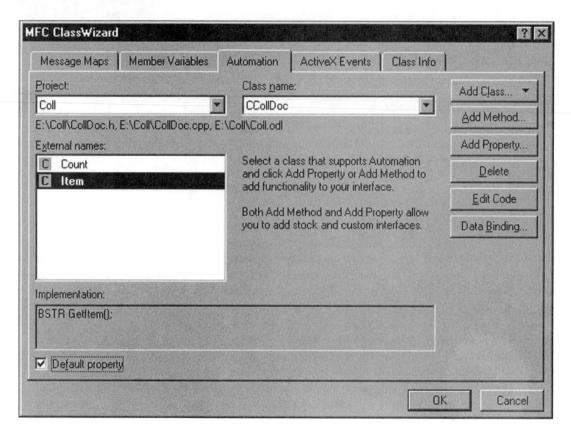

Adding _NewEnum

The final task is to implement the **_NewEnum()** function. This function is one of the stock Automation functions, and it should be given a **dispID** of -4. You'll find that ClassWizard isn't too happy about allowing you to add a method called **_NewEnum**, so you'll need to add this method by hand.

Add the following entry for **_NewEnum()** to the **IColl** dispinterface in the ODL file. It should be in the **methods** section, but outside the ClassWizard comments:

```
methods:
    // NOTE - ClassWizard will maintain method information here.
    //    Use extreme caution when editing this section.
    //{{AFX_ODL_METHOD(CCollDoc)
    [id(2), propget] BSTR Item(VARIANT vtIdx);
    [id(0), propget] BSTR _Item(VARIANT vtIdx);
    //}}AFX_ODL_METHOD
    [id(-4), propget, restricted] LPUNKNOWN _NewEnum();
```

Note the use of the correct dispID, and the **restricted** keyword, which indicates that this function shouldn't show up in type library browsing tools. The function creates a new object that supports **IEnumVARIANT**, and returns a pointer to its **IUnknown** interface.

Now we'll add the function to the source code. Add an entry to the document class header file, once again placing it outside the ClassWizard comment block:

```
// Generated OLE dispatch map functions
//{{AFX_DISPATCH(CCollDoc)
afx_msg short GetCount();
afx_msg BSTR GetItem(const VARIANT FAR& vtIdx);
//}}AFX_DISPATCH
afx_msg LPUNKNOWN _NewEnum();

DECLARE_DISPATCH_MAP()
```

Manually add an entry to the dispatch map in the document's source file, as follows:

```
BEGIN_DISPATCH_MAP(CCollDoc, CDocument)
//{{AFX_DISPATCH_MAP(CCollDoc)
DISP_PROPERTY_EX(CCollDoc, "Count", GetCount, SetNotSupported, VT_I2)
    DISP_PROPERTY_PARAM(CCollDoc, "Item", GetItem, SetNotSupported, VT_BSTR,
VTS_VARIANT)
    DISP_DEFVALUE(CCollDoc, "Item")
    //}}AFX_DISPATCH_MAP
DISP_PROPERTY_EX_ID(CCollDoc, "_NewEnum", -4, _NewEnum, SetNotSupported,
VT_UNKNOWN)
END_DISPATCH_MAP()
```

The **DISP_PROPERTY_EX_ID()** macro is used to add an entry for a property where you wish to specify the dispID explicitly, rather than letting MFC handle it.

Now we can implement **_NewEnum()** itself (also in the document's source file):

```
LPUNKNOWN CCollDoc::_NewEnum()
{
   CEnumData* pData = new CEnumData(this);

   if (pData)
   {
      pData->m_xEnumVARIANT.Reset();
      return &pData->m_xEnumVARIANT;
   }
   else
      return NULL;
}
```

What's going on here? First, we create a new **CEnumData** object, owned by this document. The object will have a nested object implementing **IEnumVARIANT**; the nested object will be called **m_xEnumVARIANT** (because of the names we chose when implementing the class), and it will have a **Reset()** function, which we call in order to reset the counter to the start of the collection. We return the address of the object, which is fine because we know that the **IUnknown** methods start at the beginning of the object, so the object and **IUnknown** addresses coincide.

Testing the Collection

We need to test the collection, and the simplest way to do it is to use a simple Visual Basic application. The test project has a very simple form:

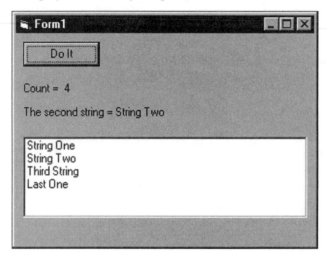

The click handler for the button does all the work:

```
Option Explicit

Private Sub Command1_Click()
On Error GoTo err_Unexpected

    ' Create the document object
    Dim strings As Object
    Set strings = CreateObject("Coll.Document")

    ' Get the count
    StringCountLabel.Caption = "Count = " & Str(strings.Count)

    ' Get an individual item
    StringLabel.Caption = "The second string = " & strings(1)

    Dim thing As Variant
    ' Use For Each to fill the listbox
    For Each thing In strings
      StringList.AddItem thing
    Next thing
Exit Sub

err_Unexpected:
    MsgBox Err.Description, vbOKOnly, "Error!"

End Sub
```

When the button is pressed, the application starts the server, and then tries three actions. First it uses the **Count** property to display the number of strings. It then retrieves one of the strings by index, using the default **Item** property. Finally, the **For Each** construct is used to iterate over the collection of strings, adding each one to the listbox.

Summary

We've seen how to add two of the more advanced Automation features to MFC programs, by doing the COM-level coding ourselves. Dual interfaces provide an efficient way for Automation clients to access methods and properties, and while these are directly supported by ATL, we need to do some extra work to add them to our MFC objects. Collections provide a useful way for Automation clients to manipulate collections of objects, and are especially useful for Visual Basic programmers.

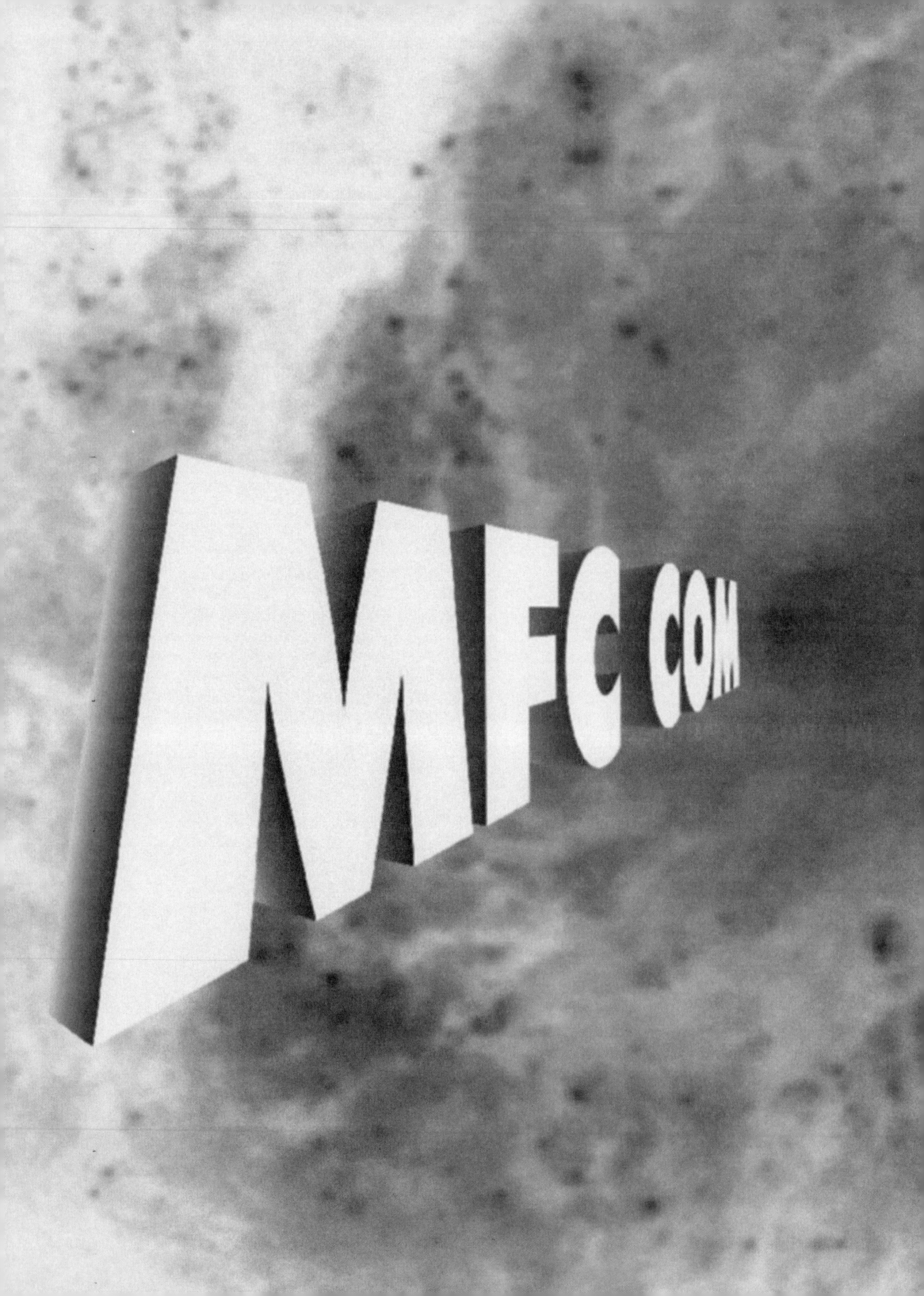
MFC COM

Win32 Memory Management

In general, using MFC frees you from having to know very much about the underlying Windows API. In particular, MFC provides C++ classes which do all the low-level Win32 memory management for us, so we never normally need to deal with functions such as **GlobalAlloc()**, which were well known to C programmers in the days before C++ class libraries like MFC were available.

Unfortunately, COM works at the level of the Windows API, and when you want to (or have to) code at the COM level, you'll find yourself coming across memory management concepts and techniques which may be unfamiliar. This appendix gives you a very quick overview of what Win32 memory management is all about.

> *If you want to know more, consult a Win32 programming textbook, such as 'Win32 Programming', by Rector and Newcomer [Addison-Wesley Developers Press, 1997]*

Memory Handles

When you ask Windows for a block of memory, using one of the Win32 functions I'll come to in a moment, you'll be returned a **memory handle**. Doubtless you'll have already come across **window handles** (**HWND**s, such as the **m_hWnd** member of the **CWnd** class), and maybe others too, like font and menu handles. In fact, Windows keeps track of *all* its resources using handles, and memory is no exception.

When you want to use the memory, you 'lock' the handle to obtain a pointer, use it, and then free the pointer and unlock the handle when you've finished. Why the complexity? Why not just use a pointer?

Originally, handles were used so that Windows could shift the location of the actual memory around in order to keep memory usage efficient. When you needed to use the memory, you locked the handle, and that made Windows fix the position of the block. Windows gave you back a pointer to the block, which you could use; when you'd finished, you unlocked the handle, and that told Windows that it could start moving the memory around again. Needless to say, it was *very* risky using your pointer once you'd unlocked the handle.

Allocating Memory

Memory is requested using the **GlobalAlloc()** API function, like this:

```
HGLOBAL hG;
hG = GlobalAlloc(flags, size);
```

The **size** argument is the number of bytes being requested, while **flags** describes the attributes of the memory block required. If the function fails, zero will be returned.

Note the type used to store the handle: **HGLOBAL**. You'll also see a **GLOBALHANDLE** type used, and in fact both of these are **typedef**s for the basic **HANDLE** type, which in turn is a **typedef** for a **void*** pointer.

> *Just about all* **Global** *functions have a* **Local** *equivalent, such as* **LocalAlloc()**.
> *Under 16-bit Windows, the different functions were used to allocate 'near' and 'far' memory. Under Win32 there is no such distinction and these functions are equivalent, the two names being kept on for compatibility's sake.*

The **flags** can be a combination of any the following values:

Flag	Meaning
GMEM_FIXED	Allocates a fixed block of memory, and the handle returned is a **void*** pointer
GMEM_ZEROINIT	Zeros out the memory
GPTR	A combination of **GMEM_FIXED** and **GMEM_ZEROINIT**
GMEM_MOVEABLE	Allocates a moveable block; the handle has to be locked to get a pointer
GHND	A combination of **GMEM_MOVEABLE** and **GMEM_ZEROINIT**
GMEM_DISCARDABLE	The memory can be discarded
GMEM_DDESHARE	Used to implement shared memory for DDE; it isn't generally meaningful in Win32

Using Fixed Memory Blocks

In 16-bit versions of Windows, using **GMEM_FIXED** was discouraged, because the memory block really *was* fixed, and Windows couldn't move it at all. Now, it may look fixed to you, but Windows can still move it behind the scenes.

Using the **GPTR** flag makes **GlobalAlloc()** work like **malloc**, returning you a pointer which you cast to the appropriate type:

```
int *pi = (int*) GlobalAlloc(GPTR, 10 * sizeof(int));
pi[0] = 3;
```

Once you've finished with the block, you free it using **GlobalFree()**:

```
    GlobalFree(pi);
```

GlobalSize() returns you the size of a block, while **GlobalReAlloc()** can be used to resize it:

```
    DWORD dwSize = GlobalSize(pi);
    pi = (int*)GlobalReAlloc(pi, 20 * sizeof(int), GPTR);
```

Note that in the **GlobalReAlloc()** call, the flags are specified after the size, unlike **GlobalAlloc()**, which has them the other way around. You also might want to note that **GlobalSize()** returns the *actual* amount of storage associated with a block; this might be larger than the amount you asked for originally, if memory is allocated in fixed increments.

Using Moveable Memory Blocks

Why might you want to use moveable memory? One good reason is that allocating memory as moveable blocks gives Windows the right to move it around, and this will help reduce the possibility of memory fragmentation, which is a growing problem in these days of large, memory-hungry applications that people run for long periods.

Moveable memory requires you to lock the handle in order to get a pointer, and to unlock it when you've finished:

```
    // Obtain a handle to a block
    HGLOBAL hG;
    hG = GlobalAlloc(GHND, dwSize);

    // We want to use the block, so lock it...
    int* pi;
    pi = (int*)GlobalLock(hG);

    // Use the memory...

    // We've finished with the block, so unlock it
    GlobalUnlock(hG);
```

It's recommended that you don't keep the block locked for any longer than you need to, and in the early days of Windows programming it was just about mandatory to lock and unlock the block within the course of processing a single Windows message. A block can be locked multiple times, and Windows will keep a count of the locking, not actually unlocking the block until the lock count reaches zero.

When you've really finished with the memory, call **GlobalFree()** on the handle to release it. If you have the pointer but not the handle, you can use the **GlobalHandle()** function to retrieve it:

```
    // pi must point to the start of a block
    hG = GlobalHandle(pi);
```

Note that unlocking a block doesn't free it for reallocation - you must call **GlobalFree()** to do that.

There are a couple of macros defined in **Windowsx.h** that you may find useful, because they provide a way to allocate and lock a block in one go, and then to unlock and free it.

```
#define GlobalAllocPtr(flags, size)  \
    (GlobalLock(GlobalAlloc((flags),(size))))

#define GlobalFreePtr(lp)  \
    (GlobalUnlockPtr(lp),  \
    (BOOL)GlobalFree(GlobalPtrHandle(lp)))
```

Discardable Memory

If a block is marked as discardable, Windows can discard it when it needs to free up some space. It does this by reallocating it to have a length of zero, thus destroying its data. This is usually true of blocks which contain program code, which can always be reloaded from disk if required; in this case, it will be quicker to reload the code block than to page the block out to disk and then get it back.

Windows won't discard a block unless its lock count is zero. However, the **GlobalDiscard()** function can be used to force the discarding of a block.

Other Memory Allocation Functions

GlobalReAlloc() can be used to change the flags associated with a memory block. To do this, pass zero as the **size**, and include **GMEM_MODIFY** in the **flags**.

The **GlobalMemoryStatus()** function will return you a pointer to a **MEMORYSTATUS** structure, from which you can find out how much physical and virtual memory are available to your application.

The **GlobalFlags()** function can be used to tell you whether a block is discardable or has been discarded, or if the **GMEM_DDESHARE** flag is set (but remember that this isn't usually meaningful under Win32). It can also be used to find the lock count for a particular block.

A Memory Allocation Example

Here's a very simple console application that shows how you can use these functions to allocate and use memory. When using handles, make sure that every **GlobalAlloc()** you code is matched by a **GlobalFree()**, and every **GlobalLock()** by a **GlobalUnlock()**.

```
#include <iostream.h>
#include <windows.h>

int main()
{
    // Find out how much memory we have...
    MEMORYSTATUS ms;

    ms.dwLength = sizeof(ms);
    GlobalMemoryStatus(&ms);
```

```
    cout << "Total virtual memory: " << ms.dwTotalVirtual << endl;
    cout << "Available virtual memory: " << ms.dwAvailVirtual << endl;

    // Allocate memory - make it an odd number to see what the system
    // actually gives us
    HGLOBAL hG = GlobalAlloc(GMEM_MOVEABLE | GMEM_ZEROINIT, 2047);
    if (hG == NULL)
    {
        cout << "Error allocating memory!" << endl;
        return -1;
    }

    // See how much the system has given us
    DWORD dwSize = GlobalSize(hG);
    cout << "Allocated block of " << dwSize << " bytes" << endl;

    // Lock it so we can use it as a block of integers
    int* pi = (int*)GlobalLock(hG);
    if (pi == NULL)
    {
        cout << "Error locking handle!" << endl;

        // We couldn't lock the handle, but remember to free it before exiting
        GlobalFree(hG);
        return -1;
    }

    // Save some values and check they work
    for(int i=0; i<10; i++)
        pi[i] = i*i;

    for(i=0; i<10; i++)
        cout << "pi[" << i << "]=" << pi[i] << endl;

    // Unlock and free the memory
    GlobalUnlock(pi);
    GlobalFree(hG);

    return 0;
}
```

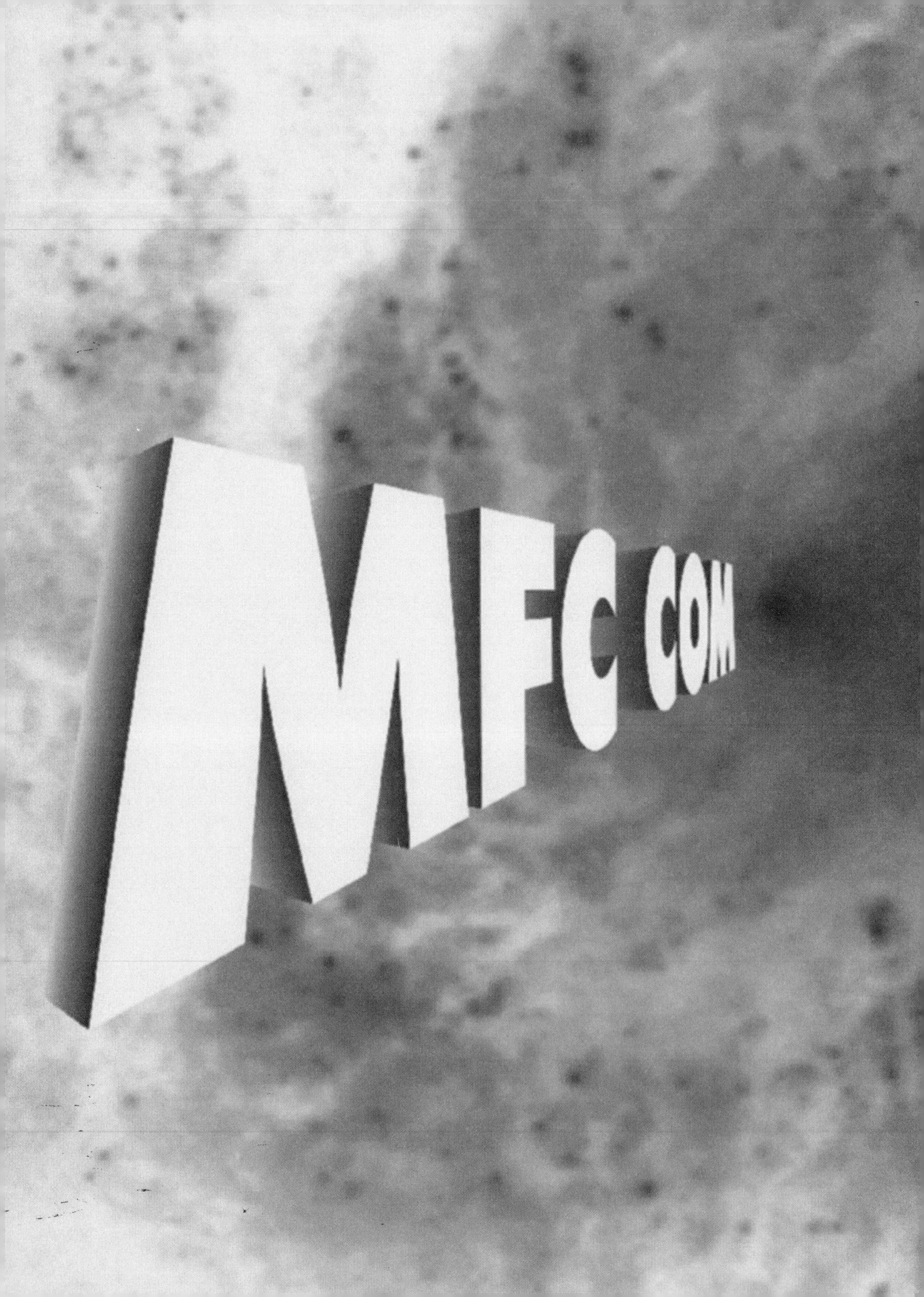
MFC COM

Compiler COM Support

The Visual C++ 5 compiler provides a range of features to make COM programming easier. These features include a new preprocessor directive, a couple of new keywords and four new classes. We'll examine these in this appendix.

We'll start by seeing compiler COM support in action in a simple application, which, in the grand tradition of programming tutorials, greets the world with a display of text. Then we'll examine each element of Microsoft's compiler COM support in turn.

> *To compile and run this example successfully, you'll need Microsoft Word 97 on your system.*

Hello World!

In this example, we're going to create a C++ equivalent of the following Visual Basic application, which consists of a form with a single command button:

```
Option Explicit

Private Sub Command1_Click()
    On Error GoTo err_Unexpected
    Dim word As New Word.Application
    Dim doc As Word.Document

    word.Visible = True
    Set doc = word.Documents.Add
    doc.Range.InsertAfter "Hello World!"
    Exit Sub

err_Unexpected:
    MsgBox "Description: " & Err.Description
End Sub
```

There are only five lines of code needed to start up Word, make it visible, create a new document, and insert the text Hello World!. The other lines just add a little bit of error handling to the event handler.

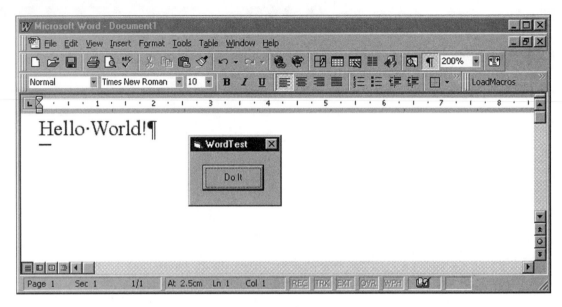

Don't be caught out. Despite the identical functionality, this example is a little different from the Word Automation examples we had back in the first couple of chapters. For a start, the **Application** and **Document** objects are declared as specific types rather than generic **Object**s. The downside to this is that we need to add the Word object library to the project's references to ensure that these types are properly defined. The upside is that we get syntax checking and extra speed, because Visual Basic can use the information in the object library to work out precisely how the methods of Word's objects need to be called.

Another difference is the use of the **New** keyword when we declare an object variable for the **Application** object. This signals to Visual Basic that we want it to create an **Application** object the first time that we use a property or method of that object - it works just like a hidden call to **CreateObject()**. Once again, this is made possible by attaching the Word object library as a reference to the project.

Finally, the actual sequence of calls to insert text in a new document is different from the earlier examples. In those projects, we used the WordBasic object to keep the examples for Word 95 and Word 97 as similar as possible. In this case, I've decided to make full use of Word 97's rich hierarchy - that's why the example won't work with Word 95. We create a new document by calling the **Add()** method of the **Documents** object, which is represented as a property of the **Application** object. The text itself is inserted using the **InsertAfter()** method of a **Range** object that we retrieve from the newly created **Document** by calling its **Range()** method.

> *You can take a look at the full extent of Word 97's object hierarchy by using the Object Browser provided with Visual Basic or the OLE/COM Object Viewer provided with Visual C++.*

We're going to produce a functionally identical application using Visual C++ 5's compiler COM support. What's more, we're going to write an identical number of lines of code in our C++ application as we did in the Visual Basic version!

The Project

Start by creating a new MFC project called **VCWordTest**. Use MFC AppWizard (exe) to create a dialog-based project, and leave all the other options with their default settings. Once you've generated the project, add the following code to the application's **InitInstance()**. This will initialize the COM libraries so that our application can start using COM whenever we're ready:

```
BOOL CVCWordTestApp::InitInstance()
{
    if (!AfxOleInit())
    {
        AfxMessageBox(_T("AfxOleInit() failed"));
        return FALSE;
    }
}
```

Next, open the source file for the dialog class and add the following statements to the file, just below the **#include**s:

```
#import "D:\Program Files\Microsoft Office\Office\MSO97.dll"
#import "C:\Program Files\Common Files\Microsoft Shared\Vba\VBEEXT1.olb"
#import "D:\Program Files\Microsoft Office\Office\Msword8.olb" \
    rename("ExitWindows","WordExitWindows")
```

Here you can see the first of the new COM features provided by Visual C++: the **#import** directive. We'll discuss precisely what this directive is doing once we've seen the finished application in action. For now, all you need to know is that we give the **#import** directive the name of some type libraries, and it will create some classes to wrap the interfaces described in them.

Now that we've done the basic setting up, we can get on with reproducing the functionality of the Visual Basic application. Open the dialog resource, delete the static text item, relabel the OK button on the dialog so that it reads Do It, and change its ID to **IDC_DOIT**. Then, create a **BN_CLICKED** handler for **IDC_DOIT** and add the following code:

```
void CWordTestDlg::OnDoit()
{
    try
    {
        // Declare a smart pointer to the _Application interface
        Word::_ApplicationPtr word;

        // Create an instance of Word's Application object and store the
        // interface in the smart pointer
        word.CreateInstance(__uuidof(Word::Application));

        // Make the application visible
        word->Visible = TRUE;

        // Declare a smart pointer to the _Document interface
        // and fill it with a pointer to a newly created Document object
        Word::_DocumentPtr doc = word->Documents->Add();

        // Insert the text "Hello World!" using the Range of the Document
        doc->Range()->InsertAfter("Hello World!");
    }
```

```
    catch (_com_error Err)
    {
        AfxMessageBox(_T("Description: ") + CString((LPCTSTR)Err.Description()));
    }
}
```

Apart from the differences in syntax, you should see that this code has a similar form to the Visual Basic code that we saw earlier; the major difference is in the use of the indirect member selection operator. We'll see precisely why the code looks like it does in a short while; for now, you can build the application and test it out to see that it works as advertised.

What's Going On?

If you're used to more traditional methods of coding Automation clients, you might find a few things about the code you've just seen surprising, or even unsettling:

▶ Where are the deeply nested **if** statements checking the return values for errors?

▶ Where are the calls that **Release()** the interface pointers?

▶ Where are all the calls to functions that take a thousand and one parameters even though it seems like they should need only one?

▶ What's going on?

The secret behind the smooth coding is in the **#import** statements. As I've already mentioned, these statements create wrapper classes for the interfaces declared in the type libraries we've imported.

#import vs. COleDispatchDriver

In a sense, **#import** works in a similar way to the **COleDispatchDriver**-derived classes that ClassWizard allows you to create from type libraries. In both cases, the classes created are responsible for calling **Release()** on the underlying interface pointer once the interface is no longer needed. However, the classes created by **#import** (which I shall refer to as COM **smart pointers** from now on) provide a number of features that the ClassWizard-generated wrappers do not:

▶ Parameters declared as **optional** in the type library remain optional in the wrapper classes

▶ Interface pointer parameters are converted to smart pointer parameters

▶ **BSTR** parameters become **_bstr_t** parameters

▶ Property wrappers can look like data members of a class

▶ Smart pointer wrapper functions are declared as **inline**

▶ COM smart pointers can wrap custom and dual interfaces as well as standard Automation interfaces

▶ In the case of custom and dual interfaces, the vtable methods are also exposed directly

▶ Smart pointers look and feel like pointers (and can even be used as arguments to functions that take **[out]** parameters)

▶ COM smart pointers have *no* dependence on MFC

The term smart pointer is used to refer to classes that behave like pointers, but take responsibility for allocating and freeing the memory that the pointer represents when it's no longer in use. The COM smart pointers that we're discussing here are a type of smart pointer that takes responsibility for freeing interface pointers. You may come across other classes that are also referred to as smart pointers that have different capabilities and uses.

Namespaces

By default, all of the output of a **#import** statement is created in a **namespace** with the same name as the type library (its internal name, *not* its filename). In our case, all the classes we're using are created within the **Word** namespace. This not only helps to avoid naming collisions, but also helps the readability of our code. If you find that the namespace is not to your liking, you can rename it or remove it completely using the **rename_namespace** or **no_namespace** attributes:

```
// This line generates the smart pointers without a namespace
#import "VBEEXT1.olb" no_namespace
// This line generates the smart pointers in a namespace called
NoCollisionsPossible
#import "Msword8.olb" rename_namespace("NoCollisionsPossible")
```

*The namespace is a relatively recent addition to Microsoft's Visual C++ compiler. Namespaces are designed to avoid naming conflicts by adding extra levels of scoping to C++ declarations. You can refer to items defined within a namespace by prefixing the identifier with the name of the namespace and the scope resolution operator (: :). Thus, a **struct** called **_Application** defined within the namespace **Word** can be referred to from outside that namespace as **Word::_Application**.*

Renaming Elements

You can also rename elements of the type library that aren't to your liking or are causing collisions by using the **rename** attribute. You've already seen this in action in the **#import** statement that we used for Word's type library. In that case, we needed to rename **ExitWindows** in Word's type library so that it didn't clash with the macro of the same name. It's mostly collisions with macros that will cause problems, since function collisions should be easily avoidable by sensible use of namespaces.

Multiple Libraries

You may be wondering why you've had to **#import** three type libraries, when we're using only a very small part of the functionality contained in Word's own type library. The simple reason is that if you don't **#import** all three type libraries, you'll get a whole chain of compiler errors!

Word's type library contains **importlib** statements to bring in other type libraries because it uses interfaces that are common to a number of applications in the Office suite. Because **#import** converts interface pointer parameters into smart pointer parameters, we'll get errors if we don't make sure that those smart pointer classes are fully defined. We can only be sure that they *are* fully defined by **#import**ing the other type libraries.

To understand the implications of this, let's compare the smart pointer classes created by **#import** with the **COleDispatchDriver**-derived classes that ClassWizard generated for us in the earlier chapters. As an example, we'll look at the **_Application** interface's **VBE** property. In both cases, a **GetVBE()** accessor function is created for this property.

In the case of the **#import**-generated class, the function returns a smart pointer:

```
VBIDE::VBEPtr GetVBE();
```

Clearly, the **VBIDE::VBEPtr** class needs to be fully defined if we're to avoid compiler errors. The **VBE** interface is defined in **VBEEXT1.olb**, so we get the definition for **VBEPtr** by **#import**ing that type library just before the **#import** for **Msword8.olb**.

In the case of the ClassWizard-generated wrapper, the function returns an **LPDISPATCH** (an **IDispatch** pointer):

```
LPDISPATCH GetVbe();
```

The disadvantage of returning a raw dispatch interface like this is that we'd need to attach this pointer to a wrapper class manually if we wanted to use its Automation features without too much coding. Alternatively, we'd have to requery for the **VBE** interface if we wanted to make use of the vtable part of this dual interface. We don't get either of these problems with the smart pointer method. The advantage, however, is that we don't have to use ClassWizard to create a wrapper for the **VBE** interface unless we feel like it.

The **#import** statement actually understands that **Msword8.olb** relies on the other two libraries, and places comments at the top of **Msword8.tlh** to inform you of that fact. It even goes so far as to give you the full path to the other libraries. However, it won't automatically **#import** them for you, in order to leave your options open. For example, in some cases, you might want to resolve the problem by removing from the output any interfaces that rely on interfaces defined in other type libraries. In our case, it was much simpler to bite the bullet and add the **#imports** for the other two libraries.

Minimizing the Output

Although, by default, **#import** will produce code for every interface and enumeration in a type library, it is possible to limit its output using the **exclude** attribute. Just follow the **#import** directive on the same line with **exclude(*namelist*)**, where **namelist** is a comma-separated list of strings of the names of the items that you want excluded from the output.

_com_ptr_t

The classes created by **#import** are all template specializations of a class called **_com_ptr_t**. This class takes two template parameters: the interface name and the IID. Smart pointer classes are usually generated using the **_COM_SMARTPTR_TYPEDEF** macro, which takes the same parameters as **_com_ptr_t** and declares a specialization of that class with the name of the interface plus a suffix of **Ptr**. Thus, in our example, **_ApplicationPtr** is a smart pointer class for Word's **_Application** interface.

.tlh and .tli Files

You can see the rafts of **_COM_SMARTPTR_TYPEDEF**s generated when we use **#import** on Word's type library by scanning the **VCWordTest** project's output directory for **.tlh** files. You'll see that there's one **.tlh** file for every type library that we imported. Each of these files contains the smart pointer class definitions for the interfaces contained in their respective type library, as well as definitions for any enumerations defined in the library. You could use the OLE/COM Object Viewer to view Word's type library directly to verify that there is a **_COM_SMARTPTR_TYPEDEF** for every interface declared in the type library.

In the output directory, you will also find a **.tli** file for each of the imported libraries. The **.tli** files contain the implementations of the wrapper functions, and it's these that we've made use of in our code to automate Word.

Function Prefixes

If you take a look at the classes generated in the **.tlh** files, you'll see that the classes expose wrappers for **propget**, **propput** and method functions, which are prefixed with **Get**, **Put** and nothing respectively. For dual and custom interfaces, you'll also be able to see that the original vtable methods are exposed with the prefixes **get_**, **put_**, and **raw_** respectively. If you should ever need the **HRESULT** from a method call, you can obtain it easily by calling these vtable methods in the normal fashion.

Although it's possible to change the prefixes used to name the wrappers and the low-level functions using the **high_method_prefix**, **high_property_prefixes**, **raw_method_prefix** and **raw_property_prefixes** attributes on the **#import** statement, it is not recommended. The standard prefixes should be clear and consistent enough for most uses.

_com_ptr_t::CreateInstance()

Now that you've seen how and where the interface wrapper classes are created by the **#import** statement, you're probably wondering how this line of code in our **VCWordTest** application works:

```
word.CreateInstance(__uuidof(Word::Application));
```

CreateInstance() is a member of **_com_ptr_t** that creates a new running instance of an object and queries the object for the smart pointer's interface type. There are a couple of overloads to this function, allowing it to take either a ProgID or a CLSID (in string or **CLSID** form).

__uuidof()

In our example, we're actually passing a **CLSID** to **CreateInstance()**. **__uuidof()** is a new operator that Microsoft has added to its compiler. It takes an argument and returns the GUID associated with that argument. The argument to **__uuidof()** can be almost anything under the C++ sun - a type, or a variable, a pointer, a reference, an array or a template specialization of that type - as long as it can be used to retrieve the attached GUID.

In this case, we're passing a **struct** called **Application**, defined in the **Word** namespace by the **#import** statement. This **struct** corresponds directly to the **Application coclass** declared in Word's type library, so **__uuidof(Word::Application)** is the CLSID of Word's **Application** object.

uuid()

GUIDS are associated with types by using a new declaration specifier, **uuid()**. Because this specifier is an extension to the C++ language, you need to wrap it up in the **__declspec()** keyword in order to use it.

> *The __declspec() keyword is used to specify that an instance of a given type is to be stored with a Microsoft-specific storage-class attribute. It just keeps all the Microsoft-specific extensions to the C++ language under one roof.*

uuid() takes a string parameter which specifies the GUID to be attached to the type. This string must be in standard registry format (with or without the curly braces). You can see that this attribute gets heavy use in the **.tlh** files produced by the **#import** statements. Here's how it's used to associate a GUID with the **_Application** interface, for example:

```
struct __declspec(uuid("00020970-0000-0000-c000-000000000046"))
/* dual interface */ _Application;
```

property()

If you look closely at the interface definitions in the **.tlh** files, you'll see that **__declspec()** isn't just used to wrap the **uuid()** attribute. There's another new specifier introduced to support COM: the **property()** attribute. You can see this at work in the extracts shown below taken from the declaration of the **_Application** interface wrapper:

```
__declspec(property(get=GetVisible,put=PutVisible))
VARIANT_BOOL Visible;
```

```
__declspec(property(get=GetDocuments))
DocumentsPtr Documents;
```

The **property()** attribute creates what Microsoft terms a **virtual data member** of a class. That is, although it looks like the class should contain a **Visible** data member of type **VARIANT_BOOL**, and you can write code that manipulates **Visible** as if it were a data member of the class, it doesn't actually exist as a data member!

Instead, the compiler converts code that manipulates **Visible** into the appropriate function calls using the information provided in the **get** and **put** statements, depending on whether **Visible** is being used as an rvalue or an lvalue. The same is true of the **Documents** property, except that it is read-only, since there's no **put** in the property specification. This means that it can only be used as an rvalue - you'll get compiler errors if you try to use it on the left side of an assignment.

If you look back at the code we wrote to manipulate Word, you'll see the following lines:

```
word->Visible = TRUE;
Word::_DocumentPtr doc = word->Documents->Add();
```

These are equivalent to this code:

```
        word->PutVisible(TRUE);
        Word::_DocumentPtr doc = word->GetDocuments()->Add();
```

Which form of code you use is entirely up to you; the compiler will treat them in exactly the same way.

> *If you use **property()** in your own code, you'll need to declare and implement the functions that you specify after **get** and **put**. These functions aren't magically created for you!*

_bstr_t

I've already pointed out that **BSTR** parameters or properties in the type library are converted into **_bstr_t** when **#import** creates the wrapper classes from the interfaces. **_bstr_t** is a class that encapsulates allocation, freeing and conversion of **BSTR**s, so it greatly simplifies passing strings between COM objects.

In our example code, we just passed a raw string to the **InsertAfter()** method without having to worry about allocating the string, converting our text to wide characters or freeing the string once the method had returned:

```
        doc->Range()->InsertAfter("Hello World!");
```

_bstr_t has a number of constructors and conversion operators that should cover almost every eventuality. In the example code, we rely on the constructor that takes a **const char*** to create a new **_bstr_t** object for our call to **InsertAfter()**. We also make use of **_bstr_t**'s **const char*** and **const wchar_t*** conversion operators to convert the return value of the error object's **Description()** method into something that the **CString** constructor can understand.

```
        AfxMessageBox(_T("Description: ") + CString((LPCTSTR)Err.Description()));
```

_com_error

Every wrapper function created by **#import** will throw a **_com_error** if the **HRESULT** from the underlying interface indicates a failure. The **_com_error** class encapsulates **HRESULT**s and features functions to access all the methods of the **IErrorInfo** interface.

If you want to get meaningful error messages for any errors that are thrown, you can use the **Description()** method, which just translates to a call to **IErrorInfo::Description()**, or you can use **_com_error::ErrorMessage()**, which uses the **FormatMessage()** API to convert the **HRESULT** into a readable description of the problem.

If you want to throw your own **_com_error**, you just need to construct it with an **HRESULT** and an optional **IErrorInfo** pointer, and you're all set.

_variant_t

The final COM support class is **_variant_t**. This doesn't really feature in our example, but it's a useful class nevertheless. **_variant_t** encapsulates all the **VARIANT** manipulation and conversion functions, making once-complex **VARIANT** manipulations simple.

Summary

Now you've seen how easy it is to control COM servers that describe themselves in a type library by using **#import** and the Visual C++ 5 compiler's COM support, it's up to you to create fantastic COM client applications.

If you want to make use of the COM support classes (**_com_ptr_t**, **_bstr_t**, **_variant_t**, **_com_error**) directly in your own applications, you can just **#include <comdef.h>** to get at all the relevant definitions. If you'd like some more information about any or all of these classes, try searching for compiler COM support classes in the Visual C++ online help.

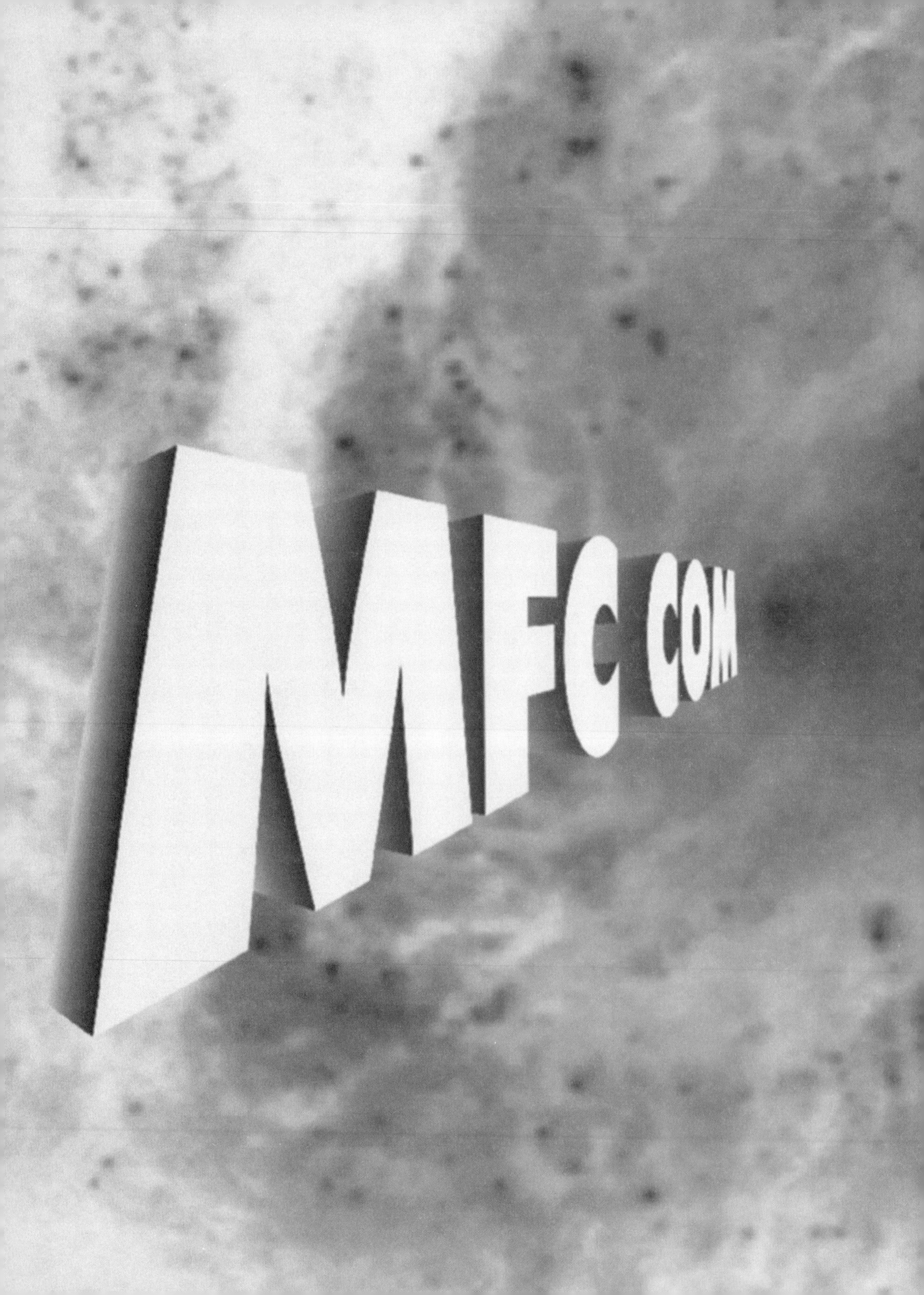
MFC COM

Further Reading

This books listed here will be useful references for anyone wishing to deepen their understanding of COM, ActiveX and OLE. They're in no particular order, and the list certainly isn't comprehensive; they're just books that I've found useful in some situations.

The Essential Distributed Objects Survival Guide
Orfali, Harkey and Edwards. John Wiley, 1996, 0-471-12993-3

This book provides a detailed overview of the two main distributed object technologies, CORBA and COM. The authors are CORBA enthusiasts, and this occasionally shows in their treatment of COM and Microsoft in general, but the book provides a very useful comparison of the technologies.

Profesional MFC with Visual C++5
Mike Blaszczak. Wrox Press, 1997, 1-861000-14-6

Features several chapters on COM, OLE and ActiveX for the advanced MFC developer, including an excellent chapter on ActiveX control containers.

Inside COM
Dale Rogerson. Microsoft Press, 1997, 1-57231-349-8

Rogerson provides a detailed and practical introduction to COM for the C++ programmer. This book is aimed at the nuts-and-bolts programmer, rather than those who want to use MFC and the Wizards to write applications.

Understanding ActiveX and OLE
David Chappell. Microsoft Press, 1996, 1-57231-216-5

Part of Microsoft's Strategic Technology Series, this book is designed to provide a firm conceptual grounding without going into implementation details. It provides a very good overview of the evolution and use of OLE technology.

Inside OLE, 2nd Edition
Kraig Brockschmidt. Microsoft Press, 1995, 1-55615-843-2

Said to be the definitive work on COM and OLE programming, this 1200-page book covers a lot of ground and is extremely comprehensive, although many people find it heavy going. Does not cover any of the ActiveX technologies, and is oriented towards C rather than C++.

Visual C++ Masterclass
Ramirez et al. Wrox Press, 1996, 1-874416-44-3

Contains several useful chapters on COM and OLE programming using MFC.

ActiveX Controls Inside Out, 2nd Edition
Adam Denning. Microsoft Press, 1997, 1-57231-350-1

Gives a very complete coverage of all aspects of ActiveX controls, at both the plain C++ and MFC levels. Highly recommended.

Professional ActiveX/COM Control Programming
Li and Economopoulos. Wrox Press, 1997, 1-861000-37-5
Contains details on developing ActiveX controls, concentrating on using ATL with Visual C++ and MFC.

Designing and Using OLE Custom Controls
Tom Armstrong. M&T Books, 1996, 1-55851-445-7

This book provides a detailed explanation of ActiveX controls using C++ and MFC, and includes numerous example programs on CD. Also gives an overview of COM and OLE, and the way in which MFC handles them.

Professional DCOM Progamming
Richard Grimes. Wrox Press, 1997, 1-861000-60-X

Provides an in-depth tour of the mysteries of DCOM and how to use it using Visual C++, MFC and ATL.

Late Night ActiveX
Tall and Ginsberg. Ziff Davis Press, 1996, 1-56276-448-9

A guide to the new Internet-related ActiveX technologies, such as controls and scripting. Unusual in that it covers both the C++ programming side and the HTML and Web side of things in some detail. Very useful for those wanting to use ActiveX technologies with the Internet.

MFC Internals
Shepherd and Wingo. Addison-Wesley, 1996, 0-201-40721-3

A thorough and readable investigation into the internals of MFC, including detailed coverage of its support for COM and OLE.

The Essence of OLE with ActiveX
David Platt. Prentice-Hall, 1997, 0-13-570862-1

A workbook covering most of the key OLE and ActiveX topics, with MFC code illustrating how to use them. Practical rather than theoretical.

Beginning Visual C++ Components
Matt Telles. Wrox Press, 1996, 1-861000-49-9

This book focuses on producing software components using MFC extensions and OLE controls. Contains instructions on writing (and code for) seven OLE controls.

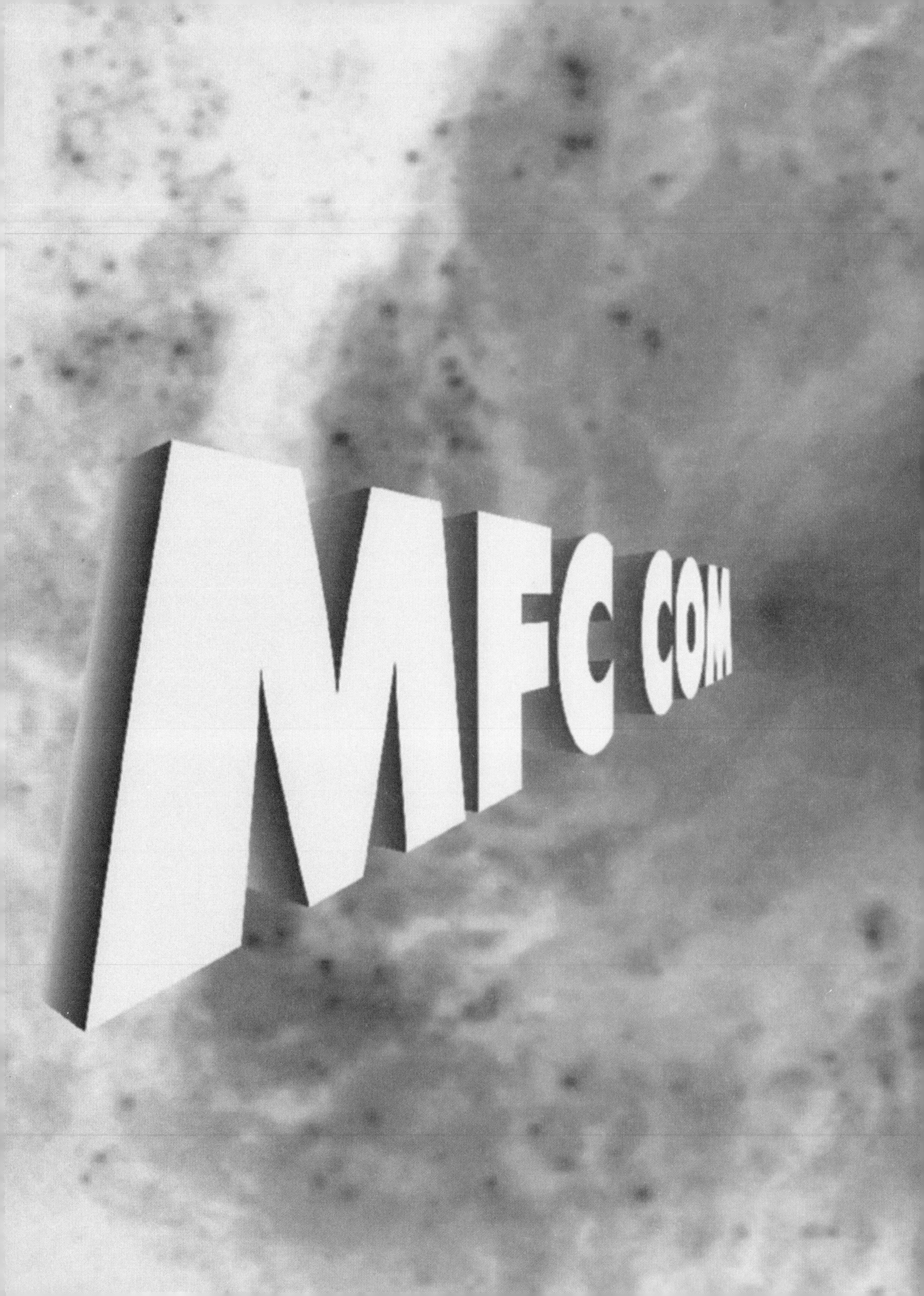
MFC COM

Beginning

MFC COM

Programming

487

Professional Visual C++ 5 ActiveX/COM Control Programming

Authors: Sing Li and
Panos Economopolous
ISBN: 1861000375
Price: $40.00 C$56.00 £36.99

"We believe that we can show you how to crack open COM and produce robust ActiveX controls to use now. It's our aim to show you the efficient route past all the pitfalls and dead-ends we've encountered and to help you succeed with the best methods. We've grappled with this technology since its inception and we know we can help you put solutions into practice. For some, it'll be the first time you've seen these new programming tools in action, but by the end of the book, you'll be using them to relieve some of your major development headaches"

Sing and Panos

This book is for anyone taking up the challenge of programming in the COM environment, using Visual C++, to produce industry-strength ActiveX controls. You should be familiar with fundamental Windows development and using MFC. You will get the full benefit of learning how to develop professional controls for Win32 with the Active Template Library (ATL) included in Visual C++ 5

Professional MFC with Visual C++ 5

Author: Mike Blaszczak
ISBN: 1861000146
Price: $59.95 C$83.95 £56.49

Written by one of Microsoft's leading MFC developers, this is the book for professionals who want to get under the covers of the library. This is the 3rd revision of the best selling title formerly known as 'Revolutionary Guide to MFC 4' and covers the new Visual C++ 5.0 development environment.

This book will give a detailed discussion of the majority of classes present in Microsoft's application framework library. While it will point out what parameters are required for the member functions of those classes, it will concentrate more on describing what utility the classes really provide. You will learn how to write a few utilities, some DLLs, an ActiveX control and even an OLE document server, as well as examining Microsoft's Open Database Connectivity (ODBC) and Data Access Objects (DAO) strategies. At the very end of the book, you'll take a look at what the Microsoft Foundation Classes provide to make programming for the Internet easier.

There's a CD_ROM included which has the complete book in HTML format - now you can use any browser to read your book on the road.

Professional DCOM Programming

Author: Dr. Richard Grimes
ISBN: 186100060X
Price: $49.95 C$69.95 £46.99

The book starts by examining why we need to be able to implement and distribute code objects, and looks at the various systems of distribution that currently exist. It then narrows the focus down to sharing data and functionality on Windows. This leads into an examination of COM, and from there, logically, to DCOM. We show how DCOM builds on the foundations of COM and RPC.

You'll quickly get to grips with the essentials of DCOM programming and we build on this base with thorough coverage of MIDL, Microsoft's Interface Definition Language. MIDL allows you to define your interfaces, create Type Libraries and provide marshaling support. All of these topics are covered in depth and backed up with strong code examples written using the latest tools.

The latter half of the book looks at the design and implementation of distributed applications. Each chapter covers a topic of prime importance to DCOM programmers. Security is fully explained, starting with the NT security model and exploring how it relates to DCOM. You'll then see how to write your DCOM servers as NT services, before being drawn into the murky world of multithreaded applications. The book shows how to use threads in Win32 and in DCOM servers, covers the different threading models and also looks at the issues of passing interface pointers between threads. Finally, you'll see how Microsoft Transaction Server can ease the life of a DCOM developer as well as the new issues introduced by this product

Instant VB5 ActiveX Control Creation

Authors: Alex Homer, Stephen Jakab
and Darren Gill
ISBN: 1861000235
Price: $29.95 C$41.95 £27.99

Aimed at experienced Visual Basic programmers who want to be able to create their own controls using the freely downloadable Visual Basic 5 CCE, this book takes you from an overview of VB5 CCE, right up to how to create your own, highly customized controls. It explains in detail how to create different types of control, including sub-classed, aggregate and owner-draw controls, and also includes coverage of the issues you need to be aware of when distributing your controls.

Beginning Java 1.1

Author: Ivor Horton
ISBN: 1861000278
Price: $36.00 C$50.40 £32.99
Available May 97

If you've enjoyed this book, you'll get a lot from Ivor's new book, Beginning Java.

Beginning Java teaches Java 1.1 from scratch, taking in all the fundamental features of the Java language, along with practical applications of Java's extensive class libraries. While it assumes some little familiarity with general programming concepts, Ivor takes time to cover the basics of the language in depth. He assumes no knowledge of object-oriented programming.

Ivor first introduces the essential bits of Java without which no program will run. Then he covers how Java handles data, and the syntax it uses to make decisions and control program flow. The essentials of object-oriented programming with Java are covered, and these concepts are reinforced throughout the book. Chapters on exceptions, threads and I/O follow, before Ivor turns to Java's graphics support and applet ability. Finally the book looks at JDBC and RMI, two additions to the Java 1.1 language which allow Java programs to communicate with databases and other Java programs.

Beginning Visual C++ 5

Author: Ivor Horton   ISBN: 1861000081
Price: $39.95 C$55.95 £36.99

Visual Basic is a great tool for generating applications quickly and easily, but if you really want to create fast, tight programs using the latest technologies, Visual C++ is the only way to go.

Ivor Horton's Beginning Visual C++ 5 is for anyone who wants to learn C++ and Windows programming with Visual C++ 5 and MFC, and the combination of the programming discipline you've learned from this book and Ivor's relaxed and informal teaching style will make it even easier for you to succeed in taming structured programming and writing real Windows applications.

The book begins with a fast-paced but comprehensive tutorial to the C++ language. You'll then go on to learn about object orientation with C++ and how this relates to Windows programming, culminating with the design and implementation of a sizable class-based C++ application. The next part of the book walks you through creating Windows applications using MFC, including sections on output to the screen and printer, how to program menus, toolbars and dialogs, and how to respond to a user's actions. The final few chapters comprise an introduction COM and examples of how to create ActiveX controls using both MFC and the Active Template Library (ATL).

'Ever thought about writing a book?'

Have you ever thought to yourself "I could do better than that"? Well, here's your chance to prove it! Wrox Press are continually looking for new authors and contributors and it doesn't matter if you've never been published before.

Interested?

contact John Franklin at Wrox Press, 30 Lincoln Road, Birmingham, B27 6PA, UK.

e-mail johnf@wrox.com

Wrox Press Developer's Journal

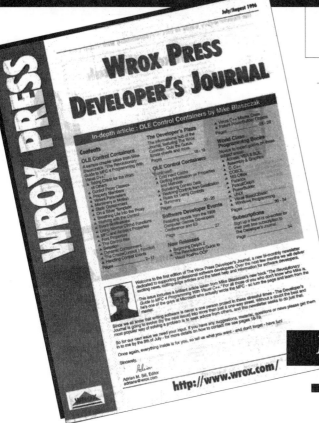

Free subscription

A 40-page bi-monthly magazine for software developers, The Wrox Press Developer's Journal features in-depth articles, news and help for everyone in the software development industry. Each issue includes extracts from our latest titles and is crammed full of practical insights into coding techniques, tricks and research.

In forthcoming editions

■ Articles on Unix, SQL Server 6.5, WordBasic, Java, Internet Information Server, Visual Basic and lots, lots more.

■ Hard hitting reports from cutting edge technical conferences from around the world.

■ Full and extensive list of all Wrox publications including a brief description of contents.

To Subscribe:

Please send in your full name and address to Wrox Press
and receive the next edition of the Wrox Press Developer's Journal.

■ Wrox Press, 30 Lincoln Rd, Olton, Birmingham, B27 6PA, UK

Contact: Pam Brand, 0121 706 6826

■ Wrox Press, 1512 North Fremont, Suite 103, Chicago, IL 60622, USA.

Contact: Michelle Giffune, 312 397 1900

or e-mail us on devjournal@wrox.com